BIBLIOTECA DELL'«ARCHIVUM ROMANICUM»
FONDATA DA
GIULIO BERTONI
Serie I - STORIA - LETTERATURA - PALEOGRAFIA   Vol. 248

STEVEN GROSSVOGEL

AMBIGUITY AND ALLUSION IN BOCCACCIO'S *FILOCOLO*

FIRENZE
LEO S. OLSCHKI EDITORE
MCMXCII

ISBN 88 222 3896 6

A Mia e ai miei

ACKNOWLEDGMENTS

Spouse, parents, and other relatives tend to appear at the very end of acknowledgments, mine instead appear at the beginning. Not only are most of them in my profession, but it is their example, inspiration, and support that have made this work possible. It is to all of them that I dedicate this book.

Then come all my other teachers, four of whom I am particularly indebted to for their guidance, instruction, and inspiration. They are, in alphabetical order, Ciriaco M. Arroyo, Calum C. Carmichael, the late Robert E. Kaske, and especially Giuseppe Mazzotta. Anyone familiar with their work will recognize in this book a valiant and often unsuccessful attempt to live up to the standards of scholarly excellence that they have set.

I would like to thank Janet L. Smarr for having read an earlier draft of the manuscript and for making many helpful suggestions on how to improve it. Her important work on the *Filocolo* has influenced the writing of this book more than any other study: the main theses I propose are premised largely on her interpretation of Boccaccio's work. I would also like to thank Victoria E. Kirkham for taking the time to read the earlier version of the manuscript. She too provided me with many useful suggestions for revising it. Her original and influential work on the *Filocolo* has also played an important role in the writing of this book.

I owe a special debt of gratitude to Robert M. Durling who painstakingly read a later version of the manuscript and made numerous corrections and suggestions. If I was unable to make all the revisions he recommended, it was for a lack of time, not a lack of good will. I would like to thank the dean of Boccaccio studies, Vittore Branca, for his encouragement during the early stages of this project. No Boccaccista can escape his influence, nor write anything which is not in some way indebted to his monumental scholarship. Finally, I would like to thank a scholar whom I have never met, but who has done more for the study of the *Filocolo* than anyone else. I am referring, of course, to Antonio Enzo Quaglio. His invaluable source studies on the *Filocolo* and his remarkable critical edition with its extensive footnotes have become indispensable tools for any student of Boccaccio's minor works. I, for one, would have never been able to write this book without them.

Generous summer funding for the writing of this book came from the University of Georgia's Sarah H. Moss Fellowship Foundation and from a University Research Grant. I am also very grateful to the Office of the Vice President for Research and the Office of the Dean of the Franklin College of Arts and Sciences at the University of Georgia for their generous grants. All this and the departmental grants I have received over the past six years would have not been possible without the support and guidance of my chairman, Jean-Pierre Piriou. I am grateful to him and to the other members in the Department of Romance Languages who have supported me throughout my years at the University of Georgia.

INTRODUCTION
THE *FILOCOLO* AND ITS CRITICS

Of all Giovanni Boccaccio's Italian works, the *Filocolo* is among the least read and least studied. Written when Boccaccio was in his late twenties and living in Naples (1336-1338), the *Filocolo* is his first and longest experiment in narrative prose prior to the *Decameron*. The plot is largely derived from the considerably shorter *cantari* of Fiorio and Biancofiore which in turn were derived from the Old French romances of Floire and Blanchefleur.[1] It narrates the love of Florio, King Felice's sole heir, and Biancifiore, the daughter of two Roman nobles, Lelio Africano and Giulia Topazia. Born on the same day, the two protagonists are raised together at Felice's court in Verona. When they fall in love with each other, the king separates them out of fear that Florio's love for the socially inferior Biancifiore will diminish their family's nobility. After sending Florio to the neighboring town of Montoro, the king and his seneschal plot to kill Biancifiore in the hope that her death will bring an end to Florio's lovesickness. Upon hearing that his beloved has been falsely accused of treason and condemned to the stake, Florio returns to Verona and rescues her. Once liberated, Biancifiore is restored to her place in court, and Florio returns to Montoro. The king, however, continues to plot against Biancifiore and sells her as a slave to two Italian merchants who in turn sell her to the Admiral of Alexandria. In the meantime, the king and queen make their son believe that Biancifiore is dead. When Florio discovers that she is not, he sets off to find her. Florio's quest for Biancifiore brings him first to Naples, where he participates in Fiammetta's court of love, and finally to Alexandria where the two

---

[1] VINCENZO CRESCINI, *Il cantare di Florio e Biancifiore*, Bologna, Romagnoli-Dall'Acqua, 1889-1899. «Scelte di curiosità letterarie inedite o rare dal secolo XIII al XIX in appendice alla Collezione di opere inedite o rare. 233, 249». This was reprinted in a facsimile edition: *Il cantare di Fiorio e Biancifiore*, Bologna, Commissione per i testi di lingua, 1969.

protagonists consummate their love. The two lovers are caught *in flagrante delicto* by the Admiral, and are sentenced to die at the stake. When Florio's friends hear about it, they come to the rescue and defeat the Admiral's forces with the help of Mars and Venus. After the lovers' liberation, the Admiral discovers that Florio is his nephew, and asks him to marry Biancifiore in public. The protagonists spend almost a year in Alexandria before beginning their long journey back to Felice's court. On their way home they stop in Rome where Biancifiore discovers her noble ancestry and where she and Florio convert to Christianity. The narrative concludes with a reconciliation scene on Felice's deathbed, and the subsequent coronation of the two protagonists.

Boccaccio added to this fairly simple plot a large number of digressions and amplifications which have made the *Filocolo* the object of considerable criticism. For well over a hundred years critics and scholars have pointed to the work's narrative and structural «weaknesses» without carefully considering the function Boccaccio intended them to have in the *Filocolo*. Such criticism has largely been due to the scholars' own embarrassment at the fact that the father of European narrative prose (as Boccaccio has often been called) should have written a work which fails to live up to the standards later set by the *Decameron*. Their criticism often reflects modern aesthetic and literary tastes, and is not responsive to the medieval qualities of this work, qualities which are harder to appreciate when juxtaposed to the «modernity» of the *Decameron*. The following overview of what critics and scholars have said about the *Filocolo* during the past fifty years will reveal some of the problems which this work has generated and which still need to be resolved.

One of the first scholars to devote serious attention to the *Filocolo* was Salvatore Battaglia. Besides his edition of this work, Battaglia also wrote one of the first important critical essays on the *Filocolo*. [2] Unlike the positivist scholars before him who attempted to interpret the *Filocolo* in autobiographical terms, Battaglia attempted to place some distance between the work and its author. [3] Instead of an autobiographical text, Battaglia saw the *Filocolo* as a lyrical expression of a sentimental journey filled with psychological adventures. The

---

[2] SALVATORE BATTAGLIA, *Schemi lirici nell'arte del Boccaccio*, «Archivium romanicum», XIX, 1935, pp. 61-78.

[3] Crescini's study is typical of this kind of autobiographical interpretation.

sentimental tone and lyrically abstract atmosphere which permeate the *Filocolo* are a significant departure from the typical medieval romances on which this work is based. The numerous digressions, episodes, characters, and descriptions are, according to Battaglia, echoes of one voice — that of the author. They constitute the literary fiction into which his personal experiences are translated; but because they are given a lyrical and abstract mein, they are never purely empirical.

Speaking about the world of the protagonists, Battaglia says that it is a reflection of the courtly world Boccaccio had become acquainted with at the Angevin court in Naples. It is also an internalized world which, according to Battaglia, reflects the protagonist's solitude and, by extension, that of the author: it is an idyllic interlude that has been externalized. Battaglia claims that Boccaccio took this from Ovid's *Metamorphosis*, where myths are projections of human passions translated from illusory and unstable experiences to perennial and immobile ones. Similar transformations in the characters of the *Filocolo* celebrate these abstract and contemplative aspects of erotic passion; and in so doing, they translate the static nature of sentimental behavior into mythic and idyllic forms. These metamorphoses, concludes Battaglia, freeze the immobile solitude of amorous contemplation within the solitary and tacit forms of Nature.

Although Battaglia rarely cites examples from the *Filocolo* to support his generalizations, anyone familiar with Boccaccio's text will find his observations quite compelling. A closer reading of the *Filocolo*, however, reveals that there is more to the world of the protagonists than fantastic, idyllic, and solitary meditations on love. Contrary to what Battaglia claims, the fantastic is not used at the expense of human values and social customs. The world of the *Filocolo* may be far from the realism of the *Decameron*, as Battaglia states, but the «communal sentimental existence» of the characters is not divorced from reality. As we shall see in this study, the *Filocolo* is actually a *speculum mundi* in the guise of a courtly romance.

With regard to the work's shortcomings, Battaglia states that it is too episodic, dispersive, and discordant in its tone and proportions. He attributes these «caratteri negativi» to the work's sources: Boccaccio's periphrases and linguistic elaborations accentuate the defects in the fluid and quick paced *cantari*. According to Battaglia, the byzantine qualities of the sources are deformed by Boccaccio's excessive use of additional literary and extra-literary material. By amplifying his meager sources, Boccaccio made each *amplificatio* a story in itself which often has no connection to the plot or the other stories in the *Filocolo*: it lacks the unity one would expect from a work which is meant to have the structure of a medieval romance. Battaglia concludes that the disorderly structure of the *Filocolo* is a reflection of the author's youthful exuberance and his inability to «discipline» his culture. Battaglia's overall impressions of the *Filocolo's* weaknesses seem justified after a cursory reading of this long and seemingly incongruous work. But as we shall see in this study, many of the amplifications and digressions in the *Filocolo* are thematically connected to the plot: the apparent lack of unity of form, style, and narrative artistry does not necessarily preclude a thematic unity of content and meaning.

Several years after Battaglia's article, Natalino Sapegno wrote an essay on the *Filocolo* which shares some of the same views. [4] Like Battaglia, Sapegno feels that Boccaccio's artistry lies in the young writer's linguistic and stylistic experiments: the oratorical, majestic, and analytical prose of the *Filocolo* will reappear in the *Decameron* in a pared and lightened form. Sapegno praises the precious sonority and hidden harmonies in this poetic prose, but claims that Boccaccio was unable to distinguish between eloquence and poetry, thereby giving rise to the prolix dialogues and «useless» descriptions which permeate the *Filocolo*.

Like Battaglia, Sapegno sees Boccaccio's elaborate narrative as a vehicle for expressing psychological experiences within the fragmentary plot of a conventional romance. The narrative is adapted and transformed, according to Sapegno, to suit Boccaccio's minute psychological analyses, his understanding of human experience, and his dialectics of love. The love story itself, however, is tenuous and gets lost in the dispersive and unbalanced structure of the narrative. Sapegno recognizes the thematic and not purely autobiographical importance of love in the *Filocolo*, and states that this love is not Dante's Platonic and heaven-bound love, but rather a carnal and fragile love which never becomes coarse or vulgar. Although Sapegno's characterization of the protagonists' love is correct, he overlooks several of the thematic implications love has in the *Filocolo*.

Like Battaglia, Sapegno too sees a lack of unity in the *Filocolo*, particularly between the plot and the overwhelming «cultura» Boccac-

---

[4] NATALINO SAPEGNO, *Il Trecento*, Milano, Vallardi, 1942, pp. 296-304.

cio attempts to incorporate in it. His criticism of Boccaccio's seemingly disorganized use of literary and extra-literary sources is echoed by later critics. Vittore Branca, the dean of Boccaccio studies, makes a similar observation when he notes that Boccaccio's «disordinato e pesante bagaglio culturale» overwhelms the narrative of the *Filocolo*. [5] Antonio Enzo Quaglio, the leading authority on the *Filocolo*, when confronting the apparent lack of unity in this work, and the seemingly disproportionate importance Boccaccio gives to the various episodes, digressions, and addenda, concludes:

> esso è nato e resta un centone di tipo medievale, la cui ossatura ricorda sia l'impianto dei romanzi di avventura e d'amore dell'epica due e trecentesca di estrazione europea, sia le enciclopedie e i florilegi di cultura scolastica in cui si stipano con fonti classiche aneddoti, leggende, proverbi dell'età di mezzo. [6]

If indeed Boccaccio can be accused of overburdening the *Filocolo* with cultural erudition, even at the expense of narrative form, we must assume that he had a reason for doing so. Is his use of erudition purely a rhetorical strategy (*imitatio*, *dilatio*, and *amplificatio*)? Or could it be that Boccaccio also used these and other rhetorical devices for reasons which critics have not taken into account? More than draw our attention to an inappropriate use of culture in the *Filocolo*, the criticism leveled against the *Filocolo* indicates the need to deal with this cultural erudition. Rather than regard it simply as rhetorical «baggage», we must see if Boccaccio's «cultura» has a more precise function in the narrative.

Similar criticism of the *Filocolo* was also expressed by Luigi Malagoli. [7] For Malagoli the narrative moves rigidly within a rhetorical frame which consists largely of speeches and conventional divine interventions in human affairs, both of which break the action. The dialogues, which follow one another in a fairly rapid succession, break the narrative and make it languid. Malagoli also criticizes the schematic and predisposed order in which events take place within the protagonists' lives. (As we shall see, however, this is actually a deliberate authorial strategy: the predisposed order of events is meant to reflect the providential plan at the heart of the plot itself.) Malagoli

---

[5] Vittore Branca, *Giovanni Boccaccio: profilo biografico*, Florence, Sansoni, 1977, p. 47.

[6] Quaglio, *Tra fonti e testo del Filocolo*, «Giornale storico della letteratura italiana», CXLI, 1963, pp. 321-sg.

[7] Luigi Malagoli, *Timbro della prosa e motivi dell'arte del Boccaccio nel «Filocolo»*, «Studi mediolatini e volgari», V-VI, 1959, pp. 97-111.

mitigates his criticism, however, by stating that the discursive parentheses in the narrative, with its repetitions and recapitulations, are another example of the work's prolonged rhythm and the author's partiality for delay and deferral, all of which have their own legitimacy in the narrative. Unfortunately, Malagoli does not tell us what this legitimacy consists of. A possible answer can be found in the classical rhetorical device of *dilatio* (delay and deferral) which, as Patricia Parker has shown, is a common attribute of the romance genre. [8] Boccaccio's use of *dilatio*, as well as other narrative devices such as *amplificatio* and *imitatio*, reflect the young writer's deliberate choice of narrative techniques. Like critics before him, Malagoli did not recognize that many of these techniques serve to convey the narrative's thematic meaning. [9]

Besides analyzing the rhetorical qualities of the *Filocolo*, Malagoli also analyzes Boccaccio's style. Malagoli takes into account Boccaccio's deliberate and, at times, innovative use of medieval stylistics, particularly the combination of various *cursus* (*planus*, *tardus*, and *trispondaicus*) with the rhythmic syntax of Boccaccio's long sentences. Malagoli sees elements of style, which became famous in the *Decameron*, already present in the *Filocolo*. Speaking about Boccaccio's early style, Malagoli indicates that the syntax and intonations are uniformly rhythmic and slow-moving, giving the *Filocolo* its fluid, musical, and at times monotonous style. The intricate interlacing of relative clauses, causative constructions, consecutive conjunctions, and gerundives within a single Ciceronian sentence are the trademark of Boccaccio's syntax. Malagoli adds that the subordination of clauses and the way these clauses are used in a sentence produce a cause and effect relation which serves to represent reality in a new and innovative manner: things are seen in terms of how they are connected to one another, but are not explored in depth. Everything is held together by a unifying chain of events, but no one thing is ever the object of particular attention. As a result, concludes Malagoli, everything represented in the *Filocolo* seems to be placed on the same narrative plane: no single event or idea stands out. This in turn makes

---

[8] PATRICIA PARKER, *Inescapable Romance: Studies in the Poetics of a Mode*, Princeton, Princeton University Press, 1979.
[9] Alluding to the wealth of motifs which appear throughout the *Filocolo*, Malagoli claims that they are mere allusions which are only developed in Boccaccio's later works. Contrary to Malagoli's claim, however, these motifs and allusions are actually well-developed themes that govern the narrative.

the narrative fluid and circular in its representation of reality, uniform and constant in its dramatization of events; all of which anticipates, according to Malagoli, the dramatic elements in the *Decameron*.

Malagoli's analysis of how Boccaccio's style affects his narrative is compelling; but by viewing Boccaccio's choice of stylistic and rhetorical devices in purely aesthetic terms, he fails to take into account the manner in which these devices are related to the meaning of the text itself. In fact, Malagoli's interpretation of the plot of *Filocolo* is actually a projection of the characters' own inability to comprehend the importance of the events in their life. The fact that both the narrator and the protagonists fail to see the significance of their own experiences (an important theme in the *Filocolo*) should not be mistaken for the author's inability to highlight the most important episodes in his work.

Many of the «caratteri negativi» which critics found in the *Filocolo* were reevaluated for the first time by Guido Di Pino. [10] Di Pino was one of the first critics to suggest that Boccaccio's narrative and poetic strategies were an integral part of the tale's meaning. Analyzing key passages from the *Filocolo*, Di Pino illustrated the poetic devices Boccaccio adopted in the portrayal of the characters. Biancifiore is portrayed in dramatic terms: her character takes shape as a result of the dismal conditions she must live in, and her dramatic confrontation with her misfortune gives her nobility. As Di Pino astutely points out, Boccaccio plays with shade imagery and *chiaroscuro* descriptions of Biancifiore in order to heighten the dramatic clash between her nobility and her ignoble condition: her «turbata bellezza» becomes the poetic essence of her character. As the narrative progresses, her personality acquires greater autonomy and self-awareness. She accepts her adversity with the same constancy of Griselda (the heroine of the last novella in the *Decameron*), while displaying the same signs of anxiety that we find in the unhappy love stories of the fourth day of the *Decameron*.

The portrayal of Florio, on the other hand, is more lyrical and elegiac: his internal solitude is constantly juxtaposed to his actions. The dichotomy between action and elegy is accentuated by the divine interventions which often determine the nature of the protagonist's actions. As a result, the world of adventure recedes and gives way to

---

[10] GUIDO DI PINO, *La polemica del Boccaccio*, Firenze, Vallecchi, 1953, pp. 79-96.

Florio's melancholy which in turn becomes the dominant and most poetic note of the romance. It is unfortunate that Di Pino's brilliant insights into the portrayal of the characters in the *Filocolo* do not also take into account the thematic issues which are emblematized by the characters' conduct: the relationship between action and elegy, love and melancholy, drama and dramatic irony, all of which are thematically important because, as we shall see, they govern the plot. [11]

Looking at the poetic qualities at work in the plot itself, Di Pino states that by elevating the tale of Florio and Biancifiore above the level of the popular *cantari*, Boccaccio was not simply elevating the style but also the dramatic tone and cultural setting of the tale. Boccaccio accomplished this by using supernatural interventions and historical, mythological and geographic digressions, all of which give the *Filocolo* its solemn tone. The elevated tone of the tale is also created by the soliloquies and dialogues which embellish the expression of the characters' sentiments. According to Di Pino, the pomp and splendor of Boccaccio's writing have only one purpose, the creation of an atmosphere which ennobles the sensual and enlivens the inner quest of each character. Although Di Pino is correct in recognizing the deliberate attempt to elevate the narrative to a higher stylistic plane, one must take issue with his claim that this is the sole purpose for these digressions. As we shall see, these digressions are thematically connected to the plot itself, and play a significant role in the narrative's overall meaning.

Carlo Muscetta made a claim similar to Di Pino's several years later. Muscetta states that by choosing to write in prose rather than in poetry, Boccaccio adopted a stylistic means which would give a nobler quality to the popular tale of Florio and Biancifiore. Muscetta sees in Boccaccio's use of epithets, rhetoric, erudite insertions, and long sentences with several different verb tenses a deliberate attempt to obliterate the humble origins of this tale (much the same way Boccaccio attempted to cover up his illegitimate birth by claiming to be born

---

[11] Di Pino's keen observations on Boccaccio's character portrayals were supplemented, some thirty years later, by Jonathan Usher who analyzed Boccaccio's use of medieval portraiture techniques. Usher notes that feminine beauty is portrayed with a double perspective: an objective account as seen through the eyes of the narrator, and a more dynamic account seen through the eyes and actions of the protagonists. The latter allows for erotic possibilities which do not exist in the former. This in turn gives the reader insight in the *notatio* or moral characterization of the protagonists. See JONATHAN USHER, *Boccaccio's Experimentation with Verbal Portraits from the Filocolo to the Decameron*, «Modern Language Review», LXXVII, 1982, pp. 585-96.

of a French noblewoman). [12] Having obliterated its humble origins, Boccaccio elevates the love story of Florio and Biancifiore by giving it a higher style and by amplifying the tenuous plot of the *cantari* with numerous digressions, new episodes, literary and extra-literary insertions, fables, and legends, all of which are set, according to Muscetta, in a «cornice» which is historic, realistic, and contemporary at the same time. Boccaccio's use of important authors, most notably Ovid, Lucan, Dante, and other acknowledged and unacknowledged writers, is, according to Muscetta, another example of Boccaccio's elevation of this tale to the dignity of the works he is using. Muscetta's observation suggests that Boccaccio is giving his work an importance which is comparable to that of his classical sources, a point Victoria Kirkham would make several years later. [13] If that is the case, it would only seem natural that the *Filocolo* should be read along the same lines these other works have been read. Instead, the biases which have plagued the *Filocolo* have also prevented it from even getting the kind of critical attention Boccaccio's other «minor» works have received.

Speaking about the «superfluous» descriptions and the «meandering» structure of the plot, Muscetta states (as Battaglia had done before him) that they are typical of Byzantine and Hellenistic narratives, but adds that Boccaccio goes to great lengths to reiterate and amplify his sources, and does so with a «youthful desire» to outdo himself. Muscetta also states that the action of the plot is revealed in monologues, epistles, dialogues, and innumerable descriptions which increase the pathos of the dramatic circumstances and give depth to the author's psychological analysis. It is hard to agree with Muscetta's assertion that these seemingly extraneous insertions in the narrative «sembrano scritti per sfoggio di bravura decorativa».

Muscetta's observations reflect the difficulty that even the best critics have in grasping the puzzling structure of the *Filocolo*. These difficulties may have been spawned, in part, by Fiammetta's own statement at the beginning of Book I: «ti priego che [...] tu affanni in comporre un picciolo libretto, volgarmente parlando, nel quale il nascimento, lo 'nnamoramento e gli accidenti de' detti due infino alla loro fine interamente si contenga» (I 1, 26). If we give any credence to

---

[12] Muscetta's observation is interesting in light of the whole question of birth and nobility, a theme which pervades the *Filocolo*.

[13] VICTORIA E. KIRKHAM, *Reckoning with Boccaccio's «Questioni d'Amore»*, «Modern Language Notes», LXXXIX, 1974, pp. 49-50.

the myth that Fiammetta (the *senhal* for Boccaccio's beloved) asked him to write «un picciolo libretto», then one could consider the more than six hundred pages which make up the *Filocolo* as the product of youthful exuberance and a lover's zeal. But in so doing we are also assuming that Boccaccio and the narrator are one. Whether Fiammetta's influence on the narrator is fact or fiction, the *senhal* should be regarded as a figure for poetic inspiration. The fact that she should have prompted the narrator to write over six hundred pages (everything but «un picciolo libretto») is part of the Boccaccio's use of irony. This and other ironic remarks in the *Filocolo* could be seen as Boccaccio's way of mocking the narrator as lover, and lovers in general. Boccaccio's ironic voice is present at the beginning of the *Filocolo* to distinguish it from the narrator's persona. As in the case of Dante and other medieval writers who served as models for Boccaccio, the figure of the beloved as the writer's prime source of inspiration is a well-established topos, a literary device with a fiction of its own. If we deem the persona of the narrator as the prime means of expression in the *Filocolo*, then it is not surprising that critics from Battaglia to Muscetta consider this work a stylistic «failure». If, on the other hand, we distinguish the narrator from Boccaccio the author, we discover that the narrative is more profound and far less superficial than these critics have led us to believe.

It seems safe to conclude that most Italian criticism on the *Filocolo*, prior to Quaglio's critical edition of 1967, was more intent on giving «un giudizio critico complessivo sul valore dell'opera» (the words are Quaglio's) than on arriving at the kind of interpretations Vittore Branca, Luigi Russo, Giovanni Getto, et al. were proposing for the *Decameron*. [14] Although many of these critical appraisals provide insight into the *Filocolo's* historical, linguistic, stylistic, and inter-textual background, they seldom consider the work's thematic significance.

Quaglio's critical edition of 1967 did more to alter the way the *Filocolo* would be read than any previous work of scholarship. Quaglio's wealth of textual and critical annotations proved that Boccaccio's first work of narrative prose fiction was not nearly as simplistic as critics had claimed. As both Quaglio and Muscetta have shown, the

---

[14] See VITTORE BRANCA, *Boccaccio medievale*, Florence, Sansoni, 1956; LUIGI RUSSO, *Letture critiche del «Decameron»*, Bari, Laterza, 1956; and GIOVANNI GETTO, *Vita di forme e forme di vita nel «Decameron»*, Torino, Petrini, 1958.

bad fortune of the *Filocolo* was in part due to Gaetano Tizzone's Renaissance edition of this work. Tizzone revised the *Filocolo* so that its style would conform to Renaissance literary tastes: many archaic words and latinisms were expurgated, and the original syntax of Boccaccio's sentences was made less precious and laborious. Since Tizzone's edition served as the basis for practically all editions of the *Filocolo* (including Battaglia's) prior to Quaglio's, it is not surprising that some of the negative criticism directed at the style of the *Filocolo* was in part due to the lack of an unadulterated text.

After Quaglio's critical edition appeared, scholars and critics working on the *Filocolo* could no longer settle for broad generalizations. Quaglio's painstaking work of identifying sources, inter-textual allusions, and footnoting practically every difficult or puzzling line in the *Filocolo* forced scholars to look at this work more closely and analyze its key passages in greater detail. To cite just a few examples, Luigi Sasso reevaluated previous interpretations of the characters' names; Giuseppe Chiecchi looked at Boccaccio's use of epistolography as an extension of the Provençal «amor de lonh» motif; Luigi Surdich analyzed the quest motif in the protagonists' journey to and from Alexandria; and Francesco Bruni has reconsidered the way Boccaccio used his Latin sources. [15] Although these studies have proven to be more accurate than the previous ones in their critical appraisal of the *Filocolo*, they still fall short of offering an overall interpretation of the text. This is best illustrated in Bruni's thought-provoking essay.

Like critics before him, Bruni underscores the overabundant and disorderly narration in the *Filocolo*, but points out (as Victoria Kirkham and Janet Smarr had done before him) that the work has symmetrical correspondences and reference points whose purpose, according to Bruni, is to balance this excessive material. [16] In addition to pointing out some of these symmetrical patterns, Bruni ascribes the importance of the allusions in the *Filocolo* to Boccaccio's desire to write in a middle style (as opposed to the higher style of Virgil,

---

[15] Luigi Sasso, *L'«interpretatio nominis» in Boccaccio*, «Studi sul Boccaccio», XII, 1980, pp. 129-174. Giuseppe Chiecchi, *Narrative, «amor de lohn», epistolografia nelle opere minori del Boccaccio*, «Studi sul Boccaccio», XII, 1980, pp. 175-195. Luigi Surdich, *La cornice di amore: Studi sul Boccaccio*, Pisa, ETS Editrice, 1987, («Saggi di letteratura italiana», 9), pp. 13-75. Francesco Bruni, *Il Filocolo e lo spazio della letteratura volgare*, «Miscellanea di studi in onore di Vittore Branca II: Boccaccio e dintorni» Firenze: Olschki, 1983, pp. 1-21.

[16] Bruni, however, does not seem to accept the thematic importance of these symmetrical correspondences.

Statius, Lucan, and the other classical writers he uses in his work). By comparing the context in which Boccaccio's literary allusions are made with the context from which they are taken, Bruni concludes that Boccaccio was not attempting to say the same things his *auctores* were saying. Following a premise which is similar to Giuseppe Velli's, Bruni claims that Boccaccio used literary allusions for poetic *imitatio*, and concludes that there is no superior moral perspective that runs through the *Filocolo*, nor any connection between a source and the way it is used in this work. [17] Boccaccio's choice of allusions and source material is strictly meant to convey a certain tone (dramatic, elegiac, etc.) and to elevate the tale of Florio and Biancifiore above the level of the *cantari*, but not high enough to deal with the same philosophical ideals or «sottigliezze» that his classical sources dealt with. Bruni claims that by detaching himself from the major classical works of Latin and early Italian literature, and by distancing himself from the committed ideology of medieval Latin culture, Boccaccio was able to delve further into the Ovidian tradition of elegiac comedy, the romance genre, and the culture of the early vernacularized editions of Latin classics, all of which acknowledged their inferiority vis-à-vis their major classical models. Bruni illustrates this by comparing the *Filocolo* to the Old French *Roman d'Eneas* which shifted its center of gravity from the *Aeneid*'s religious, political and historic concerns to Ovid's erotic concerns. By divorcing himself from the more elevated themes of the classics, Boccaccio is able to give the amorous aspects of his romance their own literary space.

Bruni's essay reflects an assumption which has persisted throughout the century among Italian critics of the *Filocolo*: the work's style matches its content--one is a reflection of the other. If we were to apply Bruni's method to Dante's *Commedia*, which, like the *Filocolo* was deliberately written in a middle style, then one would have to conclude that the *Commedia* does not deal with religious, political and historic concerns comparable to those found in the *Aeneid*. Unfortunately, Bruni's essay is symptomatic of the extent to which Boccaccio's style and narrative form have prejudiced many critics' views on the allusions, themes, issues, and «lofty» concerns which actually permeate the *Filocolo*. If we keep in mind the large number of allusions which Boccaccio makes to Dante's *Commedia* and *Vita*

---

[17] See GIUSEPPE VELLI, *Cultura e «imitatio» nel primo Boccaccio*, «Annali della Scuola Normale Superiore di Pisa», s.II, vol. XXXVII, 1968, pp. 65-93.

Nuova, we soon realize that the *Filocolo* is as much an *imitatio* of Dante as it is of the classical Latin authors Bruni cites. This in itself suggests that we should read the *Filocolo* along the same lines that Boccaccio might have read the *Vita Nuova* and the *Commedia*.

In the United States, where the study of Dante has determined to a large extent the way Boccaccio is read, we find critical approaches to the *Filocolo* which give considerably greater importance to the ethical and moral issues raised in the text. Four critics in particular, Nicolas Perella, Victoria Kirkham, Robert Hollander, and Janet Smarr, have provided us with new insights into the *Filocolo* which have significantly contributed to our understanding of this work. Nicolas Perella, the first American critic to devote serious attention to the *Filocolo*, analyzed it in thematic terms. Perella states that the main theme is «the natural or instinctive love that attracts two young people of the opposite sex and the persistence of their love against the obstacles erected by an unsympathetic law or by class conscious relatives concerned with preserving the distinctions created by social and economic position».[18] Other themes in the *Filocolo* (love, fortune, beauty, and courtliness) are essential to an understanding of Boccaccio's spiritual world, according to Perella, because they are part of the author's psychological portrayal of man's sentimental life.

Looking at the theme of love, Perella concurs with Italian critics who claim that it is far from animalism. Sexual love is made beautiful, not condemned, but the context in which it takes place is criticized. The most erotic moments, such as the near seduction of Florio by the two maidens, are free of «crude materialistic description» and are filled with the «tremulous yet passionate awe and desire for possession that accompany the awakening to the vision of beauty». Awe at feminine beauty is a motif in the *Filocolo* which, as Perella points out, Boccaccio has taken from the «dolce stil novo»: Biancifiore has a celestial splendor and divine attributes which, however, do not diminish her physical attractions or «lift her into a sphere of impalpable spirituality». Furthermore, «it is beauty primarily as a physical quality that is made to have a refining or elevating effect». As Perella correctly points out, all these courtly elements can be found in the protagonists' conduct and reasoning, and serve to ennoble both the characters and the text. What Perella does not show, however, are the

---

[18] Nicolas Perella, *The World of Boccaccio's «Filocolo»*, «PMLA», CXXVI, 1961, pp. 330-339.

ambiguous aspects of the protagonists' courtliness: while at times it may ennoble the characters, at other times it also debases them, as we shall see.

Looking at those elements which make the *Filocolo* an «immature work», Perella, like Italian critics before him, criticizes Boccaccio's inability to fuse the diverse material he brings to his work, his arbitrary juxtaposition of differing traditions, tendencies, and episodes, his enthusiastic but inordinate outpouring of culture, and his use of numerous and diverse allusions and echoes, all of which, according to Perella, have no apparent connection to one another. In the words of Perella, much of this is «irrelevant material» which may have been intended as an integral part of the work, but is simply an ornamental device. For Perella, the classical gods are a case in point: they are principle actors and ruling agents of a world which Boccaccio studies with such psychological realism that their presence is «superfluous and bothersome». According to Perella, the gods are an expedient for Boccaccio to move action without having to give logical connections or additional psychological probing: they are one more example of how Boccaccio's culture could «tyrannize him and do violence to his own genius».

Despite the prominence of these «unsubstantial literary phantasms», the pagan deities are not the real antagonists in the *Filocolo*, Fortuna is, according to Perella. Fortuna is not conceived as a Dantean-Christian «handmaiden or administrator of God operating within an intelligible providential order of things», but rather a metaphorical expression, «a personification, a rhetorical device seeking to vitalize the abstract and neutral concept of the [...] unexpected happening». It is hard to agree with Perella that Fortuna has no relationship to a transcendent order of things. As we shall see, Fortuna is closely connected to the providential plan which permeates the plot of the *Filocolo*. This, however, does not preclude Fortuna from also functioning as a metaphor: many characters in the *Filocolo* in fact treat her as such, blaming her for their own shortcomings and failures. Perella is correct, however, when he says that the reality of Fortuna is completely contingent upon the given desires of human beings. As we shall see, Fortuna does not abate her ill will against the protagonists until they have brought their appetites fully under the control of reason.

Several years later Victoria Kirkham revealed the central importance of the thirteen *questioni d'amore* which are discussed at Fiammetta's court of love in Naples. As Kirkham has shown, the *questioni* have a symmetrical structure which centers around the debate between Fiammetta (the queen of this court of love) and Caleone, whom both Kirkham and Quaglio identify as Boccaccio the narrator. The debate centers around the relative merits of *amore onesto* and *amore per diletto*, with Fiammetta supporting the former and Caleone the latter. Fiammetta rejects *amore per diletto*, which Kirkham identifies with courtly love, in favor of *amore onesto*, which Kirkham associates with Christian love. Kirkham concludes that, «The *questioni d'amore* thus appear to be structured around a double perspective involving on the one hand the relative, or peripheral, supremacy of Cupid, and on the other the absolute and central supremacy of God». [19]

Kirkham's analysis, however, is not limited to the *questioni d'amore*. She illustrates the way in which this «double perspective of courtly and Christian love» has both a structural and thematic importance in the plot itself. For example, the dream visions Florio has immediately before and after the court of love episode represent, according to Kirkham, courtly love and Christian love respectively. The concentric patterns Kirkham finds in the love court and in the dream visions that frame it also appear in the larger frame of the tale itself. As Kirkham has shown, the protagonists' movement from courtly love to Christian love (as witnessed by their conversion to Christianity) also brings them full circle when they complete the pilgrimage Lelio and Giulia had begun, and when they fulfill in Book V the numerous visions which appeared in the first four books. [20] By proposing these thematic and structural patterns within the *Filocolo*, Kirkham rectifies earlier criticism about the digressive and seemingly meaningless structure of the *Filocolo*. Kirkham's analysis proves that the innovative passages Boccaccio added to the rough material of the source tale play an integral part in both the meaning and the structure of the narrative.

A few years later, Robert Hollander incorporated Kirkham's conclusions in his contention that there are two Venuses in the *Filocolo*, a terrestrial and a celestial Venus. Hollander concludes that «whatever the aesthetic merit of the *Filocolo*, [...] Boccaccio has constructed

---

[19] VICTORIA KIRKHAM, *op. cit.*, p. 53.

[20] I agree with Kirkham that the *Filocolo* basically rejects courtly love in favor of Christian love; however, I disagree with her contention that Fileno's apparent rejection of courtly love and his subsequent conversion to Christianity can be compared to those of Florio and Biancifiore.

what we might call [...] a "Christian romance," in which the deity with whom we begin, the Venus of the *Ars amatoria*, is superseded by a better Venus, who in turn yields to the true God». [21] Hollander's thesis thus rectifies Perella's claim that the classical gods are insignificant in the narrative.

More recently, Janet Smarr has taken the theses of Kirkham and Hollander a step further. Since many of the issues and episodes discussed in her compelling study are also discussed in this book, a close look at her essay can serve as the point of departure for our analysis of the *Filocolo*. [22] Smarr begins by reaffirming the literary fiction behind the name Fiammetta and the persona of the narrator. This means, according to Smarr, that Boccaccio's work must be read on several levels, not just the literal level (as earlier scholars and critics had done). In addition to proposing a moral and allegorical reading of Boccaccio's work, Smarr sees a polarity between the Ovidian and Dantean elements that appear throughout the *Filocolo*. [23] Boccaccio's use of Ovid reflects a worldly love whose literature serves as a means of attracting the woman to the narrator, whereas his use of Dante reflects the holy love whose literature serves to move the lover to his lady, and in turn to God. According to Smarr, Boccaccio is writing «to seduce and to educate, to draw the soul toward pleasure and toward truth [...] to join the erotic with the moral». [24]

Looking at the opening chapters, Smarr sees a mixture of religious and secular narratives which reflect two different writers: the narrator as lover «who writes as a labor of love at the request of his lady Maria», and Ilario «the original author of the history [...] who within the story converted Florio and his companions to Christianity». The existence of two fictional authors (besides the real Boccaccio) implies two different intentions for the same narration: the narrator's offer to educate lovers «in the art of "perfect" love exemplified by Florio and Biancifiore» and Ilario's story which is supposed to educate future readers in the same holy love he converted Florio and Biancifiore to.

---

[21] ROBERT HOLLANDER, *Boccaccio's Two Venuses*, New York, Columbia University Press, 1977, pp 39-40.

[22] JANET L. SMARR, *Boccaccio and Fiammetta: The Narrator as Lover*, Urbana, University of Illinois Press, 1986, pp. 34-60.

[23] Smarr shows in her book how the *Filocolo* consists of many literary genres (epic, romance, erotic poetry, etc.) all of which have been allegorized.

[24] Smarr seems to depart from Kirkham's contention that Boccaccio is rejecting one form of love and literature in favor of another.

The *Filocolo*, therefore, is meant to inspire «two quite different kinds of love: human and divine».

As Smarr has shown, the doubleness of the text is reflected in similar dualities between the spiritual and erotic themes and allusions that appear in the tale itself: Priapus/Astrea, lover/monk, classic epic/Christian allegory, Florio's adventures/Christ's mission on earth, Florio and Biancifiore's love/Christ's incarnation and redemption of man, etc. This doubleness also appears in Florio's journey to Biancifiore and in his journey to God, as revealed by the double meaning of the word «salute»: besides its Dantean meaning of salvation, the word also has sexual connotations, as seen in the expressions «porto di salute» and «nave in porto».[25] Smarr's insight into the spiritual meaning of «salute» and its thematic importance in the *Filocolo* is very convincing. It is hard to agree, however, with her claim that Florio's «etterno esilio» (i.e. his journey to Biancifiore) is due to Eve's sin and is equated with the loss of Biancifiore.[26] As we shall see, Florio's journey brings him close to the «etterno esilio» of Hell (like Ulysses's journey in *Inferno* XXVI) before it brings him to God. His journey to Biancifiore must end (along with his *amor per diletto*) before he and Biancifiore can find God and *caritas* (*amor onesto*).

Looking at Fiammetta, the queen of the court of love, Smarr states that she is the same lady the narrator addresses in the introduction to his book, whereas her admirer (Caleone) is a figure for the narrator. As Smarr has convincingly shown, both women are introduced with religious resonances. The queen of the court of love is given attributes reserved to the Virgin Mary, including the notion that her love «binds together both the cosmos and human society». This in turn is supported by the fact that it is Fiammetta who advocates *amore onesto* over *amore per diletto*. Fiammetta becomes for Smarr «a miracle sent from the heaven of the celestial Venus as a demonstration of divine love, the holy alternative of Cupid's "dardi"».

There is, however, a certain amount of ambiguity in the debate between Fiammetta and Caleone, as Smarr astutely points out: if *amore onesto* is the best kind of love and *amore utile* the worst, where

---

[25] As we shall see, the word «salute» also appears in a number of other contexts which stress salvation.

[26] Smarr mistakenly attributes to Florio Fileno's misogynistic complaint against Eve in III 35, 2; see SMARR, *op. cit.*, p. 37. It is Biancifiore's Eve-like deception of Fileno that brings about his «etterno esilio». Florio's «etterno esilio», on the other hand, is brought about by the deception of his parents.

does *amore per diletto* stand? «Fiammetta's argument with Caleone attempts to classify it on one side or the other, ignoring the idea of a middle ground. Is she, then, entirely correct in her assessment or is she failing to acknowledge the possibility that such love can lead to good?» Smarr looks for answers to these crucial questions in the amorous adventures of Florio and Biancifiore. Looking at the literary antecedents of the episode narrating the protagonists' falling in love (*Inferno* V and *Aeneid* I), Smarr claims that «the negative implications of both these models are transmuted by the innocence of Boccaccio's young couple».[27] A closer look at the protagonists' conduct, however, suggests that they are not quite as innocent as Smarr and other critics have suggested. Smarr attempts to further support her claim by viewing the protagonists' secret marriage in the tower as a positive step: «The *Filocolo* celebrates their marriage as a relation that can reconcile virtue and chastity with sexual desire. Venus and Diana, the motivating deities of much of the *Filocolo's* action, join forces for the marriage of Florio and Biancifiore». Marriage is indeed the only solution to the protagonists' amorous and social hardships; however, the fact that the two lovers secretly marry because of their *amor per diletto*, and the fact that this marriage brings about a massacre and almost kills them, suggest that there is a darker side to the protagonists' clandestine activities in the tower.[28]

Smarr concludes that Boccaccio, like Dante, «is turning love stories to an ultimately Christian use, thus "saving" the pleasures of Ovid's poetry in both senses of the word: preserving them and transforming them for Christian readers», and adds that «human love can actually lead to Christian love without our needing to reject the former». I believe, instead, that in the *Filocolo* Ovidian love gives way to Christian love: *amor per diletto* is one of several stumbling blocks the lovers must overcome in their quest for beatitude (*amor onesto*). As we shall see, Ovidian love is a false (i.e. pagan) image of Christian love, and must be renounced before *caritas* can be attained.

If we interpret the duality between *amor per diletto* and *amor onesto* as a clash between courtly love and Christian love, whereby the latter rejects the former (as suggested by Kirkham), are we overlook-

---

[27] Smarr views in positive terms Florio's self-comparison to Paris, Menelaus, and Ulysses, despite the fact that these characters tended to have negative connotations in medieval literature.

[28] The protagonists' ulterior motives for getting married are even tainted by a touch of *amor utile*, as we shall see.

ing the possibility that these two kinds of love have something in common? If, on the other hand, we interpret this duality as a contrast between Ovidian and Dantean love, whereby the former leads to the latter without rejecting it (as Smarr has suggested), are we ignoring the possibility that these two loves might be irreconcilable? Although it may be argued that Ovid's works were «moralized» in the Middle Ages in order to make them more acceptable to a Christian audience, it is hard to see how Dante's love for Beatrice, or even Christian love, can be reconciled with the love described in the *Ars amatoria*. By the same token, it is hard to see how Dante's repressed sexual desire for Beatrice (as revealed in the first dream of the *Vita Nuova*) can be placed at the same level as *caritas*, even though Dante feels Christian charity and beatitude whenever he sees Beatrice. Could it be that Boccaccio viewed Dante as someone who tried unsuccessfully to bridge the gap between «human love» and Christian love?

If, as Smarr claims, Dante and Ovid coexist in the *Filocolo*, it is because the narrator's Ovidian love story barely hides Ilario's Dantean tale on which it is based. Ilario's subtext and its Christian message are a palimpsest which lies just beneath the narrator's own superficial tale of Florio and Biancifiore. It is up to the reader to go beyond the narrator's story in order to reach Ilario's more meaningful source tale. The fact that the narrator as lover is oblivious to the spiritual message of Ilario's subtext suggests that the love he valorizes in his narrative (*amor per diletto*) has little spiritual significance other than the fact that it may eventually lead to or be superseded by *caritas*. Furthermore, the fact that the narrator believes, as do the characters in the *Filocolo*, that this kind of love will bring happiness (a point that is repeatedly disproven by the misadventures of Florio, Biancifiore, Fileno, Caleone and Idalogo) suggests that he, like Caleone, does not recognize that *amor per diletto* and beatitude («true happiness») are two different things. Ultimately, it is the author, not the shortsighted narrator, who understands the moral implications of his Ovidian/classical and Dantean/Christian sources. Ilario's subtext and the narrator's own text are indeed polar opposites, representing two totally different concepts of love, as Smarr has pointed out. I believe, however, that Boccaccio's point of view is to be found in Fiammetta and Ilario's views of love, rather than in those of Caleone and the narrator. Ilario's subtext functions, therefore, as a theological objective correlative to the narrator's text: it shows the shortcomings of Florio and Biancifiore's love before their conversion.

In the *Filocolo* Christian love (*amor onesto*) is only attained after the protagonists have been converted to Christianity (almost a year after they have consummated their love in Alexandria). Their love prior to conversion undergoes three transformations: before their adventures in Alexandria, it is continent; during their adventures in Alexandria it is passionate; and after their adventures in Alexandria it attains the cardinal virtue of temperance.[29] It is not surprising, therefore, that the protagonists' conversion to Christianity and *caritas* takes place almost a year after they have been married, a year during which their appetites have been brought under the control of reason. The only passionate love that we find in Book V of the *Filocolo* is that of the three unrequited lovers who still believe in *amor per diletto*--Fileno, Caleone, and Idalogo. Rejecting *amor per diletto* for *amore onesto* does not mean, however, that the two have nothing in common. The ambiguity that Smarr noticed in the debate between Fiammetta and Caleone can be seen as a subtle recognition on the part of Boccaccio that *amor onesto* and *amor per diletto* are neither reconcilable nor completely divorced from each other: they both share an innate desire for beatitude, but totally different views of what beatitude is and how it is attained.

Besides drawing our attention to the importance of love in the narrative, Fiammetta's court of love also alludes to the importance of interpretation. Each *questione d'amore* deals with an aspect of amorous conduct which Fiammetta is asked to judge. The person asking the *questione d'amore* invariably has an interpretation of his/her own which runs counter to that of the queen, and from these differing interpretations arise the debates between Fiammetta and her interlocutor. (Even the words and deeds of the characters within the *questioni d'amore* are often equivocal and must be interpreted.) By setting the court of love in a period of time that is disjointed from the actual setting of the plot (i.e. Boccaccio's fourteenth century Naples versus Florio's sixth century Italy), Boccaccio is holding a mirror to his fourteenth century readers — the very same people in Fiammetta's entourage.[30] Boccaccio's intended audience would have probably dis-

---

[29] In the words of St. Thomas Aquinas, «*Continentia* is present when rational deliberation governs the sense-appetite, but with the latter still in revolt. It is therefore an imperfect state compared with the full virtue of *temperantia*» (*Summa Theologica* IIa, IIae, q. 155, art. 1).

[30] This is supported by Smarr's contention that Fiammetta is the same person who asked the narrator (alias Caleone) to write the *Filocolo*.

cussed aspects of the *Filocolo* the same way Fiammetta's participants discuss the issues raised at the court of love. [31] One can assume, therefore, that his readers are also expected to question and interpret the amorous conduct of the characters in the *Filocolo* in much the same way.

The importance of interpretation is further suggested by the two dream visions which immediately precede and follow the court of love: both visions beg to be interpreted. If they are not interpreted, they make no sense and have no purpose in the narrative. The same is true, to a certain extent, of many of the other episodes in the *Filocolo*. It is not surprising, therefore, that the *questioni d'amore* bear directly on the events in plot, as Kirkham, Smarr, Cherchi, and Surdich have shown. [32] As we shall see, the acts of interpretation which begin at the center of the *Filocolo* (at Fiammetta's court of love) ripple to the work's furthest edges.

By illustrating how the court of love goes about interpreting the words and deeds of other lovers, Boccaccio is not simply telling his readers that they too should debate, discuss, and interpret the amorous conduct of the characters in his work, he is also illustrating what happens when one is engaged in interpretation. Arguments which may be used to support one point, actually support the opposite point of view, as Smarr has shown in her analysis of the debate between Caleone and Fiammetta. [33] Furthermore, many of the interpretations and much of the logic used at the court of love are quite arbitrary (this is true even of some of Fiammetta's rulings on the *questioni*). This arbitrariness is made more evident by the fact that Fiammetta always has the last word (since she is the queen) and is therefore always «right». [34] Therefore, while Boccaccio is encouraging us to interpret and discuss his work, he is also showing us the pitfalls, limitations, and arbitrariness of interpretation. It is not surprising that, in the debate between Caleone and Fiammetta, the issue of *amore onesto* and *amore per diletto* is never fully resolved: any resolution would arbitrari-

---

[31] The same can be said about the ten narrators in the *Decameron* who comment on the individual novelle.

[32] See PAOLO CHERCHI, *Andrea Cappellano, i trovatori, e altri temi romanzi*, Rome, Bulzoni Editore, 1979, pp. 210-217; and SURDICH, *op. cit.*, pp. 49 sg.

[33] We shall see the same thing happen when the protagonists themselves discuss or interpret a given point.

[34] For a similar discussion of Fiammetta, see HENRY ANSGAR KELLY, *Love and Marriage in the Age of Chaucer*, Ithaca, N.Y., Cornell University Press, 1975, p. 50.

ly give more importance to one kind of love than to another. Ultimately, the *questioni d'amore* reveal the relative and arbitrary nature of interpretative judgments.

As we shall see in this study, there is a certain amount of ambiguity throughout the *Filocolo*, making any interpretation of this work quite difficult. The ambiguity of the text, as Robert M. Durling has pointed out, is not only present when an overt meaning is contradicted by ironic implications, creating a tension between the two, but also when the text presents two conflicting possibilities without offering clues that permit decision, either because the author could not decide or for some other reason (confusion, an oversight on the part of the author, etc.). [35] Sometimes the ambiguities in the *Filocolo* are simply Boccaccio's oversights, but in the majority of cases they are not. Boccaccio, in fact, uses irony (especially dramatic irony) to contradict the assumptions held by his characters and his audience. It is by analyzing these assumptions and the manner in which Boccaccio undercuts them that we can better understand the *Filocolo*.

Kirkham and Smarr have set us on the right path by showing the thematic importance of love in the narrative. The duality between *amor onesto* and *amor per diletto*, however, can be extended to include the larger duality between classical and Christian cultures. [36] By applying this polarity to a broader range of themes and issues, we will be able to interpret in a more comprehensive fashion the plot of the *Filocolo*. The juxtaposition of two different, yet extremely important cultures also allows us to see the limitations of each. Hence our interpretation of the *Filocolo* becomes, as it were, a passing of judgment on the classical, courtly, and early Christian cultures of the protagonists, not unlike the judgments passed by Fiammetta and her interlocutors in their court of love.

In this study I propose to show how classical, courtly, and Christian cultures intertwine in the world of the *Filocolo* and play a greater role in the world of the characters than previously believed. The narrative is filled with cultural allusions which would have been familiar to the well-educated readers of the fourteenth century, but

---

[35] I am grateful to Professor Durling for bringing this to my attention.

[36] The concept of love extends itself beyond the actual love story of Florio and Bianci-fiore, and encompasses the entire universe of both the author and his characters. It is important, therefore, to see how love in all its manifestations rules both the inner and exterior worlds of the protagonists.

not necessarily to those of the twentieth century. It is essential, therefore, that any critical appraisal of the *Filocolo* take into account Boccaccio's cultural milieu before it can unravel the allusive and often elusive nature of this work. Scholars have been able to reconstruct Boccaccio's literary and cultural background to the point that we now know most of the texts Boccaccio used in his various works. Not until recently, however, have scholars and critics (especially Smarr and Kirkham) attempted to use this extra-literary material to interpret his early works.

This study will examine how key philosophical concepts and important aspects of medieval culture function as governing principles in the *Filocolo*. The main themes in the *Filocolo* (fate, fortune, Providence, free choice versus determinism, acquired versus achieved nobility, divine love versus courtly love, reason versus desire, astrology and pagan divinities versus the powers of the human soul, immanent justice versus human injustice, divine and natural law versus human law, etc.) can be traced to influential works by Aristotle, Augustine, Ovid, Boethius, Aquinas, Bernard Silvester, Andreas Capellanus, and Dante. Of these writers, Boethius and Aquinas are particularly well suited to a thematic analysis of the *Filocolo*. Both philosophers had a great influence on fourteenth-century vernacular literature (especially when that literature dealt with the same themes discussed in the *Filocolo*). Since Boethius' *De consolatione philosophiae* never refers to Christianity, Boccaccio might have regarded it as a syncretic fusion of pagan and early Christian philosophies representing a culture similar to the one he was trying to portray in the *Filocolo*. Aquinas' *Summa Theologica*, on the other hand, is a synthesis of Aristotelian (i.e. pagan) and Christian thought suited to the naturalism Boccaccio seems to have been pursuing throughout his literary career. [37] Although it is not always possible to determine the extent to which Boccaccio was familiar with these influential authors at the time he was writing the *Filocolo*, the philosophical concepts discussed in their works would have been accessible to him through other sources as well. [38] Furthermore, the themes Boccaccio incorporates in the *Filocolo* were themselves issues which were discussed and debated

---

[37] For a discussion of Boccaccio's naturalism, see ALDO D. SCAGLIONE, *Nature and Love in the Late Middle Ages*, Berkeley & Los Angeles, University of California Press, 1963, pp. 48-125.

[38] This would be particularly true of famous vernacular works, such as the *Roman de la Rose*, which dealt with similar themes that can be traced to Scholastic Aristotelianism.

throughout his century. The importance these concepts have in the narrative suggests that the *Filocolo* is more than just the tale of two star-crossed lovers: it is also a representation of the world as Boccaccio understood it.

An understanding of the thematic principles in the *Filocolo* will also help explain why certain aspects of this work have given the *Filocolo* a bad name (e.g. the apparent lack of unity in the plot, the infinite digressions, episodes and amplifications which seem to be unrelated to one another, and the seemingly incongruous structure of a text which gives the impression of having no unifying meaning). I shall attempt to look at the most important episodes and digressions in order to understand their purpose in the narrative and discover how they fit in the overall structure of the tale. My contention is that each episode, chapter, and amplification in the *Filocolo* has a function that is not purely aesthetic or mimetic, but also thematic and hermeneutic.

This study analyzes the thematic patterns in the *Filocolo* in chronological order. The first chapter is devoted to an analysis of Book I and how it relates to Book V of the *Filocolo*. In it I discuss the cosmic and supernatural forces that affect the characters' behavior. The second chapter examines the thematic importance of astrology in Books I through V, and its effect on the characters. The third chapter is a close reading of Book II, and examines the characters' behavior in terms of medieval psychology. The fourth chapter analyzes the legal issues raised in Books II and III, and the way they relate to Book V. The fifth chapter analyzes Book IV, the climactic turning point in the *Filocolo*. The last chapter looks at how the *Filocolo* was incorporated into the *Decameron*, and how the differences between these two works can shed light on Boccaccio's changing perspective of his world.

Chapter One

FATE, FORTUNE, AND PROVIDENCE: BOETHIUS IN THE *FILOCOLO*

In his important study *Giovanni Boccaccio a Napoli*, Francesco Torraca reconstructed Boccaccio's literary and cultural background at the time the *Filocolo* was written. One work which Torraca believed Boccaccio might have known at that time was Boethius's *De consolatione philosophiae* since it seems to be the source of several sentences in the *Filocolo*. [1] Years later, Antonio Enzo Quaglio concurred with Torraca's suggestion. [2] Neither critic, however, went beyond identifying the verbal echoes from Boethius's famous treatise.

A closer look at the *Filocolo* shows that Boethius plays a significant role in the narrative, one which goes beyond a mere *imitatio* of certain images or sentences. One of the first things to suggest this is the spatial and temporal setting of Boccaccio's romance. As Quaglio has suggested, the tale is set in a period of time which goes from 529 to 552 A.D. [3] On the basis of inter-textual allusions and chronologies familiar to Boccaccio, Quaglio has proposed that Florio and Biancifiore were conceived in 529 A.D. and were born the following year on Pentecost. What Quaglio does not mention, however, is that the narrative actually begins five years earlier with an allusion to the marriage of Biancifiore's Christian Roman parents, Giulia Topazia

---

[1] See Francesco Torraca, *Giovanni Boccaccio a Napoli*, Napoli, L. Pierro & figli, 1915, pp. 101-102.

[2] See Antonio Enzo Quaglio, *Tra fonti e testo del «Filocolo»*, «Giornale storico della letteratura italiana», CXXXIX, 1962, p. 140, & CXL, 1963, p. 514. See also Giovanni Boccaccio, *Filocolo*, edited by Antonio Enzo Quaglio, Milan, Mondadori, 1967 («Tutte le opere di Giovanni Boccaccio», I) p. 837. All the quotations from the *Filocolo* are taken from this edition.

[3] The first person to suggest that the events in the *Filocolo* occur around this period was Aldo Rossi, *Dante nella prospettiva del Boccaccio*, «Studi danteschi», 37, 1960, p. 121. Quaglio elaborates on Rossi's suggestion in *Tra fonti e testo del «Filocolo»*, *op. cit.*, CXL, 1963, pp. 340-41.

and Quinto Lelio Africano, in the same year Boethius was executed by Theodoric the Ostrogoth (524 A.D.). The fact that Lelio and Giulia got married the year Boethius wrote the *De consolatione philosophiae* while awaiting execution suggests that Boccaccio wants his narrative to begin where Boethius's own narrative ended.

This quasi-historical time frame is complemented by an equally suggestive spatial setting: a good part of the plot unfolds in Verona, one of two cities where Felice holds court (the other city is Cordova). Verona was also one of Theodoric's most important cities. [4] When Lelio is killed by Felice at the beginning of the tale, the episode recalls the deaths of Boethius and other Christian Romans under Theodoric's orders. Needless to say, there are discrepancies in the narrative which fail to make the *Filocolo* a purely historical epic. Felice's empire, for example, includes much of eighth-century Arabic Spain as well as sixth-century Ostrogothic Italy; but such discrepancies are consonant with the poetics of the medieval romance genre. [5] As we shall see, Boccaccio's purpose for these semi-historical allusions is not so much to write a history of two star-crossed lovers, as Fiammetta asked the narrator to do, but rather to place their plight in a context which is similar to Boethius' at the time he was writing the *De consolatione philosophiae*. In addition to creating a syncretic fusion of Roman and Christian cultures similar to the one Boccaccio could have easily assumed existed during the sixth century, the author is also adopting Boethius's philosophy for the themes of his own narrative.

Some of these themes begin to appear in the first two chapters of the *Filocolo* when the narrator explains how Fiammetta (the *senhal* for Boccaccio's beloved) asked him to write «un picciolo libretto, volgarmente parlando, nel quale il nascimento, lo 'nnamoramento e gli accidenti de' detti due infino alla loro fine interamente si contenga» (I 1, 26). Her reason for requesting a new account of the adventures of Florio and Biancifiore is given in the preceding line:

Certo grande ingiuria riceve la memoria degli amorosi giovani, pensando alla grande costanza de' loro animi, i quali in uno volere per l'amorosa forza sempre

---

[4] Although Theodoric made Ravenna the capital of his kingdom, he is known as Theodoric of Verona in the *Hildebrandslied*, and he appears in the *Heldenbuch* as Dietrich of Berne (Dietrich of Verona).

[5] For a different perspective and analysis of the spatial and temporal setting of the *Filocolo*, see JAMES H. McGREGOR, *The Shades of Aeneas: The Imitation of Vergil and the History of Paganism in Boccaccio's «Filostrato», «Filocolo», and «Teseida»*, Athens, Georgia, The University of Georgia Press, 1991, pp. 23-27.

furono fermi servandosi debita fede, a non essere con debita ricordanza la loro fama essaltata da' versi d'alcun poeta, ma lasciata solamente ne' fabulosi parlari degli ignoranti. (I 1, 25)

Shortly thereafter, in his long address to the readers the narrator says:

Adunque, o giovani, i quali avete la vela della barca della vaga mente dirizzata a' venti che muovono dalle dorate penne ventilanti del giovane figliuolo di Citerea, negli amorosi pelaghi dimoranti disiosi di pervenire a porto di salute con istudioso passo, io per la sua inestimabile potenza vi priego che divotamente prestiate alquanto alla presente opera lo 'ntelletto, però che voi in essa troverete quanto la mobile fortuna abbia negli antichi amori date varie permutazioni e tempestose, alle quali poi con tranquillo mare s'è lieta rivolta a' sostenitori; onde per questo potrete vedere voi soli non essere sostenitori primi delle avverse cose, e fermamente credere di non dovere essere gli ultimi. Di che prendere potrete consolazione, se quello è vero, che a' miseri sia sollazzo d'avere compagni nelle pene; e similemente ve ne seguirà speranza di guiderdone, la quale non verrà sanza alleggiamento delle vostre pene. (I 2, 1-2)

It is clear from what both Fiammetta and the narrator say that Florio and Biancifiore are seen as *exempla* of steadfastness and faithfulness in the face of adversity: they are two lovers who have withstood the trials and tribulations of the goddess Fortuna. The Boethian image of the boat beset by the tempests of Fortuna has been modified by the narrator into a love boat which, after sailing through Fortune's tempest, finds calm seas once the Boethian goddess «s'è lieta rivolta». Boccaccio is ascribing to these lovers a fate similar to that of someone who places himself in the hands of Fortuna. In fact, fortune and love are inexorably linked to one another in a constant state of tension throughout the first four books of the *Filocolo*. Unlike the love boat Dante describes in his sonnet *Guido, i' vorrei che tu e Lapo ed io*, there is no idyllic moment «sì che fortuna od altro tempo rio / non ci potesse dare impedimento»: the unrequited lovers in the *Filocolo* are constantly at the mercy of Fortuna.

The example set by these two lovers is one of virtue and good faith, from Fiammetta's point of view, and one of hope and consolation from the point of view of the narrator. In both cases their example is consonant with the philosophy of Boethius, as we shall see. In the court of love (IV 17-70) Fiammetta is a proponent of a virtuous and charitable love (*amor onesto*), as Victoria Kirkham and Janet

Smarr have shown. [6] It is only fitting that she should emphasize the lovers' virtue and nobility of character in her request for a nobler account of their lives. The narrator, on the other hand, is an unrequited lover who seeks *amor per diletto*. He acknowledges the importance of devoting oneself to only one beloved, and seeks consolation to his suffering while awaiting his reward for love's labor. The romance he is about to narrate, therefore, is a *consolatio amoris* for himself and other unrequited lovers. Like a true courtly lover, the narrator places his hope in his beloved (Fiammetta) the same way the protagonists of his tale place their hopes in each other. The narrator's hope, like his *consolatio*, is a pale imitation of the hope Boethius's narrator places in his lady, Philosophy. It is also a false reflection of the theological virtue of hope which Florio and Biancifiore discover when they become Christians. [7] As we shall see, hope plays an important thematic role in the *Filocolo* which goes well beyond the narrator's own hopes as a courtly lover.

When the narrator actually begins narrating his version of the lives of Florio and Biancifiore, he makes the events which precede their birth part of a providential plan which shares many of the same characteristics of Boethius's Providence. The tale begins with a classicized account of Christian history from the fall of the rebellious angels to the founding of Santiago de Compostella. This brief account sets the stage for the important episode describing Lelio's tragic death. The conflict between Giove and Pluto (allegorical figures for God and Satan) is later picked up when the narrator describes Satan's attempt to prevent Lelio and Giulia from carrying out the pilgrimage they promised to make to Santiago. As Cazalé-Bérard has pointed out, the divine interventions that occur in this episode point to a providential plan which will bring about Lelio's spiritual salvation and the eventual reestablishment of order over chaos: a triumph of good over evil. [8] Cazalé-Bérard's suggestion that there is a providential scheme at work in the *Filocolo* can be supported by the way Boccaccio depicts Lelio's prayer to Saint James and the ensuing vision Lelio has of the saint. As Olin H. Moore pointed out, this episode vividly recalls the Annuncia-

---

[6] See VICTORIA KIRKHAM, *op. cit.*, pp. 47-59; and JANET SMARR, *op. cit.*, pp. 34-60.
[7] It is worth noting that in the *Amorosa visione* Fiammetta becomes the nymph who symbolizes the theological virtue of hope.
[8] See CLAUDE CAZALÉ-BÉRARD, *Les structures narratives dans le premier livre du «Filocolo» de Giovanni Boccaccio*, «Revue des études italiennes», ns. XVII, 1971, pp. 125-129.

tion of the angel to Zacharias in the first chapter of Luke's Gospel. [9]
This is followed by a second instance of divine intervention when
Lelio and his small band of men decide to fight Felice's army. Prior to
the battle, a voice from a bright cloud tells them:

Sicuramente e sanza dubbio combattete, che io sarò sempre appresso di voi
aiutandovi vendicare le vostre morti; e sanza alcuna ammirazione le presenti
parole ascoltate, che tal volta conviene che 'l sangue d'uno uomo giusto per
salvamento di tutto un popolo si spanda. Voi sarete oggi tutti meco nel vero
tempio di Colui il cui voi andate a vedere, e quivi le corone apparecchiate alla
vostra vittoria vi donerò. (I 25, 9-10)

Olin Moore correctly pointed out that «Lelio is compared to the lamb
of God which was slain for the salvation of the world», but adds that
«the Scriptural allusion is dragged into the romance by Boccaccio
without any artistic justification whatever». [10] One must take issue
with the latter point because, even though Boccaccio's purpose for
including this Scriptural detail is not clear at this point in the narrative, it becomes clear towards the end of the *Filocolo* when Felice and
his entire kingdom convert to Christianity. The voice from the cloud
anticipates this conversion «di tutto un popolo» while at the same time
anticipating the death «d'uno uomo giusto» (Lelio) that will make this
mass conversion possible. Lelio's death, in fact, sets in motion an
intricate series of events which will conclude with the conversion of
the very same man who killed him, and those foreign people («strani
popoli») rebellious to the laws of God («del tutto le siano ribelli»), as
Lelio refers to them in his prayer.

The thematic importance of salvation in this episode is stressed by
the repeated use of the word «salute», and by the interesting contexts
in which it is used. As both Antonio Enzo Quaglio and Giuseppe Velli
have shown, the episode is patterned after Lucan's *De bello civili*. [11]
The speeches Lelio makes to his men prior to the battle clearly echo
those of Pompey, as Velli has shown; even the battle between Lelio's
small band of men and Felice's army recalls the battle at Pharsalia.

---

[9] See OLIN H. MOORE, *Boccaccio's «Filocolo» and the Annunciation*, «Modern Language
Notes», XXXIII, 1918, pp. 438-440.

[10] OLIN, *op. cit.*, p. 438.

[11] See A.E. QUAGLIO, *Boccaccio e Lucano: una concordanza e una fonte dal «Filocolo»
all'«Amorosa visione»*, «Cultura neolatina», XXIII, 1963, pp. 153-171; and GIUSEPPE VELLI,
Cultura e «imitatio» nel primo Boccaccio, «Annali della Scuola Normale Superiore di Pisa», s. II,
vol. XXXVII, 1968, pp. 65-93 (later reprinted in *Petrarca e Boccaccio: Tradizione, Memoria,
Scrittura*, Padova, Antenore, 1975, pp. 61-96).

Velli suggests that these passages from Lucan are meant to heighten the elegiac and fatalistic moments in the narrative. We can find support for Velli's observation in a number of premonitory allusions to Lelio's death which become more and more ominous as he approaches his seemingly foreordained fate (I 5, 5; I 8, 2; I 15, 2-3; I 24, 8). A closer look at the episode, however, reveals that it is neither as fatalistic nor as pessimistic as its classical source. This may best be seen in an example of *amplificatio* which Velli cites to illustrate Boccaccio's imitation of Lucan: «*alla vostra salute* non manca altro che l'opera dè ferri... ("extremum ferri superest opus")». Boccaccio added the words «alla vostra salute»; and by doing so «lo scrittore discioglie la pregnante espressione del cordovese mediante aggiunte esplicative che mirano a rinsaldare la plausabilità della nuova situazione», as Velli has suggested. [12] It is more likely, however, that these loaded words were added to underscore the thematic importance of salvation in this episode.

It would seem, therefore, that Boccaccio is rewriting Lucan, not just imitating him. Instead of the tragic outcome of the battle of Pharsalia with its disastrous consequences to the Roman republic, the seemingly tragic battle in which Lelio dies is marked by hope and consolation for all the characters involved. Saint James, like Fiammetta in the *Amorosa Visione*, is also a figure for hope: as Giuseppe Mazzotta has pointed out, it is Saint James who questions Dante on the theological virtue of hope in *Paradiso* XXV. [13] Boccaccio has thus transformed Lucan's tragic and hopeless pessimism into a Christian and Boethian optimism.

If the reader of the *Filocolo* must wait until the end of the tale in order to understand the beginning, the characters themselves find it just as hard to comprehend what is happening and why. When Giulia sees Felice's army coming down the mountain to attack them in the valley, she asks Lelio: «O Lelio, ove è fuggito il tuo lungo provedimento? Or non vedi tu quella gente armata che sì furiosamente verso noi discende dell'alto monte? Che gente può ella essere? Come non provedi tu al necessario rimedio ora, se elli vengono per offenderci?» (I 17, 4). Her use of the words «provedimento» and «provedi» suggests that Lelio's «providence» is blind to the larger providential plan of

---

[12] VELLI, *op. cit.*, p. 82.
[13] I am grateful to Professor Mazzotta for bringing this to my attention.

which they are a part. [14] It also suggests that his «provedimento» is questionable: Giulia in fact takes issue with it in chapters 22 and 24 when Lelio chooses to fight against Felice's army. It is Giulia who proposes alternate courses of action which Lelio refuses to undertake. The reader is likely to interpret Giulia's counter-proposals exactly the same way Lelio does – as manifestations of fear on the verge of despair. They appear to be unrealistic: Lelio and Giulia might not have enough time to flee, nor is it likely that the attacking army would stop and parley; besides, Lelio has already considered these alternatives even before Giulia proposes them to him (I 17, 7-9). The fact, however, that Giulia insists on them suggests that the Boccaccio wants to underscore Lelio's other choices at the moment in which he exercises his «libero albitrio» (I 27, 3).

Boccaccio's use of the words «libero albitrio» is an allusion to the theological concept of free will (*liberum arbitrium*). Free will is often associated with the ability to choose between different courses of action, as Boethius states in the fifth book of the *De consolatione philosophiae*:

There is free will [...] and no rational nature can exist which does not have it. For any being which by nature has the use of reason, must also have the power of judgment by which it can make decisions and, by its own resources, distinguish between things which should be desired and things which should be avoided. (V prose 2) [15]

Therefore, the providential scheme within the tale itself, and the narrator's own providential perspective (as underscored by his premonitions) do not diminish Lelio's free will. [16] They merely indicate his inability to see the consequences of his choices, a fact that is symbolically underscored by the fog in the valley: «Lelio e la compagnia lieti a' loro danni cavalcavano per una profonda valle, la quale

---

[14] Discussing the natural law within man, Aquinas says «the rational creature is subject to divine providence in a more excellent way, in so far as it itself partakes of a share of providence by being provident both for itself and for others» (Ia, IIae, Q. 90, art. 2, resp.) *Basic Writings of Saint Thomas Aquinas*, edited by Anton C. Pegis, New York, Random House, 1945, vol. II, p. 750. All quotations from the *Summa Theologica* are taken from this translation. As we shall see, Lelio too has room to operate within the providential plan.

[15] BOETHIUS, *The Consolation of Philosophy*, translated by Richard Green, New York, Bobbs-Merrill Co., 1962, p. 103.

[16] As Frederick Copleston has shown, *liberum arbitrium* for Aquinas is the power by which man can judge freely and choose: it is an act of the will resulting from a judgment of reason (see F.C. COPLESTON, *Aquinas*, Baltimore, Penguin Books, 1955, p. 195).

piena di nebbia molto impediva le loro viste, tanto appena l'uno all'altro si poteano vedere» (I 16, 2). When it becomes apparent that Lelio's chosen course of action does not have a chance of success, we cannot help wondering whether Giulia's alternatives to fighting would not have been better since the risk of dying is the same in all three cases. Fleeing is a valid option until shortly before his death, as Lelio himself realizes in his final prayer to Giove (I 26, 44-45). [17] As for parleying, we find out towards the end of the *Filocolo* (V 51), that Ascalion, one of Felice's right-hand men, had been a close friend of Lelio; and even though he tells Giulia «io fuggii oggi per non bagnarmi nella dolente occisione» (I 30, 17), he could not have been too far from the battlefield since he is consoling her on the site where Lelio was killed a short time before. Furthermore, the fact that Ascalion knows Latin (I 30, 4) suggests that he would have probably served as an interpreter had a parley actually taken place, and would have thus recognized Lelio in much the same way the Admiral of Alexandria recognizes Florio in Book IV.

The *agnitio* which failed to occur between Lelio and Ascalion is one more element of classical tragedy which Boccaccio includes in this episode. From a Boethian perspective, however, the *agnitio* represents what would have probably happened had Lelio chosen to parley rather than fight. The fact that their friendship might have prevented this tragic event is supported by Lelio's very name which, as Janet Smarr has shown, comes from Cicero's *De amicitia* (also known as the *Laelius*, after the name of its narrator). [18] The content of Cicero's famous treatise fits in nicely with this episode. The *De amicitia* is a work of consolation like Boethius's *De consolatione*: Laelius is moved to discuss friendship after the death of his close friend Scipio Africanus the Younger. [19] Throughout the treatise Laelius claims that friendship is a means of overcoming the adversities of fortune: «When fortune is fickle the faithful friend is found». True friendship is a form of unswerving constancy and loyalty within a world of change. [20]

---

[17] If we are to assume that Ascalion is telling Giulia the truth when he says that he fled from the battlefield not to bathe himself with blood, then fleeing would not seem to be as ignoble or as useless as Lelio makes it out to be.

[18] See SMARR, *op. cit.*, p. 48.

[19] Dante read both the *De amicitia* and the *De consolatione* as «consolatione» after Beatrice's death (*Convivio* II, xii, 2-4). This would seem to confirm the importance that both works had as consolatory literature in Boccaccio's time.

[20] CICERO, *De amicitia*, with an English translation by William A. Falconer, Harvard University Press, 1965, «Loeb Classical Library», paragraphs 17; 22; 54; 64; 65.

Furthermore, it is never separated from virtue: virtue both creates the bond of friendship and preserves it even after death.

Laelius's philosophy in the *De amicitia* is similar to Lady Philosophy's in the *De consolatione*, especially with regard to Fortune. It is also in harmony with the themes which both Fiammetta and the narrator announced at the very beginning of the *Filocolo*. The hopefulness which all three narrators share in their respective works reinforces the idea that Lelio's death is marked by hope, despite the fact that it is described in tragic terms. What Laelius says about Scipio Africanus could be said of Lelio Africano: he loses nothing by dying, since he is in the company of «the gods»; and his friendship with Ascalion continues even after his death. [21] Ascalion, in fact, becomes a surrogate father for both Florio and Biancifiore, doing for them what Lelio would have done had he been alive.

Lelio's free will is always compatible with the providential plan at work in the *Filocolo*. This is in keeping with Boethius's discussion of free will and Providence in the *De consolatione*:

Just as, when you happen to see simultaneously a man walking on the street and the sun shining in the sky, even though you see both at once, you can distinguish between them and realize that one action is voluntary, and the other necessary; so the divine mind, looking down on all things, does not disturb the nature of the things which are present before it but are future with respect to time [...] the same future event is necessary with respect to God's knowledge of it, but free and undetermined if considered in its own nature [...] No necessity forces the man who is voluntarily walking to move forward; but as long as he is walking, he is necessarily moving forward. In the same way, if Providence sees anything as present, that thing must necessarily be, even though it may have no necessity by its nature. But God sees as present those future things which result from free will. Therefore, from the standpoint of divine knowledge these things are necessary because of the condition of their being known by God; but considered only in themselves, they lose nothing of the absolute freedom of their own natures [...] Similarly, all the things God sees as present will undoubtedly come to pass; but some will happen by the necessity of their natures, others by the power of those who make them happen. [22] (V prose 6)

One can conclude that, contrary to what Cazalé-Bérard has suggested,

---

[21] See CICERO, *op. cit.*, paragraph 14.
[22] BOETHIUS, *op. cit.*, pp. 117-118.

Lelio does not die because his death was determined by divine interventions, but because of his own choices and wishes.

It is worth noting that the divine interventions in the *Filocolo* come about as a direct response to the wishes, prayers, and choices of the characters. In Lelio's case, the divine interventions occur only after he has expressed his wishes and has exercised his free will: his first vision of Saint James occurs after he has prayed to the saint, after he has promised to go to Compostella of his own free will, and after he has expressed his belief that his pray will be granted (I 5, 12). Likewise, the voice from the cloud occurs as a direct response to Lelio's hope-filled prayer to God for a sign «il quale le nostre speranze conforti» (I 25, 6). Lelio has expressed his free will and his wish is granted through this second form of divine intervention. Had he prayed, instead, that the attacking army would stop and parley, his wish might have also been granted. Lelio dies, therefore, because he chose to fight against insurmountable odds, rather than choose another course of action.

The «salute», therefore, that Giulia hoped she and Lelio would find by fleeing (I 29, 17) or parleying is replaced, instead, by the spiritual «salute» (salvation) which they both find in death. [23] Boccaccio's masterful play on the various meanings of the word «salute» is probably derived from his reading of Dante's *Vita nuova*. In this episode, as in the *Vita nuova*, there is a movement away from a purely physical «salute» (i.e. life and health) and «salutare» (i.e. the *agnitio* which never took place) towards the greater spiritual «salute» which Lelio finds in the hereafter, as Beatrice had done.

Although their pilgrimage ends abruptly, their immediate wishes (a child and their «salute») are granted, but by means which they neither imagined nor anticipated. The means by which their desired ends are reached are an example of how «la fortuna» and «i fati» (words which are used interchangeably throughout this episode) operate within the providential plan. As Boethius states, Fate translates into a series of temporal events what Providence sees in an eternal present. More than a force in itself which determines what will happen on earth, Fate is the expression of diverse forces which lead up to an event:

---

[23] This is in sharp contrast to the death Florio and Biancifiore risk in Book IV (see chapter five of this study).

Just as the craftsman conceives in his mind the form of the thing he intends to make, and then sets about making it by producing in successive temporal acts that which was simply present in his mind, so God by his Providence simply and unchangeably disposes all things that are to be done, even though the things themselves are worked out by Fate in many ways and in the process of time. Therefore, whether Fate is carried out by divine spirits in the service of Providence, or by a soul, or by the whole activity of nature, by the heavenly motions of the stars, by angelic virtue or diabolic cleverness, or by some or all of these agents, one thing is certain: Providence is the immovable and simple form of all things which come into being, while Fate is the moving connection and temporal order of all things which the divine simplicity has decided to bring into being. [24] (IV prose 6)

Most of the above mentioned agents by which Fate is carried out are present in this episode of the *Filocolo*: Saint James and the voice from the cloud («divine spirits in the service of Providence»), Satan and Felice («diabolic cleverness»), Lelio («a soul»), the fog («nature»), etc. In the case of Lelio's death, Fate consists of the total sum of circumstances, both «voluntary» and «necessary», which led up to it.

From a Boethian perspective, Lelio's choices are always free and in no way determined by Providence. [25] Necessity is not imposed on events themselves: events are necessary in relation to God's vision; but from man's perspective they do not lose their nature of free choice. The fact that such events happen means, according to Boethius, that they cannot *not* happen. The sense of tragic inevitability in the description of Lelio's death is actually a diachronic perspective which reflects the pagan world view. Boccaccio superimposes on it a synchronic perspective which reflects the Christian world view. The clash, therefore, between Lelio and Felice is not simply an extension of the Manichean battle between good and evil (Giove and Pluto) as Cazalé-Bérard has suggested, but it is also a clash between pagan and Christian world views. This becomes more apparent when we look at Felice's role in this providential plan.

Juxtaposed to Lelio's divine visions is Felice's encounter with Satan who, disguised as one of his noblemen, tells the king that Verona has been sacked. This false tale is patterned after the destruc-

---

[24] BOETHIUS, *op. cit.*, p. 92.
[25] Aquinas too states that God's foreknowledge does not impose any necessity on human actions; see COPLESTON, *op. cit.*, p. 196.

tion of Troy in *Aeneid* II, as Zumbini and Quaglio have shown.[26] If Lelio's speeches are meant to recall those of Pompey prior to the battle of Pharsalia, the speech in which Satan exhorts the citizens of Verona to take up arms against the enemy is adapted from Aeneas' speech to his men when he exhorts them to fight to the death (*Filocolo* I 10, 7-8 corresponds to *Aeneid* II 348-354). Even Satan's false account of the last stand of the citizens of Verona is taken from Aeneas's account of the Trojans' last brave stand (*Filocolo* I 10, 9-12 corresponds to *Aeneid* II 361-369). Despair is the theme in both accounts: the citizens of both Verona and Troy have been abandoned by the gods and have no hope of being saved («sanza alcuna speranza di salute»). Repeating Aeneas's very words, Satan reports having told the people of Verona: «mandiamo le nostre anime alle infernali sedie: "sola salute è a' vinti non isperar salute"» (8). This invitation to send one's soul to hell because there is no possibility of salvation contrasts sharply with what the voice from the cloud tells Lelio and his men: their salvation («salute») is in being vanquished («vinti»). For Lelio and his group of Christian pilgrims there is real hope even in the most desperate moments; for Felice and his pagan army, instead, there is wrath provoked by a sense of despair which is totally unfounded. Since Satan's account is false, so is Felice's sense of hopelessness; it has no place in the Boethian and Christian world of the pilgrims. This is supported by the fact that Boccaccio chooses to put in Satan's mouth that part of *Aeneid* II which narrates Aeneas' momentary despair and rage («furor iraque mentem paecipatat», II 316-317) when he finds out that Troy is doomed. No mention is made of the hopeful conclusion of Book II which narrates Aeneas' decision not to go down with Troy, and the hero's exodus from the burning city with his father and son. Satan instead claims that his father and sons were killed in the fall of Verona.[27]

---

[26] See QUAGLIO, *Tra fonti e testo del «Filocolo», op. cit.*, CXXXIX, 1962, p. 139, and CXL, 1962, pp. 327-ff; and BONAVENTURA ZUMBINI, *Il «Filocopo» del Boccaccio*, Firenze, Le Monnier, 1879, p. 31-ff.

[27] In his commentary on the second book of the *Aeneid* Bernard Silvester says «And since speech is something true and something false, the mixture of the truth of history and the falsity of fables in the narration follows this same pattern. The Greek destruction of Troy is history, but Aeneas's honesty is fiction for Dares Phrygius narrates that Aeneas betrayed his city». EARL G. SCHREIBER and THOMAS E. MARESCA, translators, *Commentary on the First Six Books of Virgil's «Aeneid» by Bernardus Silvestris*, Lincoln, Nebraska, University of Nebraska Press, 1980, p. 16. If the fall of Troy is history, Satan's account of the sack of Verona is a false fable:

If we compare the context of Satan's speech with that of Aeneas, we see that both are rooted in deception and misunderstanding. The fall of Troy is brought about by the deception of the Greeks (Ulysses and Sinon in particular), and is hastened by the tragic attempt of Aeneas's men to disguise themselves as Greek soldiers in order to deceive the enemy. Satan's disguise as one of Felice's noblemen and his false story (not unlike the one Sinon tells the Trojans), underscore the treachery behind the ensuing tragedy. [28] Furthermore, the fact that Satan identifies himself with Aeneas throughout his speech to Felice fits in well with the allegory of the opening chapter of the *Filocolo*. The goddess Giunone is associated with the Church, as Quaglio points out, because she is the spouse of Giove (God); and her Virgilian hostility towards Aeneas is explained by the fact that Aeneas founded the pagan Roman empire. [29] Satan is thus identifying himself with the man who created the nemesis of the early Christian Church. Furthermore, by identifying himself with the fallen Trojans of «superbum Illium» (*Aeneid* III 2-3), Satan is recalling his own pride and the fall from heaven that resulted from it. [30]

Satan thus sparks the king's irascible appetite just as Aeneas sparked that of his men («Sic animis iuvenum furor additus», II 355). Felice responds by sacrificing to Mars (the god of war, and a figure for the irascible appetite throughout the *Filocolo*) before attacking the pilgrims. The unusual omens and unclear auguries which take place during and after the sacrifice force Felice to make uncertain and contradictory interpretations of their significance. When the bull

---

the two are blended together to form his deceptive narrative. Boccaccio transcribed Bernardus's commentary in his *Zibaldone*; however, we cannot be sure if he was familiar with this work at the time he was writing the *Filocolo*.

[28] A similar idea can also be found in McGregor's *The Shades of Aeneas* which came off the press as I was about to mail my manuscript to the publisher. McGregor sees Felice's interpretation of the bull prodigy as a reenactment of the Laocoön episode in *Aeneid* II. McGregor makes a compelling case for the similarities between the two episodes, and concludes that, like the Trojans before the fall, Felice «takes in something belonging to the enemy. It is the apparently innocent Giulia Topazia, but she, like the Trojan horse, has something hidden inside her. That something, Biancifiore, will eventually prove as successful in overrunning Felice's kingdom as the Greeks proved in overrunning Priam's Troy. She does not destroy the kingdom [...] she subverts Felice's reign by bringing about its conversion». See McGREGOR, *op. cit.*, p. 34.

[29] See BOCCACCIO, *Filocolo*, pp. 713-ff. B. ZUMBINI, *Il «Filocopo» del Boccaccio*, Firenze, Le Monnier, 1879, pp. 31-33.

[30] Boccaccio himself alludes to «superba Troia» in *Filocolo* II 32, 3. As for Satan's fall, it is narrated in allegorical terms in *Filocolo* I 3.

escapes from the sacrificers' hands, Felice interprets it as a bad omen (I 13, 1). Later, when the bull dies and an eagle lands on it, Felice assumes it to be a good omen (I 14, 3). After his victory over the Romans, Felice continues to be baffled by his satanic vision when he finds out that Verona was never attacked, and that the nobleman who brought him the false news never left the city. At first he believes that the gods have deceived him (I 33, 5), but then decides to interpret it as a sign that the gods wished to add this victory to his «magnificenzie» (I 33, 11).

Felice's sacrifice and prayer to Mars, and all the equivocal auguries which stem from them, are in sharp contrast to the sacrifice and prayers Lelio and his priest («santo uomo») make to Giove. Despite the pagan overtones, the priest's «degni sacrificii» and Lelio's basically Christian prayer are actually part of the celebration of the mass — the reenactment of Christ's human sacrifice. Later when Lelio realizes that he has lost the battle, he will ask Giove, «Io vi priego che le loro anime riceviate e la mia, in luogo di degno sacrificio, se vostro piacere è» (I 26, 45). This last prayer of his will also be answered: Lelio and his men, like Christ, in fact become «degni sacrificii». Therefore, even Lelio's human sacrifice is an expression of his free will.

There is, nevertheless, a certain amount of ambiguity even in the voice from the cloud. Once Lelio has decided to face Felice's attacking army, the divine voice seconds his decision by exhorting him and his men to fight to the death (there is no injunction to turn the other cheek). Lelio and his men, in fact, die killing many of Felice's men. A similar moment of ambiguity can be seen in Lelio's vision of Saint James when the Saint promises to grant him his wish without, however, telling him the great price he and Giulia will have to pay for it. How can we explain such ambiguities? Is Boccaccio portraying the Church Militant? Or is he illustrating the ambiguity of all affirmations, both human and divine? Can Lelio or any human being, for that matter, adequately interpret divine language? The fact that Lelio's Christian Roman divinities respect his free choices and grant him his wishes suggests that they are not interfering with his *liberum arbitrium*. No matter how tragic Lelio's death may be, or how questionable his chosen course of action may have been, both are the result of his free will, and both result in a greater good, for him and for others, than the one he prayed for to Saint James. As we shall see, Boccaccio's Providence grants all wishes and desires which are close to the providential plan, and realigns the ones that are not so that they will conform to that plan. This providential realignment is what ultimately determines the unusual means by which many characters (Lelio included) ultimately attain their desired end. The relationship between ends and means is one of the central themes of the *Filocolo*.

Of all the events which are triggered by Lelio's death and which will bring about Felice's conversion, the protagonists' birth and the unusual circumstances in which this occurs are probably the most important ones. Book I of the *Filocolo* is, in fact, entirely devoted to narrating the events which lead up to the birth of the two protagonists. Their «nascimento» and all the «accidenti» that stem from it are two of the three topics Fiammetta asked the narrator to discuss in his «libretto». The unusual circumstances of their birth are of thematic importance from a Boethian perspective since the lovers' trials and tribulations («accidenti»), particularly those of Biancifiore, are in fact determined by their birth. The fact that Giulia dies a captive in King Felice's court shortly after giving birth to Biancifiore means that her daughter will never have the same social status that Felice's son (Florio) has. Furthermore, Biancifiore is born without the «ereditaggio» Lelio had prayed that his child might have «dopo me» (I 5, 9-10): she loses her noble ancestry the moment she loses her parents. Although Felice acknowledges Giulia's nobility by burying her «con quello onore che a sì nobile giovane si richiedea» and by mentioning it in her epitaph (I 43, 2-3), he never acknowledges Biancifiore's noble blood as she grows up.

When the two protagonists fall in love, Felice and his wife attempt to separate them because, vis-à-vis Florio, Biancifiore «alla sua nobiltà è dispari» (II 7, 9). Both the king and the queen consider her «una romana popolaresca femina, non conosciuta e nutricata nelle nostre case come una serva» (II 7, 10; 14, 5). Since Florio's parents are not certain of Lelio's ancestry (II 15, 4) and do not give much importance to Giulia's ancestry (II 15, 5), Biancifiore is not allowed to live with Florio after they fall in love. The king and queen justify the protagonists' forced segregation on the grounds that the future heir to Felice's throne must be married to someone of his station. The cruelty, however, which is later shown Biancifiore (her death sentence and subsequent bondage) seems to be totally gratuitous.

From a Boethian perspective, however, it is the king and queen's cruelty towards her, coupled with those misfortunes which beset Biancifiore as the direct result of their cruelty, that will test her true nobility and condemn their own ignoble conduct.[31] Biancifiore's ability to withstand the king and queen's abuses of royal power and remain virtuous throughout her misfortunes, as well as her unswerving loyalty to Florio, are the ultimate proof of her nobility of heart. It is only after she has proved her true nobility that she discovers and reacquires her ancestral nobility: that nobility of blood which prevented her from being with Florio in the first place. Soon after Biancifiore reacquires her family's nobility in Rome, she becomes a queen by virtue of her marriage to Florio (Felice's successor). Therefore, the protagonists' constant struggle with Fortuna in Books II through IV is rewarded in Book V when they reacquire the noble titles which are theirs by virtue of both their blood and merit. Judging from their conduct prior to that moment, we can assume that the protagonists will live up to the nobility of heart which made them worthy of their titles, for as Boethius states: «If there is anything to be said for nobility, it lies only in the necessity imposed on the nobility to carry on the virtues of their ancestors» (III prose 6).[32]

The retrieval of Biancifiore's nobility in Rome is the result of a seemingly fortuitous encounter between Ascalion and Mennilio, one of Lelio's two brothers. The encounter, which brings back to Ascalion's mind his encounter with Giulia shortly after Lelio's death, is misinterpreted by Ascalion as a trick of Fortuna:

Disse allora Ascalion [a Florio]: — Ora sappi che di costoro fu fratello Lelio, il padre di Biancifiore, il quale dal tuo padre fu ucciso, e quella donna chiamata Clelia, la quale tanto Biancifiore onora, sorella carnale fu di Giulia sua madre. Vedi ove la fortuna ci ha mandati! Io penso che senno sarebbe omai di qui partirci, però che di leggieri, se conosciuti fossimo da loro, potremmo in questa fine del nostro cammino ricevere impedimento [...] La fortuna ci è in molte cose stata contraria: che sappiamo noi se ancora la sua ira verso noi è passata? Da fuggire è la cagione acciò che l'effetto cessi —. Queste parole udendo Filocolo si maravigliò molto, pensando alla grande nobiltà de' zii di Biancifiore, e alla miseria in che la fortuna l'avea recata, ponendola nella sua casa come serva, e così da tutti riputata; e molto in se medesimo si contentò che donna di sì nobile progenie gli fu dagl'iddii per amante mandata e poi per isposa: e con Ascalion delle iniquità del padre e della madre verso di lei usate si duole (V 51, 4-7).

---

[31] Biancifiore's suffering at the hands of Felice parallels Boethius' suffering at the hands of Theodoric: both are thrown in prison on false charges of treason.

[32] BOETHIUS, op. cit., p. 53.

As we shall see in chapter five, Fortuna has ceased to harass the protagonists' after their public marriage in Alexandria; this encounter, therefore, cannot be the work of Boethius's capricious goddess. Nor is it a chance encounter because, as Boethius states, there is no such thing as chance:

I consider it an empty word. For what room can there be for random events since God keeps all things in order? [...] Whenever anything is done for one reason, but something other than what was intended happens on account of other reasons, it is called chance [...] But it does not come from nothing since the event has its own causes whose unforeseen and unexpected concurrence seems to have produced an effect by chance [...] Therefore, we can define chance as an unexpected event brought about by a concurrence of causes which had other purposes in view. These cause come together because of that order which proceeds from inevitable connection of things, the order which flows from the source which is Providence and which disposes all things, each in its proper time and place. (V prose 1) [33]

We must therefore assume that this seemingly fortuitous encounter is another example of Fate unfolding the events «present to the vision of the divine mind». The encounter marks the return of Fate as an active participant in the narrative. After Lelio's death, in fact, Fate and Providence recede into the background so that Fortuna can take charge in Books II, III, and IV.

The total absence of Fortuna and the reappearance of Fate and Providence in Book V is significant because it indicates a return to Book I. Book V consists of a series of returns to the beginning of the *Filocolo*, before Fortuna began to harass the protagonists. It is in Rome that Biancifiore acquires her parents' religion as well as Lelio's «ereditaggio»: the actual recognition scene between her and her relatives occurs on the occasion of the protagonists' baptism. Thus the *agnitio* between Lelio and Ascalion, which did not occur in Book I, occurs a generation later between Lelio's daughter and his relatives, thanks to Ascalion. This *agnitio* is successful also thanks to Ilario's mediation between Florio's small band of pilgrims and Lelio's larger group of Roman relatives who are prepared to avenge his death (V 66, 1-3). The tables have been turned a generation later: now it is Felice's son who is a vulnerable pilgrim traveling in a foreign land under the rule of people who would like to avenge a wrong that they believe has

---

[33] BOETHIUS, *op. cit., p.* 101-102.

been done to them. It is through Ilario's mediation that the *agnitio* and the peaceful resolution of differences take place, just as they might have taken place in Book I had Lelio and Ascalion recognized each other. Ilario's Christian sense of justice thus prevails over the pagan idea of vengeance which brought about Lelio's death.

While in Rome, Florio too retrieves his past by assuming the name he was born with (Florio) and by dispensing with the name Filocolo which he assumed when he became a «pellegrino d'amore» looking for Biancifiore. The fact that both Florio and Biancifiore reacquire at the time of their baptism an identity which had been hidden suggests that the protagonists, by virtue of their conversion, are restored to their proper place within the social and providential order of things.

This idea of a return to the past is suggested not only by Biancifiore's return to her roots (which is soon followed by Florio's desire to return to his parents) but also, as Janet Smarr has pointed out, by the protagonists' pilgrimage to Compostella. [34] Right after their conversion Florio and Biancifiore go to Compostella with their infant son Lelio (V 87) and thus complete Giulia and Lelio's pilgrimage which Felice had interrupted at the beginning of the *Filocolo*. From «pellegrini d'amore», the protagonists have now become Christian pilgrims. Their passionate love for each other, which reached its climax in Alexandria, has now been replaced by an almost Virgilian «pietas» towards their parents which first manifests itself, appropriately enough, in Rome: upon completing their pilgrimage to Compostella they miraculously discover the unburied bones of Lelio, and bring them back to be buried next to Giulia's remains. They thus complete what was left undone in Book I.

Approximately twenty years after his death, Lelio's promise to Saint James is kept, and so are the Saint's promises to him: Lelio's daughter not only inherits his «ereditaggio», but she gives birth to a «figliuolo [...] il quale dopo l'ultimo nostro giorno possa il nostro nome ritenere» (I 5, 9). Once again, Lelio's wishes are granted, but by means which do not correspond to the ones he elected. The events which follow Lelio's vision and which conclude with the conversion of Felice's people at the end of the *Filocolo* are merely Fate's translation of what Providence foresaw and foretold in Book I. Fate, which one may say is synonymous with the plot of the *Filocolo*, unravels twenty-

---

[34] See SMARR, *op. cit.*, p. 48.

three years of events thus bringing the reader, as well as the characters, to that providential moment alluded to by the voice in the cloud. By the time we have come to the end of the *Filocolo*, Fate has revealed what Providence prefigured at the beginning. By coming to the end of the book, we too, like Florio and Biancifiore, return to its beginning. Like the protagonists themselves who discover the providential scheme as they begin to understand their human experience, the reader discovers the author's own providential-like vision of the narrative as the plot unfolds (a narrative device Boccaccio borrowed from Dante).

If true happiness, according to Boethius, can only be found in the *summum bonum* (i.e. God), and if the other objects of desire which men strive for are illusory shadows of that happiness, then Lelio and Felice's search for it in an heir, and Florio's search for it in Biancifiore are just as illusory. [35] Even though Lelio and Florio's greatest wishes are granted in the person of Biancifiore, these wishes come true only after Fate has realigned the means they chose to their desired end with the providential plan alluded to in Book I. The discrepancy between the characters' chosen means to their desired end and the means that Fate obliges them to follow so that their end may be reached and still be in harmony with the providential plan reflects the realignment of their wishes with those of Providence.

As one of several instruments of Fate, Biancifiore becomes the means by which Florio can convert to Christianity; his conversion, in turn, brings about the above-mentioned conversion of his «popolo». Even though Florio mistakenly thought that his happiness lay in consummating his love for Biancifiore, he is closer to achieving true happiness when he comes close to the «divine mind» (i.e. when he converts to Christianity). It is at the moment of his conversion that he becomes one with Providence through the transformation of his desire from a sensual love for Biancifiore to «celestiale amore» (V 58, 2). This is best illustrated after Florio hears Ilario's sermon on the seven *aetates mundi*:

Partironsi adunque Filocolo e Menedon da Ilario, sopra l'udite cose molto pensosi, e ripetendole fra loro più volte, quanto più le ripeteano, più piaceano:

---

[35] In *Filocolo* I 45, 4 and II 13, 4, both Florio and Felice refer to the most cherished object of their desire (Biancifiore and Florio respectively) as «l'ultimo fine de' miei disii». In the *Summa Theologica*, Ia, IIae, 1, 7, Aquinas says, as Boethius had done before him, that some men seek riches as the supreme good, others pleasure, others something else.

per che essi in loro deliberarono del tutto di volere alla santa legge passare, e di narrarlo a' compagni proposero. E accesi del celestiale amore, tornarono lieti al loro ostiere, dove essi il duca e Parmenione e Fileno e gli altri trovarono aspettargli [...] Co' quali poi che Filocolo fu alquanto dimorato, non potendo più dentro tenere l'accesa fiamma [...] così loro cominciò a parlare [...] E mirabile cosa fu che, secondo ch'egli disse poi, nella lingua gli correano le parole meglio che egli prima nell'animo non divisava di dirle; la qual cosa superinfusa grazia di Dio essere conobbe [...] I giovani baroni [...] udendo queste cose si maravigliarono molto, e guardando al ben dire di costui, similemente così com'egli, conobbero grazia di Dio nella sua lingua essere entrata; e i nobili animi [...] similemente di subito con lui entrarono in un volere della santa fede [...] (V 58-60)

Born on Pentecost, the feast of the Holy Ghost, Florio is now filled with the Holy Ghost like the Apostles at Pentecost. And just as the Apostles went out into the world to convert others after the descent of the Holy Ghost, Florio converts his parents to Christianity after he returns from Rome. Florio's sermon and amazing fluency due to the influence of Holy Ghost is a palinode to his mellifluous and deceptive speeches in Books II, III, and IV when he was under the influence of Venus, the goddess of the «mansueta verba» and the planet of rhetoric. [36] Florio is converted from the language of sensual love (*cupiditas*) to the language of *caritas*.

If it took Florio three years and three books (*Filocolo* II, III, IV) before he could consummate his love for Biancifiore, it takes him merely three days to convert to Christianity. The ease of the latter and the difficulty of the former are due to the difference in proximity to the divine mind of the two desired ends:

Human souls, however, are more free while they are engaged in contemplation of the divine mind, and less free when they are joined to bodies, and still less free when they are bound by earthly fetters. They are in utter slavery when they lose possession of their reason and give themselves wholly to vice [...] By yielding and consenting to these passions, they worsen the slavery to which they have brought themselves and are, as it were, the captives of their own freedom. (V prose 2) [37]

Looking at the first and last books of the *Filocolo* from a Boethian point of view, we must conclude that the farther the end from the divine mind, the harder the means of achieving it. The desired end is

---

[36] As we shall see in the second chapter of this book, Andalò Negro, Boccaccio's astrology teacher in Naples, associated the planet Venus with «mansueta verba». Dante associates the planet with rhetoric, see *Convivio*, II 13, 13.
[37] BOETHIUS, *op. cit.*, p. 104.

reached through means which follow a course of their own despite the wisher's chosen means. When the desired end is reached, it is through Fate's roundabout ways. It would seem, therefore, that for Boccaccio every man is able to freely fulfill his wishes once Fate has realigned them with those of Providence. Man's illusory objects of desire (sensual love, wealth, honor, heirs, etc.) are therefore reached when they serve as a stepping stone to the *summum bonum*.

This is as true for Felice (the villain in the *Filocolo*) as it is for the virtuous characters in the story (Lelio, Giulia, Florio, and Biancifiore). In contrast to the many misfortunes of the latter, we find the good fortune of the former. Throughout the *Filocolo*, in fact, Felice is depicted as having all the temporal goods that Boethius' capricious goddess can bestow on man: he has an empire that stretches from Cordova and Seville to Verona, an heir to his throne, uncontested power over his subjects, and practically everything he desires. He is the classical example of Boethius' wicked man living in prosperity but unable to find happiness («felicitas»). Felice's very name means fortunate in Latin (*felix*) and translates the Boethian concept of «felicitas». Despite his name and good fortune, Felice is never happy because he looks for his happiness in Fortune's transitory goods-- material possessions, public honors, the exercise of power, fame, and pleasure--each of which, as Boethius shows in the third book of the *De consolatione*, is limited and fails to provide the felicity it promises: «Then these false causes of happiness are mere appearances of the true good and merely seem to give certain imperfect goods to mortal men; but they cannot give true and perfect good» (III prose 9). [38] Felice attributes his unhappiness to Fortuna and to his son's conduct, when instead it is the result of his own conduct. The king's inability to accept Biancifiore on account of her social background makes it harder for him to accept his son's falling in love; and his cruelty towards Biancifiore alienates Florio. Felice's conduct throughout the *Filocolo* places him farther away from the *summum bonum* than any of the other characters in the book. As a result, he is the unhappiest of them all because, as Boethius states, true happiness can only be found in God:

For, since nothing can be thought of better than God, who can doubt that He is the good, other than whom nothing is better. And that God is good is demon-

---

[38] BOETHIUS, *op. cit.*, pp. 59.

strated by reason in such a way as to convince us that He is the perfect good. If He were not, He could not be the ruler of all things; for there would be something better than He, something possessing perfect good, which would seem to be older and greater than He. For all perfect things have been shown to come before less perfect ones. And so, if we are to avoid progression *ad infinitum*, we must agree that the most high God is full of the highest and most perfect good. But we have already established that perfect good is true happiness; therefore it follows that true happiness has its dwelling in the most high God. (III prose 10) [39]

As a Boethian figure of the wicked man in prosperity, Felice's place in the providential plan of the *Filocolo* is best explained by Lady Philosophy:

the lot of the wicked, which is sometimes painful and sometimes easy, comes from the same source and for the same reasons. No one wonders at the troubles they undergo, since everyone thinks that is just what they deserve. Such punishment both deters others from crime and prompts those who suffer it to reform. On the other hand, the prosperity of the wicked is a powerful argument for the good, because they see how they ought to evaluate the kind of good fortune which the wicked so often enjoy. Still another good purpose may be served by the prosperity of the wicked man: if his nature is reckless and violent that poverty might drive him to crime, Providence may cure this morbid tendency by making him wealthy [...] Some who have achieved prosperity unworthily have been driven by it to well deserved ruin. Some have been given the right to punish so that the good might be tested and the evil punished [...] Only to divine power are evil things good, when it uses them so as to draw good effects from them. All things are part of a certain order, so that when something moves away from its assigned place, it falls into a new order of things. Nothing in the realm of Providence is left to chance [...] It is enough to have understood only that God, the Creator of all things in nature, also governs all things, directing them to good [...] Therefore, if you fix your attention on Providence as the governor of all things, you will find that the evil which is thought to abound in the world is really nonexistent. (IV prose 5) [40]

As in the case of Florio and Lelio's greatest wishes, those of Felice come true but in ways which go against his expectations. His son will in fact marry someone worthy of his noble birth; but the person whom Felice thought would be least suitable for Florio (i.e. Biancifiore) becomes the only woman worthy of him thanks to Felice's own

---

[39] BOETHIUS, *op. cit.*, pp. 62.
[40] BOETHIUS, *op. cit.*, pp. 95-96.

wickedness. Felice's cruelty to Biancifiore serves to prove her true nobility and to discover her nobility of blood, although that was never his intention. Thus Felice's most desired goal is only reached when his wicked means of reaching it follow a course of their own (i.e. when his actions, like those of Lelio, Florio, and Biancifiore, become instruments of Fate). In Felice's case too, Fate does not deny him his ultimate wish, just the means he chose to attain that wish. Fate once again alters and realigns the character's chosen courses of action so that they concord with the providential plan: «All things are part of a certain order, so that when something moves away from its assigned place, it falls into a new order of things».

As Felice's good fortune would have it, however, the possibility of reaching the *summum bonum* is granted to him when he converts to Christianity. On his death bed he will acknowledge Biancifiore's nobility and recognize the fact that she is an appropriate wife for Florio:

A te e la tua Biancifiore, bellissima e d'alta schiatta nata, la quale tu lungamente hai amata e con sollecitudine guadagnata; guardalati, e siati cara, e sola come si conviene ti basti sanza più avanti cercare. (V 92, 17)

Felice does not actually confess his sins to Florio, but the fact that Ilario gave him «i santi sacramenti della chiesa con divozione» (V 93, 1) suggests that he has already confessed them. Felice's long sermon on the seven virtues and vices and on how his son should rule after him suggests that he is a reformed man and is that much closer to finding the *summum bonum*.

Felice's last words echo the remarks Fiammetta and the narrator made at the beginning of the *Filocolo* concerning the importance of fidelity between lovers. The protagonists' faithfulness and their overall virtue are essential to their ability to overcome the Boethian goddess Fortuna, and to establish that bond of friendship between them which Cicero discusses in the *De amicitia*. The virtue which Boethius claims is the «natural» means by which a person can reach the *summum bonum* is not, however, always attained by the two young lovers. As we shall see in the following chapters, the way in which their love is portrayed in Books II, III, and IV suggests that Florio and Biancifiore are, at times, similar to Boethius's «mali» who seek true happiness «per cupiditatem». [41]

---

[41] BOETHIUS, *op. cit.*, pp. 78-79.

CHAPTER TWO

ASTROLOGY IN BOCCACCIO'S *FILOCOLO* [1]

In his important study *Scienza e mito nel Boccaccio*, Antonio Enzo Quaglio convincingly proves that Boccaccio used Andalone Negro's astrological treatises (especially the *Introductorium ad iudicia astrologiae*) in the *Filocolo*. [2] Quaglio, however, does not fully examine the literary significance of these allusions, preferring instead to identify their sources. His source study, nevertheless, provides us with many useful excerpts from the *Introductorium ad iudicia astrologiae* that can help us interpret the astrological allusions from a critical perspective. [3] In this chapter I will show how these allusions may be used to shed light on the thematic and symbolic meaning of the *Filocolo*.

The first astrological reference appears in the opening pages of the *Filocolo* when the narrator describes the moment he first saw his beloved Fiammetta:

Avvenne che un giorno, la cui prima ora Saturno avea signoreggiata, essendo già Febo co' suoi cavalli al sedecimo grado del celestiale Montone pervenuto, e nel quale il glorioso partimento del figliuolo di Giove dagli spogliati regni di Plutone si celebrava, io, della presente opera componitore, mi ritrovai in un grazioso e bel tempio in Partenope [...] e già essendo [...] la quarta ora passata, apparve agli occhi miei la mirabile bellezza della prescritta giovane [...] (I 1, 17-18) [4]

As Quaglio has shown, the allusion is to Holy Saturday, and, as Janet Smarr has indicated, the narrator sees Fiammetta in an hour dominat-

---

[1] An abridged version of this chapter appeared in «Italiana 1987: Rosary College Italian Studies», II, 1989, pp. 143-155.

[2] See ANTONIO ENZO QUAGLIO, *Scienza e mito nel Boccaccio*, Padova, Liviana, 1967.

[3] Since Andalone's *Introductorium ad iudicia astrologiae* has never been printed (not even in the Renaissance), all my quotations from it and reference to it are taken from the excerpts that appear in Quaglio's *Scienza e mito*.

[4] BOCCACCIO, *Filocolo*, pp. 63-4.

ed by the planet Venus. [5] This combination of spiritual and astrological allusions may indeed function, as Smarr has suggested, to highlight the two different kinds of love the narrator and Fiammetta represent (*amore per diletto* and *amore onesto*). [6] However, looking at these allusions from a strictly astrological perspective, we discover that their literary importance goes beyond the thematic structure of the narrative. Saturday is the day of Saturn («Saturni dies»), a planet which Andalone associates with melancholy and other malefic influences. [7] The sadness associated with Holy Saturday and with the death of Christ (the God of *caritas*) contrasts with the melancholic sadness of the narrator which results from his unrequited, venereal love for Fiammetta. Venus's influence on the narrator is affected by Saturn; for as Andalone says, «Quando Venus iungitur cum Saturno significat damnum et anxietatem totius anni populo». [8]

Despite the allusions to Venus and Saturn, these two planets have only a marginal presence in this episode. The Sun is the only celestial body whose presence is explicitly mentioned by the narrator. Its position is significant: located sixteen degrees in Aries, it appears in its own «decan», or «facies» as Andalone calls it (a ten degree section of a zodiacal sign in which a designated planet exerts a strong influence). [9] The Sun's influence on the narrator is made even stronger by the fact that it is approaching the nineteenth degree in Aries, its point of «exaltation». [10] If Venus is present at this hour, her proximity to the Sun would make her venereal influence on the narrator even stronger. [11] Furthermore, since the influence of the Sun, as Andalone

---

[5] BOCCACCIO, *Filocolo*, p. 717. JANET L. SMARR, *op. cit.*, p. 53. Smarr bases her assertion on a passage from Boccaccio's *Genealogia Deorum* I 34, which, as Quaglio has indicated, can be traced back to Andalone and others (cfr. *Scienza e mito*, pp. 141, 200-201).

[6] SMARR, *op. cit.*, pp. 34-60.

[7] See Andalone's text in QUAGLIO, *Scienza e mito*, pp. 195-196.

[8] *Ibid*, p. 109. For a detailed study on how melancholy affects lovers see MASSIMO CIAVOLELLA, *La «malattia d'amore» dall'antichità al medioevo*, Roma, Bulzoni, 1976. For Saturn's melancholic influence, see RAYMOND KLIBANSKY, ERWIN PANOFSKY, and FRITZ SAXL, *Saturn and Melancholy: Studies in the History of Natural Philosophy, Religion, and Art*, New York, Basic Books, 1964, and GIUSEPPE MAZZOTTA, *The World at Play in Boccaccio's «Decameron»*, Princeton, Princeton University Press, 1986, pp. 30-31.

[9] See Andalone's text in QUAGLIO, *op. cit.*, p. 50.

[10] *Ibid*, p. 51. See also FIRMICUS MATERNUS, *Ancient Astrological Theory and Practice: «Matheseos Libri VIII» by Firmicus Maternus*, trans. Jean Rhys Bram, Park Ridge, N.J., Noyes Press, 1975, p. 34. As Smarr has indicated, Dante knew Firmicus, and Boccaccio may have also known the work of this important classical astrologer; see JANET L. SMARR, *Boccaccio and the Stars: Astrology in the Teseida*, «Traditio», XXXV, 1979, p. 305.

[11] See Andalone's text in QUAGLIO, *op. cit.*, pp. 106-7.

indicates, is far-reaching in the natural world, especially in making things grow, its appearance at the beginning of Spring (the traditional time for amorous activities) and at the budding of the narrator's love for Fiammetta suggests that, like everything else in the natural world, the narrator's love will also grow. [12] Fiammetta's own strong influence over the narrator is a reflection of the Sun's influence. Her very name suggests her solar-like power over him: she is, as it were, a «donna sole», not just a «small flame».

Most of the other astrological periphrases in Book I refer only to the Sun. They are used to indicate the seasons or months of the year, giving the Sun a chronological as well as astrological function in the narrative. The actual tale of Florio and Biancifiore begins, in fact, with an astrological reference to the five years which have passed since Lelio and Giulia were married:

E già era con lei, poi che Imineo coronato delle frondi di Pallade fu prima nelle sue case e le sante tede arse nella sua camera, dimorato tanto, che Febo cinque volte era nella sua casa della celestiale Vergine rientrato, e ancora di lei niuno figliuolo avea potuto avere, de' quali egli sopra tutte le cose era disideroso; (I 5, 3)

The Sun is in Virgo as the couple complete their fifth year of childless marriage. Lelio's prayer to Saint James for an heir, and the actual conception of Biancifiore occur within that same period (I 5, 9). Since the protagonists are born nine months later when the Sun is in Gemini, both their conception and birth occur within Mercury's two «domi» (the zodiacal signs in which a planet exerts its greatest influence). Although Mercury is a planet rarely mentioned by name in the *Filocolo*, the fact that it plays such a significant role in the conception and birth of the protagonists suggests that its influence is present during both these moments. Speaking about Mercury, Andalone says:

Mercurius est planeta masculus cum masculis, femininus cum femininis, diurnus, calidus et siccus, forme et nature corrutibilis, fortunatus cum fortunatis et infortunatus cum infortunatis, scribanie computationum, scientiarum, documentorum bene ratiocinatus, bene loquens et audacter, violentiarum et maleficiarum pulcre apparentie apposite persone puer. Amat libros et computationes, magisteria, res bene factas [...] et ystorie antique libros versificare, dictare et universa

---

[12] *Ibid*, p. 91.

scientia scripture mobili est in omnibus suis rebus. Per loquelam, ractiocinationem et resistentiam suam retrahit infortunium ab infortuniis et est declinabilis per naturam suam ad eum cui complectitur ex planetis et ex signis, alacer, agilis in motu et proprietate. Significat fratre minores et seniores servos, dilectionem concubinarum, celeritatem, oracula prophetarum, credulitatem, opus oratorum [...]. Et ex operibus opera que generant cognitionem, predicationem, rectoricam, negociationes, extimationem, geometriam, dispositionem, prophetiam, auguria, proverbia, scripturam, versificandi scientiam. [13]

The prophetic voice of Saint James and the narrator's ominous premonitions which follow Lelio's prayer and accompany him to the grave all suggest that Mercury's vatic powers are at work. Later, as Florio and Biancifiore grow up, they become well versed in all the liberal arts, and soon prove to be very eloquent, intelligent, and well endowed with the power of reasoning. As for Mercury's negative qualities, the two young lovers are often a step away from «dilectionem concubinarum».

A similar astrological allusion occurs a few chapters later when Lelio dies. The narrator tells us that the Sun is now in the last part of Capricorn (I 29, 1) one of Saturn's two houses (a very unfortunate «domus», if Saturn is in it). Lelio dies when the Sun is in its own decan, and Mars is in its own «term» (a section of a zodiac, smaller than a decan, where a planet exerts a significant influence). Furthermore, Mars is extremely close to, and possibly on, its point of exaltation (twenty-eight degrees in Capricorn). Even though the narrator does not tell us if Mars and Saturn are actually present, their presence is suggested throughout this episode. Prior to the battle, Felice prays to Mars, and interprets the ensuing omens to be those of the martial god (I 12 and I 13). The narrator's description of the cold, grim setting in which the battle took place (I 32) recalls Saturn's cold, grim world, as described by Andalone. [14] Furthermore, the qualities most often associated with Felice, «ira» and «malinconia» (II 27, 1 & 4), are the two most common attributes of Mars and Saturn respectively.

Lelio, on the other hand, prays to Jupiter, a classicized rendition of the Christian God (as we have seen in I 1, 17-18). The qualities which characterize Lelio are those which Andalone attributes to

---

[13] *Ibid*, p. 200. Andalone also says «Mercurius [significat] rationalitatem, dyaleticam et disciplinam» (p. 93).
[14] *Ibid*, pp. 195-6.

Jupiter («Iupiter [significat] rationem et sapientiam»).[15] From an astrological point of view, however, Jupiter is in a weak position, having just come out of its point of «debility» or «fall» (fifteen degrees in Capricorn); therefore, what actually mitigates the malefic powers of Mars and Saturn seems to be, once again, the presence of the Sun in its own decan. Although seemingly weak at this time of year (the days being short), and faint on this particular day (one covered with fog), the Sun's propitious presence is underscored by the divine promise of salvation which Lelio and his men hear from the sky just prior to the battle. Although their death is a tragic one, the salvation of their souls is assured (I 25, 10). The nexus between Sun and soul is a traditional one which even Andalone makes: «Sol significat spiritum idest animam»[16]. Furthermore, the fact that the Sun is once again the only celestial sphere referred to by name symbolically underscores the point Boccaccio is making in this particular episode, namely, that Lelio's heavenly «gloria» is far greater than Felice's earthly «vittoria».

Of all the astrological allusions in the *Filocolo*, the most important ones appear in the narrator's several accounts of the planets at the time of the protagonists' birth. The first such allusion appears in the narrator's description of Florio's birth:

s'appressò il termine del partorire alla reina, e simigliantemente a Giulia; e nel giocondo giorno eletto per festa de' cavalieri, essendo Febo nelle braccia di Castore e di Polluce insieme, non essendo ancora la tenebrosa notte partita, sentirono in una medesima ora quelle doglie che partorendo per l'altre femine si sogliono sentire. Dopo molte grida, essendo già la terza ora del giorno trapassata, la reina del gravoso affanno, partorendo un bel garzonetto, si diliberò, (I 39, 1-2)

If Quaglio is correct about the date of their birth (Pentecost), then the fourth hour on a Sunday would have to be under the influence of the Moon. This helps explain Florio's easy birth and Biancifiore's much harder birth several hours later:

Avea già il sole per lungo spazio trapassato il meridiano suo cerchio, avanti che Giulia del disiderato affanno liberare si potesse: anzi, con grandissime voci invocando il divino aiuto, sostenea grandissima doglia. Ma tra la erronea gente si dubitava non Lucina sopra i suoi altari stesse con le mani comprese, resistendo a' suoi parti [...] e con divoti fuochi s'ingegnavano di mitigare la colei ira, per liberare Giulia di tale pericolo. (I 40, 1-2)

---

[15] *Ibid*, p. 93.
[16] *Ibid*, p. 93. Firmicus states that Mars is the one planet whose negative influence is weakened when it is close to the Sun; FIRMICUS, *op. cit.*, p. 39.

Lucina, the goddess of child birth, is often associated with the Moon; and even though she smiles on Florio, she does not smile on Biancifiore, who loses her mother shortly after being born. [17] The Moon's «fortunate» influence at Florio's birth, and her «unfortunate» influence at Biancifiore's birth are indicative of the life each is born into. Florio is born into a life of wealth, power, and numerous social privileges. Biancifiore, on the other hand, is born into a life of hardship and low social station. The circumstances at the time of their birth determine their fortune and/or misfortune for a good part of their life. Since Biancifiore is born of a captive, she is regarded a slave rather than the Roman noblewoman she really is: her lowly birth is the main reason why Florio's parents continuously attempt to keep her away from their son, the sole heir to their kingdom. As we shall see later on, Biancifiore's adverse lunar fortune is not limited to her suffering at the hands of Florio's parents. She also becomes the main target of Diana's attack against the two young lovers, when Biancifiore forgets to thank the lunar goddess for helping Florio save her life.

There are, however, other planetary influences which affect the fate and fortune of the protagonists. Six years after their birth, the narrator tells us that Venus was «donna del loro ascendente» (I 45, 2). This in turn is followed by a description of the astrological «chart» at the time of their birth:

Venus era nell'auge del suo epiciclo, e nella sommità del differente nel celestiale Toro, non molto lontana al sole, quando ella fu donna, senza alcuna resistenza d'opposizione o d'aspetto o di congiunzione corporale o per orbe d'altro pianeta, dello ascendente della loro natività; il saturnino cielo, non che gli altri, pioveva amore il giorno che elli nacquero. (II 9, 2)

As Quaglio has convincingly shown in his detailed study of this passage, the fact that Venus is ascendent, in Taurus (one of her two «domi»), and in close proximity to the Sun, means that her influence on the two young lovers is very powerful. [18] As for the «saturnino cielo», Quaglio states that «persino il più odioso e malevole pianeta collaborava nei benefici effetti d'amore con Venere, sotto la cui

---

[17] Boccaccio may have found this in the work of the VATICAN MYTHOGRAPHER, *Scriptores rerum mythicarum latini tres romae Nuper Reperti*, ed. George Henry Bode, Hildesheim, Georg Olms, 1968, pp. 36 & 83. Quaglio, on the other hand, suggests some better known classical sources, *op. cit.*, p. 168.

[18] QUAGLIO, *op. cit.*, p. 106.

protezione erano nati Florio e Biancifiore». [19] No matter how powerful Venus's influence may be over the other planets, the fact that Saturn is alluded to in the «chart» suggests that his influence, however small, will mitigate in part the goddess's strong influence over her two protégés. As in the case of the narrator's own love for Fiammetta, the protagonists' love for each other is filled with moments of «malinconia», as we soon find out in the ensuing chapters. Their «malinconia», however, is also the result of the hardships brought about by Florio's parents and by the conflict which later arises between the Moon (personified by the goddess Diana) and Venus. From an allegorical point of view, this conflict is a pyschomachia between love and chastity (or *amor per diletto* and *amor onesto* as Smarr has suggested), but as we see in Book II, the Moon and Venus are also astrological forces which actually influence the conduct and fate of the two young lovers.

In Book II the Moon's influence on Florio and Biancifiore begins as a positive one: she works with Venus to help Florio save Biancifiore from Massamutino's false accusations. On the eve of the trial by combat between Florio and Massamutino, Venus tells Florio that the Moon has promised her to provide him with light so that he can travel by night from Montoro to Verona (II 42, 16). [20] Venus adds that the Moon was recently full in Aquarius («ancora pochi dì sono») and has begun to wane. This brief astrological detail is significant because it tells us, in a roundabout way, that the Sun is in Leo (i.e. in opposition to the full Moon), that Felice was born under Leo (his birthday was celebrated that very same day), and that ten months have passed since Florio's departure from Verona (when the Sun was in Libra). As Janet Smarr has indicated in her important study of astrology in the *Teseida*, Leo is «a sign of valiant knights, strong armed men, and noble kings; men under this sign "in servitio domini et iuxta magnos viros morantur," comments Andalò». [21] Although Felice only becomes a noble king towards the end of the *Filocolo*, his warrior spirit and strong-armed tactics throughout the tale make him very much of a «feroce Leone» (V 8, 20) like his zodiacal sign. Although Felice does not fight

---

[19] *Ibid*, p. 109.

[20] When Florio actually sets out on his nocturnal ride from Montoro to Verona, he prays to the gods, and begins by invoking the Moon (II 47, 4). In his prayer Florio recalls her role at his birth: she is the «principio» of both his life and his prayer; and her light, which «facea loro la via aperta e manifesta», also makes manifest «lo 'mpromesso aiuto degl'iddii». (II 47, 3).

[21] SMARR, *Boccaccio and the Stars*, p. 328.

the trial by combat, Massamutino represents him in battle carrying a shield «nel quale un leone rampante d'oro in uno azzurro campo risplendea» (II 65, 8). The battle begins when the sun is at its highest point in the sky, thereby making its influence very strong. This and the fact that the sun is in its *domus* would suggest that Felice should be favored by the outcome of this battle. In a way he is, since it is Massamutino who «in servitio domini et iuxta magnos viros moratur», and does so without revealing Felice's role in the plot to convict and kill Biancifiore. [22]

The fact that Venus and Mars appear as gods in this important episode suggests that their presence might also be astrological. If that is the case, the fact that they both appear to Florio by day, when the Sun is in its own *domus* and at its peak, means that their influence is intensified by the Sun; [23] it also suggests that they are in conjunction with the Sun, and therefore have an «unfortunate» influence on the sublunary world. [24] Florio in fact succeeds in defeating Massamutino on the battlefield largely because of Mars and Venus's divine intervention (the narrator makes it clear that Florio was too young and inexperienced in the martial arts to defeat Massamutino on his own). However, the fact that Florio also kills Massamutino at Mars' instigation, after the seneschal is defeated and has confessed his crime, and after Florio promised him mercy, suggests that the combined influence of Mars and Venus on Florio is a negative one.

Equally ambiguous is the astrological reference Felice makes the night before Biancifiore is to be executed on his orders. The king spends the long night of a guilty man anxiously awaiting for the day to come. In his monologue Felice asks if the Sun has returned to Capricorn (II 50) since the night seems so long. Aside from the obvious irony in his remark (seeing that the Sun is in Leo), the allusion recalls the last time the Sun was referred to in Capricorn--when Felice killed Lelio in combat. The king is subconsciously associating Lelio's death with Biancifiore's imminent death. This small touch adds to

---

[22] As Robert Durling has shown, there is a medieval tradition that associates the Day of Judgment with the sun in Leo. As we shall see in chapter four, this day is in fact a day of judgment for both Massamutino and King Felice. See ROBERT M. Durling, *A Long Day in the Sun: «Decameron» VIII 7»* in *Shakespeare's «Rough Magic»: Renaissance Essays in Honor of C. L. Barber*, ed. Peter Erickson and Coppélia Kahn, Newark, University of Delaware Press, 1985, pp. 269-275:273.
[23] See Andalone's text in QUAGLIO, *op. cit.*, pp. 106-7.
[24] *Ibid*, p. 148.

Boccaccio's masterful psychological portrayal of the king's feelings, while at the same time establishing a nexus between Lelio's martyrdom and his daughter's persecution.

After the trial by combat, all the gods, except Diana, are thanked for their role in liberating Biancifiore. This brings about several negative interventions on the part of Diana which affect all the characters in tale. Fileno, a young knight in love with Biancifiore, wins a tourney in honor of Mars and boasts of the attention he received from his beloved. After successfully making Florio jealous of Fileno, Diana succeeds in inspiring Felice to sell Biancifiore to two merchants. This in turn prompts Florio to embark on his long and dangerous journey in search of his beloved. Venus, Diana, the Moon, or some combination of the three are always present in these episodes. The conjunction of the Moon with Venus traditionally brings about the negative effects illustrated in Book III, including «the disturbance of hidden jealousy». [25] Whereas Mars and Venus are the most influential gods (and planets) in Book II, Diana and Venus acquire the greatest influence on the protagonists in Book III.

Before leaving Verona, Florio confronts his parents in a manner reminiscent of his first confrontation with his father prior to his first departure from Verona the year before (II 10 & ff.). In her attempts to dissuade Florio from leaving, the queen tells him:

Deh, per amor di me, non ti partire al presente. Non vedi tu le stelle Pliade, le quali pur ora cominciano a signoreggiare? Aspetta il dolce tempo nel quale Aldebaran col gran pianeto insieme surge sopra l'orizonte. (III 72, 2-3)

Basing himself on Boccaccio's *Chiose* to the *Teseida* IV 1, 2-5, Quaglio has shown that this astrological periphrasis refers to the month of October. Quaglio also points out that this allusion is similar to the one Felice made in the first confrontation scene (II 10, 12). [26] If this indeed corresponds to the month of October, then the second confrontation occurs at the same time of year the first one did. At that time Felice told Florio that the Sun had completed fourteen and one third years since his birth (II 12, 5). This would place it in Libra, one

[25] FIRMICUS, *op. cit.*, p. 231.
[26] See BOCCACCIO, *Filocolo*, pp. 759 & 840

of Venus's two houses; and though Venus's presence in both episodes is limited to that of a deity, not of a planet, her influence on the outraged lover is evident. Both episodes conclude with a self-imposed exile brought about by Florio's venereal impulse. [27]

The conflict between the various gods comes to an end in Book III, but their negative influence on the protagonists protracts itself through Book IV. Throughout the narrator's account of the protagonists' respective journeys to Alexandria, the passing of time is no longer expressed in terms of the Sun's course through the zodiac, but in terms of the waxing and waning of the Moon. In so doing, Boccaccio seems to be establishing a link between the protagonists' shifting fortune during their voyages and the continuous mutations of the Moon. The Moon is sometimes personified as Proserpina in the *Filocolo*, spending an equal amount of time on Earth with her mother Ceres (as a full Moon) and below the Earth with her husband Pluto (as a new Moon). This cyclical pattern, coupled with the numerous allusions to «fortuna» in conjunction with the passing of time, underscores the fact that the world of fortune is closely connected to the Moon. As Andalone and other astrologers point out, the «fortunate» and «unfortunate» influences of the planets all pass through the Moon's sphere, and are distributed by her to the sublunary world. [28] As the heavenly sphere which separates the immortal world from the mortal sublunary world, the Moon's continuous flux is a reflection of the change and impermanence of the protagonists' world, one which is dominated by both love and fortune (i.e. Venus and the Moon).

Once in Alexandria, Florio is advised by Dario to befriend Sadoc (the guardian of the tower in which Biancifiore is kept); but soon after deciding that this is the best course of action to follow, Florio has second thoughts and procrastinates (IV 89). The astrological allusions which appear in this episode indicate the actual length of his procrastination:

Rallegravasi Apollo nella sua casa, quando primieramente lo 'nnamorato giovane pervenne al tanto tempo cercato paese, dove avuto il consiglio di Dario tutto in sé propose di adempiere. Ma ciò sì tosto com'egli imaginava, non poté venire ad

---

[27] Janet Smarr has brought to my attention the fact that Libra is often associated with departures in Boccaccio's later works (e.g. Panfilo's departure in the *Elegia di madonna Fiammetta*).

[28] See Andalone in QUAGLIO, *op. cit.*, pp. 90, 140, 147; and THE VATICAN MYTHOGRAPHER, p. 198.

effetto, però che in diversi atti e modi la fortuna, ancora non contenta de' suoi beni, gli ruppe le vie, per che assai tempo ozioso gli convenne stare [...] E in questa vita stette infino a tanto che Febo in quello animale, che la figliuola di Agenor trasportò de' suoi regni, se ne venne a dimorare, e quivi quasi nella fine congiunto con Citerea, rinnovellato il tempo, cominciò gli amorosi animi a riscaldare e a raccendere i fuochi divenuti tiepidi nel freddo e spiacevole tempo di verno: e massimamente quello di Filocolo, il quale sì nel suo disio divenne fervente, che appena raffrenare si potea di pur non mettersi a volere il suo proponimento adempiere sanza guardare luogo o tempo. (IV 90, 1 & 6)

If Apollo is rejoicing in his «house», it means that the Sun is back in Leo. Florio spends, however, the next nine months in Alexandria without following Dario's advice. This comes to us as a surprise because the last time the Sun was in Leo Florio freed Biancifiore from imminent death with less than twenty-four hours to prepare for his first combat experience. It is apparent from the soliloquy in the preceding chapter that Florio lacks the same determination he had a year before. The narrator attributes Florio's lack of resolve to «fortuna» (IV 90, 1); but judging from the soliloquy, what actually holds him back is his clear understanding of the dangers involved in this mission.

It is only when Venus enters her house in Taurus that Florio is moved to go through with his mission. The fact that Venus is also in conjunction with the Sun adds to her power over her protégé, while at the same time making it «unfortunate». [29] It should be noted that this is the first time Boccaccio actually tells us Venus's position in the zodiac. Along with the description of the protagonists' «chart» at the time of their birth (II 9, 2), this is one of the few planetary settings we find in the *Filocolo*. It is clear that by making the astrological reference at this point in the narrative Boccaccio is preparing his readers for the dramatic events which bring about the consummation scene:

Venuto adunque già Titan ad abitare con Castore, un giorno, essendo il tempo chiaro e bello, Filocolo si mosse per andare verso la torre: alla quale essendo ancora assai lontano, verso quella rimirando, vide ad una finestra una giovane, alla quale nel viso i raggi del sole riflessi dal percosso cristallo davano mirabile luce [...] Per che tanto il disio gli crebbe di vederla più da presso e d'adempiere ciò che proposto aveva, che, abandonate insieme le redine del cavallo con quelle della sua volontà [...] col cavallo correndo infino al piè della torre se n'andò: dove

---

[29] See Andalone in QUAGLIO, *op. cit.*, p. 148.

disceso con le braccia aperte s'ingegnava d'abbracciare le mura, quelle baciando infinite fiate, e quasi nell'animo di ciò che faceva si sentiva diletto. (IV 91, 1-3)

Florio's mad rush to his «donna sole» recalls Phaeton's tragic chariot ride through the heavens: both are overpowered by solar forces over which they have no control. Florio's foolhardy behavior is in sharp contrast to his circumspection during his first eight months in Alexandria (one more indication of Venus's power over him); and even though the Sun has moved into Gemini, it is close enough to Venus to fortify her influence over her protégés.

The consummation scene occurs just a few days later when Mars and Venus are honored. This is the same pagan «festa dei cavalieri» on which Florio and Biancifiore were born. On a day which honors the union of Mars and Venus, both Florio and Biancifiore are so overcome by their passion for each other that they fail to anticipate its disastrous consequences. Florio fails to conceive of an escape plan to free Biancifiore from the tower; and Biancifiore fails to make Florio aware of the dangers they both face if they get caught. When they are caught and sentenced to be burnt at the stake, both Venus and Mars come to their rescue. The results, however, are devastating: in the ensuing battle the Admiral of Alexandria loses many of his men, and Ascalion, Florio's closest friend, is wounded. This episode reveals the negative forces of Mars and Venus: they are very similar to the negative influence traditionally associated with the conjunction of these two planets. [30]

After the protagonists' unfortunate adventures in Alexandria, the gods disappear completely from the narrative; and the only significant astrological allusion in Book V appears at the end of the *Filocolo* when the narrator tells us the planetary setting at the time of the protagonists' coronation:

Il dolce tempo era, e il cielo tutto ridente porgeva graziose ore: Citerea, tra le corna dello stellato Tauro splendidissima, dava luce, e Giove chiaro si stava trà guizzanti Pesci; Apollo nelle braccia di Castore e di Polluce più lieto ogni mattina nelle braccia della sua Aurora si vedea entrare; Febeia correa con le sue agute corna lieta alla sua ritondità. Ogni stella ridea, e il sottile aere confortava i viventi, e la terra niuna parte di sé mostrava ignuda: ogni cosa o erba o fiori si vedea, sanza i quali niuno albero si saria trovato, o sanza frutto. (V 95, 1-2)

---

[30] FIRMICUS, *op. cit.*, pp. 200, 202-3, 216 & 229. See also SMARR, *op. cit.*, pp. 310-311.

The Sun is back in Gemini, Venus is in her feminine house (Taurus), and Jupiter in his (Pisces). The Moon is waxing and about to become full, meaning that she is in Sagittarius, Jupiter's masculine house (in opposition to the Sun). Venus and Jupiter are in a fortunate aspect, sextile, or «triplicates» as Andalone calls it. Both the Sun and Moon are in a square aspect to Jupiter. Although square aspects are often regarded as «unfortunate», with Jupiter they are quite «fortunate», as Firmicus amply illustrates in the *Matheseos*. [31] Furthermore, as Andalone states, the Sun is fortunate when it is in aspect to a planet: here it is in square aspect to Jupiter, and in opposition aspect to the Moon. [32]

This fortunate astrological setting at the end of the *Filocolo* promises well for Florio and Biancifiore not only as rulers but also as husband and wife. Their love is no longer the surreptitious passion which puts their life in danger. Venus is now united with «il temperato Giove» (V 8, 18), just as the protagonists' love is tempered by reason throughout Book V («Jupiter [significat] rationem et sapientiam»). [33] It is worth noting that this union of Venus and Jupiter (which supersedes the unfortunate unions of Venus and Mars in Books II-IV) is one which has its roots in the protagonists' ancient ancestors. Florio's mother and uncle (the Admiral of Alexandria) trace their origins to Jarba («re de' Getoli») son of Jupiter (III 73, 1). [34] Giulia, Biancifiore's mother, belongs to the *gens Julia*, descendants of Aeneas, the son of Venus. [35] Considering the fact that Biancifiore's misfortunes are largely due to the fact that the king and queen do not recognize her noble pedigree, the union of the planets Venus and Jupiter is the fitting conclusion to the two lovers' trials and tribulations: their marriage and coronation were «in the stars».

Andalone's astrological philosophy is consonant with Boethius' philosophy on the relationship between human action and celestial and divine forces. [36] Like several astrologers of his time, Andalò

---

[31] FIRMICUS, *op. cit.*, pp. 185-186, 189-190, 196, 209.

[32] See Andalone's text in QUAGLIO, *op. cit.*, p. 148.

[33] The astrological setting of the coronation episode has some interesting counterparts in the *Teseida*, see SMARR, *op. cit.*, pp. 312-317.

[34] It is worth noting that Jupiter was on his way to see «Atalante» (Felice's mythic ancestor) when he saw and seduced the nymph Garamante, Jarba's mother (see Boccaccio's *Chiose* to the *Teseida* V 103, 1-2). The fact that both of Florio's parents trace their ancestry to the characters in this myth suggests that they too, like Jupiter, abused a helpless maiden.

[35] BOCCACCIO, *Filocolo*, p. 958.

[36] Andalone's philosophy is also compatible with Aquinas. In his commentary to Aristotle's *De anima*, Aquinas states: «Sense-faculties are in part corporeal, because of the bodily organs in which they exist. Therefore they are subject to the influence of the heavenly bodies,

believed that judgments of astrology were not necessary but contingent: they depended as much on the disposition of the patient as on the actions of the agent. [37] What this suggests is that astrology, like the Boethian providential plan, allows for the characters to exercise their free will without ever making their actions «necessary». As we shall see in the ensuing chapters, the protagonists' «liberum arbitrium» remains free as long as it does not succumb to the external and internal forces which affect it.

---

though even so, only indirectly, for neither the soul itself nor any of its powers is directly subject to the action of corporeal matter. Consequently, the imagination and sense-appetite are modified in various ways by the influence of the heavenly bodies» (par. 617). Aquinas goes on to say, «There is no difficulty, however, about admitting an indirect stellar influence upon intellect and will, in so far as these faculties act in conjunction with the faculties of sense. Thus any injury to the bodily organ of the imagination will impede the intellect; and the will is incited towards choosing or not choosing by sensuous desire. But since the will is never drawn of necessity, but remains free to follow or not the prompting of desire, human actions are never completely determined by astral influences» (par. 621). See *Aristotle's «De Anima» in the Version of William of Moerbeke and with the Commentary of Saint Thomas Aquinas*, translated by Foster and Humphries, London, Routledge, 1959.
[37] See LYNN THORNDIKE, *A History of Magic and Experimental Science*, III, New York, Columbia University Press, 1934, pp. 192-3; and GEORGE SARTON, *Introduction to the History of Science*, III, Baltimore, Carnegie Institution of Washington, 1947, p. 647.

CHAPTER THREE

LOVE, REASON, AND THE APPETITES

I. The Mimesis of Love

Although supernatural forces are at work throughout the *Filocolo*, they never prevent the characters from ultimately determining their fate through their choices. This is as true for Florio and Biancifiore as it is for their parents. In fact, Boccaccio is as interested in portraying the human factors, or «intrinsic principles of acts» (to use Aquinas's terminology), involved in shaping his protagonists' fate, as he is in illustrating the «extrinsic principles of acts» (i.e. the role Providence and its ministers--fate, fortune, astrology, and the pagan gods--have on the lives of the protagonists). It is the interrelationship of the external supernatural forces with the internal human emotions which gives the narrative its richness and complexity.

Of all the external and internal forces depicted in the *Filocolo*, love and its relation to the human appetites are given the greatest attention. If Book I is devoted to the circumstances of the protagonists' birth («il nascimento»), Books II, III, and IV are dedicated to «lo 'nnamoramento e gli accidenti» (the other two topics Fiammetta had asked the narrator to write about in his new rendition of the story of Florio and Biancifiore). The last sentence in Book I is, in fact, an allusion which sets the stage for the love labors narrated in the ensuing books: «Racheio [...] fece loro leggere il santo libro d'Ovidio, nel quale il sommo poeta mostra come i santi fuochi di Venere si deano ne' freddi cuori con sollecitudine accendere» (I 45, 6). [1] The fact that the

---

[1] Ussani claimed that Boccaccio was alluding to Ovid's *Ars amatoria*, see VINCENZO USSANI JR., *Alcune imitazioni ovidiane del Boccaccio*, «Maia», I, 1948, pp. 289-306: 289. See also QUAGLIO, *Filocolo*, p. 755. Francesco Bruni supports Ussani's claim on the grounds that the minor works of Ovid were often used as readers for youngsters learning Latin; see *Il «Filocolo»*

protagonists learn how to express themselves by reading Ovid's love poetry indicates that they are educated not only in the way love is born, but also in the way the innermost feelings of passion and melancholy can be expressed. As we soon find out, the protagonists master both the content and the style of Ovid's work by mimetically adapting them to their own life. Ovid's work, therefore, is not just the traditional school book for children learning to read and write, it is also the first means of linguistic expression and imitation which the protagonists learn and later adopt when they fall in love. The protagonists are thus introduced to language and desire almost simultaneously. The nexus between language and desire in turn determines how the protagonists relate to the world around them.

Book II opens with Venus's first appearance in the *Filocolo*. She asks her son Cupid, the external force of Love, to make the two protagonists one of their number («d'essere del numero de' nostri suggetti»). The fact that Cupid does so by disguising himself as King Felice and by breathing his amorous breath on Florio and Biancifiore suggests that his power over the two protagonists is as strong and ambiguous as that of the king. Cupid's «mentita forma» distinctly recalls Pluto's «vana forma» in I 36: in both instances a supernatural force assumes a «lying» human form. Both Pluto and Cupid reenact a role taken from the second book of the *Aeneid*: Cupid does exactly the same thing he did when he assumed the form of Ascanius, Aeneas's son.[2] But instead of assuming the body of the son in order that the father may fall in love, Cupid is now assuming the body of the father so that the son will fall in love. The new twist Boccaccio gives to the famous Vergilian episode anticipates the different course Florio's love will follow: unlike Aeneas, who sacrifices his love of Dido for the future empire the gods have promised him and his son, Florio is prepared to sacrifice for Biancifiore the empire his father wants him to inherit (II 18, 3). As in the case of Aeneas, the danger of losing the

e lo spazio della letteratura volgare, «Miscellanea di studi in onore di Vittore Branca», II, Firenze, Leo S. Olschki, 1983, pp. 1-21. Nicola Zingarelli showed, however, that even Ovid's *Metamorphoses* is present in the *Filocolo*, see his article *La fonte classica di un episodio del «Filocolo»*, «Romania», XIV, 1885, pp. 433-441.

[2] McGregor sees this reenactment of the famous episode in the *Aeneid* as Venus «once again using Cupid [...] to overthrow a kingdom hostile to the mission of her people». McGregor views the *Filocolo* as an epic struggle between two Trojan remnants: the descendants of Aeneas (e.g. Biancifiore), who founded Rome and set the foundation for a Christian empire, and another group (represented by Felice) that reverted back to to a pre-Christian paganism. In this episode Venus is helping her son's descendants; see McGREGOR, *op. cit.*, pp. 36-7.

empire for the love of a woman is ever present in the *Filocolo*. The importance of the empire in both works is clear from the very beginning of each work: for both Felice and Aeneas love and empire cannot coexist. [3] As the narrative progresses, it becomes obvious why Boccaccio has patterned the protagonists' falling in love after that of Dido and Aeneas: like their Vergilian counterparts, Florio and Biancifiore are destined to become rulers, but the nature of their love will lead them astray, thereby endangering the future of the people they are destined to rule. [4] Furthermore, by trying to mimetically pattern their behavior after that of the two Vergilian lovers, Florio and Biancifiore are making the same dangerous mistake that Dante's Paolo and Francesca made after reading about Lancelot and Guinevere. [5] Like their Vergilian counterparts, the two young protagonists discover that the road to their foreordained end (i.e. reign over a large empire) is made longer because of their passion.

As Cupid assumes the «falsa forma» of Felice, Venus makes the real king fall asleep and dream of the consequences of the amorous encounter which is taking place. It seems only natural that Venus is responsible for this vision since she is, in effect, responsible for the love which develops between Florio and Biancifiore. The fact that the dream is an allegorical vision of the events which will occur from the time Felice wakes up to the end of the *Filocolo* suggests that Venus is a minister of Providence since she is able to disclose the providential plan. This vision, therefore, acquires an eschatological and teleological dimension similar to that found in Lelio's vision of Saint James and in the voice from the cloud which Lelio and his men hear before the battle. [6] The fact that Felice is chosen to see the entire course of events which will result from the protagonists' falling in love is significant since it is he who will try to go against the providential

---

[3] In fact, when the king finds out that his only son is in love with a commoner, he devotes all his efforts to bringing an end to their relationship.

[4] This may explain why, after the consummation scene, the two protagonists undergo a long physical and spiritual journey home in Book V: they must prepare themselves for when they become rulers.

[5] It should be noted that Florio and Biancifiore appear in Boccaccio's *Amorosa Visione* XXIX 32 right after Dido and Aeneas, and immediately before Lancelot and Guinevere (the two lovers Paolo and Francesca had imitated in their tragic love affair). All three pairs of lovers are examples of the Triumph of Love; however, they are also examples of dangerous love and, in the case of Florio and Biancifiore, of the dangers involved in mimetically reproducing the love they read about (a mistake Paolo and Francesca had made).

[6] Venus's visions reveal what is hidden from the characters; this is also true of Florio's first vision of her (II 42).

plan. The king cannot interpret the allegorical meaning of the vision at this point in the story, nor does he make any effort to interpret it or have someone else interpret it for him. Felice, in effect, disregards his vision completely, and in so doing he is ultimately negating the providential nature of the protagonists' love. By describing the dream before Felice attempts to alter the course of this love, Boccaccio is underscoring the futility of Felice's actions. Like the protagonists in the *Aeneid*, Felice and the two young lovers will misdirect their actions as a result of their respective desires, thereby delaying the eventual attainment of their desired end and their ultimate end as ordained by Providence. Providence, in turn, will realign the course leading to each characters' most desired object with that leading to the *summum bonum*.

If, on the eschatological level, the dream is meant to illustrate the providential nature of the protagonists' love, on the allegorical and moral levels it tells us something about the nature of that love. The dream is filled with images of animals that are metamorphosed into human beings towards the end of the dream. [7] The vision is an inversion of Ovid's *Metamorphosis* in which sensual love transforms the lover, or the beloved, into a plant, animal, or other non-human element of the natural world. The metamorphosis in the dream implies that the characters themselves will undergo a transformation in their lives. Since the metamorphosis corresponds to the moment of conversion to Christianity (V 71), the first part of this allegorical vision suggests that the love of the protagonists and their conduct prior to their conversion is characterized by those appetites which all men share with animals (i.e. the sensitive appetites). The protagonists become human only after those appetites are brought under the full control of their will and reason, the powers which only rational creatures (i.e. human beings) possess. The moral and allegorical implications of this vision are significant: the protagonists' love is not under the full control of reason before their conversion. Only after their conversion is their love realigned with the greater love of God that governs the universe.

The ambiguous nature of the protagonists' love prior to conversion is anticipated in the actual description of how Florio and Biancifiore fall in love:

---

[7] For a related discussion, see VICTORIA KIRKHAM, *Numerology and Allegory in Boccaccio's «Caccia di Diana»*, «Traditio», XXXIV, 1978, pp. 303-29.

Taciti e soli lasciò Amore i due novelli amanti, i quali riguardando l'un l'altro fiso, Florio primieramente chiuse il libro, e disse: — Deh, che nuova bellezza t'è egli cresciuta, o Biancifiore, da poco in qua, che tu mi piaci tanto? Tu non mi solevi tanto piacere; ma ora gli occhi miei non possono saziarsi di riguardarti! —. Biancifiore rispose: — Io non so, se non che di te poss'io dire che in me sia avvenuto il simigliante. Credo che la virtù de' santi versi, che noi divotamente leggiamo, abbia accese le nostre menti di nuovo fuoco, e adoperato in noi quello già veggiamo che in altrui adoperarono —. (II 4, 1-2)

As Quaglio has shown, the moment is patterned after the Paolo and Francesca episode in *Inferno* V. Critics have tended to view this moment of sexual awakening as an innocent and idyllic one. [8] Boccaccio may have indeed mitigated the negative implications of comparing the protagonists to Paolo and Francesca; however, the fact that they are indirectly compared to Dante's tragic lovers suggests that, no matter how innocent and chaste the protagonists' love may be at its inception, it has a darker side to it.

Like their Dantean counterparts, Florio and Biancifiore fall in love while reading a work about love: their desire is mediated by the very same «santi versi» on which their education is based. The fiction they are reading becomes a reality over which they have a limited control. Besides picking up on Dante's warning of the dangers of love poetry and the way it is read, Boccaccio is also illustrating the dangerous discrepancies between fiction and the reality it attempts to represent. These discrepancies create a tension throughout the second, third and fourth books which is an important trait of the young lovers' amorous experience and of the narrative itself. What now may be an innocent moment of sexual awakening, has all the ear-marks of something that can destroy that very innocence.

The first signs of lost innocence appear, in fact, shortly after Florio and Biancifiore have fallen in love. When Felice discovers that his son is in love with Biancifiore, he confronts Florio. During the confrontation scene both father and son reveal their bad faith and deception in the things they tell each other. Felice tries to conceal his real motives for sending Florio to Montoro by claiming that he wants his son to learn the «santi principii di Pittagora» (philosophy, accord-

---

[8] Cfr. SAPEGNO, *op. cit.*, p. 300 and PERELLA, *op. cit.*, p. 333. Even when the two protagonists consummate this love several years later, the consummation scene, as critics have pointed out, is not described in pornographic or overly erotic terms.

ing to Quaglio). [9] Florio, on the other hand, conceals his true motives for wanting to stay in Verona by pretending to be concerned for his father's well being, and by claiming that he loves his father above anyone else (II 11, 6). Florio's lie is taken from a sincere remark Dido makes to Aeneas in *Aeneid* IV 365-8 when she exposes her lover's surreptitious attempt to leave Carthage and abandon her. The confrontation scene between Felice and Florio is, in fact, patterned after Dido's famous confrontation with Aeneas. Like Dido, Florio does not want to be separated from the object of his greatest desire, and unlike Aeneas, who wanted to leave Dido and Carthage, Florio wants to remain with Biancifiore in Verona. Like Aeneas, however, Florio is not straightforward, and his deception is exposed by Felice just as Aeneas's insincerity is exposed by Dido. Whereas Aeneas's decision to leave Dido and Carthage may be viewed as an act of *pietas* made in response to the wishes of the gods and his dead father Anchises, Florio's desire *not* to leave Biancifiore and Verona goes against the wishes of his father and is expressed by a false act of filial piety. When Florio uses the word «pietosa» (II 11, 8), Felice unmasks his son's false *pietas* by revealing the hollowness of that word (II 12, 1-2). One cannot help agreeing with Felice that love has taught Florio to be deceptive (II 14, 2).

To further undercut the reasoning of the two, Boccaccio has both Florio and Felice cite examples of classical heroes which undercut the very points both father and son are trying to assert. Felice cites the example of Androgeus (Minos' son) and Jason, to justify sending Florio to study away from home. Felice could not have chosen two more inappropriate examples, since the departure of these two classical heroes from their homes proved to be tragic. [10] Florio, on the other hand, justifies his love on the grounds that even great men like Hercules and Ajax fell in love. Rather than proving his point, Florio's allusion to these two heroes (both of whom became mad) proves the very point Felice had made earlier:

della qual cosa doppiamente sè da riprendere e principalmente d'aver avuto sì poca costanza in te, che a sì vile passione, com'è amare una femina oltre misura,

---

[9] See BOCCACCIO, *Filocolo*, 759.

[10] Androgeus was killed in Athens by his fellow schoolmates, giving rise to Minos' cruel vengeance against the Athenians. As for Jason, he was forced to leave his homeland because his father's throne had been usurped, not because he was «più disposto all'armi che a' filosofichi studii» as Felice claims.

hai lasciato vincere il tuo virile animo, non ponendo mente quanti e quali sieno i pericoli che da questo amare sieno già proceduti e procedano. (II 14, 3) [11]

The unintented ambiguity of their allusions underscores the duplicity and fallacy of their reasoning, while unwittingly revealing the truth in the other's point. If Florio leaves Verona, the consequences may be tragic; and if he loves Biancifiore «oltre misura», he, too, like Hercules and Ajax, risks madness. [12]

Boccaccio adds a touch of dramatic irony to Florio and Felice's speeches during their confrontation. Florio states that he would be prepared to travel even farther than the epic heroes in order to find «la cosa da me disiata e a quietare la mia volontà» (II 13, 2). Little does he know that this is exactly what he will do in the first half of Book IV. Like Aeneas, Florio too will travel far and wide in search of his desired end; his voyage, however, begins as a reversal of Aeneas's voyage since he leaves Italy for the Orient. It is only after his misfortunes in Alexandria that Florio follows Aeneas's footsteps back to Italy. It is in Rome that Florio, like Aeneas, discovers his ultimate end. That end will be marked by Florio's conversion to Christianity and the subsequent conversion to Christianity of his father's empire. Just as Aeneas's journey ends on the site of his future pagan empire (Rome), Florio's journey will end with the foundation of a new Christian empire. [13] Before reaching their ultimate end, however, both journeys are marked by an amorous experience on the north African coast and by several significant detours in southern Italy.

We also find dramatic irony in Felice's false warning to Florio of the dangers of loving «oltra misura». Little does Felice know what dangers Florio will actually incur when he embarks on his *peregrinatio amoris*. As in the case of Florio's dramatically ironic remark, Felice's reason for making his statement has nothing to do with its inherent truth. Both Florio and Felice make these statements in order to conceal the true reasons for which they are said. The fact that their

---

[11] These two heroes had one thing in common – they both became mad (Boccaccio was probably familiar with the Senecan tragedies which describe their madness). Florio's passion is often referred to as «follia», and can be traced back to the «amour follie» of the Old French romances.

[12] Felice's words «oltre misura» are repeated by Dario in Alexandria when he realizes that Florio is in love with Biancifiore «beyond measure».

[13] The juxtaposition of these two journeys is anticipated in the opening sentence of the *Filocolo* (I 1, 1) when Boccaccio alludes to Aeneas's foundation of pagan Rome and Juno's role in the foundation of Christian (i.e. papal) Rome (see BOCCACCIO, *Filocolo*, p. 713).

lies contain a subliminal truth not only reveals Boccaccio's perceptive understanding of the human psyche, but it also reveals the contiguousness of the characters' words and the Logos (as manifested in the providential plan). The truth is never fully divorced from the lies the characters tell each other, just as statements which claim absolute truth are never fully free from lies: one discloses what the other attempts to conceal, and vice versa. In so doing, Boccaccio is making a significant statement about the nature of language: like desire, language too is unstable and ambiguous. [14] And just as desire ceases to wander only after it has found the *summum bonum*, language too can never be anchored to absolute truth or unequivocal meaning except when it is at one with the Logos. [15] The closest any of the characters comes to such a union is in V 59 when Florio is possessed by the Holy Ghost and delivers a sermon which inspires all his friends to become Christians.

The father-son confrontation takes a turn in that direction when Florio finally discloses the truth about his love for Biancifiore. Instead of being deceptive, Florio engages in a sincere discussion on the superiority of Biancifiore's nobility of heart (*probitas*) over the nobility of blood found in people like himself and his father. Instead of continuing to use his exceptional powers of reason towards a negative end (i.e. to deceive his father), Florio uses «right reason» to justify his true feelings about Biancifiore. [16] Florio pleads his case by upholding achieved nobility over acquired nobility, and by alluding to the courtly-love claim that his love for Biancifiore is ennobling (i.e. it makes him a better person). His point of view, which reflects one of the most important love topoi of Boccaccio's time, is in sharp contrast to the king's equally established view of the effeminate and destructive power of «folle amore» (the Old French «fole amor») as reflected

---

[14] For a related discussion in the *Decameron*, see GIUSEPPE MAZZOTTA, *The World at Play in Boccaccio's «Decameron»*, Princeton, Princeton University Press, 1986, pp. 47-74; and MILLICENT JOY MARCUS, *An Allegory of Form: Literary Self-Consciousness in the «Decameron»*, Saratoga, California, Anma Libri, 1979 («Stanford French and Italian Studies», 18), pp. 20-25, *passim*.

[15] For a similar treatment of the logos in the *Decameron*, see MAZZOTTA, *op. cit.*, p. 49; and in Dante, see Mazzotta's *Dante, Poet of the Desert: History and Allegory in the Divine Comedy*, Princeton, Princeton University Press, 1979, p. 268.

[16] «Right reason» is the term Aquinas uses to indicate the use of reason to direct human acts to the attainment of man's objective good (i.e. the *summum bonum*). It is distinct from rational behavior in general: even a criminal may use his rational faculties to perform a crime; but in so doing, he is not using right reason because he is not directing his actions towards attaining the supreme good found in God.

in Hercules' love for Megara and Omphale, and Ajax's mad desire. Felice fails to accept his son's well argued case (*discussio*), in part because it does not conform to his narrow-minded understanding of «nobiltà», in part because Florio has lost credibility on the issue of ennobling love by lying to his father, and in part because Felice, as king, is the judge and the ultimate *autoritas* of the law, and can therefore make whatever *determinatio* or *sententia* he wants. [17]

By narrating this quasi-legal debate along such lines, Boccaccio has taken away from both Florio and Felice the moral claims their respective cases may have had, while at the same time illustrating the complex and often ambiguous relationship between reason and desire. The debate, however, also raises other questions that need to be addressed. For example, to what extent is Florio's love for Biancifiore truly ennobling, and to what extent is it «follia»? What are the inherent dangers that exist in the protagonists' love for each other? What is the relation between love and the power of reason? Between love and nobility? By placing this debate at the beginning of the protagonists' «innamoramento», Boccaccio is bringing to our attention issues that will become the thematic focal points of the narrative throughout the *Filocolo*.

The confrontation between Felice and Florio also serves to illustrate the various psychological forces at work within the protagonist's mind. In addition to portraying Florio's use of his power of practical and speculative reason in the name of love, the confrontation scene also reveals how Florio is moved by his appetitive powers. [18] When Florio is confronted with the possibility of being separated from Biancifiore, we are told that he is filled with «ira e amore» (II 13, 1). The two sensitive appetites (the irascible and the concupiscible) are, in fact, at work in Florio in a manner which is consonant with traditional medieval psychology. Since the irascible appetite is a means to a concupiscible end, as Thomas Aquinas points out, it manifests itself in Florio in direct proportion to the threat of losing the object of his

---

[17] For an analysis of the legal trappings which were part of a medieval debate, quodlibet, *tenso, joc partite*, etc., see R. Howard Bloch, *Medieval French Literature and Law*, Berkeley, University of California Press, 1977, p. 165.

[18] The terms practical reason and speculative reason are used by Aquinas to distinguish between reason concerned with the knowledge and consideration of truth (i.e. speculative reason) and reason concerned with the application of what is apprehended either in moral conduct or in artistic or technical production. See Frederick C. Copleston, S.J., *Aquinas*, London, Penguin, 1964, p. 224.

concupiscible appetite (Biancifiore). [19] The tension produced by these two appetites at work within the protagonist are checked by the third appetite, the intellectual appetite (i.e. the will), which works in conjunction with Florio's faculty of reason in an attempt not to lose Biancifiore.

Will and reason are also at work in Florio when he makes the important decision to go to Montoro as his father has requested. Aquinas says that free choice is an act of the will which results from a free judgment of reason (*Summa Theologica* Ia, 83, art. 1). [20] Both Florio and Biancifiore are fully aware of this, as we see in their respective monologues immediately after the confrontation scene (II 17 & II 18). Both recognize that Florio's consent makes him largely responsible for the lovers' separation. By consenting, Florio is, in effect, exercising his *liberum arbitrium* and determining the ensuing course of events. [21] Like the other characters in the *Filocolo*, Florio has a choice (either go to Montoro or stay in Verona), and makes his choice the moment he acquiesces to his father's request.

For both Boethius and Aquinas, free will means choosing. Aristotle in the *Ethics* III 2, and Thomas Aquinas in the *Summa Theologica* Ia, Q. 82, art. 1, res. 3, state that free choice (or the power of election) regards the means to the ultimate end, but not that end itself: «Consequently, the desire of the ultimate end is not among those actions of which we are masters». [22] The ultimate end for

---

[19] See *Aristotle's «De Anima» in the Version of William of Moerbeke and with the Commentary of Saint Thomas Aquinas*, translated by Foster and Humphries, London, Routledge, 1959, par. 803-805.

[20] Thomas Aquinas says that two things occur when man makes a free choice: «On the part of the cognitive power, counsel is required, by which we judge one thing to be preferred to another; on the part of the appetitive power it is required that the appetite should accept the judgment of counsel» (Ia, Q. 83, art. 3 resp.); see AQUINAS, *Summa Theologica*, I, p. 790. Aquinas's statement is very similar to the one Boethius makes in the *De consolatione* as we have seen in chapter one. For a more detailed analysis of Aquinas's understanding of the relationship between reason and will, see COPLESTON, *op. cit.*, pp. 185-198.

[21] For a more detailed discussion of consent and will, see Aquinas, *Summa Theologica* Ia, IIae, Q 15.

[22] THOMAS AQUINAS, *op. cit.*, p. 778. Although free choice is the power of election, Aquinas distinguishes it from the will: «In like manner, on the part of the appetite, to *will* implies the simple appetite for something, and so the will is said to regard the end, which is desired for itself. But to *elect* is to desire something for the sake of obtaining something else, and so properly speaking, it regards the means to the end» (Q. 83, Art. 4); see AQUINAS, *op. cit.*, p. 791. Boccaccio adds to this scholastic understanding of free will the Boethian ideas we saw in chapter 1: the chosen means do not always bring about the desired end, especially when that end is an apparent good which is far from the universal and perfect good of *beatitudo* (or

Aquinas is *beatitudo* (Boethius' *summum bonum*) which exists only in God. The desire for this end is the same innate desire Boethius wrote about, and which Aquinas identifies as an inclination of the will (man's intellectual appetite). Because this inclination towards *beatitudo* is a natural desire for the universal and perfect good, the will is said to desire *beatitudo* of necessity (Ia, 82, art. 3). Like Boethius, Aquinas says that the will is free to desire particular goods which are not the universal and perfect good, but it does not adhere of necessity to any of them. [23] The only time the will adheres of necessity to something is when man sees «God in His essence»; at which point, says Aquinas, it adheres to God of necessity. And even though the will may never find God, it always aims for a universal and perfect good: it apprehends what is good under a general idea of goodness (*sub specie boni*).

On the other hand, the two sensitive appetites (the concupiscible and the irascible) apprehend particular goods (ones which are pleasant to the senses) or particular evils (ones which are unpleasant to the senses). The concupiscible answers to a good which simply affords pleasure, whereas the irascible answers to a good by means of which one is able to enjoy pleasant things. For Aristotle and Aquinas, the irascible is a means to a concupiscible end. [24] Unlike the intellectual appetite (i.e. the will), the sensitive appetites may incline man to choose one thing over another, but can never actually move him in that direction: only the intellectual appetite can move him to elect one thing over another. Hence the concupiscible and the irascible can influence free choice, but never determine it. [25] Similarly, Florio and Biancifiore choose to love each other by allowing their will to be

---

the *summum bonum*). Man's desired end and his means for obtaining it are realigned by fate and fortune in order to conform to the providential plan. This realignment, in turn, is the path to *beatitudo* or the *summum bonum* (i.e. the end which the will ultimately desires).

[23] In this respect, Aquinas's *beatitudo* shares the same nature as Boethius's *summum bonum*; and like Boethius, Aquinas too points to the different ways in which this can be mistaken for other things which are apparently good: «Some men seek riches as the supreme good, others pleasure, others something else» (*Summa Theologica* Ia, IIae, 1, 7).

[24] See ARISTOTLE, *De Anima*, par. 803-804.

[25] In his commentary to Aristotle's *De anima*, Aquinas says that «rational deliberation may yield to the lower desire, may be overcome by it and drawn away from its own decision. Again, conversely, the superior appetite that follows rational deliberation sometimes sways the lower one that follows sensuous images [...] This happens in the case of «continence»; for the continent are those in whom deliberation gets the best of passion»; see ARISTOTLE, *op. cit.*, par. 843.

swayed by their sensitive appetites. For Boccaccio, *falling in love* is an act of free choice. [26]

The events in the narrative, like the desires of the characters themselves, ultimately move in the same direction--towards the *summum bonum*. In the *Filocolo*, narrative and desire are diachronic and without a complete resolution. The closest we come to a resolution or closure to both narrative and desire is when the protagonists convert to Christianity: this is the closest Florio and Biancifiore come to finding *beatitudo* or the *summum bonum* in their world. Narrative and desire cease to exist only when the soul is united with God: that union is a purely synchronic state where all movement ceases (regardless of whether it is the restless movement of desire or the meandering *dilatio* of the narrative). Appropriately enough, the *Filocolo* ends when both the characters and the narrative are as close to that eschatological end as is humanly possible within the immanent world. This in itself is indicative of Boccaccio's understanding of the limits which keep language (e.g. narrative) and desire from transcending the confines of the immanent world. In this respect, the young Boccaccio seems to be distancing himself from Dante, his mentor.

Since God's love is the first movement of the appetites (both sensitive and intellectual), as Aquinas states (Ia, 20, art.1), the desire of each character in the *Filocolo* is in some way connected to the cosmic love that binds the universe. Both Florio and Felice are moved by desire and by what they believe is their ultimate good: for Florio it is Biancifiore, for Felice it is an obedient heir: «And in as much as all seek the good in the possession of which happiness lies, all can be said, in an interpretative sense, to seek God». [27] It is not surprising, therefore, that the narrative does not end with the consummation scene in Book IV. After having reached what they erroneously thought was their ultimate desire, the protagonists' quest for their *beatitudo* continues for at least another year, and it does not end with their conversion. Their conversion simply transforms their *peregrinatio amoris* into a *peregrinatio Dei*: both move, either directly or indirectly, towards the *summum bonum*.

---

[26] Another case in point is Fiammetta's falling in love with Panfilo in the *Elegia di Madonna Fiammetta*, see HOLLANDER, *op. cit.*, p. 42-45.

[27] Frederick Copleston's words could be applied to all the characters in the *Filocolo*; see COPLESTON, *op. cit.*, p. 187. My use of Aquinas' theory of *beatitudo* is based on Copleston's interpretation of it.

Besides being the expression of his *liberum arbitrium*, Florio's decision to go to Montoro is also an act of filial obedience which contrasts sharply to his false filial piety at the beginning of the confrontation scene. Florio's act of *pietas* is, however, an act of abandonment patterned after Aeneas' abandoning of Dido in response to his *pietas* and the call of the gods. The analogy becomes more apparent when Biancifiore actually compares herself to Dido. Both her monologue and her speech to Florio are patterned after those of Dido in *Aeneid* IV: she accuses Florio of abandoning her, characterizes her falling in love as an act of «follia» (II 18, 11-12), and even contemplates suicide.

Critics have characterized Boccaccio's portrayal of the protagonists' love language as a somewhat artificial stylistic exercise which betrays the author's awkward *imitatio* of the classics. What they have failed to realize, however, is that Boccaccio's characters are the ones who are actually imitating the classical figures in the books they have read; and they do so in a clumsy and even comic manner which reflects *their* apprenticeship in love and language. Biancifiore's reprimand of Florio (II 18) and her monologue (II 17) smack of epic grandiloquence, borrowed from Virgil, and elegiac melodrama, borrowed from Ovid. As a fourteen year old who has elevated her plight to that of Dido and the abandoned women of Ovid's *Heroides*, Biancifiore's lovelorn behavior is comical. [28] This is not to suggest that Boccaccio is making a parody of the lovers' conduct. The *Filocolo* is not *Aucassin et Nicolette* (a work which was intended to be a parody of the Floire and Blanchefleur romances). Instead, Boccaccio is depicting the mimetic power of love and literature.

The nexus between the two is made more vivid by Biancifiore's wish to be a book which Florio can hold in his hands and look at wherever he goes (II 17, 14). The idea of a lover identifying herself with a book in order to be with her beloved recalls the envoy at the end of *Filocolo*, as well as the *envoi* at the end of many medieval romances and love poems: it functions both as a messenger and as a mediator of love. The fact, however, that Biancifiore would like to become one with the book suggests that her desire is to collapse the fiction of her Vergilian and Ovidian heroines with the reality of her world. By mimetically living the mythic fictions they read, Florio and

---

[28] Ussani and Quaglio have shown how parts of her speech are patterned after Ovid's *Heroides*. See, QUAGLIO, *op. cit.*, p. 767, and USSANI, *op. cit.*, p. 297.

Biancifiore come a step closer to the dangerous love of Paolo and Francesca. For, in addition to being less than exemplary models of human conduct, the *exempla* that Florio and Biancifiore refer to in their dialogues and monologues are mythic models which cannot be fully imitated. The difficulty of reproducing the myth in their world (i.e. transforming the fiction into a reality), and the difficulty of mitigating desire through an *imitatio* of the language of myths are two of the problems brought about by the tension between desire and language.

Florio's behavior and the way it determines the protagonists' future, is discussed by Biancifiore in her monologue. After correctly pointing out that Florio consented to do what his father wanted him to do, Biancifiore concludes by swearing on her mother's soul that she will reach her desired end by whichever means she elects («elegga», II 17, 18). [29] Her declaration raises again the issue of how an individual attains the object of his/her desire. Biancifiore's will is directed towards Florio (much the same way his «volontà» is directed towards her): she creates a mistaken idea of him as her ultimate end (i.e. the *summum bonum*). Her power of election («elegga») lies in the choice of means («modo») by which she hopes to reach this desired end. However, like the other characters in the *Filocolo*, she too attains her happiness (i.e. *beatitudo*) through a course of events which does not correspond to anything she had imagined. This is largely due to the fact that she neither possesses the means to attain her desired end, nor a correct understanding of *beatitudo*. Whereas Florio has a greater degree of autonomy throughout the *Filocolo*, Biancifiore's choices are very few. Since she is at the mercy of the king and queen, her fate is determined by what she does to please or displease them. The fact that she has chosen to love Florio in spite of the king and queen's objections, determines in large part what happens to her: by choosing to follow her concupiscible appetite, she is exercising her *liberum arbitrium* and is consequently determining her own fate. [30]

---

[29] According to Biancifiore, had Florio told his father that he could not leave her, Felice could not accuse him of filial disobedience «però che, quando cosa impossibile si dimanda, è lecito il disdirla» (II 17, 10). Her scholastic-like logic underscores the fact that Florio has a choice and is therefore free to decide what he wants to do.

[30] Biancifiore's reasoning may be correct from a logical, Aristotelian point of view, but it is totally unrealistic. In II 17, 9 she says that Florio should have pleaded with his father to let her go with him: according to Biancifiore, the king would have been moved by pity and would have granted Florio's request. In the events that follow, however, it becomes apparent that the king has no pity and that Biancifiore has misjudged Felice's character.

Love as concupiscence is a force which can be controlled: it can sway the will without determining it. Love as the innate desire for *beatitudo*, however, is an uncontrollable inclination which can desire a particular good apprehended by reason, but provided by the concupiscible appetite. [31] Therefore, when the protagonists choose to love each other, they are not only exercising their free will, but are also following their will's innate longing for the ultimate end (*beatitudo*) about which they still know nothing. This does not imply that Florio and Biancifiore have necessarily chosen to fall in love with each other after due deliberation and free judgment proceeding from reason. It simply means that they chose to accept loving each other after discovering the concupiscible impulse within themselves: they willed it, as opposed to not willing it. Hence, their love is not yet the uncontrollable passion found in the mythic heroes and heroines they allude to: it is still under the control of the will in so far as any good is consciously apprehended by reason. This delicate balance between concupiscence and will (or libido and super-ego, to use the Freudian terms) breaks down when the reason gives way to uncontrolled passion (as we see in the events which immediately precede the consummation scene). Boccaccio's depiction of the protagonists' budding love underscores the fragile balance which exists between love and reason in the young lovers' souls. If they imitate the heroes and heroines of the classical epics, it is because they actually believe that these figures are indeed examples of noble men and women in love. If they believe (and there is no reason to doubt them) that their love is ennobling and self-perfecting, it is not surprising that they assent to loving one another, because, from a Thomistic point of view, «"Good" in the context of human choice means the development or "perfecting" of human nature, the actualization of man's potentialities as a human person, or that possession of which actualizes these potentialities and perfects man's nature». [32] But since the will does not have an explicit understanding of the ultimate end and perfect good which it desires, it is possible to form a mistaken idea of it. [33] In Florio and Biancifiore's case, this mistaken idea of the ultimate good is to be identified in their desire for each other. No matter how well balanced their love may be for each other, it is but a faint image of God's love as manifested in

---

[31] See COPLESTON, *op. cit.*, pp. 185-6.
[32] See COPLESTON, *op. cit.*, p. 192.
[33] See COPLESTON, *op. cit.*, p. 192.

the *summmum bonum*. In fact, it is only after they have «possessed» each other, that they will realize to what extent their «potentialities» as human beings have not been met. Boccaccio does not wait for the consummation episode to show us this: he gives us examples of it from the very beginning of their «innamoramento».

From the point of view of the larger providential plan, Bianci-fiore's failure to attain her desired end by her chosen means can also be explained in terms of her mistaken understanding of *beatitudo*. Like Florio and Felice, she too is far from the divine mind Boethius refers to in the *De consolatione*. The providential nature of the protagonists' love and their future empire in no way precludes the existence of obstacles and stumbling blocks which they must over-come before they are converted from «animals» into human beings. (Felice's dream, in fact, illustrates allegorically most of these obsta-cles.) Until her love for Florio is realigned with the path that will bring her to the *summum bonum*, and until the «good» she seeks does in fact actualize her potentialities as a human person, Biancifiore, like Florio and Felice, will always be far from the «good» her will ultimately desires. Finally, the lack of revelation and supernatural grace is ultima-tely the single most important factor keeping the characters from actually knowing and attaining *beatitudo*.[34] Since the possession of *beatitudo* is not possible without supernatural grace, the protagonists must wait until their conversion in Rome before reaching their ulti-mate end.

Biancifiore also exercises her *liberum arbitrium* when she, like Florio, consents to his departure from Verona. After hearing Bianci-fiore reprimand him for his decision to leave, Florio tells her:

Se a te tanto dispiace la mia andata, commanda che io non vi vada: egli [Felice] potrà assai urtare il capo al muro, che io sanza te vi vada! E se tu consenti che io vi vada, egli m'ha promesso di mandarmiti: la qual cosa se egli non fa, io volgerò tosto i passi indietro. (II 19, 9)

Florio is asking her to consent to his departure, just as he consented to his father's request. Biancifiore refuses to order him to stay since that would mean forcing his will, and asking him to break his promise to his father.[35] Biancifiore, in fact, consents «willingly» to his departure

---

[34] See COPLESTON, *op. cit.*, p. 202-205.

[35] Biancifiore refuses to tell Florio to stay in Montoro, but in II 17 she told herself that Florio should have refused to go to Montoro and «per consolazione di me misera, farviti quasi

three times, using the word «volentieri» each time. The repeated use of this word draws our attention to her «volontà» (will), and proves that she too agrees to Florio's departure. Like Florio, she too is given a choice (either order Florio to stay, or accept his choice to leave), and chooses to respect the decision he made of his own free will. Like all the decisions made in the *Filocolo*, this one too is made in accordance with the individual's *liberum arbitrium*, and it consequently determines the individual's fate.

Biancifiore's lovelorn conduct is not limited to her expressions of free will and sorrow. After agreeing to Florio's departure from Verona, she asks him to be faithful. Unlike the angelic women of the *dolce stil novo* tradition, Biancifiore's description of what she would do, if Florio were unfaithful to her, is quite comic:

però che se io sentissi che alcuna con la sua bellezza di nuovo t'infiammasse, come furioso m'ingegnerei di venire dove tu e ella fosse; e se io la trovassi, con le proprie mani tutta la squarcerei, né niuno ordine varrebbe a' composti capelli che io, tutti tirandoglieli di capo, non gli rompessi; e dopo questo, per vituperevole e etterna sua memoria, co' propii denti del naso la priverei: e questo fatto, me medesima m'ucciderei. (II 21, 4-5)

The exaggerated and unladylike conduct she promises to wreak on her hypothetical rival is so unlike Biancifiore. It is yet another example of how her *imitatio* of classical women in love affects her personality. [36] Aside from its comic nature, Biancifiore's claim that she would become «furiosa» suggests that her love may actually be capable of Medean-like jealousy. [37] The «furor» of jealousy will in fact manifest itself in Book III when Florio finds out that Biancifiore gave Fileno her veil. Although Biancifiore never actually becomes jealous of Florio (since she never finds out about his momentary infidelity in III 11), her remarks in this scene further underscore the nexus between the irascible and concupiscible appetites. If we keep in mind that neither

---

per forza menare». On the one hand she refuses to force Florio's will, and on the other she would prefer for Felice to force it rather than see Florio consent to his father's request. Her ambiguous thoughts are yet another consequence of her love for Florio.

[36] One cannot help being reminded of Dido's passionate desire for vengeance on Aeneas as he leaves Carthage, or Medea's vengeance on Jason.

[37] The direct and indirect allusions to Jason and Medea throughout this episode suggest a number of possible analogies with Florio and Biancifiore. Florio compares himself to Jason without knowing that he too will be momentarily unfaithful (III 11), and the person to whom he will be unfaithful (Biancifiore) describes her jealousy in a manner which recalls Medea's jealousy.

Biancifiore nor Florio has gone beyond «simple» embraces and «innocent» kisses (II 4, 7), the manner in which they portray their passion suggests that, despite the comic overtones, their love may indeed become as overpowering a force as they imagine it to be. [38]

The scene concludes with the two young lovers fainting in each other's arms. When Florio regains his senses, he embarks on a passionate soliloquy similar to the one we find in Ovid's tale of Pyramus and Thisbe. Like Pyramus, Florio thinks that his beloved is dead, and therefore wishes to commit suicide. Is Florio merely acting like an Ovidian lover, or would he have actually committed suicide had Biancifiore not regained her senses? [39] By deliberately leaving this question unanswered, Boccaccio has blurred the line separating comedy from tragedy, and has underscored the ambiguity of the lovers' conduct. The lovers, in turn, have blurred the line separating fiction from reality to the extent that they have confused the two. Regardless of whether or not Florio and Biancifiore would have actually committed suicide, the fact that they refer to it on several occasions suggests that their mimetic desire is dangerous and only a step away from death.

II. *Lealtà e onore*

The fidelity the protagonists promise each other prior to Florio's departure is put to the test in several different ways soon after they are separated. By continually recalling the moments they spent together, both Florio and Biancifiore defeat the king and queen's attempts to make them forget each other. Memory now becomes the single most important faculty in the lovers' mind since it keeps their love alive during their two year separation. [40] In Book II their loyalty

---

[38] Before leaving for Montoro, Florio kissed and embraced Biancifiore in the presence of his parents (II 22, 3). Later, after having settled in Montoro we are told: «Egli da quel dì che Amore occultamente gli accese del suo fuoco infino a quell'ora non la baciò mai, né fece alcun altro amoroso atto», (II 26, 2). This seems to contradict what was said earlier, as well as what was said about the protagonists shortly after they fell in love: «abbracciandosi si porgeano semplici baci, ma più avanti non procedeano» (II 4, 7). This is one of several inconsistencies we find in the *Filocolo*.

[39] Florio expresses a similar wish to commit suicide when his parents tell him that Biancifiore is dead (III 63, 14).

[40] Aquinas states that memory (*vis memorativa*) is one of the interior senses along with the common sense (*sensus communis*), the imagination (or phantasy), and the estimative sense (*vis aestimativa*) which Aquinas also calls the *vis cogitativa* and the «particular reason» (see *Summa*

is also tested in a more dramatic way when Felice plots to have Biancifiore condemned to the stake.

Having failed to make the two lovers forget each other by separating them, the king attempts to destroy their fidelity with treachery. With the help of Massamutino, the seneschal whose very name smacks of treachery (as Quaglio has shown), Felice hatches a plot to dishonor Biancifiore and sentence her to death. [41] The ensuing events, which encompass the second half of Book II, are centered around the concepts of *lealtà* and *onore*, words which are used repeatedly to describe the inter-relationships among the characters. Loyalty and honor were at the center of the nobility's ideology during the Middle Ages. [42] Loyalty was the most important virtue a vassal could show his liege lord since their relationship depended almost entirely on it. [43] Honor, on the other hand, was not simply a virtue which noblemen were supposed to live by, it was also a quality associated with the office of the king: the king's honor demanded respect regardless of the king's behavior. [44] Whereas Florio, Biancifiore, and even Massamutino demonstrate their *lealtà* to their king and their respect for his *onor*, the king reveals a complete lack of *lealtà* and *onor* towards them.

Felice reveals his lack of *lealtà* towards his son by refusing to send him Biancifiore as he had promised, and by trying to dishonor and discredit her. The *onor* and special attention Biancifiore used to receive at Felice's court soon disappear, much the same way her *nobiltà* is lost after the death of her parents. The honor associated with nobility is a precarious gift of the goddess Fortuna which is taken away from Biancifiore at the very moment Florio is taken from her. [45] This deprivation, or downturn on Fortune's wheel, is a direct result of what the king and queen consider to be their own downturn on the fickle goddess's wheel. Speaking to his seneschal, Felice says:

Theologica Ia, 78, art. 4). Boccaccio also alludes to the estimative sense («l'estimativa») in II 65, 5; IV 23, 2; IV 31, 12; IV 35, 4. This suggests that Boccaccio was familiar with the Aristotelian faculties of the soul.

[41] See BOCCACCIO, *Filocolo*, p. 778.

[42] See J. HUIZINGA, *The Waning of the Middle Ages*, New York, Double Day Anchor Books, 1954, pp. 21-22, 39, 69, 76-78, 80, 85, 104-105, *passim*.

[43] See MARC BLOCH, *Feudal Society*, II, Chicago, Univ. of Chicago Press, 1964, pp. 145-163, *passim*.

[44] See HUIZINGA, *op. cit.*, p. 58.

[45] When Biancifiore is in prison contemplating her misfortune (in a passage ultimately derived from Boethius), she realizes that all the *onore* she received until now was simply a transitory good of the fickle goddess Fortuna (II 48, 4-7).

Ciascuno, il quale vuole sua vita saviamente menare seguendo le virtù, dee i vizi abandonare, acciò che fine onorevole gli seguisca; ma quando avvenisse che viziosa via per venire a porto di salute tenere gli convenisse, non si disdice il saviamente passare per quella acciò che maggior pericolo si fugga: e fra gli altri mondani prencipi che più nelle virtuose opere si sono dilettati, sono stato io uno di quelli, e tu il sai. Ma ora nuovo accidente a forza mi conduce a cessarmi alquanto da virtuosa via, temendo di più grave che non sarà il fallo che fare intendo; e dicoti così, che a me ha la fortuna mandato tra le mani due malvagi partiti, i quali sono questi: o voglio io ingiustamente far morire Biancifiore, la quale in verità io ho amato molto e amo ancora, o voglio che Florio, mio figliuolo, per lei vilmente si perda; e sopra le due cose avendo lungamente pensato, ho preveduto che meno danno sarà la morte di Biancifiore che la perdenza di Florio, e più mio onore e di coloro che dopo la mia morte deono suoi sudditi rimanere: e ascolta perché. Tu sai manifestamente quanto Florio ama Biancifiore [...] ma però che di picciola e popolaresca condizione, sì come io estimo, è discesa, in niuno atto è a lui, di reale progenie nato, convenevole per isposa (II 29, 3-7).

Felice then tells the seneschal to prepare a poisoned peacock for Biancifiore to present to the king on his birthday. This in turn will enable Felice to accuse her of treason, and sentence her to death. Felice's ruthless logic that the end justifies the means, and his false declaration of paternal love for Biancifiore are all part of the bad faith he uses to justify his treachery (i.e. his lack of *lealtà* towards Biancifiore). [46] His bad faith is further revealed in his assertion that he is forced by «fortuna» to choose between two distasteful courses of action, when in reality he is acting on his own free will. There is in fact a third, more sensible course of action--marrying Florio to Biancifiore; but Felice rules it out much the same way Lelio ruled out the third and most sensible course of action prior to his battle against Felice. Like Lelio before him, Felice has a choice between three courses of action, rules out the best of the three, and consequently suffers a great defeat because of his bad choice. It is not *fortuna* that is to blame, but rather Felice's own negative attitude towards Biancifiore; fortuna is merely an excuse for his treachery. [47] The king, in

---

[46] Felice's argument that the means justify the ends goes against even the most fundamental moral principles. As Aquinas says, bad acts performed with good intentions are as bad as good acts performed with bad intentions (Ia, IIae, 20, 1 & 2).

[47] A similar use of *fortuna* as the force to blame for one's failures appears in IV 90, 1 when Florio is unable to muster the courage to meet Sadoc. Once again the fickle goddess is blamed, when instead it is Florio's own inner weakness which prevents him from executing the plan he and his companions have prepared.

effect, makes a free choice based on his warped understanding of *onore* and *nobiltà*. [48]

The king's free choice is also affected by the «ira» and «melanconia» he feels when he realizes that Florio is pining away for Biancifiore (II 27, 1, 4). As in the case of the young lovers, Felice allows his free will to be swayed by his sensitive appetites, particularly the irascible appetite. Felice's fear of the evil that may befall Florio (i.e. death by lovesickness), and his hope of some good coming out of his treacherous plan are, from a Thomistic point of view, the result of his irascible appetite. His «malinconia», on the other hand, may be associated with the concupiscible appetite since «every movement of the irascible appetite starts from and ends in a movement of the concupiscible appetite. Anger springs from sadness and ceases in a pleasure; for the angry find their satisfaction in punishing». [49] Felice's «ira» springs from his «malinconia», and will cease, momentarily, in his cruel punishment of Biancifiore.

In his speech to the seneschal Felice refers four times to his *onore* and to that of his family. Aside from the obvious hypocrisy and bad faith which accompany these remarks, the allusions underscore the great importance that honor plays in the ensuing events. It is during Felice's birthday celebration, a moment when the king is honored, that Biancifiore is dishonored. [50] While his noble birth is exalted, Biancifiore's noble birth is deprecated. Ironically, it is by vilifying Biancifiore's allegedly low birth that Felice is vilifying his own birth and nobility. The king also sets in motion a series of events which will actually exalt Biancifiore's true nobility of character, and will eventually disclose the nobility of blood she lost at birth. [51] For now, however, the succession and «ereditaggio», which should have taken

---

[48] The king cannot claim ignorance about Biancifiore's noble birth since he himself acknowledged Giulia's nobility on her tomb, and even Florio reminds him of Biancifiore's Roman nobility. Nevertheless, Felice does not consider her worthy of marrying the future heir to one of the largest empires in Europe. Is it because she was born to a captive? Or is it because he does not consider her noble blood to be as noble as Florio's? Boccaccio never tell us why Felice acts in such an ambiguous way when it comes to Biancifiore's pedigree.

[49] ARISTOTLE, *op. cit.*, par. 803-5. In this respect, Felice is very similar to his brother-in-law, the Admiral of Alexandria, when he discovers the protagonists asleep in each other's arms (IV 126).

[50] Both Felice and Biancifiore state this in II 29, 13 and II 53, 5-6 respectively.

[51] The true *onor* which she will earn by suffering at the hands of Felice, *fortuna*, et al. is the kind that cannot be taken away by *fortuna*. Her nobility of character is tested by *fortuna* so that it can eventually withstand *fortuna*.

place after the deaths of Lelio and Giulia, are being denied to Biancifiore in the name of Felice's own successor and heir (Florio):

E se egli [Florio] avvenisse che io gliele donassi, o che egli da me occultamente la si prendesse, primieramente a me e a' miei sanza fallo gran vergogna ne seguirebbe, pensando al nostro onore, tanto abassato per isposa discesa di sì picciola condizione, come sarebbe nascendo di lei. E s'io non gliele dono per isposa, egli niun'altra ne vorrà, e non prendendone alcuna altra, sanza alcuna erede seguirà l'ultimo giorno: e così la nostra signoria mancherà [...] (II 29, 9-10)

The clash between achieved and acquired nobility is further reflected in the royal chamber where the peacock episode is set.[52] Boccaccio makes a point of describing it in considerable detail. The stories, which are carved in marble, depict wars described by classical epic poets (Statius' Thebes, Homer's Troy, Lucan's Pharsalia). Even some of Alexander the Great's victories are included. The martial nature of this *ekphrasis* (or *descriptio*) befits Felice's own warlike nature.[53] It is ironic, however, that one of the heroes depicted in the sculpture of the battle at Pharsalia is Julius Caesar, Biancifiore's most «noble» ancestor. Boccaccio does not refer to Caesar by name, but alludes to him in a periphrasis which underscores the concealed nature of Biancifiore's own heroic ancestry: «e' prencipi crucciati, l'uno in fuga e l'altro spogliare il ricco campo degli orientali tesori» (II 32, 4). Caesar is alluded to as a «prencipe» (prince), the very same title Felice attributes to himself in his conversation with the seneschal. The fact that Biancifiore's downfall is about to take place in a room which exalts her noble ancestry is one more example of how Boccaccio uses dramatic irony to heighten the tension of key episodes such as this one, and to underscore the ambiguity of a character's conduct. The *ekphrasis*, however, also functions as allegory: it is a sign of a concealed truth which will be disclosed through the unfolding of the providential

---

[52] In her analysis of the banquet scene, Laura Sanguineti White views the banquet hall as an «esibizione di ricchezza e potere intimidatorio» which makes Biancifiore's fall that much more dramatic. See SANGUINETI WHITE, *La scena conviviale e la sua funzione nel mondo del Boccaccio*, Firenze, Leo S. Olschki Editiore, 1983 (Saggi di «Lettere Italiane», XXXII), p. 18.

[53] As Quaglio has indicated, two of Felice's seven barons sitting at his table have the same names as two of Alexander the Great's generals (see BOCCACCIO, *Filocolo*, p. 777). This detail enhances the analogy between Felice and Alexander. Like Alexander, whom Dante seems to have placed among the violent and the irascible in *Inferno* XII 107, Felice too is irascible and war-like.

plan. [54] The fact that «Giove» (the pagan god who is a figure for the Christian God throughout the *Filocolo*) is carved in glory «sopra tutte queste cose» suggests that Felice's great injustice will be circumvented by the very deity who represents justice.

The actual moment of Biancifiore's downfall is itself concealed in a moment when she is exalted. Before Biancifiore brings out the poisoned peacock, the queen has her dress «nobilmente d'un vermiglio sciamito» with a «piccola coronetta ricca di preziose pietre» (II 33, 2). [55] Biancifiore's clothing and the *onore* she receives when she presents the peacock to the king conceal the great dishonor the king and queen have prepared for her. [56] When Biancifiore brings the peacock to the king and his six barons, each of them solemnly promises her something. Felice, the first to make a «vanto» (vow), determines the nature of the subsequent vows. Swearing by the image of «Giove» alluded to earlier, Felice promises that he will marry Biancifiore to «uno de' maggiori baroni del mio reame». His solemn oath is followed by the «vanti» of his six barons, all of whom swear to perform a feat at her marriage. Ironically, Felice begins his vow by praising Biancifiore's «bellezza adorna di virtuosi costumi», the very same beauty he and the queen had cursed for its effect on Florio, and the very same virtuous conduct (i.e. *probitas*) which they refuse to accept as the basis of her true *nobiltà*. By praising the qualities which in fact justify the *onore* she receives that day from the king, queen, and barons, Felice successfully conceals both his treachery and his erroneous belief that inherited nobility is superior to achieved nobility.

Upon hearing the king's oath, Biancifiore immediately assumes that she will have Florio as her husband, «però nullo è maggiore di lui» (35, 6). Her response heightens the pathos of her situation while at the same time revealing her naiveté about the king's intentions. This is somewhat surprising since it was Biancifiore who had seen through

---

[54] The use of *ekphrasis* as a vehicle for allegory was quite common in medieval and Renaissance literature: see ERNST ROBERT CURTIUS, *European Literature and the Latin Middle Ages*, New York, Harper, 1963, pp. 69 sgg.; and RONNIE H. TERPENING, *Poliziano's Treatment of a Classical Topos: «Ekphrasis», Portal to the «Stanze»*, «Italian Quarterly» LXV, 1973, pp. 39-72.

[55] Besides its regal significance, the «coronetta» is also associated with weddings (see *Decameron* X 9, 85, 111, and X 10, 14). It is thus an appropriate ornament for Biancifiore to wear during the «vanti», all of which have as their focus her eventual marriage.

[56] As Sanguineti White has indicated, the king's generosity is meant to make Biancifiore look even worse for her alleged crime. The topos of the banquet is thus used to destroy the

the king's earlier deception when he told Florio that he would send her to Montoro (II 17, 4-6). The fact that she actually believes Felice in her moment of false glory suggests that she is affected by a touch of vanity. This self-deluding moment, no matter how innocent it may be, accentuates her downfall. [57]

The solemnity of Felice's oath suggests, however, that Providence will hold the king to his promise, regardless of the fact that Felice has no intention of keeping it. [58] This is supported by the narrator's own remark that Felice is happy when he and his barons make these promises, «però che già vedea per la pensata via appressarsi il disiderato fine» (II 35, 2). [59] Little does Felice know that both the means («via») and the end («fine») will follow a course of their own so that his promise, like those of his barons, will be kept. The fact that the promises made in Books I and II are kept in the subsequent books suggests that the covenants made between man and God are protected by Providence.

The clash between the king's will and the providential plan is alluded to more explicitly when the narrator says, «Assai coperse il re con queste parole il suo malvagio volere, ignorando quello che i fati gli apparecchiavano» (II 35, 5). Here too, as throughout this episode, the allusions to concealment and disclosure are present: what the king hides from his subjects is not hidden from Providence. This in itself is ironic since Felice has ignored the providential plan revealed to him in

---

social values that were associated with it (magnanimity, liberality, and social harmony). See SANGUINETI WHITE, op. cit., pp. 20-22.

[57] This fine touch in Boccaccio's portrayal of Biancifiore anticipates the proud figure of Fiammetta in the first book of the Elegia di Madonna Fiammetta.

[58] It is worth noting that after the seneschal hears the king's plan, he praises Felice's foresight: «onde io il lodo, e dicovi che saviamente proveduto avete, con ciò sia cosa che non solamente il giudicare le preterite cose e le presenti con diritto stile è da riputare sapienza, tanto quanto è le future con perspicace intendimento riguardare» (II 30, 2). Neither he nor the king, however, are able to foresee the consequences of their actions. Later, when the narrator addresses Giove in chapter 36 and explains why this god allowed Biancifiore to be accused unjustly, he says «Ma tu forse per fare con gli avversi casi conoscere le prosperità, pruovi le forze degli umani animi, poi con maggior merito guiderdonandoli» (II 36, 8). The narrator's explanation for Biancifiore's suffering is Boethian. As we saw in chapter one, the importance of Boethius is crucial to an understanding of how the suffering of a virtuous person fits into the providential plan.

[59] Sanguineti White has suggested that this sentence reveals an ambiguity of appearances and reality in the two antagonists (Felice and Biancifiore): Felice appears «lieto» because he sees his plot materialize, whereas Biancifiore is «lieta» because she believes that she has been promised to Florio (op. cit., p. 20).

Venus's dream. [60] Biancifiore will, in fact, marry Florio as the indirect result of Felice's words and deeds during this episode. [61] The relationship between *res et verba* extends itself into the realm of Providence: the Logos, as the perfect fusion of word and deed, realigns the deeds of those who fail to live by their word.

The choice of a peacock as the *pièce de résistance* of both the meal and the king's treachery is not without significance. [62] The peacock is Juno's bird, as the characters themselves point out several times. As the goddess of marriages, Juno's symbolic presence, by way of the peacock, is one more example of how Boccaccio's allusions create dramatic irony in key episodes. The «vanto» which Felice makes in the name of the peacock concerns Biancifiore's marriage, but is as tainted as the peacock itself. In addition to profaning the name of Jove with his false oath and false justice, Felice also profanes the name of the god's legitimate wife with his false promise of matrimony. Ironically, the king and queen's attempts at keeping Biancifiore from marrying Florio will be circumvented by the heavenly king and queen Felice has dishonored that day. [63]

When the people at the table discover that the peacock is poisoned, Felice's hypocritical condemnation of Biancifiore and the lies he tells in order to conceal his treachery are a projection of his true self:

Sanza dubbio credo che a voi sia manifesto che io oggi sono stato in vostra presenza voluto avvelenare; e chi questo abbia voluto fare, ancora è apertissimo

---

[60] The earlier allusion to Alexander the Great and the similarity of this setting with the Torre dell'Arabo in Alexandria where Florio and Biancifiore consummate their love suggest that Boccaccio is establishing a nexus between this episode and the consummation scene. We find a similar moment of concealed ancestry disclosed in the carved representations of the Admiral's ancestors in the Torre dell'Arabo. Furthermore, many of the things which take place in Alexandria are both the direct and indirect result of what takes place here. See SANGUINETI WHITE, *op. cit.*, p. 21-22; and LUIGI SURDICH, *op. cit.*, pp. 57-62.

[61] Besides Felice's promise coming true in Book IV, those of his six barons are also fulfilled: some are fulfilled after their first marriage (when all six of them attack the Torre dell'Arabo) and the rest after their second marriage.

[62] When she devised this plan, the queen had suggested «o pollo o altra cosa» (II 28, 8). As Quaglio points out in a footnote, the introduction of the peacock is Boccaccio's own invention: it does not appear in any of the sources. According to Saint Augustine, the flesh of the peacock was regarded as incorruptible (see *City of God* XXI 4). The act of poisoning the flesh of an animal which cannot be made corrupt is symbolic of Felice's attempt to corrupt an otherwise incorruptible Biancifiore.

[63] Jove and Juno are often alluded to, but they never actually appear in the *Filocolo* as Venus, Mars and Diana do. Their presence in the narrative is manifested in what they

per molte ragioni che Biancifiore è stata; la qual cosa molto mi pare iniqua a sostenere che sanza debita punizione si trapassi, pensando al grande onore che io nella mia corte l'ho fatto, sì come di recarla da serva a libertate, farla ammaestrare in iscienza e continuamente vestirla di vestimenti reali col mio figliuolo, datala in compagnia alla mia sposa, credendo di lei non nimica ma cara figliuola avere. (II 37, 4-5) [64]

Later, when the sentence is passed, Biancifiore is accused of attempting to kill the king by honoring him («sotto spezie d'onorarlo» [52, 2]). Although Felice and Biancifiore are diametrically opposed individuals, Felice's way of depicting Biancifiore makes her his mirror image. She is, as it were, his mimetic self-creation: like the young lovers themselves, the king too is guilty of creating mimetic fictions which clash with reality. These fictions are real only in so far as they are reflections of their creator's true self.

As for the *onor* Felice claims Biancifiore received from him, it is the kind of honor that is associated with «nobiltà di sangue». It is something she acquired not because of her merit (as Florio claimed) but because of her love for Florio (as she herself pointed out to Florio in II 18, 8), a love which the two protagonists view as ennobling, and thus a sign of her «nobiltà di cuore», but which the king and queen view as ignoble. [65] Paradoxically, Biancifiore is both honored and dishonored because of her relationship with Florio: she falls out of her lord's good graces the moment her relationship to Florio ceases to be considered appropriate. Boccaccio's social commentary is obvious: the gifts and honors bestowed by the nobility are instances of *fortuna*, and the conduct of the nobility is just as volatile as that of the fickle goddess. The fact that the narrator engages in an invective against

---

represent: Giove, a figure for the Christian God, and Giunone, a figure for the Church (cfr. BOCCACCIO, *Filocolo*, p. 713).

[64] Even the seneschal uses expressions denoting concealment and disclosure in order to conceal his treachery and convince the barons that Biancifiore is guilty of treason: «Il fallo, il quale Biancifiore ha fatto, è tanto manifesto, che in alcuno atto ricoprire non si puote, né simigliantemente si può occultare il grande onore da voi fatto a lei: per lo quale avendo ella voluto si fatto fallo fare, merita maggiore pena» (II 38, 4).

[65] Before leaving Verona, Florio told Biancifiore that Felice would continue to honor her even after his departure (II 19, 1-2). Despite the fact that events since that time have proven him wrong, Florio still tells Biancifiore the same thing in II 72, 6. Does he actually believe that the king will change his attitude towards her? Or is he simply obeying Venus, as he obeyed Mars when the god told him to kill Massamutino? The fact that Florio repeats what he said in II 19, 1-2 reveals his own naiveté and the extent to which he too, like Biancifiore, is under the the powerful influence of Venus.

fortuna at this point in the narrative (pointing out Biancifiore's sudden change of status from an exalted princess-like maiden to a wretched outcast) is merely a cover Boccaccio uses to conceal his criticism of the nobility. Biancifiore is stripped of her temporal gifts by Felice, an agent of *fortuna*. As the Latin etymology of his name indicates, Felice (*felix*) is a figure of *fortuna*: it is he that gave Biancifiore these temporal goods in the first place, and it is he who upholds the principles of «nobiltà di sangue» which are associated with these gifts. [66]

The close relationship between *fortuna* and inherited nobility is also revealed in the response of the six barons to the king's accusations: they remain silent, for fear of offending Felice, instead of coming to Biancifiore's defense. As we shall see in the next chapter, the barons have a choice: they can either challenge the accusations and propose a trial by combat to defend Biancifiore's *onor* (as Florio will do), or they can let the charges go uncontested. They choose to do the latter (their silence is tantamount to consent, as the narrator indicates in II 39, 1). The barons thus exercise their free will by choosing to accept the king's «volontà»: *quod principi placuit legis habet vigorem*. [67] Only Ascalion and the Duke (Florio's two friends from Montoro) part company with their king without congé («sanza prendere alcun congedo»). This break with protocol is an expression of disapproval which may be seen as a third course of action available to the barons. It does little, however, to help Biancifiore (especially since neither Ascalion nor the Duke inform Florio of her fate). [68] In effect, all the barons condemn themselves with their silence: whereas before they were prepared to promise Biancifiore great honors, now they fail to utter a

---

[66] It is worth noting that both Ascalion (II 42, 16) and Biancifiore (II 48, 4) speak about the *onor* she has received from the king. Ascalion tells Florio that just because Biancifiore has received such *onor* does not make her noble.

[67] This Latin phrase is taken from Justinian's *lex regia* at the beginning of the *Corpus Iuris Civilis: Institutiones*. Aquinas refers to it in his discussion of tyrannical laws; see *Summa Theologica* Ia, IIae, 90, 1. Even the queen exercises her free will by choosing between two courses of action. When the seneschal comes to ask her if Biancifiore can serve the peacock, we are told: «La reina, che ben sapeva come l'opera dovea andare, sì come quella che ordinata l'avea, stette alquanto sanza rispondere; ma poi che la crudele volontà vinse la pietà che di Biancifiore le venne [...] disse: — Certo questo ci piace molto —» (II 33, 7). She too is confronted with an important choice: either defeat or execute her own cruel plan; her «volontà» chooses the latter.

[68] As we shall see in the next chapter, the barons are «the king's men» and can only challenge him if he is guilty of *infidelitas*. Although they suspect him of it, they neither have the proof nor the courage to accuse him of it.

single word in her defense (noble promises, but no noble deeds). [69] Their silence, however, is mitigated by the fact that the chivalric vows the barons made in honor of Biancifiore are now in conflict with the vows of homage they took when they became the «king's men». [70] Their dilemma can be seen as Boccaccio's criticism of the conflicting codes of honor which govern the nobility.

Silence and secrecy not only govern Biancifiore's relationship with the nobility, they also govern, to a lesser extent, the relationship between Felice and Massamutino. Although Felice is quite open with Massamutino and holds him in his highest trust, he never alludes to the fact that Biancifiore has spurned him. Nor does Massamutino speak about his love lost on Biancifiore, except at the king's council, after she has been imprisoned (II 38, 6). Both men know, however, that this jilting is the king's main reason for choosing Massamutino to execute his treacherous plan. Thus the trust Felice has in his seneschal, and the loyalty Massamutino has towards his liege lord are strengthened by a mutual hatred for Biancifiore. [71] This is in sharp contrast to Florio and Biancifiore's loyalty and trust which are founded on their love for each other. By juxtaposing the lovers' *lealtà* to the feudal *lealtà* between Massamutino and Felice, Boccaccio is not only contrasting the two, but he is also adopting a common medieval love topos whereby the lover's loyalty to his lady is placed at the same level as a vassal's loyalty to his liege lord. [72] Felice wants the lovers' loyalty towards their king and father to take precedence over their loyalty towards each other; but it soon becomes apparent that these two kinds of loyalty cannot coexist since each is in conflict with the other. [73]

---

[69] Biancifiore says something similar to this when she wonders where Florio's friends are now that she is in prison (II 48, 12). She does not expect these «friends» to rescue her for her own sake, but rather for their love of Florio. Here too, Biancifiore recognizes that her importance (or lack of importance) in the eyes of others depends entirely on her relationship to Florio. Here too Boccaccio is critical of how human worth is determined by the nobility.

[70] See HUIZINGA, *op. cit.*, pp. 85-93.

[71] Felice begins his speech to the seneschal by describing him as his closest confidant: «Tu sai che mai a' tuoi orecchi niuno mio segreto fu celato, né mai alcuna cosa sanza il tuo fedel consiglio feci: e questo solamente è avvenuto per la gran leanza la quale io ho trovata in te» (II 29, 1). The seneschal responds by reaffirming the king's remarks: «Signor mio, sanza dubbio conosco la gran fede, la quale in me continuamente avuta avete, la quale sempre con quella debita lealtà che buon servidore dee a naturale signore servare, ho guardata e guarderò mentre in vita dimorerò» (II 30, 1). The narrator, however, makes it clear that the loyalty of the lovers will prevail: «Ma i fati non serbavano a sì leale amore, quale era quello intra' due amanti, sì corta fine né sì turpissima, come costoro loro voleano sanza cagione apparecchiare» (II 40, 4).

[72] See HUIZINGA, *op. cit.*, pp. 77-84.

[73] For a similar clash between feudal homage and courtly love homage, see PIERRE JONIN,

This conflict of loyalties is particularly evident in the clash between Florio and the man who is both his father and his king. Their conflict throughout this episode is part of an on-going Oedipal struggle between father and son. This is most evident when Felice unwittingly grants Massamutino permission to fight and kill Florio in battle. The king's conduct towards his adoptive daughter accentuates this conflict. [74] Biancifiore, in fact, is seen as a sexual threat to the status quo of the royal family: the social discrepancy between Florio and Biancifiore is similar to an incest taboo between brother and sister since the two are prohibited from getting married. The brother-sister relationship between the two protagonists is also suggested by the fact that they were born on the same day, and were reared together under the same roof. The fact that Biancifiore addresses Felice as «padre» and the king refers to her as his «figliuola» adds to the familial bonds which exist between Biancifiore and *all* the members of the royal family. It is not surprising, therefore, that when the two protagonists fall in love, their love is viewed in the same terms that incest might be viewed. [75] If their sexual love prevails, the very existence of the royal family is undermined (much the same way the existence of any family is threatened when the incest taboo is violated). This may explain why the narrator in II 48 does not reject the importance of nobility by birth. As we see in Book V, Biancifiore must rediscover her nobility of blood in Rome before she can be crowned an empress. Had Biancifiore simply been a «liberata», or freedman, her status as empress would have been diminished, as well as Florio's status as emperor and that of their infant son Lelio. (This is a point that even the king makes during his private conversation with the seneschal.) Boccaccio's position in the great debate between nobility by birth and «nobiltà di cuore» (or *probitas*) does not make one exclusive of the other. It would seem that for Boccaccio the two must coexist: the nobility should have

---

Le Vassalage de Lancelot dans le «Conte de la Charrette», «Le Moyen Age: Revue d'Histoire et de Philologie», LVIII, 1952, pp. 281-298.

[74] Felice threatens to kill Florio if he refuses to go to Montoro (II 14, 7), but this is obviously meant to scare the king's only heir into obedience.

[75] In IV 94, 1 we are told that Sadoc sees a physical resemblance between Florio and Biancifiore. The fact that they were both born on the same day under the sign of Gemini suggests a sibling-like relationship between the two. The Felice-Biancifiore-Florio triangle is similar to the Tancredi-Ghismonda-Guiscardo triangle in *Decameron* IV 1. When Tancredi sees that his Oedipal relationship with his daughter is threatened by her love for Guiscardo, he becomes as violent as Felice. Guiscardo's lack of inherited nobility becomes Tancredi's excuse for killing him.

probitas, and the *probitas* of those who are not noble by birth should be acknowledged and rewarded by the nobility. [76] Felice, however, fails on both counts.

Throughout the Middle Ages there existed a well recognized distinction between a king's behavior and the *onor* which accompanied the office of his «estate». [77] From the point of view of the king, the queen, the seneschal, and even Florio and Biancifiore, Felice's *onor* must be preserved at all costs. Book II in fact concludes with the successful preservation of the king's honor by all the parties involved in Biancifiore's trial. The queen fights back her pity for Biancifiore so that her husband's compromised honor will be saved (54, 6); the seneschal dies defending his liege lord's honor by taking up Florio's *diffidatio* (something that none of the king's barons were prepared to do), and by keeping Felice's involvement in the plot a secret (70, 1-4); Florio returns Biancifiore to Felice without revealing his identity or the king's dishonorable role in the plot (72, 8--74, 1); and even Biancifiore keeps to herself Venus's revelation of the king's involvement in the plot. [78] In so doing, Biancifiore ultimately proves her «troppa lealtà e onore a colui che ora mi fa morire» (II 53, 7). [79] As the adjective «troppa» suggests, loyalty and honor, like love, can go beyond measure. The fact that all these characters (including the barons) respect the king's *onor* even when he is most dishonorable suggests that the subterfuge used to conceal «tanta malvagità [che] occultamente in lui regnava» (71, 4) is a crime in itself. [80]

---

[76] One should not forget that Niccola Acciaiuoli, Boccaccio's closest friend at the time he was writing the *Filocolo*, achieved the title of *cavaliere* despite his humble bourgeois background. See VITTORE BRANCA, «Giovanni Boccaccio: profilo biografico» in *Tutte le opere di Giovanni Boccaccio*, I, Milano, Mondadori, 1967, pp. 23-24. As Surdich has pointed out, the Angevin aristocracy not only rewarded meritorious members of the bourgeoisie, but also integrated them in their society. This in turn had a significant impact on the ideologies of both classes. According to Surdich, this fusion of aristocratic and middle-class ideologies permeates the *Filocolo* (see SURDICH, *op. cit.*, pp. 43-49).

[77] See HUIZINGA, *op. cit.*, p. 58.

[78] The seneschal brings to Felice's attention the fact that both he and the king have been dishonored by the blow he received in public (II 62, 14). As an officer who has been offended while performing his legal duties on behalf of the king, Massamutino's point is well taken. When Felice gives him permission to fight the mysterious offender, he tells him «fa che onore acquisti con vittoria» (II 64, 1).

[79] Honor is at the heart of Biancifiore's trial. She repeatedly alludes to the *onor* she showed the king (II 53, 11; II 54, 3-4, 6) as a way of exculpating herself.

[80] Although these words are used by the king with regard to the seneschal after his death, they are really projections of himself (like so many of Felice's hypocritical remarks).

III. Venus and Mars: *ars amandi et ars bellandi*

The interplay of disclosure and concealment in the narrative is not limited to the concealed treachery of the king and seneschal, the concealed poison in the peacock, or Biancifiore's obscured innocence and nobility. We also find it in the events which immediately follow Biancifiore's condemnation. When Ascalion and the Duke return to Montoro, they keep the events of the day hidden from Florio without realizing that he already knows about them through Venus's vision. The goddess's divine revelation is in sharp contrast to his friends' surreptitious conduct. The fact that Boccaccio has made this revelation part of the characters' real world suggests that it is meant to be viewed literally and allegorically.[81] Like her revelation to Felice, Venus's revelation to Florio is a reflection of the truth and, consequently, is closely tied to the providential plan.

Everything Florio does from this moment of revelation to the moment he saves Biancifiore from the stake is the direct result of Mars and Venus's divine interventions. Florio's conduct is determined entirely by what these two gods tell him to do. Consequently, everything he does between these two moments is guaranteed to succeed: nothing is left to chance or *fortuna*. The presence of Mars and Venus throughout this episode is so explicit that it is hard to think of these gods solely as planetary influences (i.e. extrinsic principles of acts) affecting human behavior, or as metaphors for the irascible and concupiscible appetites (i.e. intrinsic principles of acts). They are also characters, very much like the protagonists themselves. Their existence in the narrative is both allegorical and literal throughout Books II, III, and IV. The fact that Mars and Venus are actual beings whose presence is discernible by all the mortals around them (not just Florio and Biancifiore) raises two questions.[82] First, what is the function of the gods in this episode and the rest of the *Filocolo*? Second, what is significant about their literal as well as metaphoric presence in the narrative?

A closer look at the gods' role in Book II can provide us with some answers. During Florio's vision, Venus tells the young lover that when

---

[81] We shall look at the allegorical significance of this vision in the next chapter.

[82] Although Mars is alluded to in Book I as the god that Felice prays to before the battle against Lelio, he never appeared *in persona* as he does in Book II where several characters (not just Florio and Ascalion) are capable of seeing him. He has a physical presence which cannot be mistaken for the characters' imagination.

he wakes up he will find a sword made by her husband (Vulcan) but belonging to her lover (Mars). [83] Venus is portrayed as the adulterous goddess we find in the «santo libro d'Ovidio». She is clearly the earthly Venus (there is hardly anything «celestial» about her). [84] There are, however, allusions to a celestial figure of love: Florio addresses Venus as «santa madre del mio signore» (II 42, 9). The goddess is addressed the same way the Virgin Mary would be addressed: Boccaccio is deliberately contrasting the mother of Cupid (the god of earthly love) to the mother of Christ (the God of *caritas*, or Christian love). At this point in the narrative, however, Florio's knowledge of love is limited to the venereal love of the pagan goddess he worships. Only after the negative consequences of this love in Alexandria, do Florio and Biancifiore learn about Christian love, at which point Venus and Cupid are replaced by Mary and Christ.

In the *City of God* Saint Augustine states that devils often disguised themselves as pagan gods (including Venus) in order to perform prodigies which would pass for miracles (XXI 6). The fact that pagan gods may also be demons adds to their ambiguity in the *Filocolo*. As we shall see in chapter five, Boccaccio portrays Cupid as a demonic-like figure. [85] The negative consequences of Florio and Biancifiore's venereal love further suggests Cupid's demonic-like power over the protagonists. What then becomes of the courtly ideal of ennobling love? Is all venereal love tainted by a negative numinous source? Boccaccio's description of sexual love in the *Filocolo* suggests that the conduct of the courtly lover oscillates between two extremes:

---

[83] As McGregor has pointed out, Venus gives Florio the same sword that was used to defeat the Titans when they rebelled against Giove. Since Felice is a direct descendant of Atalante (Atlas), one of the Titans, the sword «helps to identify the battle against Felice with that exemplary struggle», see McGREGOR, *op. cit.*, pp 38-9 and 121n. To this I would add that like his ancestor, Felice too commits treason against Giove's *sacrosanctitas* by making a false oath in the god's name. Felice is eventually defeated with the very same sword that defeated his ancestor.

[84] For a discussion on the two Venuses see EARL G. SCHREIBER, *Venus in the Medieval Mythographic Tradition*, «Journal of English and Germanic Philology», LXXIV, 1975, pp. 519-535; and ROBERT HOLLANDER, *Boccaccio's Two Venuses*, New York, Columbia University Press, 1977. The only celestial attribute one can find in this Venus is in her claim that she has descended from heaven to arrange for Biancifiore's liberation: «discesa giù dal cielo, ordinai la tua diliberazione» (II 48, 23). For all practical purposes, she is as much a divine figure as any of the other pagan gods that descend from the heavens in classical literature. Her miracles and apparitions, however, prove to be quite ambiguous.

[85] This negative view is echoed in the first chapter of the *Elegia di Madonna Fiammetta* when Fiammetta's nurse portrays Amore (Cupid) as «da infernale furia sospinto», and describes him using such epithets as «pazzia» and «pestilenza».

it may either succumb to concupiscence or it may be transformed into the ultimate theological virtue of *caritas*. Boccaccio's portrayal of Venus and Cupid suggests that they represent love without *caritas*: a pagan, pre-Christian understanding of love which is as distant from God's universal love as the desired objects of sexual love are from the *summum bonum*. Venus and Cupid are corrupt images of a greater love which the protagonists have not yet discovered. What Florio and Biancifiore suffer at the hands of Venus and Cupid is but the first leg in a quest which brings them from concupiscence to *caritas*, a quest which reflects the will's desire for *beatitudo*. Like Saint James and Satan (alias Pluto) in Book I, Cupid, Venus, and Mars are lesser instruments of Providence that sway the characters in a direction which is in turn realigned by Providence so that the characters come closer to God.

This becomes more apparent when Venus appears to Biancifiore in prison. The scene recalls the opening scene in the *De consolatione philosophiae* when Boethius is visited in prison by Lady Philosophy. [86] Venus's *consolatio amoris* is significant because it is the only kind of consolation Biancifiore has any knowledge of at this point in her life. Unlike Florio, she was not sent to Montoro to study the «santi principii di Pittagora» (II 10, 6): her education has remained at the level of the «santo libro d'Ovidio». It is love («Ovidio»), not philosophy («Pittagora»), that comes to console her. Venus is now the most important spiritual force in Biancifiore's life. It is not surprising, therefore, that Venus is also the first deity Biancifiore prays to in prison.

As in the case of Florio's address to Venus, Biancifiore's prayer to the love goddess also has Christian overtones:

O misericordiosa dea, lodata sia la tua potenza. Niuno conforto era a me misera rimaso, se tu venendo non m'avessi riconfortata. Ahi, quanto ti dobbiamo essere tenuti pensando alla tua benignità, la quale non isdegnò di venire de' gloriosi regni in questa oscurità e solitudine a darmi conforto, non avendo io tanta grazia già mai meritata. (II 48, 19-20)

The goddess is viewed by Biancifiore with the same attributes one would associate with the Virgin Mary: she is «misericordiosa», filled

---

[86] McGREGOR, *op. cit.*, p. 39. When she appears to Florio, Venus appears in a torn gown (a sign of mourning) which recalls Lady Philosophy's gown torn at the hem by lesser philosophers.

with «benignità» and «grazia», and she resides in the «gloriosi regni». Venus is a corrupt image of the Middle Ages' greatest feminine source of spiritual consolation, as well as a poor surrogate for the consolation Boethius found in jail.

When Venus appears to Biancifiore, the goddess is described as wearing a crown of laurels while holding an olive branch in her hand. The crown of laurels, a symbol of victory, is worn in anticipation of the moment when the goddess's two protégés will be victorious over the adversities of *fortuna*; the olive branch, as Quaglio points out, anticipates the peace which will follow these adversities. [87] Venus is able to anticipate the future, and assure Biancifiore of the positive outcome of her trial. This apparition may be seen, at first, to be a «trionfo dell'amore sulla fortuna» as both Boccaccio (in the *Amorosa visione*) and Petrarch (in the *Trionfi*) would later illustrate in more allegorical terms. Venus's victory and peace, however, are short lived: in Book III Biancifiore suffers more of Fortune's slings, and in Book IV she and Florio find themselves sentenced to die at the stake. This suggests that venereal love and *fortuna* are so inexorably linked to each other that one can never defeat the other. This episode is in fact just the first in a series of misfortunes (or trials of *fortuna*) which are the direct result of the protagonists' venereal love. Venus says so herself when she explains to Biancifiore why she is in prison:

Niuna altra cagione ci è, se non per che tu e Florio siete al mio servigio disposti; ma non sotto questa spezie s'ingegna il re di nuocerti, ma il modo trovato da lui, col quale egli si ricuopre, è falso e malvagio: ma egli è ben conosciuto tanto avanti, che alla tua fama non può nuocere, e ancora sarà più manifesto. (II 48, 22)

As we shall see at the end of Book IV, the protagonists' trials and tribulations at the hands of Fortuna cease only when their venereal love comes to an end.

As she had done with Florio, Venus reveals to Biancifiore Felice's role in the plot against her. [88] The goddess thus becomes a figure of divine revelation, disclosing to mortals what Felice conceals («ricuopre») from them. Venus's revelations, promises, and assurances

---

[87] See BOCCACCIO, *Filocolo*, p. 789-790
[88] Here too Boccaccio uses the word «manifesto» to allude to the goddess's divine revelation. Boccaccio's conscious use of Christian vocabulary further underscores the tension and distance between venereal love and Christian *caritas* in the *Filocolo*.

are, however, ambiguous: on the one hand they are partial reflections of the providential plan, and on the other they are meant to strengthen the young lovers' hope and faith in her, regardless of the consequences of such devotion. Venus's divine revelations, therefore, cannot be placed at the same level as Christian revelation. This does not diminish, however, the goddess's role in the providential plan: Venus is as much an indirect means to the protagonists' ultimate end and eventual salvation as Satan (Pluto) and Mars were for the salvation of Lelio and his enemies. Venus's pseudo-Christian attributes are simply distorted images of Christian concepts which the protagonists will learn of in Book V.

Biancifiore's devotion to Venus is tested shortly after the goddess's apparition; and her hope is shaken when she is brought to the stake. Recalling what Venus had promised her, Biancifiore «cominciò [...] a prendere speranza della sua salute» (54, 23). These words echo the ones her mother (Giulia) used prior to the battle between Lelio and Felice (a battle which is very similar to the one between Florio and Massamutino). In this context, as elsewhere in Book II, the Christian overtones of «speranza» and «salute» are muted: Biancifiore's salvation is strictly an earthly one which further confirms Venus's pagan nature in the providential plan. [89]

The apparition of Venus is followed by a similar apparition of Mars. Like Venus, Mars too reveals to Florio a concealed aspect of Felice's plot (i.e. Massamutino's role in it). Besides disclosing a concealed truth, Mars' role in this episode is that of an instigator. Just as Cupid had breathed on the protagonists his «segreto veleno» II 2, 5 and aroused their concupiscible appetite, Mars literally breathes wrath into Florio and arouses his irascible appetite. [90] Mars' loan to Florio of a divine bow, against which no mortal can resist, recalls Cupid's bow and further establishes the nexus between these two gods and these two important moments in Florio's life. Their divine breath «in-

---

[89] While tied to the stake, Biancifiore asks Jove (rather than Venus) to help her as he had helped Anchises during the fall of Troy (II 67, 3). By comparing her fate at the stake to that of Anchises during the «crudeli fuochi dell'antica Troia», Biancifiore is associating herself with a helpless old man who was saved by his son. Besides suggesting that her mysterious savior (Florio) is an Aeneas-like figure, her association is a reversal of the father-son relationship in the *Aeneid*: Felice, Biancifiore's surrogate father, hopes to burn to death someone he once regarded as his daughter; Aeneas instead saved his father from the fires in Troy.

[90] Mars has Florio provoke the seneschal into battle, and later orders him to kill Massamutino after the seneschal is vanquished and disgraced.

spires», in the eytmological sense of the word, Florio to become like these gods. Their divine breath, however, is also a perversion of the Holy Spirit which later inspires Florio to convert his friends to Christianity.

Like Venus, Mars too has religious attributes with Biblical connotations. The red cloud in II 59, 4, which conceals the martian god and which all the characters regard as a sign («manifesto segnale») signifying («in signifanza») salvation («salute»), recalls the cloud in Book I that promised salvation to Lelio and his men. It also recalls the pillar of fire and cloud in Exodus 14, 24 which the Israelites saw as a sign of their God and of their deliverance from the Pharaoh's army. Boccaccio's use of the Biblical words «diliberare» and «salute» to describe Biancifiore's «deliverance» and «salvation» from the king and his men suggests that Mars' «giustizia» (as the god himself calls it) is similar to that of the Israelite God on the Pharaoh and his people. (As we shall see in the next chapter, both forms of justice are far from the merciful Christian justice which the protagonists discover in Rome when Ilario reconciles Lelio's vengeful relatives to Florio.) Boccaccio's repeated use of the words «segnale» and «significanza», with reference to the red cloud, also establishes a connection between signifier and signified which extends beyond the figure of Mars. The Martian cloud is a sign pointing to other signs (the cloud in Book I and the pillar of fire and cloud in Exodus) which in turn are signs of the greater «salvation» all the characters in the *Filocolo* are moving towards. All these signs point to God; and it is only in God that the distance between signifier and signified is collapsed. Everything the characters do (all their acts and the entire action in the plot) is part of a larger motion moving towards the First Mover, the One who sets in motion all movement. [91]

Mars' irascible influence, however, is not limited to Florio: Massamutino too is described as being filled with «rabbiosa ira» (II 59, 3 & 7; II 62, 4). As in the case of Florio's irascible appetite, the seneschal's irascibility is the result of his past love for Biancifiore. Whereas Florio's irascible appetite fights to save the object desired by his concupiscible appetite, Massamutino's irascible appetite turns against what was once the object of his concupiscence. Having been spurned by Biancifiore, «every movement of [Massamutino's] irascible appetite starts from and ends in a movement of the concupiscible appetite». [92]

---

[91] For this concept, see AQUINAS, *Summa Theologica*, Ia, 2, art. 3.
[92] The words are those of Aquinas, see *Aristotle's «De Anima»*, para. 803-805.

Like Felice, Massamutino too wishes to punish Biancifiore (but for a different reason); and when Florio, disguised as a knight, strikes him in public, the seneschal wishes to avenge himself of this other offense. («Anger springs from sadness and ceases in a pleasure; for the angry find their satisfaction in punishing».) Furthermore, since the fear of evil is also associated with the irascible appetite, we find both fear and ire in Massamutino: he is «crucciato e impaurito» when he recognizes that the gods are on the side of his adversary. The seneschal will use his irascible appetite to conceal and overcome his fear of these divine forces.

Massamutino's response to the insurmountable odds he must face is marked by a sense of inevitable doom which verges on despair. His pessimistic monologues recall Pluto's false Vergilian account of the fall of Verona (I 10).[93] Like Pluto, Massamutino narrates to Felice his version of the events which have just occurred in Verona, and hopes that by doing so he may move the king to grant him permission to fight his offender. Massamutino has several courses of action to choose from, including the withdrawal of his false charges against Biancifiore (the king does not oblige him to follow any one course of action). But like the tragic pagan figure that he is, Massamutino chooses the most desperate one:

Già mi manifestò il cuore stamane incontanente che io vidi la vermiglia luce, che quello era segno di soccorso divino a Biancifiore. Io veggio costui che d'iniquità o d'altro arde tutto nel primo aringo: or che farà egli quando più sarà riscaldato nella battaglia? [...] Volentieri vorrei di tale impresa esser digiuno, ma più non posso. (68, 8-9)

One cannot help remembering Lelio's tragic choice prior to his defeat at the hands of Felice who, like Florio, was also aided by Mars. Although the seneschal's conduct prior to the battle recalls, appropriately enough, Pluto's, he looks more like Lelio after he has been defeated. Furthermore, when Florio kills Massamutino after having promised him mercy, he proves to be as merciless as his father was when he killed Lelio.[94] The analogy between Massamutino and Lelio becomes greater in their respective deaths: like Lelio, Massamutino's

---

[93] Janet Smarr has brought to my attention the fact that Massamutino's conduct is very similar to that of Turnus in his tragic duel with Aeneas.

[94] Rather than accentuate differences, this conflict actually reduces the differences between the opposing parties by revealing their similarities.

life is sacrificed for a «noble» cause. However, instead of dying for the eventual salvation of his enemies, Massamutino dies to save Felice's *onor* and to remain in the king's good graces. The seneschal does this by claiming that he falsely accused Biancifiore of treason because she had rejected his love. [95] Although this is only half of the truth, it is the main reason why Felice chose Massamutino to execute his plot. Both Felice and Massamutino were aware of this when they discussed the plot, but neither of them ever spoke about it. The secret they concealed from each other is instead disclosed to the public. Everything else which the king discussed with his faithful seneschal is forever concealed in the silence of Massamutino's death. Massamutino's disgraceful defeat, therefore, conceals his sovereign's dishonorable role in the plot and safeguards Felice's *onor*.

Ironically, Massamutino dies a public disgrace because he does not wish to be out of his lord's grace: «ché non volea rimanere nella disgrazia sua» (70,2). However, since the seneschal's reason for this *beau geste* is determined by self-interest, his deed falls short of self-redemption. [96] Similarly, Florio's cruel *colpo di grazia* or *coup de grâce* and the king's «grazia» (like the divine grace of Roman emperors and absolute monarchs) are perversions of Christian grace and mercy. [97] Massamutino's understanding of grace and honor is terrestrial: it is not the spiritual grace Lelio finds dying a defeated man in honor of his Lord.

Biancifiore is the one who is actually restored to the king's graces (against his will). She is rehabilitated in the eyes of the very same public that came to watch her die, and that failed to defend her *onor*. This would explain why Venus orders Florio to return Biancifiore to the king: she must be restored to the state from which she had

---

[95] This confession of love for Biancifiore will be echoed by the Admiral of Alexandria in IV 121, 4 when he discovers the protagonists lying naked in bed.

[96] The seneschal's ulterior motive for his confession reflects his pagan culture and Boccaccio's realistic psychological portrayal of human behavior. No matter how noble his act may seem, it is ultimately determined by self-interest. Here too, Boccaccio is underscoring the false nature of the nobility's *onor*.

[97] One might argue that in medieval combat the *coup de grâce* was considered a «mercy killing»; even the names of the weapons (e.g. misericords) used for that purpose suggest this. However, when Florio promises mercy to Massamutino, his *colpo di grazia* is not what either knight had in mind. This is underscored by the fact that Massamutino's death by fire is very painful (not a traditional *coup de grâce*). The fact that Florio first promises mercy (in order to elicit a confession) and then throws Massamutino in the fire suggests that he can be as deceptive and cruel as his father.

fallen. [98] The fact that Biancifiore is no longer in disgrace, but rather in her lord's good graces, further underscores the fickle nature of the *onor* she has regained. Like any gift of Fortuna, this honor and the good graces of her surrogate father (Felice) are unstable goods which are but a pale reflection of the greater spiritual honor and grace her real father (Lelio) died for. The fact that Venus should insist on restoring Biancifiore to her previous position, despite the dangers she faces by returning to court, underscores the nexus between Love and Fortune.

As for Felice's disgraceful conduct, Florio too is an accomplice in concealing it. When Florio hears Massamutino's confession, he realizes that the seneschal is protecting the king's honor by assuming all the blame for Biancifiore's suffering. It is all the more surprising, therefore, that Florio kills him, especially after promising him mercy. Since Florio does so on orders from Mars (70, 3-4), one has to conclude that Boccaccio is using this gratuitous slaying as a way of highlighting the negative consequence of Florio's irascible appetite. [99] Florio's conduct in this scene also reveals the extent to which he has been altered after Cupid and Mars have breathed their «veleno» on him.

Book II begins with a seemingly innocent love between two young teenagers, but ends with the slaying of a wounded man who has been disgraced in public. By the end of Book II, Florio has lost his innocence without losing his virginity. By allowing the irascible to fight on behalf of the concupiscible, Florio has revealed the worst aspects of both appetites. Protecting a virgin's honor and living a chaste life may have been typical deeds performed by the virtuous knight in the chivalric romance, but in Boccaccio's portrayal of Florio these deeds undercut the passions and virtues they were supposed to glorify.

IV. Love and Virtue

The courtly ideal that love is an ennobling power which can lead the lover to virtue has a theological correlative. Aquinas assigns the cardinal virtues of fortitude and temperance to the irascible and

---

[98] From a chivalric point of view, one of the knight's prime duties was to protect a virgin «in distress» and restore her to her previous state (see HUIZINGA, *op. cit.*, pp. 79 *passim*). Florio accomplishes this by following all of Venus's directives.

[99] One might even suspect Florio of killing Massamutino in order to insure that his father's dishonorable conduct would never be revealed. However, there is nothing in the text to support this.

concupiscible powers respectively, whereas justice is in the will «for it applies the will to its proper end», and prudence is in the reason: [100]

For the formal principle of the virtue of which we speak now is the good as defined by reason. This good can be considered in two ways. First, as existing in the consideration itself of reason, and thus we have one principle virtue called *prudence*. Secondly, according as the reason puts its order into something else, and this either into operations, and then we have *justice*, or into passions, and then we need two virtues. For the need of putting the order of reason into the passions is due to their thwarting reason; and this occurs in two ways. First, when the passions incite to something against reason, and then they need a curb, which we thus call *temperance*; secondly, when the passions withdraw us from following the dictate of reason, *e.g.*, through fear of danger or toil, and then man needs to be strengthened for that which reason dictates, lest he turn back, and to this end there is *fortitude*. In the like manner, we find the same number if we consider the subjects of virtue. For there are four subjects of the virtue of which we now speak, viz., the power which is rational in its essence, and this is perfected by *prudence*; and that which is rational by participation, and is threefold, the will, subject of *justice*, the concupiscible power, subject of *temperance*, and the irascible power, subject of *fortitude*. (Ia, IIae, 61, 2)

Boccaccio seems to have made a similar correspondence between the four cardinal virtues, which a pagan like Florio is capable of knowing, and the four main parts of the soul. One could argue that Florio demonstrates all four virtues during this episode like a «virtuous» knight in a chivalric romance: his will is directed at justice (rectifying the wrong done to Biancifiore), his irascible appetite (like that of the seneschal) is directed at overcoming fear and doubt; his concupiscible appetite is directed at controlling his desire for Biancifiore; and his rational deliberations could be seen as acts of prudence. On the surface Florio could be seen as a knight with all four cardinal virtues, but the ambiguity which surrounds his «chivalric» deeds suggests that these four virtues have not been perfected in him. If justice is a virtue «whose object is the perfect due, which can be paid in the equivalent», as Aquinas states, Florio's killing of Massamutino does not seem to correspond to the «perfect due» for someone guilty of perjury or treachery. [101] The fact that Florio returns Biancifiore to his father while assuring her that «non avrai altro che onore» (72, 5), an

---

[100] AQUINAS, *Summa Theologica*, Ia, IIae, 56, 4, *sed contra* and Ia, IIae, 50, 5.
[101] As we shall see in the next chapter, defeat in a judicial combat was regarded as a conviction of perjury. The traditional punishment for perjury was the loss of one hand.

assurance he had made to her prior to his first departure from Verona, suggests a lack of prudence and reason. (Felice, in fact, continues to persecute Biancifiore even after Florio's second departure from Verona.) The fact that both actions are done under orders of Mars and Venus respectively suggests that Florio has allowed the influence of these two gods to lead him beyond reason.

Florio and, to a lesser extent, Biancifiore show an unquestioning *lealtà* to Venus and Mars that is best reflected in the way the two young lovers carry out to the letter whatever the gods tell them to do (the same way Massamutino carried out Felice's orders). Whether one wishes to consider these two gods as demonic-like deities, planetary influences, metaphors for the sensitive appetites, or a combination of all three (as Boccaccio seems to have done), it becomes apparent at the end of Book II that the protagonists are practically possessed by them.

When Florio offers thanks to Venus for his victory in battle, the goddess crowns him «acciò che tu per inanzi ne' nostri servigii e nelle virtuose opere prenda migliore speranza, e più ferma fede nelle nostre parole» (75, 4). Just as Florio's slaying of Massamutino undercuts her notion of «virtuose opere», her idea of «fede» and «speranza» are also questionable. The fact that these words are similar to the ones she told Biancifiore in prison is indicative of Venus's continued attempt to strengthen her devotées' faith («fede») and hope («speranza») in her and in what she represents («amor»). The love goddess's repeated use of the words «fede» and «speranza» are obviously said with reference to the eventual consummation of the protagonists' love. However, the Christian overtones of these words bring to mind the three theological virtues Florio later dreams of during his quest for Biancifiore (IV 74). Like everything else that is divine in Book II, Florio and Biancifiore's introduction to the virtues of hope, faith, and charity, through Venus's distorted understanding of «virtù», will be rectified when the protagonists convert to Christianity in Book V. For now, however, the three theological virtues, like the four cardinal virtues we saw in Florio, are far from perfect. Like the objective perfect good the protagonists hope to attain in their desire for each other, the subjective perfect good in themselves is still very far away.

The ambiguous nexus between passion and virtue is as true for Biancifiore as it is for Florio. By saving Biancifiore from the stake, Venus rewards her, in effect, for her venereal love. Biancifiore's ordeal by fire is a test of her faith in this kind of love, and Venus's rescue is similar to the divine intervention associated with a trial by fire. Biancifiore's ordeal and salvation mark her initiation into the cult of Venus, and are a confirmation of her faith in the religion of courtly love. At the end of Book II Biancifiore has indeed become «del numero de' nostri suggetti», just as Venus had wanted at the beginning of Book II. On the other hand, by condemning Biancifiore to the stake like a heretic because she loves Florio, Felice's «auto da fé» becomes a condemnation of venereal love. [102] By choosing *amor per diletto* over *amor onesto*, Biancifiore's choice could be seen as a heresy within the greater religion of *caritas*. [103] Furthermore, the fact that Biancifiore's *lealtà* to Venus and Florio has revealed some flaws (e.g. her momentary loss of «speranza» at the stake, and her false assertion that Florio is a faithless lover because he has not come to rescue her) suggests that her worship of this goddess cannot provide her with the same spiritual strength and security she and Florio learn about when they convert to Christianity. In fact, prior to their conversion, the protagonists undergo a very similar ordeal by fire and similar divine interventions (IV 126-153) which further suggest that placing «fede» and «speranza» in Venus is questionable, to say the least.

When Florio first left Verona, Biancifiore's doubts about him were partly determined by her *imitatio* of the classical heroines she had read about. When she is at the stake, however, her remarks are the result of her new awareness that she may actually die on account of her *amor per diletto*. Book II began by describing how Florio and Biancifiore fell in love while reading Ovid (a moment which Boccaccio deliberately patterned after Paolo and Francesca's act of falling in love). Like Dante's two damned lovers, Boccaccio's protagonists act out the roles of the lovers they read about; but when reality catches up with their amorous illusions, the consequences of their passion become a matter of life and death. [104] The second book of the *Filocolo* illustrates, ultimately, the clash between love's pleasant fictions and its harsh realities.

---

[102] The idea of heresy can also be seen in Boccaccio's portrayal of Felice, whom McGregor views as a heretic; see MCGREGOR, *op. cit.*, p. 33

[103] As Mazzotta has pointed out, Jerome, Isidore of Seville, and Aquinas viewed heresy as a sin of choice: «as a misinterpretation of Scripture, it is a denial of the truth on which faith is founded and, in this sense, it designates an intellectual error»; MAZZOTTA, *Dante, Poet of the Desert*, pp. 283-84. Even though Biancifiore is ignorant of Scripture and Christian *caritas*, she is punished by Felice for choosing to love Florio the way she does.

[104] In fact, Florio and Biancifiore both risk dying like Paolo and Francesca when they are caught *in flagrante delicto* by the Admiral of Alexandria (IV 126). But unlike Dante's adulterous couple, Florio and Biancifiore are saved a second time by Mars and Venus (themselves adulterers).

CHAPTER FOUR

IMMANENT JUSTICE, THE LAW, AND THE
REGULAE AMORIS

The psychological terms Boccaccio uses to portray the behavior of his characters in Book II are also endowed with legal meaning. For example, when Felice asserts his tyrannical will at the council convened to deliberate on Biancifiore's guilt or innocence, his actions are a corruption of Aquinas' discussion on the relationship between will, deliberation and counsel (Ia, 83, art. 3 res.); and the violence inflicted on Biancifiore's intellectual appetite (i.e. her will) is centered around the seneschal's false charge that she intentionally tried to kill Felice with the poisoned peacock. Furthermore, the Thomistic idea that all human judgments proceed from reason is further corrupted when Felice arrogates the role of judge in order to falsely convict Biancifiore of treason and sentence her to death. All this suggests that Book II of the *Filocolo* raises several legal issues that need to be considered.

I. *Laesa maiestas*

Boccaccio had had extensive legal training by the time he was writing the *Filocolo*. As Vittore Branca has shown, Boccaccio studied canon law in Naples for six years, and studied the *Digest* with Cino da Pistoia during that time. [1] The fact that Boccaccio was familiar with both Roman and canon law at the time he was writing the *Filocolo*

---

[1] VITTORE BRANCA, *L'incontro napoletano con Cino da Pistoia*, «Studi sul Boccaccio», V, 1969, pp. 1-12. The *Digest* was the fundamental textbook of law students in the Middle Ages, see CHARLES H. HASKINS, *The Renaissance of the Twelfth Century*, New York, Meridian, 1970, p. 202. To this one should add that Boccaccio's exposure to the life at the court of Robert of Anjou would have provided him with a knowledge of feudal law as it existed both in court and in literature. Therefore, it is not surprising to find in Book II a fusion of feudal, Roman and theological principles of law which were prevalent not only in the treatises of the time, but even in the vernacular literature.

suggests that his description of the legal procedures adopted before, during and after Biancifiore's trial are based on actual legal procedures that were familiar to him. This is also suggested by the legal terms Biancifiore herself uses during her ordeal. While in prison she says «Io mai né con parole né con operazioni non lesi la reale maestà» (II 48, 3); and later, when she is brought to the stake, she tells the king «che mai a' vostri onori non ruppi fede» (II 54, 4). As Quaglio has pointed out, the first allusion «è formula appartenente al linguaggio giuridico». [2] Although Quaglio does not specify which juridical formula, it obviously refers to *crimen laesae maiestatis*, the legal term for treason in Roman law. Her second allusion is to the customary feudal law of fealty to one's liege lord. As we shall see, both allusions refer to important legal concepts which are at the heart of the treason charges brought against Biancifiore.

The most famous Roman law against *laesa maiestas*, and the one that Boccaccio would have probably known from his study of the *Digest*, was the *lex Julia maiestatis* (*Digest* 48, 4), named after Biancifiore's noble ancestors. The dramatic irony of her allusion is obvious: she is accused of *laesa maiestas* because of her unacknowledged kinship ties to the *gens Julia*. The irony, however, is not limited to her misfortune: like so many of Felice's self-projections on Biancifiore, his false charges of treason are a reflection of the actual treason he is committing against her and God. Since the concept of *maiestas*, like that of *sacrosanctitas*, derived from the sacred order of the divine law (*fas*), treason, in Roman law, could be directed against both men and gods. [3] Felice's false oath to Jupiter during the peacock episode is *impietas*, an offense against the god's *maiestas*. [4] The king's treachery against Biancifiore, on the other hand, is *infidelitas*, or the Germanic *Treubruch*, which was similar to, but not the same as *laesa maiestas*. [5]

As Floyd S. Lear has shown, *laesa maiestas* was a violation of a deferential allegiance to public authority (in the figure of the emperor), whereas *Treubruch* (*infidelitas*) was based on a contractual idea between a subject and his king. [6] Whereas the laws against *laesa*

---

[2] See BOCCACCIO, *Filocolo*, pp. 789. Quaglio sees other juridical expressions in II 39 & 51 (cf. pp. 781-791).
[3] See FLOYD SEYWARD LEAR, *Treason in Roman and Germanic Law: Collected Papers*, Austin, University of Texas Press, 1965, pp. xix, 15, 70.
[4] For a discussion of *impietas* and how it relates to *maiestas*, see LEAR, *op. cit.*, p. 70.
[5] For a discussion of *infidelitas* and *Treubruch*, see LEAR, *op. cit.*, pp. 39-ff.
[6] LEAR, *op. cit.*, p. 43.

maiestas permitted the emperor to determine what constituted an offense to his majesty (since he stood above the law), in Germanic law the fealty which governed the relationship between a liege lord and his vassal went both ways (since sovereignty belonged to the law): if the king broke his troth, he too could be charged with *Treubruch* or *infidelitas*, and his authority could be «defied» by his vassals through the formal renunciation of fealty known as *diffidatio*. *Diffidatio* was an open renunciation of faith in a faithless king (something which was not possible in *laesa maiestas*). [7] Felice's faithlessness towards Biancifiore is in fact challenged by Florio's *diffidatio* in the second half of Book II.

In theory, though not always in practice, *diffidatio* could occur without incurring the accusation of *traïson* (the feudal equivalent of *treubruch* and *infidelitas*). [8] In addition to its standard meaning of renunciation of fealty, the medieval vernacular equivalent of *diffidatio*, *desfi* and *defiance* in Old French (*disfida* or *sfida* in Italian) also referred to the warning which a knight was required to make before attacking another knight. [9] Killing a man without *desfi* was *traïson*: an act synonymous with the Latin *murdrum* and the Old French *murdre* (from which we get the word murder). As R. Howard Bloch has shown, the distinction between homicide (i.e. manslaughter) and murder in feudal law up to the fourteenth century hinged on the idea of an open as opposed to a hidden killing. [10] Murder (i.e. killing someone without *desfi*) was therefore synonymous with treason; *traïson*, however, could only exist if a murder actually took place. [11] It was only with the revived interest in Roman law during the later Middle Ages that treason also included acts of plotting to kill an individual, even if harm was not inflicted. [12]

It is hard to say with any certainty which treason laws Boccaccio had in mind when he was narrating Biancifiore's trial. There is a remote possibility that he was limiting himself to the Roman and Germanic laws of the period described in the *Filocolo* (a period which roughly corresponds to the sixth century). This is suggested by the

---

[7] LEAR, *op. cit.*, p. 40; and MARC BLOCH, *Feudal Society*, translated by L.A. Manyon, Chicago, Univ. of Chicago Press, pp. 227-230.
[8] R. HOWARD BLOCH, *Medieval French Literature and Law*, Berkeley, University of California Press, 1977, p. 242.
[9] R. HOWARD BLOCH, *op. cit.*, pp. 145-146.
[10] R. HOWARD BLOCH, *op. cit.*, pp. 34-ff.
[11] R. HOWARD BLOCH, *op. cit.*, pp. 34-41.
[12] R. HOWARD BLOCH, *op. cit.*, pp. 40-41.

allusion to *laesa maiestas*, the thematic importance of *infidelitas*, and the absence of Christian elements in the judicial combat scene. However, since Boccaccio probably did not know the Visigothic code or any of the other Germanic laws which combined *Treubruch* and *laesa maiestas*, it seems more likely that his fusion of Roman and feudal laws in the *Filocolo* actually reflects fourteenth century laws which he modified (by eliminating the Christian elements) so that they would pass for sixth-century pagan laws. This would be in keeping with the other semi-historic allusions to Roman and Germanic cultures which we find in the *Filocolo*. The discrepancies between Boccaccio's rendition of these laws, and the actual treason laws of the fourteenth century would be consonant with the poetics of fourteenth century narrative prose. Since Boccaccio was living in an age when Roman law had modified the earlier feudal concept of *traïson*, it is quite likely that the laws he incorporated in the narratives were those which associated treason with *laesa maiestas*.

The combination of feudal and Roman laws is most evident in the way in which Biancifiore is charged with treason. Although she does not actually kill the king, the fact that she gives him poisoned food is tantamount to *traïson* because she has attacked him without *desfi*. This in turn enables Felice to accuse her of treason rather than attempted homicide. What R. Howard Bloch says of Guinevere, in his compelling analysis of the queen's first trial in *La mort le roi Artu*, can also be said of Biancifiore: she is materially guilty but morally innocent of treason. [13] Although the king can legally prove Biancifiore's material guilt by virtue of the fact that she gave him the poisoned peacock in the presence of his barons, he cannot prove that she actually *wanted* to kill him (an accusation which both he and the seneschal make). [14] The Roman concepts of *culpa*, *dolus*, and *casus*, which permeated later feudal laws, have been distorted by both the king and his seneschal in order to make a stronger case against Biancifiore. [15] By accusing her of a crime done with criminal intent (*dolus malus*) rather than one done out of negligence (*culpa*), the king and his seneschal have grounds for asking the death penalty (the main objective of their plot). The fact

---

[13] R. HOWARD BLOCH, *op. cit.*, pp. 41.

[14] Here too Biancifiore finds herself in a situation which is similar to Guinevere's. As Howard Bloch has shown, the issues of criminal intent and material guilt are not clearly distinguished by all the characters in *La mort le roi Artu*; cfr. BLOCH, *op. cit.*, pp. 32-ff.

[15] For a discussion of the terms *culpa*, *dolus*, and *casus*, see R. HOWARD BLOCH, *op. cit.*, p. 39; LEAR, *op. cit.*, pp. 32, 45.

that Felice suppresses any attempt on Biancifiore's part to prove her lack of criminal intent is itself proof of the importance that *dolus malus* has for both the plaintiff and the defendant in this case. If Biancifiore were allowed to prove her *culpa*, it would be very difficult for the judges to sentence her to death, especially since she did not inflict any harm on Felice. By insisting that her act was both intentional and concealed, the king and his seneschal are not only seeking a death sentence for Biancifiore, but they are also projecting their own *traïson* and attempted *murdrum* on her. Not only are they attempting to kill her by means of a concealed attack, but they do so without *desfi*, since Biancifiore does not know that the charges brought against her are part of a secret plot to have her killed. Before Venus revealed to her the king's *dolus malus*, Biancifiore assumed that the charges were a mistake: a case of the king's *culpa*. Ironically, she projects her own *culpa*, and consequently her moral innocence, while her accusers project their *dolus malus*. In so doing, both plaintiff and defendant project on the case and on each other the concealed truth concerning their respective guilt and innocence.

The fact that Felice must plot Biancifiore's death by means of an elaborate legal scheme underscores the fact that he does not have the absolute power of a Roman emperor.[16] Like many fourteenth century feudal lords, Felice is obliged to follow certain legal procedures, or risk the renunciation of fealty from his barons. This is one reason why he calls upon the aid of his seneschal: besides counting on Massamutino's hostile feelings towards Biancifiore to win him over, the king also uses Massamutino's office as a means to his treacherous end. In Italy the seneschal's duties were not limited to catering; they also included some of the most important administrative offices at a king's court.[17] It is quite likely that Massamutino's office enabled him to prosecute Biancifiore on behalf of the king, thereby making it easier for the king to conceal his role in the plot.[18]

---

[16] It may be argued that he is doing this for fear that his son will find out about it. The narrator in fact gives this as one of the reasons for preventing Biancifiore from being heard by the judges (II 51, 4). Felice, however, has just demonstrated his power over his son by pressuring him to go to Montoro. It is more likely that Felice engages in his elaborate scheme in order that neither his son nor his barons will consider him guilty of *infidelitas*.

[17] Marc Bloch, *op. cit.*, pp. 340 and 343-344. For the role of seneschals in France, where they were employed as bailiffs, see MARC BLOCH, *op. cit.*, p. 425 and HENRY C. LEA, *Superstition and Force: Essays on the Wager of Law, the Wager of Battle, the Ordeal, Torture*, 1870, New York, Greenwood, 1968, p. 181. See also R. HOWARD BLOCH, *op. cit.*, pp. 128-9.

[18] It is more than likely that Boccaccio knew about Frederick Barbarossa's famous seneschal, Markward of Anweiler. Markward died regent of Sicily, duke of Ravenna, and

In order to conceal Massamutino's own role in the plot, the king has him arrested along with Biancifiore and Salpadin (the three people directly involved in the preparation and presentation of the poisoned peacock). Salpadin and the seneschal are found innocent after their «scuse» (excuses) have been heard (II 37). Biancifiore's «scuse», however, are neither heard nor solicited. The king, in fact, locks her up in a dungeon so that no one can speak to her. The double standard which Felice applies to Biancifiore cannot be explained in terms of her sex or inferior social status. She is, instead, the victim of an illegal procedure intentionally used by the king to prevent her case from being heard by others. The correct legal procedure would have been to allow Biancifiore to confront her accuser and swear her innocence under oath, or to deny the charges and challenge the accuser with an ordeal or a judicial combat.[19] Had Felice not placed Biancifiore in solitary confinement, she would have probably been able to exculpate herself.

Since no action can be taken against an individual unless someone steps forward to accuse him or her, the king holds an inquest to deliberate Biancifiore's case.[20] Since the poisoned peacock was given to him, Felice is the plaintiff and therefore has the right to accuse her. After accusing her, the king seeks the advice of his barons before punishing her:

Laonde io intendo, come detto v'ho, di volerla di ciò gravemente punire, acciò che mai alcuna altra a sì fatto inganno fare non si metta. Ma però che di ciò dubito non mi seguisse più vergogna che onore, se subitamente il facessi, però che parrà a molti impossibile a credere questo per la sua falsa piacevolezza, la quale ha molto presi gli animi, n'ho voluto e voglio primieramente il vostro consiglio, e ciò tutti fidelmente porgere mi dovete, disiderando il mio onore e la mia vita, sì come membri e vero corpo di me, vostro capo. (II 37, 8-9)

The image of the body politic, which the king alludes to at the end of his speech, suggests that the offense is not just against him but also against his barons. Like the *comitatus* (kin-group) that was collectively responsible for seeking redress, the barons must help their king

---

marquis of Ancona. As Marc Bloch has shown, in addition to having considerable power, a few of them were actually great barons. The way Massamutino speaks to Felice's six barons during the council (II 39), however, makes it clear that he is of an inferior rank.

[19] For a discussion of this procedure, see R. HOWARD BLOCH, *op. cit.*, p. 122-125.

[20] See R. HOWARD BLOCH, *op. cit.*, p. 16. This is also confirmed by Marc Bloch who states that «even the most imperious of tyrants found it impossible to dispense with a collective judgment» (*op. cit.*, p. 369).

vindicate the wrong that has been done to him. [21] Furthermore, as R. Howard Bloch has shown, the presence of barons at any inquest functions «as a repository of collective truth, the custom of the community as expressed by the judge. Their attendance validates the entire proceeding, and no legal action can be admitted without them». [22] Finally, by using Biancifiore as an example of a faithless subject, while reminding his barons of the vows of fealty they took when they became the «king's men», Felice makes it hard for any of the barons to challenge his *infidelitas*. [23] However circumstantial the evidence against Biancifiore may be, the barons know that it is sufficient for the king to accuse her of treason. Furthermore, the fact that Biancifiore was seen giving the king a poisoned peacock eliminates the need for either the king or the seneschal to have people testify against her: her material guilt is «manifesto»:

Di questo ciascuno si maravigliò, non potendo alcuno pensare né credere che Biancifiore avesse tal malvagità pensata; ma pure il manifesto presentare del paone facea a molti non potere disdire quello che è medesimi non avrebbero voluto credere. (II 37, 2)

It is not surprising, therefore, that the barons tacitly consent to the king's statements. If they did not, their own fidelity would be questioned. As long as the king can keep Biancifiore from swearing her innocence and/or challenging her accusers, he can expect to get the tacit support of his men. It is through this artful manipulation of customary feudal law that Felice is able to affirm his authority over his people and attain his desired end.

After Felice is through speaking, there is a long moment of silence which is broken by the seneschal. Speaking in his capacity as the officer who represents the king in matters of justice, the seneschal subtly challenges the audience to defy Felice. In so doing, Massamutino initiates a procedure which will eventually make him Felice's champion, ready to defend any challenge to the king's authority: [24]

---

[21] For the role of the *comitatus* see R. HOWARD BLOCH, *op. cit.*, pp. 113-128. It should be pointed out that some of the king's barons are actually related to him.

[22] R. HOWARD BLOCH, *op. cit.*, p. 49.

[23] The barons suspect that the king had something to do with these charges, but have no evidence to prove it.

[24] For a discussion of this procedure, see LEA, *op. cit.*, 158-159; and R. HOWARD BLOCH, *op. cit.*, p. 129.

— Caro signore, io so che 'l mio consiglio sarà forse tenuto da questi gentili uomini qui presenti sospetto per la presura che di me subita fare faceste sanza colpa, e so che diranno che ciò che io consiglierò, io il faccia a fine di scaricare me e di levare voi di sospezione [...] E così m'aiutino gl'immortali iddii, com'io se non quello che diritta coscienza mi giudicherà non dirò; e dico così: «Il fallo, il quale Biancifiore ha fatto, è tanto manifesto, che in alcuno atto ricoprire non si puote, né simigliantemente si può occultare il grande onore da voi fatto a lei: per lo quale avendo ella voluto sì fatto fallo fare, merita maggiore pena. E certo, se quello che in effetto s'ingegnò di mettere, avesse solamente pensato, merita di morire». (II 38, 2-5)

His declaration is meant to be an example for the barons to follow. By upholding the king's accusations, the seneschal is forcing the issue on them: the barons must now make a choice, either support their king, or defy him in order to defend Biancifiore. Like the lukewarm angels in Dante's limbo, the silent barons neither side with the plaintiff nor the defendant, «ma tacendo tutti, di questa opera stupefatti, dierono segno di consentire al detto del siniscalco» (II 39, 1). [25]

It may be argued that the barons could have testified in Biancifiore's favor through compurgation (the act of swearing to her innocence after she herself has sworn to it). This procedure would have been less provocative than the actual act of *diffidatio*; and even though Frederick II was one of the first rulers to curtail the use of compurgation in his Neapolitan domains, its use throughout Europe was widespread. [26] The fact that the six barons believe in Biancifiore's innocence and would like to speak on her behalf, but do not, suggests that they can only become her compurgators after she herself has taken the oath. Since Biancifiore is not a serf («serva») but a freedman («liberata»), as Felice himself admits during the inquest (II 37, 5), an oath from the six barons would have made up for her lack of nobility. As Lea has shown, it was common for a defendant of a lower social class to seek compurgators among the nobility, especially if the accuser was a member of the nobility. However, by preventing the barons from communicating with Biancifiore, Felice has made it virtually impossible for them to «purge» her of the charges. Furthermore, in accor-

---

[25] Apparently, tacit consent was a fairly common practice at such inquests: see R. H. BLOCH, *op. cit.*, pp. 49-50.

[26] LEA, *op. cit.*, p. 71. For a discussion on the uses and abuses of this common practice, see LEA *op. cit.*, pp. 13-84. See also LEAR, *op. cit.*, p. 206, and R. HOWARD BLOCH, *op. cit.*, pp. 125 and 132. Lea believes that the absence of compurgation in Frederick's constitution is due to the widespread abuse of this procedure by the most hardened criminals.

dance with feudal law, Biancifiore can automatically be convicted if she is unable to challenge her accusers or have someone challenge them for her. [27] As long as Felice can persuade his men not to stand up for Biancifiore, her conviction is assured.

The seneschal sets the stage for her conviction by declaring that even the thought of killing an emperor is worthy of capital punishment («E certo, se quello che in effetto s'ingegnò di mettere, avesse solamente pensato, merita di morire»). This is a Roman concept found in the later interpretations of the *lex Julia maiestatis*. [28] In keeping with the *lex Julia maiestatis*, Massamutino concludes that Biancifiore should be burnt to the stake, the standard punishment for *humiliores* (the lower classes) guilty of *laesa maiestas*. [29] Here too there is dramatic irony in the fact that Biancifiore is condemned to die an ignoble death according to the laws of her noble ancestors.

Biancifiore, in effect, is falsely accused of *laesa maiestas* because her ancestry to the *gens Julia* is never recognized. This in turn reveals the importance of family affiliation in legal feudal matters concerning marriage, succession, and even the private right of vengeance (which often took the form of a *faida* or blood feud). Since marriage, succession, and vengeance existed as private rights (as opposed to laws enforced by a sovereign) it was the prerogative, if not the responsibility, of the *comitatus* or the members of the *gens* to exercise these rights. [30] In his speech to the seneschal, Felice justifies his cruelty to Biancifiore on the grounds that he must choose someone worthy of marrying his son, the only heir to his throne. Felice is exercising both his private right as a father and his public duty as a king in upholding a custom which has the force of law among the very people he rules. [31] Felice's responsibility as a sovereign towards his people is to insure the

---

[27] For this aspect of feudal law, see R. HOWARD BLOCH, *op. cit.*, p. 18.

[28] See LEAR, *op. cit.*, pp. 20, 44-48.

[29] For this kind of punishment, see LEAR, *op. cit.*, pp. 33-35. The upper class was either banned to perpetual exile, or hanged. This practice was modified slightly in the Middle Ages; but the burning of women was not uncommon; see LEA, *op. cit.*, p. 132.

[30] For a similar discussion, see R. HOWARD BLOCH, *op. cit.*, pp. 128-131. As we shall see, Lelio's relatives feel that it is their obligation to avenge Lelio's death on Florio: the private right to vengeance was upheld by both Roman and feudal laws.

[31] This is the only way to explain Felice's cruel behavior towards Biancifiore. Even though Felice acknowledged her mother's nobility on Giulia's tombstone, and even though he does not contradict Florio when he says that Biancifiore is a descendant of great Roman noblemen, the fact that she was born to a «schiava romana» (i.e. when her mother was made a captive) diminishes her birth considerably.

social status of the royal family. [32] As he tells his seneschal, if Florio were to have a child by Biancifiore, it would be a dishonor to the throne. Anything less than an heir of regal birth («di reale progenie nato») would undermine the prestige and power of both the ruler and the kingdom. Furthermore, if Florio were to die on account of his unrequited love for Biancifiore, the kingdom would have to seek «signore strano» (a foreign sovereign). From Felice's point of view the commonweal must take precedence over the private right of the individual: Florio and Biancifiore's private right to love each other must be denied in favor of the general welfare of their people. [33] Furthermore, by giving the seneschal the power to deny to Biancifiore what she had denied to Massamutino (requited love), Felice is allowing the seneschal to avenge himself in return for Massamutino's full support. Therefore, while claiming to act on behalf of the commonweal, Felice is actually bestowing the private right of vengeance on both himself and the seneschal at the expense of the protagonists' private right to love each other. Individual private rights and the more abstract laws of love clash with the concept of the commonweal, the *comitatus*, and the customary feudal rights of a sovereign. [34] As we shall see, these customary laws and rights also clash with the moral and positive laws which permeate the *Filocolo*.

When Felice sees that no one is going to challenge him, he calls the judges «i quali di presente la giudichino, che sanza giudiciale sentenzia io non intendo di farla di fatto morire» (II 39, 3). Now that the verdict has been reached by virtue of the barons' tacit consent, the sentence must be passed so that Biancifiore can be executed. Although Felice expects the judges to automatically pass the death sentence, their role is more than a rubber stamp for the king's verdict. The judges in fact tell the king that they cannot sentence Biancifiore without first hearing her confess the crime of which she is accused. [35] Their objection takes Felice by surprise, proof that this was one legal point which the king had overlooked in his otherwise carefully pre-

---

[32] I am grateful to Professor Ciriaco Moron Arroyo for bringing this to my attention.

[33] For the importance of the commonweal in Roman and Germanic law, see LEAR, *op. cit.*, pp. 21-22, 133-134.

[34] See R. Howard Bloch's analysis of the tension between the courtly romance's tendency to individualize and the epic's emphasis on the collective (*op. cit.*, pp. 141-ff).

[35] In most treason trials their function was not restricted to passing a sentence (as Felice is asking them to do): they were also expected to determine whether or not the accused was guilty of the charges.

pared case against Biancifiore. Confronted with this legal impediment, Felice orders them to sentence Biancifiore without hearing a confession, on the grounds that the evidence points to her guilt. [36] In so doing, the king discards a legal procedure which would have saved Biancifiore from the stake. He does so «temendo forte che Biancifiore ascoltata non fosse». His fear that Biancifiore might be heard, and consequently exculpated, makes his blatant breach of procedure all the more significant since it exposes to the public his denial of the defendant's most fundamental right to challenge her accusers. The king has thus abandoned his role as plaintiff in order to assume that of a corrupt judge.

II. The *Iudicium Dei*

Once the sentence has been passed, Biancifiore is left without any legal recourse. In fact, when Florio finally arrives to challenge the seneschal's accusations, he comes too late (as the seneschal points out in II 62, 6). The fact that Florio was asleep when Biancifiore was being sentenced, taints his right to challenge the verdict in Biancifiore's case. [37] Challenging a charge, whether by compurgation, judicial combat, or an ordeal, usually took place before the accused was sentenced or punished. [38] (The punishment of the defeated party in a judicial battle occurred after the battle was concluded). [39] Florio, in effect, is matching his father's illegal procedure with an illegal procedure of his own. As we shall see, this is just one of several illegal procedures Florio adopts in this episode.

In the events which follow, it is not clear to what extent Florio's actions are a *diffidatio* against Felice; nor is it clear to what extent his duel with Massamutino is a judicial combat. When Florio listens to Biancifiore's side of the story, it is obvious that he is following a

---

[36] One might argue that the king could have accepted the judges' request for a confession by having Biancifiore tortured so as to extract a false confession that would automatically condemn her. Despite the widespread use of torture to extract a confession from the accused, such cruelty on the part of Felice would have put him in a very bad light vis-à-vis his people. This explains the prevalence of torture in those medieval laws which were influenced by Roman law: it was often the only way to extract a confession from the accused before being able to sentence him. For the judicial use of torture in Roman and medieval times, see Lea, *op. cit.*, pp. 323-459.

[37] This may explain why the narrator digresses from his narrative and devotes a whole chapter to reprimanding Florio for sleeping while Biancifiore is being sentenced (see II 56).

[38] See LEA, *op. cit.*, p. 91; and R. HOWARD BLOCH, *op. cit.*, p. 18.

[39] See LEA, *op. cit.*, pp. 128-9.

formal procedure, since he already knows that she is innocent. The fact that he engages in this interrogation suggests that he must hear her plead her innocence before he can become her champion and challenge the charges brought against her. Florio then turns to the crowd and formally states his belief in the truth of what Biancifiore has told him, and accuses the seneschal of being the wrongdoer. [40] He concludes by telling the crowd, «io sono presto e apparecchiato di difendere che quello ch'io ho detto sia la verità, e in ciò arrischierò la persona e la vita» (II 61, 2). Although neither he nor Biancifiore actually swears the traditional oath denying the charges against her, Florio's words up to this point are similar to the standard formula which preceded most judicial combats. [41] The fact that this formula does not include the standard Christian oaths of the *iudicium Dei* underscores the strictly pagan nature of this judicial combat. [42]

Massamutino responds to Florio's denial of accusal by reaffirming the original allegation against Biancifiore. His response is similar to the standard formula one finds in a medieval *iudicium Dei*; but here too the customary Christian oath is omitted. [43] The exchange of charges and counter-charges gives way to physical contact: after Massamutino pushes Florio with his horse, Florio strikes the seneschal on the head and tries to push him into the fire. From the way Boccaccio describes this initial clash, it is not clear whether the exchange of blows is the symbolic act of *diffidatio*, or the traditional *ictus regis* which took place at the beginning of a judicial combat. [44] Florio's blow is given spontaneously, out of anger, rather than as a calculated renunciation of fealty towards the king or as a warning (*desfi*) to the seneschal. The fact that the public intervenes to separate the two men, suggests that Florio's actions toward the seneschal do not fall under any category legally recognized by the public. Furthermore, the fact

---

[40] For this standard procedure, see LEA, *op. cit.*, p. 126-128 and 140.

[41] For a discussion of these formulas, see LEA, *op. cit.*, p. 126. R. Howard Bloch, *op. cit.*, pp. 47-50.

[42] As Lea has shown (*op. cit.*, p. 91), the *iudicium Dei* was mainly a post classical, feudal practice; but traces of its existence in Roman times may be found in Livy's *History of Rome*, XXVII 21. Boccaccio's familiarity with Livy at the time he was writing the *Filocolo* and Livy's references to Scipio Africanus and Mars in XXVII 21 all suggest that Boccaccio may have had this classical model in mind for the judicial combat episode in the *Filocolo*.

[43] For a discussion of the oaths that preceded a trial by combat, see R. HOWARD BLOCH, *op. cit.*, p. 47.

[44] For a discussion on the the *ictus regis* and *diffidatio* the see MARC BLOCH, *op. cit.*, p. 229 and LEA, *op. cit.*, p. 125-6.

that Florio strikes Massamutino while the seneschal is performing his public duty as the king's representative in his case against Biancifiore means that Florio is committing an offense against the king, not just his legal representative. Even though Florio neither reveals his identity nor openly renounces fealty to his king and father, his act can easily be interpreted as a surreptitious *diffidatio*. Even if the blow was not intended as a formal act of *diffidatio*, Florio clearly intends to defy the actions of both the king and the seneschal on account of their *mala fides* and *infidelitas* towards Biancifiore.

Massamutino, on the other hand, cannot exercise his private right of vengeance for the blow he received because the blow occurred while he was acting as the king's representative. Therefore, before seeking redress, the offended seneschal must first seek the king's permission to fight the mysterious knight. Massamutino uses the judicial combat as a means of exercising his private right of vengeance while claiming to Felice that he is upholding the public image of the king. Similarly deceptive motives are found in Florio's reasons for engaging in the judicial combat. He tells Biancifiore and the others present that he has been sent by Florio to represent her. By saying this, Florio purports to be a champion who is not emotionally involved in this case (as required of all champions in a judicial combat). [45] However, since Florio despises the seneschal for what he has done to Biancifiore, much as Massamutino despises Biancifiore for what she did to him, neither Florio nor Massamutino can truthfully claim to be disinterested champions of either the defendant or the plaintiff. In public, each knight claims to defend what he believes to be a just cause (in accordance with the standard oath of the *iudicium Dei*), but privately both man are so emotionally involved with Biancifiore that their true motives for engaging in judicial combat are not always what they claim to be. Here too the purported truth is distant from the actual truth each champion conceals from the other.

According to the Veronese code of 1228 champions were a professional institution which consisted of individuals selected and appointed by a judge; they were hired by principles for a fixed fee. [46] To

---

[45] As Lea points out, any kind of relationship between the contestants was an impediment; see LEA, *op. cit.*, p. 109. This may explain, in part, why Florio is incognito when he goes against his father in this combat.

[46] LEA, *op. cit.*, pp. 144-5. See also LEA, *op. cit.*, pp. 136-153 and R. H. BLOCH, *op. cit.*, pp. 25-28 for the theory and practice behind the use of champions.

insure equalization between champions, the judge chose two champions of equal capabilities, and the defendant was allowed to choose between the two.[47] In Frederick II's constitution for his Neapolitan provinces, champions were required to give the maximum injury possible to each other so as to prevent them from agreeing between themselves on the outcome of the combat.[48] All these procedures illustrate the basic purpose of a judicial combat: to disclose the truth through an impartial procedure. The selection of disinterested and equal champions was aimed at guaranteeing this impartiality. However, by revealing these champions' personal motives for engaging in judicial battle, Boccaccio is showing how the original purpose of the *iudicium Dei* is being subverted. Instead of being an impartial trial by battle which is undertaken to determine whether or not Biancifiore is actually guilty of treason, we have a duel between two men who are seeking vengeance.[49] Despite his claim that he is the champion of truth (II 66, 3), Florio is misusing a legal procedure designed to reveal the truth rather than serve as a vehicle for personal redress. Boccaccio is not only illustrating a prevalent abuse of judicial combat, but he is also showing how this legal procedure can be used to conceal as well as disclose the truth.[50]

When the seneschal returns, armed and ready for battle, he expresses his readiness to prove Florio wrong by the sword. Florio in turn gives him the lie, a required formality in judicial combat.[51] Their verbal exchange is very similar to the defendant's reiteration of the original denial of accusal and the plaintiff's affirmation of the original allegation, both of which were standard procedures in a *iudicium Dei*.[52] Furthermore, the fact that the combat begins at around noon is

---

[47] LEA, *op. cit.*, p. 149.

[48] LEA, *op. cit.*, p. 141.

[49] As Lea points out, judicial combat was considered, in theory, to be distinct from the duel: the latter is derived from the right of private vengeance, the former from the desire to discover the truth and the impartial ministration of justice (*op. cit.*, p. 88). But, as Lea indicates throughout his study, the line separating duel from judicial combat was often blurred, and many combatants crossed that line without the least compunction.

[50] This and similar abuses of the *iudicium Dei* moved Frederick II to abolish the judicial combat in his Neapolitan provinces in 1231. He made exceptions, however, for it in cases of murder and treason where other proof was unattainable; in such cases it was at the option of the accuser, not the accused (see Lea, *op. cit.*, p. 170). Frederick even provided champions, at public expense, to widows, children, and paupers (see LEA, *op. cit.*, p. 145).

[51] Giving the lie (i.e. accusing the accuser of lying) was one of the required formalities; see LEA, *op. cit.* p. 185.

[52] Lea states that in Frederick II's constitution of 1231 the champion was required to «swear on the field of battle as to his belief in the justice of the quarrel which he was about to

in keeping with the traditional hour of day when judicial combats were supposed to take place. [53] However, despite these standard procedures, there are some major discrepancies. Regardless of whether we wish to consider this combat as a judicial combat or a duel, the great disparity of weapons between the two sides goes against all the fundamental rules of engagement of either the duel or the *iudicium Dei*. Florio is armed with two divine weapons which make him invincible: the outcome of the battle has already been determined by the gods (Mars in particular) through the use of these weapons. Ironically, only the *ictus regis* is done with weapons of equal worth--the lances--both of which actually belong to the king. All the other blows are given with weapons of totally different capacities. According to most codes governing judicial combat (including the Veronese code of 1228) both champions were supposed to be equally armed so that the actual combat would be totally impartial. [54] The fact that Florio does nothing to try to equalize the battle between him and Massamutino suggest that he too is acting in bad faith.

Florio's *mala fides* is also revealed when he kills Massamutino after promising him mercy. As Lea has shown, defeating one's opponent (as opposed to killing him) was the main objective of judicial combat, especially if champions were employed. [55] The vanquished party was usually punished after being defeated; and in some cases, if he was killed during the combat without confessing the truth, he was pronounced innocent by virtue of the fact that he had died vindicating the truth. [56] By defeating Massamutino, and by getting him to confess

---

defend», *op. cit.*, p. 139. This is similar to what Florio had done before, and is doing now. See also R. HOWARD BLOCH, *op. cit.*, p. 47. Their verbal exchange can also be considered a *desfi*, in the sense of a formal warning which precedes combat so that neither combatant can be accused of *traïson*. Massamutino's *desfi* to Florio, however, immediately follows a blatant example of *traïson* towards Biancifiore: he orders his men to throw her into the fire when everyone's attention is directed at the combat (something Felice had told him to do in II 64, 2).

[53] R. HOWARD BLOCH, *op. cit.*, pp. 46-47.

[54] LEA, *op. cit.*, p. 149. In the constitution of Frederick II judicial combat «is placed at the option of the accuser alone, as if to render it a punishment and not a trial» (*op. cit.*, p. 170). The defendant, however, had the choice of arms (*op. cit.*, p. 135). This seems to be the case in the battle between Massamutino (the accuser) and Florio (the defendant with the divine arms): each is more interested in punishing the other than in actually serving as disinterested champions. This is also suggested by the Aristotelian and Thomistic idea that the irascible appetite finds satisfaction in punishing others (see ARISTOTLE, *op. cit.*, par. 803-805).

[55] This was in part due to the fact that the offense for which the vanquished party was accused was not necessarily a capital offense. As Lea points out, the defeated party was usually considered a perjurer, and the traditional penalty for perjury was the loss of a hand (*op. cit.*, p. 128-9).

[56] LEA, *op. cit.*, p. 172.

his role in the plot against Biancifiore, Florio achieves the main objectives of a *iudicium Dei*. But when he punishes Massamutino by throwing him in the fire, Florio goes beyond the limits of the customary law since it was not up to the victorious champion to punish his vanquished counterpart. [57] Like Yvain during his combat with Esclados, Florio's conduct during the judicial combat with Massamutino is ambiguous.

III. *Fides et mala fides*

Although Florio has legal grounds for challenging the king's *infidelitas* and *mala fides*, his *diffidatio* against his faithless father could also be regarded as a lack of filial *pietas* (even the seneschal proves to be more loyal to Felice than Florio). [58] This may be another reason why Florio keeps his identity a secret: he does not want to dishonor his father by publicly defying him. The entire trial episode is centered around this ambiguity of faith: Florio's fidelity as a son and lover is tarnished by his faithlessness to the seneschal and by his defiance of his father, whereas the seneschal's treachery towards Biancifiore is mitigated in part by his confession and by his faithfulness to his liege lord (as Massamutino himself points out, he is the only person to stand up for the king when everyone else, including the barons, have failed to do so [II 62, 12]). The fact that the seneschal stands by his king even in the face of certain death and against the insurmountable forces which the gods have arrayed against him gives him a tragic and even heroic mein which mitigates his negative traits. [59] By portraying Florio and Massamutino in such an ambiguous way, Boccaccio has eliminated any Manichean notion of a good knight fighting a bad one. The line separating good from evil has been blurred. [60]

---

[57] LEA, *op. cit.*, pp. 140, 149. Similar rules apply to the judicial combats which appear in the works of Chrétien de Troyes. See GUSTAVE COHN *Le Duel judiciaire chez Chrétien de Troyes* «Annales de l'Université de Paris», VIII, 1933, pp. 510-527; and ANNA-SUSANNA MATTHIAS, *Yvains Rechtsbrüche*, «Beiträge zum romanischen Mittelalter», ZRP anniversary volume, Tübingen, Niemeyer, 1977, pp. 156-192. In this respect, Florio behaves as Yvain did in his battle against Esclados.

[58] Accusations of this sort, even among the highest nobility, were often settled through judicial battle, as Lea has shown (LEA, *op. cit.*, p. 89). The custom of judicial battle between the prince and his vassals was also prevalent under Frederick II (LEA, *op. cit.*, p. 115).

[59] Boccaccio is careful, however, not to make Massamutino look like a man who has been converted from his former ways: it is obvious that the seneschal confesses his role in the plot so that he will remain in his lord's graces. Massamutino, therefore, does not redeem himself in any Christian sense of the word: he simply tries not to lose what he has been fighting for.

[60] This ambiguity of faith can also be seen in Biancifiore who did not have enough faith in

This ambiguity, however, is not limited to the main characters in this episode. We also find it in the behavior of the populace, whose choral remarks on the trial are depicted with a certain amount of irony. After the king's inquest has come to an end, all the people present at the council begin discussing among themselves what they should have discussed during the council. Although the public chorus in II 49 does not agree on who is responsible for bringing the treason charges against Biancifiore (some say it is the king, others the sene- schal) it is of one accord when it comes to Biancifiore's innocence. The irony is obvious: instead of deliberating over Biancifiore's inno- cence during the inquest (when it might have helped her), the public waits until after the inquest to proclaim her innocence, thereby reducing its deliberation to mere gossip. Furthermore, its silence during the inquest is the ultimate proof that Felice wants Biancifiore dead: it is obvious to the public «che al re piaceano queste cose e che con sua volontà eran fatte» (II 39, 1), a remark which is repeated several times (II 38, 1 & 49, 4). The truth cannot be concealed from the public: it can deduce everything, including the king's inner-most wishes, Florio's love for Biancifiore, and the seneschal's hatred for her after she spurned him (II 49, 3). The voice of the people is ultimately the voice of truth (*vox popoli, vox Dei*); but the way the public arrives at the truth is as ambiguous as the other means by which the truth is attained during this episode. This is particularly true during the judicial combat, a moment in which the truth is supposed to be reached through divine intervention. The public's presence during this important moment is indicative of its own *mala fides*: it comes to watch someone, whom it deems innocent, die at the stake. Florio, in fact, begins his *desfi* by condemning the public for its base curiosity, and does so by saying the same things the mysterious suicide in *Inferno* XIII 138-140 said to Dante and Virgil. [61] Both Florio and the suicide keep their identity a secret, while insinuating to their audience the inappropriateness of its curiosity (II 61, 1). Among the people present at Biancifiore's execution are the same «nobili uomini [...] che vantati s'erano al paone» as well as the «giudici che sentenziata l'aveano». All

---

the goddess she worships (Venus) nor in the man she loves. As we have seen in the previous chapter, she not only loses hope in Venus when she is dragged to the stake, but she also accuses Florio of being a faithless lover because he has not come to rescue her.

[61] As Quaglio has indicated, Florio's initial remark is taken straight from *Inferno* XIII 138-140; see BOCCACCIO, *Filocolo*, p. 796.

of them are prepared to watch her die, without doing anything to stop the execution; however, when Florio comes on the scene to disrupt their legal proceedings (II 62, 1-3), they propose a stay of execution (something they would never have considered had Florio not appeared). As if to underscore the bad faith of the public, Boccaccio says that even those who separated Florio from Massamutino during their initial scuffle did so «quasi più per iscusa di loro che per buona volontà» (II 62, 9). The public intervenes on behalf of the seneschal only for fear that it might be blamed for not helping a king's officer. However, the moment the course of events turns against the seneschal, so does the public. The public's reversal of position is most evident when the seneschal is defeated and mortally wounded. Only then does the public dare to speak out against him, and, in a choral voice, to call for his death. Mars hears this («udite avea queste cose» II 70, 2) and answers their cruel prayer by telling Florio, «Di così fatti uomini niuna pietà si vuole avere» (II 70, 4). The *vox popoli* has now become the *vox dei*. By granting the public their wish, Mars administers through Florio a cruel form of «giustitia» (the word used by Mars to define Massamutino's execution) better known as the *lex talionis*. Massamutino is in fact killed exactly as Biancifiore would have been killed for the same alleged crime. The law of retaliatory justice (associated with both Roman law and the Old Law) is far from the justice of the New Law which Christ and Dante couple with mercy (a quality which is ostensibly absent in this episode). [62] By failing to live up to his promise of mercy, Florio places himself farther away from the New Law. It is only in Book V that Florio will learn about the nexus between «giustitia e misericordia».

The fact that Florio exercises his feudal right of private vengeance under the pretext of a judicial combat is Boccaccio's way of criticizing both the legal means of determining the truth (the *iudicium Dei*) and the inherent injustice of the Old Law (the *lex talionis*). By making Mars the determining force of immanent justice, rather than Jove or Astrea, Boccaccio is not simply underscoring the martial cruelty and

---

[62] For the New Law concept of mercy and justice, see RODOLFO DE MATTEI, *«Misericordia e giustitia» nella patristica e in Dante*, «Giornale storico della letteratura italiana» CIX, 1937, pp. 239-252; and VITTORIO FROSINI, *Misericordia e giustitia in Dante*, «Rivista internazionale di filosofia del diritto», s. III, vol. XLII, 1965, pp. 310-320.

irascible vindictiveness of this judicial combat, he is also questioning the extent to which judicial combat in general is actually a form of «giustitia» or simply a form of «vendetta». The difficulty of separating an impartial quest for truth from a duel of vengeance was a legal problem which received the attention of many rulers throughout the Middle Ages. [63] Even though Mars' immanent justice successfully discloses Biancifiore's concealed innocence, the actual means used to prove her innocence prove to be as ambiguous as Felice's chosen means to prevent Florio from marrying someone beneath him. In both cases, Boccaccio is criticizing the ends and the means which father and son choose in order to do what each deems to be right. In the conflict which results from their radically different understanding of what is right, both father and son prove to be wrong.

In addition to exposing the cruelty of the *lex talionis*, Boccaccio's portrayal of public opinion during the judicial battle also underscores the fickle nature of human justice. Like Fortuna, both the public and the judges change their views on the accused and the accuser from one moment to the next. However, whereas Fortuna functions in a seemingly irrational and gratuitous manner, the public's change of position vis-à-vis Biancifiore and the seneschal is determined by its fear of prevailing force (as seen first in the acts of the king and his seneschal, and later in those of Mars and Florio). Ultimately, might makes right, and the course of justice is determined by the boldest, just as the bold are favored by Fortuna (*fortuna favet fortibus*). [64] The final confirmation of this is to be found in the narrator's ironic remark after Massamutino's death: Florio and Ascalion now have «molti altri compagni» (II 72, 1), whereas before the combat they were all alone.

A choral public that knows the truth but puts it to bad use is not unlike the «ignoranti» whose «fabulosi parlari», according to Fiammetta, do injustice («ingiuria») to the faith and constancy of the two young lovers («alla costanza de' loro animi, i quali in uno volere per l'amorosa forza sempre furono fermi servandosi debita fede», I 1, 25). The public's choral commentary on the events in Book II will in fact launch the protagonists' «fama» throughout the world. [65] The voice of

<hr>

[63] LEA, *op. cit.*, pp. 86-sg.

[64] The idea that fortune favors the bold will reappear in IV 101, 8 when Florio decides to undertake the dangerous mission in Alexandria.

[65] This is made even more vivid later in Book V when Idalogos remarks that Biancifiore's fame has already reached his «ears». Even Felice hears about Florio and Biancifiore's exploits in Alexandria before the two have returned to Verona.

the people, with its shifting points of view, will also give birth to diverse representations and interpretations of the lives of these two lovers, ranging from the *cantari* (i.e. the «fabulosi parlari») to the *Filocolo* itself. Boccaccio's depiction of the *vox popoli* is, therefore, a statement of how dramatic events can be interpreted by a collective voice that ultimately determines the subsequent nature of historic narrative. The transition from oral to written narrative (i.e. from the «fabulosi parlari» to the *Filocolo*), however, poses problems concerning the representation and interpretation of the truth. Besides sharing Fiammetta's desire for an account worthy of the lovers' faith and constancy, Boccaccio also seems to share Fiammetta's contempt for public opinion because it gives a distorted picture of the truth. By exposing the public's lack of faith and constancy, Boccaccio shows the limitations of all representations of the truth. [66]

The problem of determining and representing the truth is not limited to Boccaccio's description of the judicial battle and the public's vacillating views of it. Even though Mars' visible presence throughout the trial by combat is repeatedly viewed as a «manifesto segnale» of immanent justice, the god's «giustitia» is incomplete as well as ambiguous. The truth, which was supposed to be made manifest through immanent justice, is never fully revealed: both Florio and the seneschal conceal the king's involvement in the plot, as well as their own emotional involvement. If truth and justice in their totality cannot be found in Mars's immanent justice, where are we supposed to find it? The answer lies, once again, in the providential plan of which Mars is merely an agent (like Venus and Pluto) with only a partial knowledge of it. Only Providence and the omniscient author know the whole truth behind the characters' words and deeds. Boccaccio has thus placed the feudal concept of immanent justice several rungs below the providential plan, and by doing so he is questioning man's ability to interpret the *iudicium Dei* in particular and divine law in general.

IV. *Lex divina, naturalis, et humana*

Speaking about the three types of law (*lex divina, naturalis, et humana*), Thomas Aquinas says that it is only through revelation and

---

[66] For a related discussion of gossip and historic representation in the *Decameron*, see MILLICENT MARCUS, *An Allegory of Form: Literary Self-Consciousness in the «Decameron»*, Saratoga (CA), Anma Libri, 1979, pp. 103-105.

grace that man can have full knowledge of divine law and, consequently, of the providential plan. Divine law and grace are necessary means by which God instructs man to move towards *beatitudo*, the possession of which fulfills man's potentialities (Ia, IIae, 90). Aquinas defines divine law as the plan of the divine wisdom considered as directing all the acts and motions of creatures to the attainment of their ultimate end and good through the development of these potentialities (Ia, IIae, 93, 1). [67] Florio only attains full knowledge of the *lex divina*, the providential plan, and of his ultimate end when he is converted to Christianity. It is only when Florio hears Ilario's sermon and is possessed by the Holy Ghost that he has the grace and revelation necessary for him to see what before then was merely a distorted reflection of the plan of divine wisdom.

Divine law, in turn, is closely connected to natural law: «For every knowledge of truth is a kind of reflection and participation of divine law, which is the unchangeable truth [...] Now all men know the truth to a certain extent, at least as to the common principles of the natural law». Natural law is the rational creatures' participation in the divine law. Since rational creatures (e.g. man) have a share of eternal reason and a natural inclination to their proper act and end (i.e. beatitudo), they naturally know what is good and what is evil: «the light of natural reason, whereby we discern what is good and what is evil, which is the function of natural law, is nothing else than an imprint on us of the divine light» (Ia, IIae, 91, 2). Natural law consists of self-evident principles of practical reason, the first of which is that «good is that which all things seek after» and evil is that which all things avoid (Ia, IIae, 94, 2). [68] The first precept of natural law, therefore, is that «good is to be done and promoted, and evil is to be avoided». All the other precepts of natural law are founded on this one. [69]

---

[67] Divine law is given to help man direct his acts toward God; to help man in in his proper acts by means of an unerring law; to help man curb and direct interior acts (i.e. passions, virtues, etc); and to punish or forbid all evil deeds (Ia, IIae, 91, 4).

[68] Aquinas says that practical reason is directed to action; and every agent acts for an end which has a nature of good; and therefore «all the things which the practical reason naturally apprehends as man's good belongs to the precepts of natural law under the form of things to be done or avoided». Copleston distinguishes between practical reason and speculative reason in the following way: «The latter is reason as concerned simply with the knowledge and consideration of truth, while the former is reason as concerned with the application of what it apprehends either in moral conduct or in artistic or technical production» (*op. cit.*, p. 224).

[69] Since all those things towards which man has a natural inclination are apprehended by reason as being good (and therefore as things to pursue), the order of the other precepts follows

Furthermore, since all the inclinations of any part of human nature (even the concupiscible and irascible appetites, when they are under the control of reason) belong to the natural law, the love of Florio and Biancifiore is also part of the natural law when it is in harmony with reason: their love is a good they naturally pursue. Furthermore, since there is in every man a natural inclination to act according to reason, and this, according to Aquinas, is to act according to virtue, then the protagonists' love for each other is also virtuous when it is mediated by reason. (Aquinas' understanding of the concupiscible appetite and its relation to natural law, reason, and virtue are not unlike the courtly ideal of ennobling love.) Furthermore, since natural law is man's participation in the divine law, the protagonists' love shares in the divine wisdom when it is close to the divine mind. Their love is defined by law as something which shares in the greater love of God when the former is under reason's control.

Since law is an ordinance of reason, and reason is the promulgator of natural law, human reason proceeds from the precepts of the natural law in order to arrive at more «particular determinations of certain matters» which Aquinas calls the human or moral law (Ia, IIae, 91, 3). Aquinas defines the *lex humana* as «a measure or rule of human acts, a measure or rule conceived by reason and promulgated with a view to the common good» (Ia, IIae, 90, 4). [70] Aquinas adds that law must also concern itself with the order that is in *beatitudo*, which is the order directed to universal happiness. Furthermore, since living in society is prescribed by natural law, human laws should be structured accordingly, for as Aquinas says: «Man is by nature a social animal. Hence in a state of innocence (if there had been no Fall) men would have lived in society. But a common social life of many individuals could not exist unless there were someone in control to attend to the

---

the order of man's natural inclinations. For example, man's natural inclination towards the ultimate good, as far as his physical nature (or «substance») is concerned, is reflected in his desire to conserve his existence. Therefore, his reason tells him that, based on this natural inclination, he should conserve his life and avoid death. As for his sensitive appetites, man has a natural inclination to sexual intercourse and the education of children; consequently, reason promulgates the precept that children are to be put in the world and educated. With regard to his rational being, man has a natural inclination to know the truth about God and to live in society. Consequently reason promulgates the precept that the truth should be sought, ignorance avoided, and man's life ordered in such a way as to live in society with other men. See *Summa Theologica* Ia, IIae, 94, 2.

[70] «The proper effect of law is to lead its subjects to their proper virtue; and since virtue is that which makes its subject good, it follows that the proper effect of law is to make those, to whom it is given, good, either absolutely or in some particular respect» (Ia, IIae, 92, 1).

common good» (Ia, IIae, 96, 4). All positive or human laws, therefore, must be structured in accordance to the natural law and even the divine law. [71]

Since the divine law is God's plan of government, all plans of human government and human law derive from it «in so far as they partake of right reason» (Ia, IIae, 93, 3). But because man's natural inclination to that which is in harmony with divine law and his natural knowledge of what is good can both be corrupted by «passions and habits of sin», unjust laws exist which are a perversion of the law (Ia, IIae, 93, 6). «Hence the force of law depends on the extent of its justice» and «in human affairs a thing is said to be just from being right, according to the rule of reason [...] The first rule of reason is the law of nature [...] every human law has just so much of the nature of law as it is derived from the law of nature» (Ia, IIae, 95, 2). [72] Aquinas concludes that when a law departs from the law of nature and does not exist according to reason, it is no longer a law but a perversion of law; such is the case of tyrannical laws (Ia, IIae, 92, 2). Alluding to Justinian's *lex regia* in the *Corpus Iuris Civilis Institutiones I*, Aquinas states that «In order that the volition of what is commanded may have the nature of law, it needs to be in accord with some rule of reason. And in this sense is to be understood the saying that the will of the sovereign has the force of law [*quod principi placuit legis habet vigorem*]; or otherwise the sovereign's will would savor of lawlessness rather than of law» (Ia, IIae, 90, 1). [73]

Felice fits Aquinas' definition of the tyrannical sovereign to the letter. Like all «rational creatures», Felice is endowed with enough reason to know that what he is doing to Biancifiore is wrong, and therefore in violation of right reason. He corrupts the legal concept of commonweal when he justifies his actions to the seneschal, and he corrupts right reason when he says: «e però vengano immantamente i giudici, i quali di presente la giudichino, che sanza giudiciale sentenzia io non intendo di farla di fatto morire, acciò che alcuno non potesse dire che io i termini della ragione in ciò trapassassi [...]» (II 39, 3). His

---

[71] The fact that Fiammetta alludes to natural and positive laws in her concluding analysis of the last *questione d'amore* (*Filocolo* IV 70, 1) further underscores their importance in the narrative.

[72] Aquinas adds that law, not judges, should determine how a person is judged.

[73] Aquinas' understanding of the ruler's limitation under natural law can also be found in Cicero; see LEAR, *op. cit.*, p. 21.

false claim is a perversion of the importance that right reason plays in human law. [74] By debasing reason, Felice not only fails to follow the human or positive laws which require, among other things, that Biancifiore confess her crime before she can be sentenced to die, but he also goes against the natural law. The goddess Natura, in fact, rebels against the king's injustice with a series of cataclysms witnessed by Florio during his first vision. Venus explains to Florio the reason for Natura's conduct:

Florio, non credere che il pianto mio e degli altri dei sia perché noi crediamo che Biancifiore deggia morire, ché noi abbiamo già la sua morte cacciata con delibera-to consiglio, e proveduto al suo scampo, come appresso udirai; ma noi piangiamo però che la natura, vedendosi sopra sì bella creatura, come è Biancifiore, offendere dalla crudeltà del tuo padre, quando a morte ordinò che sentenziata fosse, ci si mostrò, sagliendo a' nostri scanni, sì mesta e dolorosa, che a lagrimare ci mosse tutti, e fececi intenti alla sua diliberazione. (II 42, 11-12)

The goddess Natura assumes the role of plaintiff, and the gods respond to her case with a «deliberato consiglio» which rectifies the unjust deliberation at Felice's council. The ensuing divine interven-tion, in the traditional form of immanent justice, is meant to counter-act Felice's «giustitia». Felice's injustice is not simply an offense against the *lex naturalis et humana*, but also an offense against the *lex divina* (the pagan gods, like Natura and Fortuna, are ministers of Providence). Felice's power may be similar to that of a theocratic

---

[74] Felice is not the only character to declare that he is acting according to reason in his ministration of justice. Florio, Massamutino, and even the choral public make similar claims just prior to the judicial combat. In his *desfi* Florio says that he is willing to defend the truth with life and limb «imperciò che la manifesta ragione mi stringe ad essere pietoso della ingiusta ingiuria fatta a costei; e [...] mi priega ch'io l'aiuti e difenda la ragione: e io così son presto di fare, e in ragione e in torto, contro a chiunque la vuol far morire» (II 61, 3). Upon hearing Florio's *desfi*, «tutti dissero che il cavaliere dicea bene, e che ragionevole cosa era che 'l siniscalco, o altri per lui sua ragione, contro a quelli che la contradicea, difendesse» (II 62, 1). Massamutino responds to both the public and Florio by saying «Il cavaliere mente per la gola di tutto ciò che ha detto; ché Biancifiore dee ragionevolmente morire» (II 62, 5). Massamutino not only gives Florio the lie (a standard remark which usually preceded a judicial combat); but he also declares that Biancifiore's death sentence is right. The meaning of the words «ragione» and «ragionevole» in these contexts refer to the «rightness» of a given action, as opposed to its «reasonableness». However, since the word «ragione» means both «right» and «reason», the two meanings are not mutually exclusive: what is right is what stems from reason; and right reason is that which should govern all laws. The fact that Florio, the public, and, to a lesser extent, Massamutino believe that their differing positions are justified, adds to the irony of this episode: none of them are right, because none of their acts proceed from right reason.

monarch (i.e. above positive law and below natural law) but he is still an individual who must conform to the greater sovereignty of Providence. Like all monarchs, it is his duty to recognize that his power must conform to Providence, from which it derives. His failure to do so brings about the divine interventions we have seen in Book II.

The fact that Felice was privileged by having a vision of the providential plan makes him all the more culpable of offending the *lex divina* (since one is a reflection of the other). Felice's failure to use right reason in the laws and government he applies to his subject (Biancifiore) is a corruption of God's plan of government and the divine law. Furthermore, since Felice manipulates the human laws against *laesa maiestatis* in order to reach his own lawless end, he acts against the spirit of the law, and therefore against the rational principles which associate this law with the natural laws from which it descends. Instead of ruling a kingdom directed toward the order of *beatitudo* or the *summum bonum*, Felice's rule has corrupted both that order and the laws which should direct his subjects towards their ultimate good. Since the commonweal is a reflection of man's ultimate end in society, the corruption of one prevents the development of the other. Felice is as much an antithesis of Providence as the council of barons is to the council of pagan gods.

If Venus's first vision to Felice was an allegory of the providential plan, her first vision to Florio is an allegory of the three kinds of law which derive from it. Both visions pose problems of interpretation for the dreamer: Felice chooses to ignore his vision completely and spends the rest of his life contending with the providential plan. Florio, on the other hand, follows to the letter all the goddess's commandments given to him during the vision. The king (like his seneschal) is fully aware, before and after the *iudicium Dei*, that the gods are against him and on Biancifiore's side, and yet, despite this awareness, he insists on harassing her and is never deterred from trying to subvert the divine will. By making Felice fully cognizant of the divine law, Boccaccio makes it clear that both the king and his seneschal are in a position to refrain from going against the gods: both men are free to withdraw their false charges against Biancifiore. The fact that they do not is one more example of how the expression of their *liberum arbitrium* against the divine law (and consequently against the providential plan) is both futile and self-defeating. Florio, on the other hand, recognizes that the gods are on his side and does everything they tell him to do. Each man represents an extreme postion: Felice represents a disregard of the providential plan and his contempt for the divine law, whereas Florio represents a literal interpretation and unquestioning adherence to the letter of divine law. As we have seen, both positions are misguided. The ambiguity of Florio and Felice's conduct vis-à-vis the law and its sacred nature reflects the inherent dangers of both literal and manipulative interpretations of the law. The ambiguous actions of both men may thus be judged according to the manner in which each adheres to or rebels against the most fundamental principles of law in all three of its far reaching ramifications (human, natural, and divine).

What is true of legal and divine interpretations is also true of literary interpretations. As readers we risk of doing to Boccaccio's text what Felice and Florio do to the law and divine injunctions: ignore it, interpret it literally, or manipulate it in order to arrive at a desired interpretation. By interpreting the text as a medieval glossator might interpret a law, the reader is forced to choose from a wide range of possible interpretations, including those prompted by his own *mala fides*. But if the spirit of the *littera scripta*, like the spirit of the law, is what keeps us from the dangers of literalness and textual manipulation, then a textual reading similar to the legal exegesis of the glossators could also be applied to the *Filocolo*. The glossators of the *Corpus Juris Civilis* (the great body of Roman law which includes the *Digest*) separated law from rhetoric, clarified the verbal sense of difficult passages while relating them to the greater context of the *Corpus*, and solved the apparent contradictions and ambiguities within the text. [75] Considering that Boccaccio's intellectual background at the time of the *Filocolo* was both juridical and literary, any textual interpretation he might have wanted us to adopt in our reading of the *Filocolo* would undoubtedly have shared some of these and other interpretative strategies adopted by the glossators, particularly in the use of dialectics and logic. The glossators' exegetical and expository approach to textual analysis easily complemented the allegorical readings of patristic texts since both aimed at the spirit of the *littera scripta*. The combination of both an allegorical and an exegetical *expositio* of the *Filocolo* seems to be the way in which Boccaccio wanted his readers to interpret his text. Furthermore, if a combina-

---

[75] For a discussion of the importance of interpretation in the glossators' study of Roman law, see HASKINS, *op. cit.*, pp. 199-212.

tion of good faith and right reason is important to both the creation and interpretation of the human, natural, and divine law, its application to textual analysis would suit the didactic and dialectical nature of the *Filocolo*.

The ambiguity of interpretation which we find in Florio and Felice's interpretations of Venus's visions is also found in the way all the characters respond to divine interventions. The vision of Saint James which promises Lelio a child, but fails to tell him that he will die before the child is born, the voice from the cloud, telling Lelio and his men to fight and die (i.e. to kill and be killed), and the ambiguous «giustitia» which Mars and Florio mete out to Massamutino are all literal interpretations of a divine message. The reader, however, must interpret them differently in order to mitigate their ambiguity. From the temporal diachronic perspective of the characters, the divine is as ambiguous as the acts of Fortuna herself. All divine interventions in the *Filocolo* (whether those of saints or pagan gods) are as difficult to fathom as Fortuna herself: they are irrational from the point of view of human reason, and can only be understood and made rational from the perspective of the providential plan. Therefore, even Mars' ambiguous «giustitia» is «just» because it is an agent by which Fate translates the providential plan into a series of temporal events. Only from the greater perspective of Providence and the privileged perspective of the omniscient author does the god's «giustizia» become comprehensible: Mars represents the Old Law as well as the pagan laws which, according to Aquinas, participate fully in the natural law but not completely in the supernatural divine law. [76]

The same can be said about the voice from the cloud which, instead of telling Lelio to turn the other cheek and die like a Christian martyr, says: «Sicuramente e sanza dubbio combattete, che io sarò sempre appresso di voi aiutandovi vendicare le vostre morti» (I 25, 9). It is the voice of the *lex talionis* (i.e. of the Old Law) the same Law which Lelio's relatives evoke when they wish to avenge his death on

---

[76] Boccaccio's depiction of the Old Law is similar to Aquinas' views regarding pagan and Moslem law (both of which are represented in Florio's parents: his mother is Arabian and his father is pagan). The best pagan and Moslem laws are products of natural law: their imperfections are due to the lack of grace and revelation, two qualities that are necessary in order to perfect all human laws derived from the natural law («Gratia non tollit naturam sed perficit»). Furthermore, since natural law is a participation in the divine law, pagans and Moslems are not completely ignorant of the divine law.

Florio in Book V. It is a far cry from the New Law of «misericordia e giustitia» to which Florio is introduced by Ilario.

All these representations of pre-Christian and early Christian laws reflect the lack of total assimilation of the New Law. The laws we find in the first four books of the *Filocolo* are, at best, a stepping stone to a divine law which is never fully attainable in the immanent world. The deities Florio worships, and even the Christianized pagan deities Lelio and his Roman relatives worship, are representives of laws that are never fully superseded by the New Law. The fact that Ilario must convince Lelio's relatives of the incompatibility of the *lex talionis* with the New Law is itself proof that even in Rome the Old Law has not given way to the New Law. The Old Law, as it appears in the first four books of the *Filocolo*, is a distorted image of the *lex divina*: it reflects the pagan and Christian-Roman cultures of the characters themselves, and must be realigned with the greater *lex divina* of the providential plan.

The agents of Fate (Venus, Mars, Fortuna, etc.) at work within the world of the protagonists are supernatural per se, but they are not the divine law since they are not the supernatural means to the attainment of *beatitudo*, as are, instead, grace and the sacraments. The gods' revelations to the characters are not the same as the Christian revelation Florio receives in Rome when he discovers his supernatural and natural end. It is in this context that the pagan gods should be viewed: like their counterparts in *The City of God*, they are ambiguous spirits whose words and deeds are, for the most part, negative (like those of Fortuna), but whose existence can be viewed positively when placed in the larger context of the providential plan.

Boccaccio has thus depicted a world with many religious beliefs, all of which are distorted reflections of the Christian faith. These religious beliefs are as prone to error as the pagan gods and the protagonists in the first four books of the *Filocolo*. It is only after the disappearance of the pagan gods in Book IV and the conversion of the protagonists in Book V that religion and law are realigned to the Christian faith.

V. The Laws of Love

The importance of the law as it pertains to love has many ramifications in the *Filocolo*. The amorous ordeals which the two young lovers must endure become a legal ordeal which they successfully surmount. [77] When Felice violates the *lex humana* in his actions against Biancifiore, he violates the bonds of love which are supposed to unite, rather than divide, his family. By adopting illegal procedures against Biancifiore, Felice also violates the *lex naturalis* which, among other things, moves Florio and Biancifiore to love each other; and by contending with the providential plan, Felice not only contends with the providentiality of the protagonists' love for each other, but also with the *lex divina* and the cosmic love that binds the universe.

The laws we have examined thus far do not take into account the legalistic *regulae amoris* which came from courts of love similar to Fiammetta's, and which were regarded as «legal bodies with binding jurisdictional authority». [78] Like the *lex humana*, the *regulae amoris* were closely connected to conflict, and, according to Howard Bloch, were intended to resolve or minimize it. [79] Furthermore, as Bloch points out, love in medieval literature is not simply a unilateral attachment, but a contest against a third party (i.e. the rival). [80] In the *Filocolo* similar contests and conflicts over love take shape between Florio and his father in Book II, between Florio and Fileno in Book III, and between Florio and his uncle, the Admiral of Alexandria, in Book IV. In all three contests, Biancifiore is the third party of these love/hate triangles. We have already examined the conflict between father and son; the conflict between uncle and nephew will be examined in the next chapter; here we will examine the conflict between Florio and his only real rival in love, Fileno. It is this conflict that best reflects the importance of the *regulae amoris* in the narrative.

Fileno first appears in the *Filocolo* as «un giovane cavaliere chiamato Fileno, gentile e bello, e di virtuosi costumi ornato, a cui l'ardente amore di Florio e di Biancifiore era occulto, però che di lontane parti era, pochi giorni poi la crudel sentenza di Biancifiore, venuto» (III 16, 2). The moment he sees Biancifiore, «sanza misura la incominciò ad amare, e in diversi atti s'ingegnava di piacerle, avvegna

---

[77] For a related discussion in medieval French literature, see R. HOWARD BLOCH, *op. cit.*, pp. 181-182.

[78] See the last chapter of VICTORIA E. KIRKHAM, *The «Filocolo» of Giovanni Boccaccio with an English Translation of the Thirteen «Questioni d'Amore»*, Dissertation, The Johns Hopkins University, 1971; and *Literature and Law in the Middle Ages: A Bibliography of Scholarship*, ed. John A. Alford and Dennis P. Seniff, New York: Garland, 1984, p. 204.

[79] For a related discussion in medieval French literature, see HOWARD BLOCH, *op. cit.* pp. 174 and 191.

[80] HOWARD BLOCH, *op. cit.*, pp. 188.

che Biancifiore di ciò niente si curava, ma saviamente protandosi, mostrava che di queste cose ella non conoscesse quanto facea» (III 16, 3). [81] The king and queen try to bring the two together in the hope that Biancifiore will forget Florio for Fileno. [82] During their meeting Fileno thinks that Biancifiore sighs on his account, when instead her sighs are for Florio. Fileno's egocentric interpretation of Biancifiore's conduct is complicated by the fact that Biancifiore pretends to love Fileno «per conforto della reina» (16, 5). Her deception, coupled with Fileno's own self-deception, violates the fundamental virtue of *onestà* required of all courtly lovers. Biancifiore's conduct also violates one of Andreas Capellanus' *regulae amoris*: «V. Mendacia omnino vitare memento». [83] The fact that she is not impelled to love by the persuasion of love goes against the *regula* «IX. Amare nemo potest, nisi qui amoris suasione compellitur». [84] Furthermore, the impossibility of being bound by a double love recalls the *regula* «III. Nemo duplici potest amore ligari». [85] Biancifiore's behavior is surprising in light of the fact that she had no difficulty rejecting Massamutino's love for her. It is clear that her ambiguous conduct is meant to mirror Florio's equally ambiguous behavior in the preceding episode when he almost allows himself to be seduced by Edea and Calmena (III 11). In both episodes, the friends and relatives who are encouraging Florio and Biancifiore to become involved in these new amorous relationships are placing their hopes in Andreas' *regula* «XVII. Novus amor veterem compellit abire». [86]

Biancifiore continues to deceive Fileno when she gives him her veil to wear as a «soprasegnale» during a tournament in honor of Mars. Although Biancifiore feels «costretta dal parlare della reina», it is still an act of her free will. Her gift conveys the wrong message about her true feelings: instead of being the courtly-love gift the damsel would give her knight before combat («ché usanza è degli amanti insieme donarsi tal fiata delle loro gioie»), it is a sign which generates an

---

[81] The words «senza misura» are the words used by Felice and Dario to describe Florio's love for Biancifiore.

[82] This scene, and the whole Fileno episode, is meant to mirror the episode in the preceding chapters (III 8-11) when the Duke and Ascalion try to get Florio interested in other women.

[83] ANDREA CAPPELLANO, *De amore*, edited by Graziano Ruffini, Milano, Guanda, 1980, p. 94.

[84] CAPPELLANO, *op. cit.*, p. 282.

[85] CAPPELLANO, *op. cit.*, p. 282.

[86] CAPPELLANO, *op. cit.*, p. 282.

equivocal meaning (as the word «soprasegnale» itself suggests). Fileno, in fact, misinterprets its significance, and after winning the tournament, he uses it to boast about his amorous and martial exploits to Florio and the other young knights at Montoro. In the process, he fails to observe two fundamental *regulae amoris* when he carelessly («disaveduatamente») betrays the identity of his beloved: [87]

La fortuna, non contenta delle tribulazioni di Florio, condusse Fileno a Montoro pochi giorni poi la ricevuta vittoria. Il quale là onorevolmente ricevuto da molti, nella gran sala del duca, incominciò a narrare a' giovani cavalieri suoi amici quanto fosse stato l'acquistato onore, disegnando con parole e con atti quanta forza e ingegno adoperasse per ricevere in sé tutta la vittoria, come fece. Poi, entrati in altri diversi ragionamenti, venuti a parlare d'amore, similmente sé propose esser assai più che altro innamorato, e di più bella donna, e come da lei niuna grazia era che conceduta non gli fosse se domandata l'avesse; e dopo molte parole disaveduatamente gli venne ricordata Biancifiore. E Florio, che non era troppo lontano, e avea udite tutte queste cose, e piagneasi in se medesimo d'amore, che lui peggio che alcuno altro trattava, come udì ricordare Biancifiore, e per le precedenti parole conobbe lei essere quella donna di cui Fileno tanto si lodava, (17, 1-3)

As we shall see, this serious breach of courtly-love conduct determines Fileno's fate throughout the *Filocolo*. To make matters even worse, Fileno tells Florio that Biancifiore told him «che io per amore di lei mi dovessi portar bene». Biancifiore never said this; but Fileno lies in order to make an impression on the young knights and to assert his previous claim that «sopra tutti gli altri giovani io amo». Besides violating, as Biancifiore had done, the courtly-love injunction against lying, Fileno's lie also turns Florio against him. Furthermore, Fileno's claim that he loves more than anyone else is both presumptuous and inaccurate since his amorous experience is not unique. The fact that he makes this claim to Florio underscores Fileno's egocentricity as well as his inability to imagine that others might be equally in love with Biancifiore: «XXXI. Unam feminam nil prohibet a duobus amari et a duabus mulieribus unum.» [88]

When asked by Florio how he can tell that Biancifiore actually loves him, Fileno mentions three *signa amoris* which, according to him,

---

[87] The actual *regulae amoris* he violates are: «Amor raro consuevit durare vulgatus» (CAPPELLANO, *op. cit.*, p. 282) and «Amoris tui secretarios noli plures habere» (CAPPELLANO, *op. cit.*, p. 94).

[88] CAPPELLANO, *op. cit.*, p. 284.

unequivocally signify Biancifiore's love--her sighs, her gift, and her happiness «d'ogni felice caso che m'avvegna» (17, 8). As it so happens, these three signs of love are similar to several of Andreas Capellanus' rules of love. The «timido sguardare con focosi sospiri» recalls «XV. Omnis consuevit amans in coamantis aspectus pallescere» and «XVI. In repentina coamantis visione cor contremescit amantis».[89] The «ricevute gioie, le quali sanza amore da gentile donna mai donate on sarieno» recalls «XXVI. Amor nil posset amori denegare».[90] And Biancifiore's «allegrezza [...] d'ogni felice caso che m'avvegna» recalls «XXV. Verus amans nil bonum credit nisi, quod cogitat coamanti placere».[91] Although Fileno's three signs actually correspond more closely to what Andreas discusses in his dialogues than in his *regulae amoris*, the fact that Fileno treats them as signs of true love is in keeping with the traditional medieval belief that love manifests itself through *signa amoris* which can in turn be codified as *regulae amoris*.[92] For Fileno the laws of love are as unequivocal as the laws of nature. It is only later that Fileno realizes that «Le leggi d'amore sono variate [*diverse*] da quelle della natura in molte cose» (III 31, 5). By portraying Fileno in this manner, Boccaccio is not only criticizing the young knight's egocentric love, but also the belief that love can be reduced to a set of laws (i.e. *regulae amoris*) which make it easy to identify and predict. The fact that even Florio accepts Biancifiore's acts as infallible proof of her love for Fileno underscores the dangers of giving undue importance to the *regulae amoris*.

Florio's earlier fears that Biancifiore might love another man «per li conforti della mia madre» (III 2, 11) are thus confirmed by both his and Fileno's misinterpretation of Biancifiore's «soprasegnale». Florio's *dubitare* and *dubbi* (words that refer to both doubt and fear) are in keeping with Andreas' *regulae*: «XX. Amorosus semper est timorosus».[93] With some help from the goddess Diana, Florio also becomes jealous, thereby living up to Andreas' famous *regula* «II. Qui non zelat, amare non potest». Under the inspiration of Venus, he writes a letter to Biancifiore in which he criticizes her for loving someone who

---

[89] CAPPELLANO, *op. cit.*, p. 282.
[90] CAPPELLANO, *op. cit.*, p. 284.
[91] CAPPELLANO, *op. cit.*, p. 284.
[92] In addition to functioning as rules which governed the behavior of a courtly lover, the *regulae amoris* were also meant to shed light on the psychological condition of a true lover.
[93] CAPPELLANO, *op. cit.*, p. 282.

is socially inferior to him (III 20, 21). [94] Florio's attitude not only reflects his jealousy and social prejudice, but also a well-established courtly-love conceit that lovers must always seek to love someone from a higher social station. [95] As a «semplice cavaliere» (18, 5), Fileno is not only inferior to Florio, but also to Biancifiore who is, as Florio reminds her, «degli altissimi imperadori romani discesa» (III 18, 8). Although it is appropriate for Fileno to love her, it is inappropriate for Biancifiore to love him. Biancifiore responds to Florio's letter with a letter of her own in which she tries to alleviate his *dubbi*; but the fact that she deliberately deceived someone (Fileno), diminishes her credibility in Florio's eyes. The result of Florio's jealousy is that he is indeed deprived «della pura fede», in accordance with Diana's orders to Gelosia (III 24, 10). Jealousy is thus an enemy of faith, just as Diana is an enemy of the two young lovers at this point in the narrative. The «pure faith» of the two young lovers has been tainted as much by their own actions as by those of Fileno.

Rather than mitigate Florio's jealousy, Biancifiore's letter just makes it worse. His lack of «pura fede» now threatens his relationship with Biancifiore, and moves him to contemplate suicide (III 18, 30-31; 20, 27-28) and murder (III 31, 6). It is, in fact, after receiving Biancifiore's letter that Florio wants to see Fileno dead. Like Felice, Florio plots the murder of a fairly innocent lover when he believes that this third party is in the way of his desired end. When Fileno finds out about the plot, he asks a rhetorical question which will often be repeated: «Oimè, or che farà Florio ad uno che l'abbia [Biancifiore] in odio, se a me che l'amo ha pensata la morte?» (III 31, 5). The fact that this question recurs in III 34, 2; V 33, 5; and V 36, 9 suggests that we are meant to see a connection between Florio's relationship with Fileno and his relationship with Massamutino. From a lover who killed a man (Massamutino) who hated Biancifiore, Florio has now become a lover who is prepared to kill a man (Fileno) who loves her.

---

[94] This is not the first time Florio draws attention to his superior *nobiltà di sangue*: he refers to it in his monologue shortly after speaking to Fileno (III 18, 5-9), and he even alludes to it when speaking to Fileno (III 17, 19). The fact that jealousy moves him to action for the first time since he rescued Biancifiore is significant: it is only through such emotional impulses that Florio is able to act. As we shall see in the next chapter, Florio is moved to act in Alexandria only after he sees Biancifiore looking from the Torre dell'Arabo. There too, he is moved by a reflex act, or *actus hominis* as Aquinas calls it, rather than by a deliberate act proceeding from his will and reason (i.e. an *actus humani*).

[95] Boccaccio returns to this idea in the Proem to the *Decameron*; see BRANCA, *Decameron*, p. 6n.

Even though Biancifiore's behavior towards Fileno is totally different from her conduct towards Massamutino, Florio's feelings toward both men are the same. One can conclude that if Fileno had not fled from Verona, Florio would have killed him too. By portraying Florio's jealous behavior in such negative terms, Boccaccio is ultimately criticizing Andreas' three *regulae amoris* concerning jealousy: «II. Qui non zelat, amare non potest»; «XXI. Ex vero zelotypia affectus semper crescit amandi»; and «XXII. De coamante suspicione percepta zelus et affectus crescit amandi». [96] If jealousy is the substance of love, as Andreas states in his dialogues, one must conclude that the substance of Florio's love, at this point in the narrative, is bad.

Andreas' assertion, both in his dialogues and in the *regulae amoris*, that true love cannot exist without jealousy was first undercut by Dante in the *Vita nuova*. Sonnets such as *Tanto gentile e tanto onesta pare*; *Vede perfettamente onne salute*; and *Ne li occhi porta la mia donna Amore* reveal a love that destroys envy and has the power to instill *caritas* in all men, not just Dante. Dante is never jealous when he describes Beatrice's amorous effect on others. It is clear from Florio's conduct, however, that love does not have the same effect on him that it had on Dante. [97] Florio's hostility towards those who fall under Biancifiore's influence is proof that his love has only brought out the worst in him.

Florio's jealousy is later mitigated by Fileno's exile from Verona; and their conflict comes close to a resolution when the two rivals meet on the future site of Certaldo. In is there that Fileno has been transformed into a spring, like an Ovidian lover who has actually become the metaphor for his grief. As David Wallace has pointed out, Florio encounters a close image of himself as he bends over the clear fountain. [98] Like Fileno, Florio has in fact been forced to undertake a *peregrinatio amoris* for love of Biancifiore, and like his rival, Florio also grieves for his love's labor lost. Throughout their meeting Florio knows that he is speaking to Fileno, but it is not clear whether or not

---

[96] These *regulae* are from Andreas' long list; see CAPPELLANO, *op. cit.*, p. 282.

[97] By the same token, Biancifiore's negative effect on Massamutino and her lack of *onestà* towards Fileno make any comparison of her to Beatrice absurd.

[98] DAVID WALLACE, *Chaucer and the Early Writings of Boccaccio*, Suffolk, D. S. Brewer, 1985 («Chaucer Studies XII»), p. 62. One should add that these two rivals in love do mirror each other to a certain extent even before their *peregrinatio amoris*. Both are only sons («unigenito») in love with the same woman, and both don armor for love of Biancifiore: the joust Fileno wins in honor of Mars comes shortly after Florio's combat against Massamutino which also honored Mars.

Fileno knows that he is speaking to Florio. [99] Their meeting is, in many respects, a palinode, if not an inversion, of their first meeting in Montoro. Rather than misinterpret, exaggerate, or lie about his relationship with Biancifiore, Fileno now tells the truth about it, and even admits his fatal mistake: «se io fossi taciuto, ancora in Marmorina dimorerei» (IV 3, 5). By narrating his plight in such truthful terms, Fileno discloses his rival's cruel jealousy and makes Florio look bad in the eyes of the six barons who are accompanying him. After this meeting, when the barons begin discussing Fileno's fate (IV 5, 4-5), Florio changes the subject of conversation as if to avoid any further embarrassment. Realizing how delicate the situation is, Ascalion diplomatically suggests to Florio and his companions to return to the fountain after they have found «la ricercata cosa» (i.e. Biancifiore).

If Florio looks bad in the eyes of others, Fileno now reveals his better side (something he failed to do when he was in Montoro boasting about his exploits). Whereas in Montoro he was trying to make an impression on others by revealing what would turn out to be his worst side, during this second meeting with Florio he unwittingly gets the attention he sought in Montoro by humbly revealing the truth of himself and his rival. Florio recognizes that Fileno is telling the truth (IV 4, 1) and is moved to tears «quasi per pietà». His pity, however, is not enough to move him to help Fileno regain his human form.

Florio eventually returns to help Fileno, but only after he has found and married Biancifiore. During that time, Florio's jealousy has not disappeared completely: he still has *dubbi* about Biancifiore's feelings for Fileno. As they approach the fountain, Florio in fact asks Biancifiore: «O lungamente da me disiderata giovane, dimmi, per quello amore che tu mi porti, il vero di ciò ch'io ti domanderò [...] Etti uscito della memoria Fileno, a cui tu con le propie mani donasti per amore il caro velo? O sospirasti mai per lui poi che di Marmorina temendomi si partì?» (V 33, 1-2). [100] Biancifiore turns red «per vergogna» and answers that she remembers Fileno, but never loved him. She also reaffirms the things she told Florio in her letter. When Florio

---

[99] Fileno does recognize the voices of Menedon and Biancifiore when they speak to him in V 36-37; but it could be that Florio's voice was altered when he first spoke to Fileno. Florio keeps his identity a secret throughout their first meeting, pretending to be someone who knows about Florio. Whether Fileno can see through this subterfuge, or whether he too is engaged in a similar subterfuge is not clear.

[100] Florio's own fall in the arms of another woman may have made him aware of how vulnerable even the most steadfast lover can be to the charms of a third party.

asks her if she would like to see Fileno, she answers «Certo sì, nella vostra grazia». It is at this point in their conversation that Biancifiore shifts from the familiar *tu* to the formal *voi*. She is no longer speaking to Florio as her lover and husband, but as her liege lord. By expressing her desire to see Fileno returned to Florio's graces, Biancifiore acknowledges her husband's role as a ruler capable of determining the fate of his subjects. Biancifiore concludes by saying: «Or che avria la fortuna fatto alli nocenti, se elli m'avesse odiata? Concedano gl'iddii e a voi e a me che da tutti siamo di buono amore amati, e se essere non può che amati siamo di qualunque amore, amando noi ciascuno come si conviene.» (33, 5). As Quaglio has shown, the question is similar to the one Fileno had asked about Florio. [101] She replaces, however, the name of her husband with that of *fortuna*. Like his father before him, Florio is a figure of fortune that has capriciously determined the fate of an innocent lover. Biancifiore's hope that everyone might love her and Florio, and that the two of them may in turn love everyone as is fitting, is an appeal for *agape*: she is basically asking Florio not to make the same mistakes he and Felice made in the first three books of the *Filocolo*. Her appeal is also meant to move Florio to correct his misguided love and jealousy, thereby bringing him closer to the *caritas* and *zelus* which are later manifested in him when he is filled with the Holy Spirit. Amorous jealousy and religious zeal not only share the same Latin etymology (*zelus*), but the former is a corrupt reflection of the latter: Florio must overcome one before he can attain the other. This second encounter with Fileno makes the change from jealousy to brotherly love possible: it is one more step which Florio must take in his spiritual development and in his quest for *beatitudo*.

Florio accepts his wife's request by saying: «Ottimamente parli [...] e io la mia grazia e la tua presenza gli renderò, certo della tua fede, della quale ben fui per adietro certo; ma noi amanti ogni cosa temiamo, e però odiai.» (33, 5). There is a certain amount of ambiguity in his remark: if he was so sure of her «fede», why did he interrogate her? Florio's contradictory remarks are further evidence that his jealousy has not disappeared completely. As for justifying his hatred, he alludes to Andreas' *regula* «XX. Amorosus semper est timorosus». Andreas discusses extensively the fears that beset a lover, but he never establishes a connection between fear and hatred, as Boccaccio

---

[101] BOCCACCIO, *Filocolo*, p. 935.

seems to have done when he illustrates how the irascible appetite increases in direct proportion to the frustration of the concupiscible appetite.

Florio proceeds to thank the gods «per la salvazione di sé e de' suoi compagni» and adds, «Ora per voi sento pace, e ho la lunga sollecitudine abandonata, però che gli occhi miei veggono ciò che per adietro lungamente disiderarono, e le mie braccia stringono la sua salute» (V 34, 1-2). [102] Florio's unintentional use of Christian vocabulary in his prayer anticipates his conversion. As it so happens, this is the last pagan sacrifice he makes before his conversion to Christianity. This is also the last time he thanks the pagan gods (Mars and Venus included) for their help. The fact that he prays at an abandoned temple once dedicated to the father of Venus suggests that this moment signals the imminent end of both his pagan worship and pagan love: Florio has abandoned «la lunga sollecitudine» (his love labors) just as the temple had been abandoned by its worshipers prior to Florio's arrival. [103]

After his prayer, Florio proceeds to restore «la salute di Fileno» at Menedon's request. Fileno, who has heard Menedon's request and has recognized his voice, asks him to intercede on his behalf so that he may be pardoned and restored to «la grazia del tuo signor». Florio responds by pardoning Fileno and telling Biancifiore to announce the good news («lieta novella») to Fileno. When she does, Fileno acknowledges «la riavuta grazia m'ha annunziata». The Christian vocabulary, the beloved's mediation between lord and sinner, and the annunciation of grace all culminate in the miraculous conversion of Fileno. David Wallace says that Florio «triumphantly reverses the Ovidian process with Fileno's extraordinary demetamorphosis [...] This remarkable spectacle--of a regenerate Fileno rising up out of the waters--clearly prefigures the general conversion and baptism of the company which occurs at the end of this book; it is immediately preceded by a speech of forgiveness which recalls the words of Saint Paul». [104] To this one should add that the episode also recalls the equally dramatic

---

[102] As Quaglio has indicated, the last allusion is to Biancifiore; see BOCCACCIO, *Filocolo*, p. 936.

[103] As the narrator indicated in IV 1, the temple had been abandoned for so long that it was covered with vegetation.

[104] Wallace views the use of Ovid here as «smoothing the path from paganism to orthodoxy». See WALLACE, *op. cit.*, p 47.

moment prior to Massamutino's death when the seneschal too confessed his sins in the hope of staying in his lord's graces. At that time, however, Florio showed no mercy, and killed a man who instead could have been pardoned. Florio has come a long way since then, and has begun to understand the need to combine mercy with justice.

Whereas Florio is clearly on the road to conversion, Fileno's conversion is more ambiguous:

Al quale egli [Fileno], come il [Florio] vide, s'inginocchio davanti e con pietose voci dimando perdono, e appresso di Filocolo la benivolenza: le quali cose benignamente Filocolo gli concesse. Egli fu di nuovi vestimenti adorno, e i raviluppati capelli e la male stante barba furono rimessi in ordine [...] e lieto si diede con gli altri cavalieri a far festa, maravigliandosi non poco qual caso quivi gli avesse menati insieme con Biancifiore. Il cui viso poi ch'egli ebbe veduto, stimandolo più bello che mai gli fosse paruto, contento tacitamente si dispose al vecchio amore, credendo sanza quello niuna cosa valere. (V 37, 6-7)

Fileno has come full circle: he is not only restored to his previous state, but also to his previous condition as a courtly lover. His physical conversion is symbolic of his transformation as a lover: having learned from his mistakes, he now knows better than to boast about his beloved. Like a true courtly lover, Fileno is resolved to love Biancifiore «tacitamente». His secret is matched by Florio's own secret: Fileno believes that Florio's arrival on that spot was fortuitous («maravigliandosi non poco qual caso quivi gli avesse menati») when instead Florio deliberately returned there. Neither Florio nor his companions tell this to Fileno since it would reveal their previous visit. Their silence is understandable since their first visit was an embarrassing moment for Florio and one in which he did nothing to help Fileno return to his previous state. The fact that both Florio and Fileno still have secrets to hide from each other, notwithstanding their incredible adventures, suggests that they have not changed very much since their previous meeting.

If Fileno's Ovidian transformation into a fountain was symbolic of his pagan love for Biancifiore, his conversion back to his former state could be seen as a return to his former self. Fileno, in fact, does not actually change the way he feels about Biancifiore, just the way he expresses (or does not express) his love for her. His regeneration, therefore, is not a real conversion in the Christian sense of the word (i.e. a death of the old self followed by a rebirth of a new man). The fact that he decides to continue loving Biancifiore even now that she is married means that his love is adulterous and a potential threat to Florio's marriage. When Fileno eventually converts to Christianity, along with Florio's other companions, it is not clear to what extent this conversion is also a conversion from *amor per diletto* to *amor onesto*. The fact that Fileno was unable to give up loving Biancifiore after his demetamorphosis suggests that he may not have ceased loving her after his Christian conversion. The fact that Fileno's physical transformation into a fountain, as a result of the wrong kind of love, is now followed by a metaphoric transformation at the baptismal font for what should be the right kind of love does not resolve the moral argument about his love for Biancifiore. Since we do not know Fileno's feelings for Biancifiore after he becomes a Christian, one can only assume that if he continued to love her «tacitamente», it was a well kept secret.

If the moral argument of Fileno's love for Biancifiore is ambiguous and unresolved after his Christian conversion, the moral argument of the protagonists' love for each another has a clearer resolution as we shall see in the events which immediately precede and follow the consummation episode.

CHAPTER FIVE

CLIMAX AND CONSUMMATION IN THE *FILOCOLO*

As we have seen in the Introduction, Victoria Kirkham establishes a thematic and structural connection between the *questioni d'amore* in the first half of Book IV and the dream visions which immediately precede and follow Fiammetta's court of love. [1] There are, however, other correspondences between the *questioni d'amore* and the plot itself, as Paolo Cherchi has shown. [2] For example, Florio's condition as a doubt-filled lover is reflected in the novella which accompanies his *questione d'amore* (IV 19). [3] The novella is about a woman who took a «ghirlanda» from one lover and gave it to another. Florio's question, which of the two men did the lady love, is a projection of his own uncertainty as to which man Biancifiore really loves — Fileno or Florio. The fact that Biancifiore's gesture is misinterpreted by both Fileno and Florio illustrates the difficulty of interpretation. Similarly, the two lovers in Florio's novella do not know how to interpret their lady's ambiguous act, hence the *questione d'amore*.

Although none of the thirteen questions in the first half of Book IV has a precise one-to-one correspondence with the events in the plot, there are elements in each of the novelle accompanying the *questione d'amore* which suggest that Boccaccio wanted his readers to relate them to the plot itself. [4] By leaving enough ambiguity in each novella to suggest a similarity between it and the love-life of the protagonists, Boccaccio is minimizing the anachronistic nature of the setting (fourteenth-century Naples versus sixth-century Italy) while at the same time suggesting that his readers judge the protagonists in

---

[1] See KIRKHAM, *op. cit.*, pp. 54-56.
[2] See PAOLO CHERCHI, *Andrea Cappellano, i trovatori e altri temi romanzi*, Roma: Bulzoni Editore, 1979, pp. 210-217.
[3] See CHERCHI, *op. cit.*, pp. 214-215.
[4] For a similar discussion see CHERCHI, *op. cit.*, p. 213.

terms of the discussion taking place at Fiammetta's court of love. The fact that Boccaccio set this court of love just prior to the climactic events in Alexandria also suggests, as Luigi Surdich has indicated, that Florio is being educated in the art of love (like Walter in Andreas' *De arte oneste amandi*) before he actually consummates his love. [5] To what extent Florio's didactic experience in Naples (the place where Boccaccio himself was educated in both love and literature) actually prepares him for what awaits him in Alexandria becomes the focus of Book IV.

Whereas the first half of Book IV is devoted to the idealized rulings of Fiammetta's court of love and the laws mandated by her own chaste understanding of love, the second half of Book IV is devoted to the actual practice of lovemaking. By juxtaposing these two halves of Book IV, Boccaccio is illustrating the extent to which the theory and practice of love merge and diverge. As we shall see, the ambiguity between theory and practice is just as prevalent when the lovers are brought together as it was when they were separated. [6]

I. *Ingegno, Intelletto, e Memoria*

After leaving Fiammetta's court of love in Naples, Florio's search for Biancifiore brings him and his companions to Alexandria where he finds out from Dario, a native of that city, that she is kept by the Admiral of Alexandria in a tower along with ninety-nine other virgins. [7] In his speech to Florio, Dario gives a detailed account of the marvelously wrought tower (one of the seven wonders of the world) and the paradisiacal splendor in which Biancifiore is living. In his description of the central hall Dario says:

In questa sala ne' pareti dintorno, quante antiche storie possono alle presenti memorie ricordare, tutte con sottilissimi intagli adorne d'oro e di pietre vi

---

[5] See LUIGI SURDICH, *op. cit.*, pp. 49 sg.

[6] Finding a climax or turning point in the *Filocolo* is not easy. The medley of loosely connected episodes, digressions, and tales within tales seem to deliberately mute any sense of a climax in this work. When we read, however, the alleged sources of the *Filocolo* (the two Old French romances of Floire et Blanchefleur and the Italian cantari of Fiorio e Biancofiore) there can be no doubt that the climax takes place in Alexandria when the two protagonists consummate their love affair. Our reading of the corresponding episode in the *Filocolo* will show that it too is the turning point in the narrative.

[7] During Boccaccio's time, two thousand female slaves were bought each year in Alexandria; see HENRY H. HART, *Marco Polo: Venetian Adventurer*, Norman, University of Oklahoma Press, 1967, p. 10n.

vedresti, e sopra tutte scritto di sopra quello che le figure di sotto vogliono significare. Quivi ancora sopra ogni altra figura posti, co' quali gli avoli e antichi padri del nostro amiraglio tutti vedere potresti. (IV 85, 4)

What Dario does not know is that Florio would also be able to see his own «avoli e antichi padri». In a subtle moment of dramatic irony, Dario unwittingly alludes to Florio's own genealogy. These carvings in fact reveal the common ancestry which both Florio and the Admiral share. We the readers are as unaware of this as the characters themselves, and it is only after reading the entire episode that we discover, along with the characters, that the Admiral is Florio's maternal uncle. Until the *agnitio* occurs, however, these carvings are the only clue to Florio's unknown matrilineal kinship tie. [8]

These carvings also recall those in Felice's banquet hall. As Quaglio and Surdich have shown, the two halls are described in similar terms. [9] Surdich suggests that the similarities between these two halls are meant to mark the moments when the two lovers begin and end their separation. [10] The nexus between these two halls, however, also lies in the carvings themselves which conceal the noble ancestors of the lover whose fate is determined in each hall: the carvings of Julius Ceasar in Felice's hall conceal Biancifiore's noble birth when instead they could save her from the consequences of her love for Florio; and the carvings of the Admiral's ancestors suggest that if Florio had known about them, he would have been spared the consequences of consummating his love in Alexandria. The carvings in both halls are signs («figure») whose meaning («significare») bears directly on the situation at hand.

The play between signifier and signified, which Boccaccio is engaged in at the beginning of this crucial episode, is significant for several reasons. First, it sets the stage for a series of intricate acts of concealment and disclosure which occur throughout this episode and which mimetically reflect the providential unfolding of history as well as Boccaccio's own «chiuso parlare» in the *Filocolo*. Second, the hidden kinship tie puts Florio in a situation which is very similar to

---

[8] The possibility of an *agnitio* is made stronger by the fact that Florio has the ring his mother gave him before he left Verona: that would have been sufficient proof of his kinship tie to her brother, the Admiral of Alexandria.
[9] See BOCCACCIO, *Filocolo*, p. 890n; and SURDICH, *op. cit.*, p. 57-60.
[10] See SURDICH, *op. cit.*, p. 60.

that of his beloved. Like Biancifiore, whose bondage and other hardships are due to ignorance of her noble blood, the ensuing hardships
which Florio is about to endure are also due to his ancestry being
unknown. The ensuing adventures in Alexandria, therefore, become a
Boethian test of Florio's character, much as Biancifiore's hardships
prior to Alexandria were a test of her character.

This becomes more apparent when we look at Dario's concluding
remarks:

> Signori, io non discerno qui se non tre vie, delle quali l'una ci conviene pigliare, e
> mancandoci queste, niuna altra ce ne so pensare. Le quali tre, queste, sono esse: o
> per prieghi riaverla dall'amiraglio, o per forza rapirla della torre, o con ingegno
> acquistare l'amicizia del castellano, la quale avendo, non dubito che a fine si
> verria del vostro intendimento. (IV 87, 1)

Dario makes a case for the third course of action because he believes
that the first two would be pointless: the Admiral would never give up
Biancifiore, the most prized of his one hundred virgins, nor would
Florio have enough men to take the tower by force. Florio, in fact,
takes Dario's advice and opts for the third course of action which,
from his point of view, is the one which makes the most sense. From
the providential perspective of the author, however, only the first
course of action is appropriate. The Admiral in fact tells Florio, eighty
chapters later, that he would have given him Biancifiore had he asked
for her. As in the case of Lelio's crucial choice in Book I, Florio too
chooses between three possible courses of action, but the one which
seems most feasible proves to be the most disastrous. As in Lelio's
case, Florio exercises his free will by choosing between several courses
of action and eventually reaches his desired end in a manner which
goes against his expectations.

Florio's choice of *ingegno* as the means to his desired end is
significant in itself. Judging from the contexts in which *ingegno* appears, the word seems to signify an intuitive form of understanding
which is distinct from «intellect» and «reason». The concept of *ingegno*
is largely the product of the Platonic school of Chartres in the twelfth
century. [11] Of the Chartrians, Boccaccio was most familiar with the

---

[11] See THEODORE SILVERSTEIN, *Fabulous Cosmogony*, «Modern Philology», XLVI, 1948-
49, pp. 97-98. WINTHROP WETHERBEE, *Platonism and Poetry in the Twelfth Century*, Princeton,
Princeton University Press, 1972, pp. 94-98, 116-118.

works of Bernard Silvester and Guillaume de Conches. We not only have Boccaccio's transcription of Bernard Silvester's *Megacosmus et microcosmus*, but, as Giorgio Padoan has shown, Boccaccio knew Bernard Silvester's commentary on the first six books of the *Aeneid*, or a commentary which was based on that of Bernard. [12] The same is true for Guillaume de Conches' commentary on Boethius' *De consolatione philosophiae*: Boccaccio either knew it, or knew of a commentary which was very similar to it. [13] Boccaccio's familiarity with some of the most important works of this school suggests that he may have had the Chartrian notion of *ingenium* in mind when referring to *ingegno*.

In his commentary on the *Aeneid*, Bernard Silvester states: «In the brain there are three chambers which others call ventricles: in the anterior chamber is the exercise of wit; in the middle, the exercise of reason; in the posterior, the means of memory». [14] In the *Microscosmos* Bernardus says practically the same thing:

So too, following an inscrutable design, she encased the substance of the brain, which she had made soft and fluid, with a hard earthen casing. She had decided to employ a soft and transparent material in creating the brain, so that the images of things might impress themselves more easily upon it. Then, dividing the whole cavity of the skull into three chambers, she assigned these to the three functions of the soul. In the frontal chamber provision was made for imagination to receive the shapes of things, and transmit all that it beheld to the reason. Memory's chamber was set at the very back of the head, lest, dwelling at the threshold of perception, she should be troubled by a continual invasion of images. Reason dwelt between the two, to impose its firm judgment on the workings of the others. She also set the organs of sensory perception close about the palace of the head, that judging intellect might maintain close contact with the messenger senses. For as these are prone to many sorts of error, it is best that they should not be far removed from the seat of wisdom. [15]

The standard tripartite structure of the brain (*memoria, imaginatio* or *phantasia*, and *ratio* or *cogitatio*) originated with Galen and was later

---

[12] See GIORGIO PADOAN, *Tradizione e fortuna del commento all'«Eneide» di Bernardo Silvestre*, «Italia medievale e umanistica», II, 1960, pp. 235-6. See also GIOVANNI BOCCACCIO, *Esposizioni sopra la Comedia di Dante*, edited by Giorgio Padoan, Milan, Mondadori, 1965, («Tutte le opere di Giovanni Boccaccio», VI), p. 810.

[13] See ROBERT HOLLANDER, *op. cit.*, pp. 210-211.

[14] BERNARDUS SILVESTRIS, *Commentary on the First Six Books of Virgil's «Aeneid» by Bernardus Silvestris*, translated by Earl G. Schreiber and Thomas E. Maresca, Lincoln, University of Nebraska Press, 1980, p. 47.

[15] WINTHROP WETHERBEE, *The Cosmography of Bernardus Silvestris*, New York, Columbia University Press, 1973, p. 122.

adopted in Chartrian psychology.[16] As Theodore Silverstein and Winthrop Wetherbee have shown, the Chartrians (Bernardus Silvestris and Guillaume de Conches in particular) often substituted the first part (*imaginatio* or *phantasia*) for *ingenium*.[17] According to Wetherbee, Guillaume defines *ingenium* as a mental power which perceives things immediately.[18] Wetherbee adds that Guillaume identified *ingenium* with the natural desire Boethius says exists in all men for the *summum bonum*. Since man is free to look for the *summum bonum* in something that is moral or immoral, *ingenium* can be said to move either towards a moral good or an immoral one.[19] Guillaume's suggestive connection between *ingenium* and man's innate desire for God could be extended to include human desire in general. Though there is no evidence that Boccaccio actually identifies *ingegno* with *disio*, the two are interwoven in the narrative fabric of the *Filocolo*.[20]

By choosing to attain the object of his desire by means of his *ingegno* rather than by *prieghi* or by *forza*, Florio resorts to a faculty of the mind that makes him socially equal to all men. Furthermore, by

---

[16] This tripartite division of the brain is similar to Aquinas' four-part division of the «interior» sensitive powers: common sense, imagination, memory, and the estimative power. Aquinas not only collapses Avicenna's phantasy and imagination into one power, but he makes the estimative power the equivalent of the cogitative power, which he associates with practical reason, and reaffirms the belief of the «medical men» that it is located in middle part of the brain (*Summa Theologica* I, q. 78, art. 4). The fact that Boccaccio explicitly refers to the estimative power on several occasions suggests that he has combined both Thomistic (i.e. Aristotelian) and Chartrian (i.e. Platonic) vocabulary in his representation of the human mind.

[17] See SILVERSTEIN, *op. cit.*, pp. 97-98 and WETHERBEE, *Platonism and Poetry in the Twelfth Century*, pp. 96-98.

[18] See WETHERBEE, *op. cit.*, pp. 97.

[19] See WETHERBEE, *op. cit.*, pp. 98. This natural desire for God is often expressed in the love of a person or the desire for a terrestrial good, neither of which can give true satisfaction or complete contentment.

[20] There is evidence that Boccaccio associated *ingegno* with the tripartite division of the brain. In the introduction to his commentary on Dante's *Commedia* he says, «Se Platone confessa se, più che alcun altro, avere del divino aiuto bisogno, io che debbo di me presumere, conoscendo il mio intelletto tardo, lo 'ngegno piccolo e la memoria labile?» (*Esposizioni*, p. 1). Further on, in his commentary on Dante's famous verse «O muse, o alto ingegno, or m'aiutate» (*Inferno* II 7), Boccaccio defines *ingegno* as «è lo 'ngegno dell'uomo una forza intrinseca dell'animo per la quale noi spesse volte troviamo di nuovo quello che mai da alcuno non abbiamo apparato» II i, 35 (*Esposizioni*, p. 102). It is very similar to Francesco da Buti's commentary on the same verse «Ingegno, secondo Papia, è una virtù interiore d'animo per la quale l'uomo dà sé trova quello che dalli altri non ha imparato; e perchè l'autore trovava cose nuove, che mai da altrui non avea imparate, però dice: "o alto ingegno"»; see *Commento di Francesco da Buti sopra La Divina Comedia di Dante Allighieri*, I, ed. Crescentino Giannini, 1858, Pisa, Nistri Lischi Editori, 1989, p. 60. Their definition of *ingegno* is similar to Guillaume de Conches' definition of it in his *Glosae super Platonem*: «Ingenium est vis naturalis ad aliquid cito intelligendum unde dicitur ingenium quasi "intus genitum"» (Prologue IX).

changing his name from Florio to Filocolo, he not only assumes a name which suits him better (according to Florio's own interpretation, Filocolo is supposed to mean «love's labor»), but he also hides his noble pedigree and royal rank. [21] As a result, the means he chooses to attain his desired end does away with all social boundaries and class distinctions. By hiding his acquired nobility and exercising his *ingegno*, Florio (alias Filocolo) is putting his achieved nobility (i.e. his *probitas*) to the test. [22] In so doing, Florio would seem to be living up to the important courtly-love ideal which makes *probitas*, not lineage, the true mark of nobility. [23] A careful look at what follows, however, reveals that Florio never completely does away with his nobility of blood, nor are his amorous endeavors as noble as one might expect of a courtly lover.

After listening to Dario's counsel and after rationally deliberating which course of action to take, Florio freely chooses the means to the end his will desires (i.e. Biancifiore) in true Scholastic fashion. When Florio eventually implements his choice, however, all three courses of action take place in reverse order. Once he has completed the third course of action (using *ingegno* to befriend Sadoc and gain access to Biancifiore) the second course of action follows (Dario and Florio's six «compagni» attack the army guarding the tower) and finally, after the *agnitio*, Florio remarries Biancifiore with the Admiral's consent, thereby enacting the first and most appropriate course of action. Like Lelio's choice, Florio's original choice follows a course of its own, bringing him to his desired end in a way which he neither anticipated nor planned for. Florio's choices and the way they affect him are

---

[21] Much has been written on the incorrect meaning Florio gives to his alias: rather than «love's labor», Filocolo actually means «wrath of love». Critics have been prone to attribute this incorrect meaning to Boccaccio's poor knowledge of Greek. If we could assume, however, that Boccaccio actually knew the correct meaning of Filocolo in Greek, and that he deliberately had Florio misinterpret its meaning, then the protagonist's misinterpretation becomes quite ironic. Florio's assumed name reflects his own interpretation of his amorous experience: from his perspective it is a labor of love. From the author's perspective, however, Florio's experience is a destructive one, as we shall see. (For a complete bibliography on the issues raised by the name Filocolo, see BOCCACCIO, *Filocolo*, p. 842n.).

[22] *Ingegno* becomes the means by which any man can prove his worth. Boccaccio would not have found this connection between *ingenium* and *probitas* in Andreas; instead he might have gotten it from Seneca's *De Beneficiis* III 28 where such an association is made. Boccaccio may have also found it in the fourteenth-century Tuscan translation of Andreas' *De Amore* where *probitas* is translated as «senno» (a more appropriate translation of *ingenium* than of *probitas*).

[23] See ANDREA CAPPELLANO, *De Amore*, edited by Graziano Ruffini, Milan, Guanda, 1980, pp. 18-19.

consonant with the Boethian and Thomistic philosophies at work throughout the *Filocolo*.

The fact that his chosen course of action should result in such an unusual sequence of events is best explained by the fact that Florio has become a slave of his passions. His innate desire for the *summum bonum* (or Aquinas's *beatitudo*) has translated itself into concupiscence, and his will is moved to action more as a result of his desire for Biancifiore than a concern for her well-being. Throughout the episode, in fact, Florio never thinks about rescuing Biancifiore, only about how he can consummate his love, regardless of the consequences to both him and her. It is not surprising, therefore, that the events which result from his chosen course of action are so remote from anything he and his companions had expected: the motives behind Florio's deeds are wrong and therefore far from the divine mind Boethius speaks about in the *De consolatione*. The fact that this important episode ends with the Admiral asking Florio to remarry Biancifiore in the presence of all his people, suggests that the right course of action (the first of the three mentioned above) eventually prevails. It would seem, therefore, that for Boccaccio there is such a thing as a right or wrong choice, and that the latter never precludes the former from coming about. [24] Boccaccio thus strikes a balance between free choice and determinism.

Boccaccio's illustration of means versus ends, free choice versus determinism, does not end here. After agreeing with Dario and the six barons on the means to adopt to fulfill his desired end, Florio begins to have second thoughts about his original endeavor. Boccaccio portrays the competing thoughts which take place in the protagonist's mind as a classical *psychomachy*. If the preceding chapters (81-87) focused on the means to the end, these subsequent chapters (88-91) focus on the end itself and Florio's vacillating will. Florio's inaction is not new; Boccaccio has already given examples of it in II 26 and III 7. What is new, instead, is Florio's awareness of his love madness, «né ancora ha alcuna volta ne' suoi pensieri conosciuti i suoi folli disii come ora conosce» (88, 3). [25] This new self-awareness, however, is

---

[24] A similar philosophy seems to be echoed in the *Amorosa visione*. In it the narrator as lover comes to a crossroad and chooses the wrong path. As Robert Hollander has shown, the protagonist's wrong choice becomes a learning experience which eventually brings about a conversion in the lover. See HOLLANDER, *op. cit.*, pp. 86-87.

[25] Florio himself will confess to «la mia lunga follia» (V 75, 5) after his conversion to Christianity.

limited to only the dangers which *he* might incur: he fails to realize that Biancifiore too runs the same risks.

Florio's moment of hesitation has a model in the courtly-love literature of the time. In Chrétien de Troyes' *Le Chevalier de la Charrete* Lancelot hesitates before taking the socially unacceptable ride in a peasant's cart. Since the cart is the only means of transportation which will bring him to his beloved Guinevere, Lancelot swallows his pride and accepts the demeaning ride. After making love to Guinevere in the tower where she is held captive, Lancelot is reprimanded by her for his moment of hesitation. A similar moment of recrimination takes place after Florio and Biancifiore have consummated their love affair in the tower (Biancifiore's prison). But instead of one lover reprimanding the other for his or her uncertainty, the two lovers reprimand themselves for following their concupiscence at the expense of their beloved's well-being. The protagonists' recriminations are an indictment of their own courtly love and of the code of conduct by which courtly lovers live.

Remaining within the courtly-love tradition, the *psychomachy* also recalls the debate between Caleone and Fiammetta as well as the debate between the Lover and Reason in the *Roman de la Rose* (4191-7200). [26] Like the Lover's desire in the *Roman*, Florio's desire for Biancifiore also wins over his reason. The *psychomachy*, in fact, comes to an end when Florio has a vision of Biancifiore in the arms of Venus: it is only then that he reaffirms his original decision to befriend Sadoc. [27]

What follows this vision, however, is a period of «ozio» typical of courtly lovers. The fact that Florio continues to delay any attempt at befriending Sadoc suggests that both the *psychomachy* and Florio's vision of Venus did little to move him to action. According to

---

[26] I am grateful to Janet Smarr for bringing to my attention the similarities between the *Roman de la Rose* and Book IV of the *Filocolo*. For a more detailed study of the inter-textuality between the *Roman* and the *Filocolo*, see DAVID WALLACE, *Chaucer and the Early Writings of Boccaccio*, Suffolk, D. S. Brewer, 1985, pp. 39-72.

[27] The fact that Florio's estimative power is alluded to during the *psychomachy* (IV 88, 2) suggests that we can also view the protagonist's thought-processes from an Aristotelian and Thomistic perspective. The fact that Florio hesitates on account of his «paura» suggests that the *psychomachy* is a conflict between his appetites. Whereas his desire to enter the tower and be with Biancifiore is the product of his concupiscible appetite, the fear of the evil which may result from this enterprise is the product of his irascible appetite. Consequently, after listening to Dario's counsel, after rationally deliberating on which means to adopt in order to attain his desired end, and after electing the means to reach that end, Florio's sensitive appetites begin to sway his intellectual appetite (i.e. his will) in a direction which does not correspond to the one

Aquinas, in every human act the will is directed towards an end apprehended by reason, and the actual deed must procede from an interior act of the will. What we have in Florio's case is an interior act of the will without the exterior deed issuing from it. [28] Ironically, when Florio finally acts, the exterior deed does not proceed from an interior act of the will. Instead, Florio is moved to action by an impulse which results from the sight of Biancifiore looking from a window in the tower (a typical courtly-love setting):

Per che tanto il disio gli crebbe di vederla più da presso e d'adempiere ciò che proposto aveva, che, abandonate insieme le redine del cavallo con quelle della sua volontà, disse: − Certo, se io dovessi morire, poi che io non posso te avere, o Biancifiore, e' converrà che io il luogo ove tu dimori abbracci per tuo amore − . E in questo proponimento col cavallo correndo infino al piè della torre se n'andò: dove disceso con le braccia aperte s'ingegnava d'abbracciare le mura, quelle baciando infinite fiate, e quasi nell'animo di ciò che faceva si sentiva diletto. (91, 1-2) [29]

Boccaccio explicitly associates the bridle on the horse with the symbolic bridle of Florio's will («volontà»), the very same bridle which kept Florio from going through with his original plan. [30] From a Thomistic perspective, Florio's act is an «actus hominis» (a reflex act) as opposed to an «actus humani» (a carefully deliberated choice proceeding from the will and reason, as in the choice he made after his deliberation with Dario). [31] Here too, as in the *psychomachy*, the concupiscible appetite wins over Florio's fear of evil (in his irascible appetite) and his will («volontà»). [32]

---

originally suggested by his intellect and reason. It is only when Florio has his vision of Venus holding Biancifiore in her arms that his concupiscible appetite eventually prevails. This vision underscores the erotic drive behind Florio's actions.

[28] For a discussion of this in Aquinas, see COPLESTON, *op. cit.*, p. 201.

[29] The five chapters which describe Florio and Sadoc's sudden introduction (IV 91-95) fill only two pages in Quaglio's critical edition. Their brevity corresponds to the quicker pace of the narrative during this dramatic event: action is being narrated without any attention to descriptive details. Here, as elsewhere in the *Filocolo*, the length of a set of chapters often determines the pace of the narrative itself.

[30] Florio's unbridled will echoes Biancifiore's «isfrenata volontà» in II 18, 10. This image of the soul (whose rider is reason and whose horses are the appetites) can be found in Andreas Capellanus: «Asseris te namque novum amoris militem novaque ipsius sauciatum sagitta illius nescire apte gubernare frena caballi nec ullum posse tibi remedium invenire»; see ANDREA CAPPELLANO, *op. cit.*, p. 4. It is also found in *Purgatorio* VI 88, where the image is applied to Italy (a horse without a rider).

[31] See AQUINAS, *Summa Theologica*, Ia, IIae, 1, 1.

[32] This dramatic moment recalls a similar episode in II 26, 19-21 when Florio sneaks from

In the events which lead up to this dramatic moment, the narrator blames fortune's «diversi atti e modi» for Florio's procrastination (90, 1). As we have seen, however, Florio's reason for not implementing his chosen course of action has more to do with his «volontà» than with *fortuna*. Rather than take the initiative himself and make a concerted effort to befriend Sadoc, Florio allows an «actus hominis» (i.e. his concupiscible impulse) to bring him to Sadoc. Later that day, when Dario asks him where he has been, Florio answers «nelle mani della fortuna» (98, 2), alluding to his seemingly fortuitous encounter with Sadoc. By having both Florio and the shortsighted narrator attribute these actions to *fortuna*, Boccaccio shows what an easy excuse fortune becomes for failure. As we soon find out, Florio's misadventures in Alexandria are entirely due to his passion. By implicitly criticizing Florio's amorous conduct, Boccaccio is criticizing those traditional courtly qualities (*ozio, dilatio, amor per diletto*, etc.) that make a lover the victim of *fortuna*.[33]

II. Florio as *homo ludens*

The psychological interplay of the appetites extends itself to the other characters as they become directly involved in Florio's endeavor. This is particularly true for Sadoc, as we can see when he and Florio meet for the first time:

con una mazza ferrata in mano gli sopravenne crucciato molto e pieno d'ira; e quasi furioso nol corse a ferire, dicendo: — Ahi, villano giovane, e oltre al dovere ardito, vago più di vituperevole morte che di laudevole vita, quale arroganza t'ha tanto sospinto avanti, che in mia presenza alla torre ti sia appropinquato? Io non so quale iddio delle mie mani la tua vita ha campata: tirati indietro, villano! — (92, 12)

The words «crucciato», «ira», and «furioso» clearly indicate that Sadoc is as dominated by his irascible appetite as Florio is by his concupiscible appetite. As a eunuch, Sadoc is unable to be affected by concupis-

Montoro to Verona, and kisses the palace doors that separate him from Biancifiore. At that time he feared Felice's wrath much as he now fears Sadoc's ire. In both episodes Florio's deed is depicted as a foolish act, one which underscores the ambiguous power love has over him.
[33] For the nexus between courtly lovers and the goddess Fortuna, see HOWARD R. PATCH, *The Goddess Fortuna in Medieval Literature*, Cambridge, Harvard University Press, 1927, pp. 99.

cence; and as the man in charge of defending the Admiral's most prized possessions (the one hundred virgins locked in the tower), his irascibility is easily aroused when he fears that evil may come to him or the tower. He is the mirror image of Florio, whose fear of evil seems to have disappeared completely in this moment of concupiscible rapture. [34]

Nevertheless, Florio is able to appease Sadoc's wrath with the same eloquence he has used thus far to win the support of the other people he has met on his journey to Biancifiore. Speaking as only a nobleman of Andreas Capellanus' higher nobility can, Florio lets Sadoc know that he is not a «villano»: «E avendo il castellano le belle maniere di Filocolo vedute, imagino lui dovere essere nobile giovane. Per la qual cosa quivi assai l'onorò [...]» (95, 1). Once invited inside the tower, Florio points to a beautiful chess set and lures Sadoc into playing several games with him. As we already know from Dario's portrayal of Sadoc, chess is the eunuch's favorite game, and the money he wins playing it is his greatest weakness. For in addition to being irascible, Sadoc is a man of cupidity. In order to gain access to Biancifiore, Florio attempts to win Sadoc's friendship by allowing him to win all three games and, with each game, a large amount of money. Florio's largesse, a trait common to courtly lovers, is in net contrast to the eunuch's cupidity. The gold, however, is the same gold Felice received from the Italian merchants when he sold them Biancifiore; the fact that Florio is using it to buy back Biancifiore undercuts his largesse. Florio's deceptive use of largesse as the means to his desired end (Biancifiore) adds to the ambiguity of his courtly conduct.

Sadoc, on the other hand, attempts to get from Florio the object of his greatest desire – the gold. Sadoc's love of gold is a sensual one, as we see when Parmenione, Florio's friend, gives the eunuch a «coppa» full of gold coins:

Parmenione [...] nelle sue mani recò la bellissima coppa e grande d'oro [...] e quella piena di bisanti d'oro [...] coperta con uno sottilissimo velo, davanti Sadoc la presentò, dicendo: – Bel signore, quel giovane al quale voi ieri per vostra benignità la vita servaste [...] questa coppa con questi frutti che dentro ci sono [...] vi presenta [...] Vedendo questo Sadoc, e ascoltando le parole da Parmenione

---

[34] If, as Aquinas states, the irascible is a fear of evil and a hope for good, then the desire to avoid what is harmful would probably be expressed by the irascible appetite.

dette, tutto rimase allenito e con cupido occhio rimirò quella, nel cuore lieto di tal presente. (99, 2-3)

The words «sottilissimo velo» appear a number of times in the *Filocolo* in contexts which vividly recall Beatrice's transparent veil in Dante's first dream of the *Vita nuova*. This and the pun on «cupido» suggest that Sadoc has sublimated sexual desire into a love for money. [35] Sadoc's sublimation is all the more compelling when we consider that he is a eunuch, and that money is also sterile. Medieval theologians considered usury a sin because money could not bear fruit: money was supposed to be a means of exchange, not one of procreation and multiplication. [36] The sterility of the «bisanti» is drawn to our attention by Parmenione's ironic use of the word «frutti». Parmenione in fact brings the goblet full of gold coins at a moment in the meal when fruit would ordinarily be served («con ciò fosse cosa che altro non restasse al levare delle tavole se non le frutta» 99,1). The sterile «fruit» from Florio's native land is more pleasing to Sadoc than the real fruit they were about to eat: it is the perfect gift for this eunuch.

Juxtaposed to Sadoc's sterile love of gold is Florio's concupiscence, the gratification of which lies in a person of flesh and blood, and the fruit of which will be a son (Lelio). At this point in the narrative, however, each chess player possesses the most cherished object of the other. They eventually succeed in exchanging «desired objects» through the mediation of the chess games. The chess games, therefore, mediate their desire by functioning as the means to each player's well-established end, while at the same time mitigating that desire. [37] Because in addition to being a *remedia amoris* for the melancholic lover, chess also obliges each player to exercise his intellect rather than his appetites. [38]

---

[35] Both the adjective for cupidity and the noun for Cupid are spelled the same way and share the same Latin etymology, «cupere».

[36] See JOHN THOMAS NOONAN, *The Scholastic Analysis of Usury*, Cambridge, Harvard University Press, 1957, pp. 38-60.

[37] My analysis of mediated desire in the *Filocolo* owes much to René Girard's seminal study *Deceit, Desire, and the Novel: Self and Other in Literary Structure*, trans. Yvonne Freccero, Baltimore, The Johns Hopkins Press, 1965, pp. 1-54 in particular.

[38] The nexus between chess and love is quite common in medieval literature, see MERRITT R. BLAKESLEE, *Lo dous jocx sotils: La partie d'échecs amoureuse dans la la poésie des troubadours*, «Cahiers de civilization médiévale», XXVIII, 1985, pp. 213-222. The nexus between chess and the irascible appetite is also common: the game was often referred to as «scacchi alla rabbiosa» due to the violent reaction of defeated players like Sadoc. For chess as a *remedia amoris*, see MAZZOTTA, *The World at Play in the Decameron*, pp. 32-34.

The chess games also function as a narrative device which reveals the other games Florio and Sadoc are playing with each other. The chess pieces and all their movements on the board, which Boccaccio goes to great lengths to describe, are a miniature model of the various individuals Florio must overcome before he can win the main «game» he has set out to play — the consummation of his love for Biancifiore. The pieces most often mentioned are the «rocco» (rook) which, of course, is the well-guarded tower, the «cavaliere» (knight) representing the Admiral of Alexandria, and the «alfino» (standard bearer, or bishop in English) representing Sadoc. There are also several «pedoni» (pawns) or foot soldiers guarding the tower. The «re» (king), the most important piece in the game and one of the strongest pieces in medieval chess, represents the Sultan of Babylon who will receive Biancifiore as tribute paid by the Admiral. The queen, the weakest piece in medieval chess, is the only piece that is not mentioned in Boccaccio's elaborate description of the three chess games. Like the queen, Biancifiore too is the weakest piece in this game because she has no say in it; and yet her future status depends entirely on how well Florio plays these various games. [39] If he loses (i.e. fails to win Sadoc over), Biancifiore will inevitably become one of the Sultan's consorts (his «queen»). If, on the other hand, Florio wins, she will become his wife and, eventually, a real queen. Boccaccio's omission of any allusion to the chess queen underscores Biancifiore's absence as a player in the larger «chess» game Florio is playing with Sadoc. She is, as it were, a pawn. [40]

Besides mediating the players' desires, and reflecting the other games in which Florio is engaged, the chess games also function as a medium through which Florio and Sadoc can communicate. This is particularly true of Florio who must win Sadoc's friendship to such a

---

[39] In 14th century chess the queen was the weakest piece, being able to move only one square diagonally. The bishop and pawn were also very weak pieces. The king, rook, and knight, however, were the strongest pieces: each was able to move two or three spaces.

[40] The most popular chess treatise in the Middle Ages, and the first work ever to be printed in the English language, was Jacobus de Cessolis' *De Ludo Scaccorum* which, more than being a guide to playing chess, is a thirteenth century allegory of the hierarchic structure of the social classes in the Middle Ages. Caxton's *Game and Playe of the Chesse* was first printed in 1474. It was based on an Old French translation of Jacobus' Latin text. A fourteenth-century Tuscan translation of this work survives and seems to have been popular. We do not know if Boccaccio knew this treatise, but it is obvious that he is using the game of chess in the same socio-allegorical manner. See the introduction to the *Volgarizzamento del libro de' costumi e degli offizii de' nobili sopra il giuoco degli scacchi*, edited by Pietro Marocco, Milan, Ferrario, 1829.

degree that Sadoc will be prepared to betray the Admiral's great trust in him. Here, as elsewhere in his quest for Biancifiore, Florio accomplishes this by revealing his noble birth. Sadoc, who understands Florio's hidden messages, can either acknowledge them or pretend that he is not aware of them. For example, in the first game we are told that Florio can checkmate Sadoc with his knight, but chooses instead to move his rook on the only square left for his king to escape to, thereby allowing Sadoc to checkmate him instead. Sadoc, aware of Florio's mistake, wins both the game and the pile of gold, and tells his opponent: « – Giovane, tu non sai del giuoco – , avvegna che ben s'era aveduto di ciò che Filocolo avea fatto, ma per cupidigia de' bisanti l'avea sofferto, infignendosi di non avedersene». The narrator tells us that Sadoc pretended not to be aware of what Florio had done; Florio, however, has no way of knowing this for sure, and so he is more explicit in the second game: «e avendo quasi a fine recato il giuoco, e essendo per mattare il castellano, mostrando con alcuno atto di ciò avvedersi, tavolò il giuoco». This time Sadoc cannot pretend that he did not catch Florio's message, and is forced to acknowledge it in some way:

Conosce in se medesimo il castellano la cortesia di Filocolo, il quale più tosto perdere che vincere disidera, e fra sé dice: – Nobilissimo giovane e cortese è costui più che alcuno ch'io mai ne vedessi – . Racconciansi gli scacchi al terzo giuoco [...] nel principio del quale il castellano disse a Filocolo: – Giovane, io ti priego e scongiuro per la potenza de' tuoi iddi, che tu giuochi come tu sai il meglio, né, come hai infino a qui fatto, non mi risparmiare – .

Since games can channel reprehensible social conduct into acceptable forms of behavior, these three chess games have become for Sadoc a way of indulging his greed without having to excuse himself for it. At this point in the game, however, he cannot continue doing so without exposing himself. He knows that if he does not acknowledge Florio's gesture, it will become obvious that he is simply playing for the gold.

The third and final game is a reversal of the second one:

Cominciasi a crucciare e a tignersi nel viso, e assottigliarsi se potesse il giuoco per maestria recuperare. E quanto più giuoca, tanto n'ha il peggiore. Filocolo gli leva con uno alfino il cavaliere, e dagli scacco rocco. Il castellano, per questo tratto crucciato oltre misura più per la perdenza de' bisanti che del giuoco, diè delle mani negli scacchi, e quelli e lo scacchiere gittò per terra. Questo vedendo Filocolo disse: – Signor mio, però che usanza è de' più savi il crucciarsi a questo giuoco, però voi men savio non reputo, perché contro gli scacchi crucciato siate. Ma se voi aveste bene riguardato il giuoco, prima che guastatolo, voi avreste conosciuto che io era in due tratti matto da voi. Credo che 'l vedeste, ma per essermi cortese, mostrandovi crucciato, volete avere il giuoco perduto, ma ciò non fia così: questi bisanti sono tutti vostri. – E mostrando di volere i suoi adeguare alla quantità di quelli del castellano, ben tre tanti ve ne mise de' suoi, i quali il castellano, mostrando d'intendere ad altre parole, gli prese dicendo: – Giovane, io ti giuro per l'anima del mio padre, che io ho de' miei giorni con molti giucato, ma mai non trovai chi a questo giuoco mi mattasse se non tu, né similmente più cortese giovane di te trovai ne' giorni miei. – (96, 8-11)

Sadoc does what Florio did in the previous game, and Florio says what Sadoc should have said when Florio tabled that game. Florio is deliberately projecting himself on Sadoc so as to make the eunuch fully aware of his intentions. Here too Florio is expressing himself through a mediating sphere: he is acknowledging his own «cortesia» by projecting it on Sadoc's less than courteous gesture. Besides making sure that Sadoc is aware of what the young lover is doing, Florio's behavior is also meant to elicit Sadoc's admiration so that when the eunuch finds out what Florio really wants from him, he will not react as he does when he loses. The danger that Sadoc's irascibility poses to Florio's concupiscible enterprise is suggested by the chess pieces themselves: after removing the «cavaliere» from the board with an «alfino», Florio puts his opponent's «rocco» in check. In other words, with the help of Sadoc (the «alfino») Florio plans to bypass the Admiral (the «cavaliere») and attack the tower (the «rocco»). The chess game ends with Sadoc's violent gesture which foreshadows the violent consequences of Florio's penetration of the tower walls.

If the most characteristic feature of Florio and Sadoc's first encounter is the way they communicate to each other through a mediating sphere, the same holds true for their second meeting. It is during this meeting that Parmenione enters with the golden vase filled with sterile «frutti». It is obvious that Parmenione came with the right object at the right time because Florio so instructed him in advance. During the short verbal exchange between Sadoc and Parmenione, the latter speaks on behalf of Florio, and Sadoc expresses his thanks to Florio through Parmenione. Both Sadoc and Parmenione communicate as if Florio were not present. This continuously mediated communication sets the stage for the greater act of mediation which follows.

It is, in fact, after the third chess game that Florio stops playing games, as it were, and asks Sadoc to become his go-between, the mediator of his desire. [41] Even though Sadoc never considers Florio's gold as payment for his services, his role is very much that of a procurer: it is only through Sadoc that Florio can gain access to Biancifiore. Biancifiore, in fact, is still an object that can be bought: her status as such has not changed since she was sold by Felice. (Sadoc's mediation, in fact, is bought with the very same gold with which Biancifiore had been bought in Verona.) Later, when the Admiral catches her in bed with Florio, he calls her a whore and sentences both her and Florio to die at the stake. Although Biancifiore is not a prostitute, she is practically treated like one by both Florio and Sadoc during their transactions. This further underscores the less than courtly nature of these *échecs amoureuse*.

Sadoc eventually agrees to help Florio for reasons which have little to do with his avarice. The eunuch helps the young lover because he is inspired by Florio's «nobiltà». Aware of the fact that he is old and has little to lose if he gets caught, Sadoc decides to engage in Florio's dangerous enterprise in order to do something which will immortalize him after he dies. Sadoc's concept of immortality, like his understanding of «nobiltà», is very limited: he does not hope for eternal glory in a hereafter, but rather an immortality in human time. Likewise, the nobility which he sees in Florio and which inspires him to undertake Florio's cause is superficial. It is based on Florio's great wealth, courtesy, and education, all of which are associated with his class (i.e. «nobiltà di sangue») not with his *probitas*. This is most evident in Sadoc's appreciation of Florio: when Florio forfeits the chess games, Sadoc tells him, «né similmente più cortese giovane di te trovai ne' giorni miei». Earlier, the narrator said: «conosce in sé medesimo il castellano la cortesia di Filocolo, il quale più tosto perdere che vincere desidera, e fra sé dice: — Nobilissimo giovan e cortese è costui più che alcuno ch'io vedessi — » (96, 6). Later, after Parmenione has left, Sadoc tells Florio:

---

[41] The scene is very similar to one in the *Filostrato* in which Troiolo cleverly has Pandaro beg him to reveal his love sorrows. In both books the lover skillfully manipulates his interlocutor in order to bring about the consummation of his love affair. It is evident from Boccaccio's creation of these two literary go-betweens that he is interested in the various aspects of mediated desire.

– Giovane, per quella fé che tu dei agl'iddii e per l'amore che tu porti a me, aprimisi la tua nobiltà acciò che io, di quella pigliando essemplo, possa nobile divenire. Io vidi già ne' miei dì molti nobili uomini, che per antico sangue, chi per infiniti tesori, che per be' costumi, e chi per una maniera e chi per un'altra; ma e' non mi soviene che io mai così nobile cosa, come tu se', vedessi.

Florio replies with a certain amount of false modesty:

Signor mio, non vogliate me rozzo ancora ne' costumi con queste parole scherni-re. Io non seguo nobiltà di cuore in queste operazioni, però che non ci è, che io sono di piccola radice pianta, ma ricordomi d'avere già così veduto fare a mio padre, i cui essempli io seguito: e similmente conosco che io non potrei mai fare tanto che alla vostra nobiltà aggiugner potessi, o che d'onore a quella più non si convenisse. (101, 3)

As the sole heir of the most powerful king in Europe, Florio is everything but «di piccola radice pianta». There is, nevertheless, a certain amount of unintended truth in his false modesty. Throughout their meetings, Florio has done nothing which might be associated with «nobiltà di cuore» or *probitas*. Instead, Florio is actually imitating his father's ignoble behavior: he is deceiving Sadoc with the same gold King Felice received from the merchants when he deceived Florio and made him believe that Biancifiore was dead. Furthermore, Florio's actions are about to place Biancifiore exactly where Felice placed her in Book II – condemned to die at the stake. Although their motives are different, both father and son hide their less than noble conduct behind the mask of their inherited nobility.

For Sadoc, the facade which Florio projects is the epitome of «nobiltà». He is unable to distinguish between it and *probitas*, and is therefore unable to see through Florio. Sadoc's superficial understand-ing of «nobiltà» reflects the sterile nature of acquired nobility, as well as the eunuch's own spiritual sterility. Sadoc is, in this respect, very similar to the Pardoner in Chaucer's *Canterbury Tales*. Besides being eunuchs, both characters are filled with «cupiditas». Like Chaucer's Pardoner, Sadoc too excels in «multiplicationes terrenae», because, as Robert P. Miller has shown, the spiritually sterile excel in the increase of earthly treasure. [42] Sadoc also shares the Pardoner's inability to

---

[42] ROBERT P. MILLER, *Chaucer's Pardoner, The Spiritual Eunuch, and the Pardoner's Tale*, in *Chaucer Criticism: The Canterbury Tales*, Notre Dame, Notre Dame University Press, 1960, pp. 221-244.

distinguish between spiritual and material values. [43] In Sadoc's case it is an inability to distinguish between *probitas* and the facade of «nobiltà» which Florio has shown him. It is only when Florio removes this mask that Sadoc realizes that what Florio really has is «sottile ingegno». [44] *Ingegno* thus prevails over inherited nobility, but not as the traditional courtly means of enhancing Florio's *probitas*.

If the chess games reveal Sadoc's true nature and Biancifiore's true condition, they also reveal Florio's true character. As a model *homo ludens*, Florio is both a master of disguise and a master of all the games he plays during his Alexandrian adventures. The ambiguity of these games, like that of his noble facade, undercuts the courtly ideals he uses to get Biancifiore. As a young man of «sottile ingegno», he is the prototype of the more famous tricksters and manipulators Boccaccio will portray in the *Decameron*. The chess games, therefore, are not simply part of the *Filocolo's* extended debate on love and nobility, they are also an analysis of seduction and corruption. [45]

III. *Avventura e Fortuna*

When Sadoc attempts to pry loose Florio's secret in the ensuing chapters, he is confronted with one of the protagonist's moments of fear and doubt. [46] Florio's reluctance to tell Sadoc the truth echoes Troiolo's reluctance in the *Filostrato* to tell Pandaro that he is in love with Criseida. However, unlike Troiolo, who has cleverly made Pan-

---

[43] The move from *cupiditas* to *caritas* will eventually be made after the consummation scene when the protagonists disavow their sexual cupidity and discover Christian charity. By the same token, the classical and pagan ideas of immortality which Sadoc believes in will give way to a Christian understanding of immortality.

[44] When Florio was at Fiammetta's court of love, he said that his beloved was taken from him by means of «sottile ingegno» (IV 76, 5). The fact that he uses «sottile ingegno» to get her back, further reflects the similarities between father and son.

[45] Florio's actions towards Sadoc and all the people he meets on his quest for Biancifiore can be seen as attempts to «corrupt» and/or «seduce» the obstacles that stand between him and Biancifiore. That same «corruption» and/or «seduction» will also be applied to Biancifiore when Glorizia sets her up for Florio's surprise visit. The corrupting of courtly ideals takes place even during the consummation scene which, despite its sexual innocence, reveals a certain amount of manipulation on the part of both Florio, who wishes to consummate their love immediately, and Biancifiore, who wants to get married before doing anything.

[46] As Branca has shown in his critical edition of the *Decameron*, the verb «dubitare» is synonymous with «temere» (Intro., 55; I 1, 27; II 1, 20; II 4, 22; II 5, 70; etc.), whereas the noun «dubbio» is often synonymous with «pericolo» (II 3, 17) and the adjective «dubbioso» with «pericoloso» (II 2, 3). See BRANCA, *Decameron*, p. 1281.

daro beg him to reveal the name of his beloved, Florio is actually afraid to tell Sadoc the truth. [47] Florio finally gives in to Sadoc's request when he recalls, by chance, a proverb:

Filocolo, così incalciato, e più ognora dubitando, per avventura si ricordò d'un verso già da lui letto in Ovidio, ove i paurosi dispregia dicendo: 'La fortuna aiuta gli audaci, e i timidi caccia via'; e vedendo manifestamente che tra lui e la fine del suo disio era questo in mezzo e che parlare gli convenia s'egli servigio volea ricevere, allargò le forze al desiderante cuore, e propose di dare via alle parole [...] (101, 8)

Similar proverbs can be found in Ovid's *Metamorphosis*, X 586 and Virgil's *Aeneid*, X 284. [48] By attributing this proverb to Ovid, Boccaccio is reminding his readers of the poet's strong influence on the protagonists. [49] Since the works on which the protagonists were raised («il santo libro d'Ovidio» I 45, 6) also served as sources for medieval love treatises and courtly romances, it is not surprising that Florio falls back on the ultimate *auctoritas* for matters of love, albeit pagan love.

Once again, it is «per avventura» that Florio breaks the impasse brought about by his fear. [50] This time, however, it is *memoria* (not *ingegno* or an *actus hominis*) which rids him of his fears. The seemingly fortuitous nature of his entire enterprise and of his decision to open up to Sadoc is underscored by his concluding remark: «Io nelle vostre mani e della fortuna la mia vita rimetto» (102, 3). [51] It is here that Sadoc says to himself, «io sono omai vecchio, ne mai notabil cosa per alcuno feci: ora nella fine de' miei anni, in servigio di sì nobile giovane come costui è, voglio il rimanente della mia vita mettere in avventura» (103, 2). Like Florio, Sadoc too decides to put his life in the hands of *fortuna*, but the word he uses is *avventura*. His words recall those of Ascalion to Florio in II 44, 14 when the experienced old knight asked

---

[47] From the perspective of the *Filostrato* one might be tempted to say that Florio's hesitation and uncertainty are a clever ploy to make his interlocutor force him into revealing something reprehensible. It is clear, however, from what Boccaccio has shown us thus far that Florio is still plagued by many doubts.

[48] PATCH, *op. cit.*, p. 83.

[49] Ovid is the only poet the protagonists refer to by name.

[50] Besides its use in the events which lead up to the encounter between Florio and Sadoc, the words «per avventura» appear in the other seduction scene (III 11, 10) when Edea, who has carefully calculated all her moves, begins to work on Florio in the same deceptive way that Florio works on Sadoc.

[51] This remark recalls the one Florio made to Dario after his first encounter with the eunuch (98, 2). This is just one of several remarks which recall Florio's discussion with Dario.

the inexperienced bachelor if he was prepared to put his life «in avventura» in order save Biancifiore from the stake. The similarities between these two episodes are not fortuitous: Sadoc the eunuch has now become, amusingly enough, Florio's surrogate father much the same way Ascalion had been during the rescue episode («E sì come il tenero padre i suoi figliuoli ammonisce e insegna, così Ascalion dicea a Florio» II 45, 4). Although Sadoc has not dedicated his life to Mars as Ascalion has done, he does have an irascible disposition associated with the Martian god. [52] These ambiguous similarities anticipate the similarly ambiguous course Florio's new adventure will take.

Besides its modern meaning of adventure, the word *avventura* is often synonymous with *fortuna* in fourteenth-century vernacular literature. [53] (This is particularly true in Old French, Middle English, and Italian romances.) By risking his life in adventures, the protagonist of the chivalric romances could prove his valor by facing the unknown. *Avventura* implies not knowing the future (*avvenire*): the protagonist never knows what comes next (*advenire* or *ad venire*). He is constantly faced with the uncertainty of the outside world and, in the best romances, with the uncertainties within himself. *Avventura*, therefore, was a way of actively coming to grips with *fortuna* by testing one's *probitas*. In Florio's case, however, his adventure in Alexandria undermines his *probitas* because passion has allowed *fortuna* to rule over him.

Florio's fears (*dubitare*) are directly associated with the dangerous (*dubbioso*) nature of his *avventura*. Sadoc's own remarks suggest that this adventure is dangerous:

Se a te dà il cuore di metterti a tanta *ventura*, io mi sono ricordato che di qui a pochi giorni in queste parti si celebra una festa grandissima, la quale noi chiamiamo de' cavalieri. In quel giorno i templi di Marte e di Venere sono visitati con fiori e con frondi e con maravigliosa allegrezza: il quale giorno io avrò fatto per li vicini paesi le rose e' fiori tutti cogliere, e in tante ceste porre, quante damigelle nella torre dimorano; e guardole in questo prato davanti al torre, dove l'amiraglio coronato e vestito di reali drappi con grandissima compagnia viene, e di ciascuna cesta prende rose con mano a suo piacere, e secondo che egli comanda, così poi le collo sopra la torre, faccendo chiamare quella a cui che data sia. E però che la tua Biancifiore la più bella è di tutte, sempre prima che alcuna

---

[52] Ascalion tells Fiammetta «che più ne' servigi di Marte che in quelli di Venere avea i suoi anni spesi» (IV 17, 7).
[53] See PATCH, *op. cit.*, pp. 39-41; and SURDICH, *op. cit.*, pp. 68-69.

altra è presentata, io ti porrò, se tu vuoi, in questa cesta che a Biancifiore presentare si dee, e coprirotti di rose e di fiori quando meglio si potrà. Ma s'egli *avvenisse* che la fortuna, nimica de' nostri avvisi, ti scoprisse e facesseti al signore vedere, niuna redenzione saria alla nostra vita. Vedi omai il pericolo: pensa quello che da fare ti pare. Se egli non se n'avvedrà, tu potrai con lei essere alquanti giorni: poi *s'avviene* che esso alcuna volta, si come egli suole spesso a mangiare salirvi, vi salga, in forma d'uno de' miei sergenti te ne trarrò. Altra via nulla ci è [...] Filocolo, pieno d'ardente disio, a niuno pericolo, a niuna strabocchevole cosa che *avvenire* possa, pensa, ma subito risponde che egli a questo pericolo e ad ogni maggiore che *avvenire* potesse è presto, affermando che per grandissimi pericoli e affanni si convenga pervenire all'alte cose. (IV 104, 3-7) [54]

Besides the repeated use of the verb *avvenire*, Sadoc also uses the same words Dario used to indicate the rash nature of Florio's conduct («strabocchevola cosa»). [55] Sadoc's concluding remark, «Altra via nulla ci è», recalls Dario's concluding remark after he had told Florio what courses of action were available to him. It also suggests that there is a better course of action which has not been considered (i.e. freeing Biancifiore and Glorizia from the tower). Sadoc's plan, like Dario's, is based on assumptions which will prove to be incorrect. As in Dario's plan, no consideration is given to Biancifiore's fate; consequently, this plan too is vulnerable to the future (*avvenire*) and to *fortuna*. [56]

IV. The Concealment of Desire

Besides illustrating the negative aspects of Florio's enterprise, Sadoc's long speech to Florio also describes the setting in which the consummation scene will take place. The «festa [...] de' cavalieri»,

---

[54] The italics in all the quotations from the *Filocolo* are my own.
[55] Dario uses these words in his prayer to Venus: «Tempera i fuochi tuoi nelle umane menti, acciò che per soverchio del tuo valore non si mettano alle strabocchevole cose!» (83, 1). He obviously has Florio in mind when he says this. The concept is similar to Roland's «desmesure» in *La Chanson de Roland*.
[56] The long conversation between Florio and Sadoc, which sets the stage for the consummation scene, reappears in the *Elegia di Madonna Fiammetta* in an abridged form. In this later work the protagonist narrates the consummation of her love affair with Panfilo in a single veiled sentence: «Esso adunque, in ciò poco alle mie parole credevole, luogo e tempo convenevole riguardato, più in ciò che gli avvenne avventurato che savio, e con più ardire che ingegno, ebbe da me quello che io, sì come egli, benchè del contrario infignessimi, disiava». The economy and discretion of this sentence reflects Fiammetta's own sense of modesty while revealing the steps which lead to consummation in Boccaccio's world of love. For Florio, as for Panfilo, *ardire* takes the place of his *ingegno*, and what is *avventurato* takes the place of what is *savio*.

which Sadoc refers to, happens to be Florio and Biancifiore's birthday, as Quaglio has indicated. [57] This pagan festivity consists of honoring the gods Mars and Venus with «rose e fiori». The repeated use of the words «rose e fiori» recalls the names of our two protagonists: King Felice named them Florio and Biancifiore because they were born on that day. The fact that these flowers play an integral part in the festivities honoring Mars and Venus suggests that Boccaccio is making a connection between his two protagonists and the two gods whom they are about to honor in ways which go beyond their expectations. [58] As we shall see, these «flower children» are also children of Mars and Venus. [59]

The day of the festivities, Sadoc hides Florio in a basket of flowers destined for Biancifiore, and has all the baskets brought before the Admiral. When the Admiral comes to Biancifiore's basket, we are told:

Mise allora l'amiraglio le mani in quella, e pensando a Biancifiore, a cui mandare la dovea, tanto effettuosamente di quelle prese, che de' biondi capelli seco tirò, ma nol vide [...] ma la santa dea, presente, il ricoperse con non veduta mano; e levato da Sadoc e da molti altri del cospetto dell'amiraglio, il quale avea comandato che per amore di lui a Biancifiore si presentasse, fu portato a piè della torre. (109, 1-2)

The Admiral's gesture of plunging his hand «effetuosamente» (affectionately) into the flowers betrays his repressed desire for Biancifiore. Since the Admiral has denied himself the pleasure of running his hand through Biancifiore's hair, he runs it through the very same «rose e fiori» after which she and Florio were named. [60] However, instead of Biancifiore's hair, he touches the hair of her look-alike (Florio) whom Venus has concealed in the flowers. It is as if Venus had metamorphosed Florio into his namesake, like a hapless Ovidian lover. By unwittingly giving Florio to Biancifiore, the Admiral unknowingly has

---

[57] See BOCCACCIO, *Filocolo*, pp. 897n.

[58] The words «rose e fiori» evoke the colors red and white, the colors of flesh and blood (the colors of Christ's banner at the Resurrection--the reconstitution of flesh and blood). They are, moreover, the colors used by Chrétien de Troyes and other writers of courtly romances to describe the complexion of their protagonists. Furthermore, red and white are the colors most often associated with Mars and Venus respectively in the *Filocolo*.

[59] This is also suggested, in part, by the astrological setting at the time of their birth (I 45, 2).

[60] The flowers remind the Admiral of Biancifiore much the same way the «bianco fiore» in III 11 reminded Florio of her in the other seduction scene.

a third party enact his own hidden desire.[61] This act of mediated desire which the Admiral unknowingly delegates to his still unknown nephew is further reinforced by the mediating role of Venus. Her act of concealing Florio is just one of the several acts of mediation and concealment which take place in the moments leading up to the consummation scene.

Once Florio has been hoisted up the tower and passed through the window of Biancifiore's bedroom, he reveals his presence to Glorizia. The ensuing encounter between Florio and Glorizia mirrors the one that took place between Florio and Sadoc.[62] Glorizia will in fact conclude within the tower what Sadoc began outside the tower. She does this by deceptively preparing Biancifiore for Florio without telling her that he is already in her bedroom. Glorizia, in effect, becomes a go-between like Sadoc in an illicit and dangerous love affair.[63]

The emphatic use of the words «conosca» and «conoscendo» (111, 5) during Florio's reunion with Glorizia suggestively anticipates the carnal knowledge which will result from her mediation. Despite Florio's claim that he wishes to «see» Biancifiore, Glorizia knows the real reason for his presence in the tower, and acts accordingly.[64] Like every moment in the love life of the two protagonists, Florio's concupiscence has a theological correlative. From a Thomistic perspective,

---

[61] It is worth noting that the Admiral's present relationship with Florio, his nephew, is very similar to the initial relationship between King Marc and his nephew Tristan. Just as Marc had sent Tristan to marry Iseult by proxy, the Admiral is sending Florio to make love to Biancifiore by proxy. The consequences of this act prove to be as devastating as those which resulted from the love between Tristan and Iseult.

[62] We are told that Florio «si scoperse il viso. La qual cosa quando Glorizia vide, non riconoscendolo, subito gittò un grandissimo strido, e ritornatole alla memoria chi costui era, ricopertogli il viso, che già dalle sante mani era stato ricoperto, tacitamente il riconfortò dicendo: – Non dubitare, io ti conosco» (109, 3-4). Boccaccio's use of five words with the same «ri» prefix suggests that a doubling is taking place: this scene is a reflection of what took place outside the tower. In the ensuing encounter, Glorizia, like Sadoc, proposes a secret plan to bring Florio and Biancifiore together; Florio, in turn, promises Glorizia to keep it a secret just as he had promised secrecy to Sadoc.

[63] Glorizia is a Roman woman whose role as a surrogate mother for Biancifiore recalls that of the nurse-confidant of the heroines in classical Greek and Roman literature. In the ensuing scene, however, Glorizia also comes close to becoming another classical stock figure – that of the old procuress, like the one we find in Ovid. Her role in this dramatic episode is as ambiguous as that of the other characters involved in this love affair.

[64] Glorizia tells Florio: «Quivi tacitamente dimorerai tanto che coricata e dormire la vedrai, e poi che addormentata sarà, siati licito fare il tuo disio. Sono certa che ella, destandosi nelle tue braccia, diverrà piena di paura avanti che ti conosca, ma poi veggendoti, conoscendo,

the will tends towards its desired object, but the intellect actually possesses it in cognition; there is always a union between the knower and the known: «the knower becomes the known by mental or spiritual assimilation, without, however, ceasing to be himself. Natural knowledge is thus a faint anticipation of the vision of God in heaven which is the final end of man». [65] As we have seen, the final happiness of man consists primarily in the intellectual vision of God: it is complete love born from the fruit of complete knowledge. [66] Similarly, the will of the two protagonists tends toward each other, but when Florio and Biancifiore finally see each other after so many years of separation, they actually find it hard to believe that they are reunited: they doubt their own perception (i.e. knowledge) of reality. Once they overcome this moment of bewilderment, they proceed to consummate their love in the belief that, by finally possessing, both physically and mentally, what their will has tended towards for so many years, they will find complete happiness. As they themselves discover, however, what they assumed was their desired «final end» becomes instead the final end of death, not beatitude. Ironically, it is only when they confront death that they acquire true knowledge of themselves and of the nature of their love.

Once Glorizia has concealed Florio in the bedroom, she goes to console Biancifiore who is lamenting the absence of her beloved on their birthday. In her lament Biancifiore expresses her fear that Florio may have forgotten about her, and that the gods may have lied to her when they promised her that she would one day be united with Florio (II 48). In her moment of doubt Biancifiore too uses the verb *avvenire* four times to express the same sense of uncertainty in the future which Sadoc had expressed to Florio. Glorizia comforts her much the same way Sadoc comforted Florio during their conversation. Unlike Sadoc, however, who hides nothing from Florio, Glorizia plays a very

---

la paura, a poco a poco partendosi, darà luogo moderatamente all'allegrezza» (111, 5). Her plan is meant to keep the two lovers from doing anything that might endanger their lives during their reunion. Glorizia is quite aware of Florio's love madness, and therefore acts accordingly. One might, in fact, misconstrue her mediating role as a lack of fidelity to Biancifiore (the most important person in her life) and a pandering to Florio's desires at Biancifiore's expense. In reality, however, Glorizia has a limited set of options. As a captive of King Felice, and an attendant to Giulia (Biancifiore's mother), Glorizia's position on the social ladder is quite low compared to Florio's. Even though Florio never exercises his regal power over her, Glorizia acquiesces to Florio because she cannot reason with him.

[65] COPLESTON, *op. cit.*, p. 185.
[66] COPLESTON, *op. cit.*, p. 185.

elaborate game of concealment with Biancifiore which verges on deception and which recalls Florio's deceptive chess games with Sadoc.

Glorizia counters Biancifiore's fear «che gl'iddii come gli uomini abbiano apparato a mentire» by asserting the truthfulness of «Iddio», the Christian God. [67] Ironically, Glorizia asserts the veracity of divine promises while deceiving Biancifiore for the first time in her life. She does so by describing to Biancifiore a vision which she invents for the occasion, and which she prophetically claims will come true. Her false vision also serves to assert the veracity of Biancifiore's false gods who, for Glorizia, are corrupt images of her Christian God. [68] Her fabricated vision, like the real ones which have appeared in the *Filocolo* thus far, accurately anticipates the events which will occur that evening (events which are carefully orchestrated by Glorizia herself); however, her preordained plan fails to anticipate or take into account the final outcome of these events. As in the case of Dario and Sadoc before her, Glorizia's attempts to determine the *avvenire* of this amorous *avventura* meet with only partial success. The lovers will be united the way she planned, but the disastrous outcome of their union will go against her expectations. Here too the means and ends will follow a course of their own because they are far from the divine mind despite Glorizia's claims. [69]

Before leaving Biancifiore, Glorizia plays her most redeeming part as a go-between by asking Biancifiore how she would feel if Florio

---

[67] Biancifiore's words echo the narrator's «de' bugiardi iddei» in III 33, 14, and recall Virgil's «li dèi falsi e bugiardi» in *Inferno* I 72. Glorizia's «Iddio», on the other hand, is the first direct allusion to the Christian God since the opening chapters of the *Filocolo*. As Quaglio indicates in his critical edition, the allusion is in keeping with Glorizia's Christian Roman background. The contrast created by this allusion is as sharp as the one Dante establishes between Virgil's «dèi falsi e bugiardi» and Dante's Trinitarian God. This conflation of Christian and pagan deities is not new in the *Filocolo*, as we have seen in Book I.

[68] Her syncretism suggests that the promises of the pagan gods are subordinate to a larger providential plan which we as readers, like the characters themselves, will only discover after the plan has actually unfolded.

[69] The fact that Glorizia finds it necessary to deceive Biancifiore suggests that despite her Christian faith, she too is far from the divine mind Boethius refers to in the *Consolatio philosophiae*. This is also suggested by the dramatic irony in Glorizia's reminder to Biancifiore of the time the gods rescued her from the stake in Verona. By alluding to this moment in Biancifiore's past, Glorizia is unwittingly prophesying what will actually happen to Biancifiore after the consummation scene (her condemnation to the stake and her divine rescue). By recalling the past deeds of those gods whose veracity she is asserting, Glorizia is unknowingly predicting their future assistance. This is another instance of how Boccaccio weaves dramatic irony into the narrative in order to underscore his characters' failure to determine the *avvenire*.

were with her. Her question prompts a predictable response from Biancifiore which in turn allows Glorizia to warn her about the great dangers Florio's presence would pose: «vorresti tu metter Florio a tanto pericolo, quanto gli potrebbe seguire, se egli venisse qui? Non pensi tu che, se l'amiraglio in alcun modo se n'avedesse, tu e egli morreste sanza alcuna redenzione?» (115, 4). Glorizia's words echo those Sadoc told Florio: «Ma s'egli avvenisse che la fortuna, nimica de' nostri avvisi, ti scoprisse e facesseti al signore vedere, niuna redenzione saria alla nostra vita» (104, 5). As in the case of Sadoc's warning, Glorizia's falls on deaf ears. It is obvious from the way Biancifiore is portrayed that her state of mind is similar to Florio's: neither of them seems concerned about the negative consequences that their passion may have on their beloved. The protagonists' inability to reason, or to be reasoned with, further underscores their total surrender to the concupiscible appetite.

After Glorizia has left the bedroom and Biancifiore has fallen asleep, Florio gets his first glimpse of his beloved since he saved her from the stake:

di pietà tale nel viso divenne, quale colui che morto à fuochi è portato; e la debolezza dello innamorato cuore cacciò fuori di lui un sudore che tutto il bagnò, e con tramortita voce, gittato un gran sospiro, disse pianamente: — Oimè, ch'io sento i segnali dell'antica fiamma! — (114, 2-3)

Florio's emotional response reflects courtly-love conceits which can be traced to Andreas Capellanus's fifteenth and sixteenth rules of love. [70] The words Florio utters, as Quaglio has pointed out, are the ones Dido uttered the moment she fell in love with Aeneas, «Adgnosco veteris vestigia flammae» (*Aeneid*, IV 23), as well as the ones Dante utters in *Purgatorio* XXX 48 when he finally meets Beatrice in the terrestrial paradise. Virgil's famous verse indicates a rekindling of a former love experience which will transform the lover. [71] By associating the protagonist's love experience with Dido's, Boccaccio is underscoring the self-destructive nature of Florio's love. By associating it with Dante's love for Beatrice, Boccaccio is alluding to an Edenic

---

[70] XV: Omnis consuevit amans in coamantis aspectus pallescere. XVI: In repentina coamantis visione cor contremescit amantis.
[71] It is worth noting that in the procession of lovers in the *Amorosa visione* Florio and Biancifiore appear beside Dido and Aeneas.

experience which will mark a turning point in the lovers' journey to God. Dario's earlier description of the lush and sensual world of the Torre dell'Arabo, with its one hundred virgins, recalls the descriptions of the Moslem paradise in the Koran. By conflating both Moslem and Christian paradisiacal worlds, Boccaccio alludes to the earth-bound nature of the protagonists' love while at the same time suggesting the possiblity of a more heaven-bound love developing from their Edenic experience.

Florio's vision of Biancifiore incites him to slip into her bed and wake her up. She does not awake right away because she is dreaming what is actually occurring in bed:

Ma l'anima, che nel sonno le parea nelle braccia di colui stare, nelle cui il corpo veramente dimorava, non la lasciava dal sonno isviluppare, parendole in non minore allegrezza essere che paresse a Filocolo, che lei tenea. (IV 118, 7)

When Biancifiore does awake, she refuses to accept the reality she has just dreamt:

– Come può essere che tu qui sii ora ch'io ti credea in Ispagna? –. – Così ci sono come gl'iddii hanno voluto – rispose Filocolo, – e però rassicurati –. Pareano impossibili queste parole ad essere vere a Biancifiore, e riguardandolo le parea desso, e rallegravasi, e non credendolo, tutta di paura tremava. (IV 118, 9)

Florio's sensual embrace in her sleep is identical to Biancifiore's analogous experience in her dream. Her oneiric world becomes one with the world of the «veglia»: the reality is the same in both worlds. [72] Boccaccio's interplay between the reality and illusion, belief and disbelief, is a common topos of the romance genre which has analogous moments in *Filocolo* II 25, 5 and III 7, 4. Used in this context, however, it reflects the lovers' inability to fully grasp the greater realities and dangers surrounding them. The line separating reality from illusion is blurred largely because their love affair until

---

[72] Earlier on, Florio had expressed his disbelief in the fact that he could see Biancifiore; now he expresses an even greater disbelief: «– O dolce amor mio, o più che altra cosa da me amata, è egli possibile a credere che tu sii nelle mie braccia? Certo io ti tengo e stringoti, e appena il credo – [...] – Certo, tu se' pur la mia Biancifiore, e non m'inganna il sonno, come già molte volte m'ha ingannato, che ora pur vegghiando ti tengo». (118, 2-3). The reality within the dream is much easier for each lover to accept than the dream which has become a reality. This particular moment, like others in the lives of the protagonists, was foreshadowed by the eleventh *questione d'amore* in Fiammetta's court of love (IV 59). The question is whether one finds greater pleasure in seeing one's beloved or in thinking about him/her.

now has been nurtured on illusions, dreams, visions, and lies of one sort or another.

Before these «flower children» are mutually deflowered (Boccaccio does not use the fourteenth-century word «disfiorare», but the idea is present in this episode), Biancifiore asks Florio if he still has the ring she gave him, and coyly recalls the promise King Felice made to her on his birthday: [73]

Omai – disse Biancifiore – non dubito che l'agurio ch'io presi delle parole di tuo padre, quando davanti gli presentai il paone, non venghino ad effetto, che disse di darmi, avanti che l'anno compiesse, per marito il maggior barone del suo regno: e certo di te intesi, di cui io non sono ora meno contenta, avvegna che passato sia l'anno, che se avanti avuto t'avessi, pure ch'io t'aggia –. A cui Filocolo disse: – Bella donna, veramente verrà ad effetto ciò che di quelle parole dicesti; né credere che io sì lungamente aggia affanato per acquistare amica, ma per acquistare inseparabile sposa, la quale tu mi sarai. E fermamente, avanti che altro fra noi sia, col tuo medesimo anello ti sposerò, alla qual cosa Imineo e la santa Giunone e Venere, nostra dea, siano presenti –. Disse adunque Biancifiore: – Mai di ciò che ora mi parli dubitai, e con ferma speranza sempre vivuta sono di dovere tua sposa morire; (120, 2-4)

Her last words belie what she told Glorizia when she expressed her fear that Florio might have forgotten about her. The fact that she needs to remind him of his father's promise suggests that Florio had not thought of marrying her, despite his disclaimer that he never considered having her as his «amica» (mistress). [74] The ambiguity behind the lovers' remarks suggests that they are not as truthful and straightforward as one might expect of two courtly lovers. Furthermore, the fact that Florio has not considered the danger Biancifiore will be in after she loses her virginity further suggests his lack of concern for her well-being. [75] Nevertheless, Florio fulfills his father's birthday promise by marrying Biancifiore on his own birthday, thus

---

[73] When Biancifiore is tied to the stake in II 53, 1, she tells Felice that she could have gotten Florio to marry her if she had wanted to, but did not do so out of loyalty to the king. Now, instead, she has Florio marry her against the Admiral's wishes, and, as a result, is tied to the stake a second time. This is just one of several details linking this episode with its counterpart in Book II.

[74] Mars and Venus are also called «amico» and «amica» in II 58, 4-10, underscoring their adulterous relationship. Clandestine marriages were valid; but, as Henry A. Kelly has shown, they were often not sincerely meant; see HENRY ANSGAR KELLY, *Love and Marriage in the Age of Chaucer*, Ithaca, N.Y., Cornell University Press, 1975, p. 224.

[75] In his description of the Torre dell'Arabo, Dario says that there is a magic fountain in the tower which can determine whether or not a maiden has lost her virginity.

making amends for the wrong Felice had done to her the day before she was sentenced to the stake. [76]

Their marriage is secret (no one knows about it except Glorizia), and takes place before the statue of Cupid (alluded to earlier in Dario's description of the tower). [77] Cupid functions as a witness to their marriage; however, Cupid is also the object of their attention immediately after consummation, when Biancifiore explains how she had used the statue as a simulacrum of Florio. The fact that these two moments frame the actual moment of consummation suggests that the climax of the protagonist's love affair is centered on this «figura» of Cupid. In addition to functioning as a surrogate witness and a simulacrum of Florio, the statue of Cupid is also a simulacrum of an «accident» (Amor) whom the protagonists worship as a «substance» (one of «li dèi bugiardi»). [78] The protagonists, however, never regard this «figura» of Cupid in figural terms; instead, they worship him as a pagan idol capable of performing prodigies like the ones performed by his parents, Mars and Venus. [79] The fact that the Admiral later catches Florio and Biancifiore in bed together (a scene that is patterned after Vulcan's discovery of Mars and Venus, according to Quaglio) heightens the ambiguity of their marriage in the presence of Cupid. [80]

By praying to a pagan statue, Florio and Biancifiore are also engaged in an act of idolatry which, from a medieval perspective, was

---

[76] Biancifiore's allusion to an important moment in her past is significant. Besides anticipating the moment when Florio will assume all of his father's duties as king, her allusion also foreshadows her second condemnation to the stake, a moment which recalls her first condemnation to the stake shortly after Felice had promised to marry her to a nobleman. Like his father before him, Florio is about to put Biancifiore in exactly the same situation. Although his intentions are not the same as those of his father, Florio's misguided actions follow a course which is similar to the one taken by Felice's actions.

[77] Immediately after the marriage and before the consummation, Glorizia is told by the two lovers that they are married. She responds to the news by saying «E come, così tacitamente da voi tanta festa sarà celebrata sanza suono? Negati ci sono gl'idraulici organi e le dolci voci della cetera d'Orfeo e qualunque altro citerista, ma io con nuova nota supplirò il diffetto» (121,5) and then strikes the four precious trees in the tower that produce a «dolcissima melodia». Her allusion to Orpheus is significant since it recalls his tragic marriage with Eurydice, and anticipates the near fatal consequences of this marriage.

[78] Dante tells his readers in Vita nuova XXV that the god Amor (alias Cupid in the Filocolo) is an accident within a substance (the way «green» is an accident within the substance «grass»). He warns his readers not to confuse the figure for love with love itself.

[79] As Boccaccio tells us in the Genealogia Deorum, Cupid is born of the adulterous union between Mars and Venus. He is, in other words, the product of the sensitive appetites, and therefore an irrational force.

[80] See BOCCACCIO, Filocolo, p. 904.

synonymous with demon worship. The sinister description of the statue of Cupid, with its red eyes glowing in the dark, suggests that a demonic presence is in fact trying to lead this young couple to their death as Satan (alias Pluto) led Biancifiore's parents to theirs. [81] This is also suggested by the statue's approval of their near-fatal marriage: «A questa ultima voce, la figura, dando con gli occhi maggiore luce che l'usato, mostrò con atti i divoti prieghi avere intesi, e movendosi alquanto, verso loro inchinando, si fece ne' sembianti più lieta» (121, 3). The fact that Florio and Biancifiore address the statue as «signore delle nostre menti» (recalling Dante's famous epithet for Beatrice) suggests that this demon has indeed become the lord of their minds: the two lovers are entirely possessed by it. Florio and Biancifiore have made Cupid both a substance and an accident: the statue is both a deity whom they worship in the hope of attaining their desired end (i.e. sexual gratification) and a figure of their idolatrous love for each other.

The idolatry is made more vivid when Biancifiore recounts how she used the statue as a simulacrum of her absent lover. By associating Florio with Cupid, Biancifiore confuses the desired object with the figure of desire itself, thereby making both Florio and Cupid idols of her own love. [82] Comparing herself to Sirofane after the death of his son, Biancifiore says:

Riguardando io questa imagine e considerando la bellezza d'essa sovente di te mi ricordava, perché, avvegna che promesse mi fosse da Venere questo effetto a che pervenuti siamo, parendomi impossibile, temendo d'averti perduto, di questa te, qual Sirofane egiziaco fece del perduto figliuolo, feci: e sì come quelli di fiori e di frondi ornava la memoria del figliuolo, davanti a lei della sua dissoluzione dolendosi, così io di questa proprio nome la chiamava Florio: e quand'io disiderava di vederti, a questa vedere correa (124, 1-2).

The «figura» of Cupid was not only a surrogate lover for Biancifiore, but also a means of keeping alive the memory of Florio in her mind («mente»). Her memory of Florio is further reinforced by the «fiori e frondi» she decorates the statue with. [83] *Memoria*, like *ingegno*, has

---

[81] For a completely different interpretation of the statue of Cupid, see DAVID WALLACE, *op. cit.*, pp. 70.

[82] See Biancifiore's prosopopeia in chapter 124.

[83] The «fiori» are similar to the «bianco fiore altra volta tra le spine veduto» which Florio sees and often contemplates during his exile in Montoro (III 11, 12): both flowers recall the lover's beloved.

played an important role in the protagonists' love affair prior to consummation: it is through memory that the protagonists' love for each other is kept alive. [84] Throughout their long separation they rely on their «mente» because they are unable to see and speak to each other. As in the case of Dante's «donna della mia mente», the lovers create a mental obsession which has become the focal point of their love life throughout their long separation. [85] When the desired object becomes attainable, however, these mental recreations cease to be important. The transition, however, from a mental obsession to a physical love is not instantaneous, as the lovers' initial incredulity and confusion between actual and illusionary worlds reveal.

V. The Disclosure of Desire

The ensuing consummation scene is not described, just alluded to. The narrator asks his readers to imagine it: «O allegrezza inestimabile, o diletto non mai sentito o amore incomparabile, con quanto effetto congiugneste voi i novelli sposi! Pensinlo le dure menti, nelle quali amore non puote entrare, pensinlo i crudi animi: e se questo pensando, non divengono molli, credasi che graziosa virtù in loro abitare non possa!» (122, 1). It is one more element in Boccaccio's play of illusion and reality: the actual moment of consummation cannot be mimetically reproduced, just imagined.

The lovers spend three nights together before the Admiral discovers them sleeping in each other's arms «la terza mattina». In this scene the Admiral's affection for Biancifiore turns into a passionate hatred which expresses itself through his irascible appetite, and which recalls Massamutino's hatred for her after she spurned his love. Although the natives of Alexandria are characterized as being irascible by nature (witness the Admiral, Sadoc, and later Dario), Boccaccio is not simply playing on a medieval stereotype regarding Arabs, he is also

---

[84] Biancifiore's gesture of laying «fiori e frondi» before a statue which reminds her of Florio also suggests that she was engaging in a funereal ceremony. By recalling Sirofane's prosopopeia, and by confessing that she was afraid of having lost Florio («temendo di averti perduto»), Biancifiore has underscored the precarious and deadly nature of their love affair.

[85] The fact that Boccaccio uses Dante's famous epithet («donna della mia mente») during this central episode is significant. Besides suggesting that Dante's own love for Beatrice was idolatrous, Boccaccio also establishes a sharp contrast between the protagonists' love for each other, which moves toward the demonic presence of Cupid, and Dante's love for Beatrice, which moves instead towards God.

establishing a nexus between the irascible and concupiscible appetites. [86] The irascible manifests itself in direct proportion to the frustration of sexual gratification. [87] This is clearly the case with the Admiral who originally went to see Biancifiore in her bedroom because he was «pieno di malinconia» (126, 1). Melancholy, the humor most often associated with lovesickness (*aegritudo amoris*) in medieval medicine, is also responsible for moving the Admiral to violence. [88] As a result of what he sees, the Admiral becomes angry and wishes to kill the young lovers on the spot. We are told, however, that he is prevented from doing this by Venus' divine intervention. His irascible appetite sways his will to desire their death, but his concupiscible appetite (in the form of Venus) keeps him from doing it himself:

E il pensiero subito si mutò all'amiraglio, parendogli vil cosa due che dormissero uccidere, e la sua spada fedare di sì vile sangue: per che egli tiratala indietro la ripose, e sanza destarli si partì della camera, infiammato contra loro, e in tutto deliberando nell'acceso animo di tal fallo farli punire. (126,7)

Like Florio and Dario before him, the Admiral «deliberates» before choosing the means to his desired end (the death of the two lovers):

ma poi che con diliberato animo *elesse* che la loro vita per fuoco finisse, comanda che nel prato siano posati, e quivi in accesi fuochi siano sanza pietà messi, acciò che di loro facciano sacrificio a quella dea, le fui forze agli sconvenevoli congiugnimenti gli condusse. (127, 8)

Boccaccio's use of the verb «eleggere» recalls Aquinas' association of free choice with the power of election. The Admiral's will (the intellectual appetite) wants the two lovers to die, and after careful deliberation he freely chooses (through his power of election) the means by which they shall die. His choice is made and executed, but the end is never actually reached. Although the stake, to which the

---

[86] Besides recalling Massamutino's «rabbia» toward Biancifiore for having spurned him, it also anticipates the moment when she will be condemned to the stake a second time as a result of the frustrated love of another angry Arab, the Admiral of Alexandria.

[87] Thomas Aquinas seems to make a similar correlation in his commentary on Aristotle's *De Anima*: «The irascible appetite fights, as it were, on behalf of the concupiscible [...] Therefore every movement of the irascible appetite starts from and ends in a movement of the concupiscible appetite. Anger springs from sadness and ceases in a pleasure; for the angry find their satisfaction in punishing» (par. 803-5).

[88] For an analysis of «aegritudo amoris» in the Middle Ages, see MASSIMO CIAVOLLELLA, *La «Malattia d'Amore» dall'Antichità al Medioevo*, Rome, Bulzoni, 1976, pp. 31-123.

protagonists are tied, is lit, Florio and Biancifiore do not die. Once again, the desired end fails to be reached by the chosen means.

The Admiral's deliberation («deliberando») is also a legal term which recalls the deliberation which took place when Biancifiore was condemned to the stake in II 46. The fact that this episode is patterned after Vulcan's discovery of Venus lying in bed with Mars (the mythical archetype of adulterous unions) suggests that, despite their marriage, Florio and Biancifiore's sexual union is tantamount to adultery.[89] This may be explained by the fact that the Admiral bought Biancifiore as a slave, and her status is that of an adulterous slave caught *in flagrante delicto*. As Howard Bloch has shown, the *Lex Julia de adulteriis* allowed for slaves and family freedmen to be slain on the spot if caught in the home.[90] The Admiral's initial desire to kill Biancifiore and her lover on the spot is in keeping with the legal punishment for this kind of «peccato» or «fallo» (words which the Admiral uses to describe her transgression). The fact that the Admiral decides not to kill the two lovers on the spot, but to have them executed in public without a trial, is also in keeping with medieval customary law.[91] As in the case of the laws which condemned Biancifiore to the stake in II 46, the ones which condemn her to the stake this time have their origins in a law which derives its name (*Lex Julia de adulteriis*) from Biancifiore's unknown ancestors. By offending the *gens* of the Admiral, Biancifiore is condemned by a law which is identical to that of her own *gens*.[92]

The Admiral's actions set in motion a series of disclosures and revelations which bring an end to the games of concealment and deception that took place prior to the moment of consummation. He not only uncovers Biancifiore's secret affair with Florio, but he openly admits for the first time his previously repressed love for her:

Tu, da me più che la vita mia per adietro amata [...] e tu, la quale io con sollecitudine ho infino a qui ingegnatomi dal congiungimento di qualunque

---

[89] Despite the fact that Biancifiore is married to Florio, the Admiral regards her as a «vilissima puttana» (126, 3).

[90] R. HOWARD BLOCH, *op. cit.*, pp. 54-55.

[91] For a discussion on this customary law, see R. HOWARD BLOCH, *op. cit.*, p. 57.

[92] Like King Arthur, who condemns Guinevere to the stake for her adultery with Lancelot, the Admiral has the right as judge to condemn Biancifiore to the stake. Like Guinevere, who is rescued by Lancelot's men, Biancifiore too will be rescued by Florio's men. For an analysis of the legal aspects governing King Arthur's trial of Guinevere, see BLOCH, *op. cit.*, p. 60.

uomo, e ancora dal mio medesimo, che d'avere i tuoi abbracciamenti tutto ardea, ho guardata, ora per tua malvagità congiuntati con non so cui, la morte debitamente hai guadagnata: e io la ti darò. (126, 4)

The «non so chi» draws our attention to Florio's still concealed identity, while at the same time anticipating its disclosure after the two lovers are exposed in public.

The events which immediately follow the Admiral's discovery are also described as part of a fall. After catching the two lovers in bed, the Admiral has them bound together and lowered to the ground from the same window through which he had sent Florio and the basket of «rose e fiori». The loss of their childhood innocence and their introduction to the postlapsarian world of culpability and death (the price Adam and Eve had to pay for their disobedience) is made more vivid by their expulsion from the paradisiacal world of the tower and by the death sentence the Admiral passes as the penalty they must pay for their «peccato» and «fallo».[93]

Their fall is also described as a downturn on the wheel of fortune. After having risen to the top of her wheel in the consummation scene, the lovers fall «sotto la più infima parte della sua ruota» (136, 5). As slaves of their passions, the two lovers have become slaves of the goddess Fortuna. (The nexus between slavery and passion is not fortuitous: Biancifiore was sold as a slave by Felice on account of her love for Florio, and the Admiral bought her as a slave to be eventually given to the Sultan for his harem.) Boccaccio's vivid description of Florio and Biancifiore hanging naked by a rope shortly after their birthday recalls their actual birth. Florio's «return to the womb» in his motherland is mirrored in his furtive penetration of the walls of the tower (symbolic of his penetration of Biancifiore's womb).[94] The fact that they are both expelled from the tower, through the same window through which Florio had entered, further suggests a reenactment of sexual intercourse and birth. Born under Gemini, but of different mothers, Florio and Biancifiore are often portrayed as twins. (Even

---

[93] The Admiral's words recall those of Massamutino in II 38, 4 when he spoke about her «fallo» at the king's council. Professor Calum Carmichael has pointed out to me that in Hebraic biblical exegesis Adam and Eve were born and married on the same day: the fact that the protagonists get married on their birthday makes their resemblance to Adam and Eve more striking.

[94] Such sexual imagery was quite common in the Middle Ages: we find it in *Decameron* (IV 1), the *Le Roman de la rose*, and it can ultimately be traced back to the Bible. The «fall» or «conquest» of a woman is often expressed as a fall of a city or other fortified structure (a case in point would be Giangiorgio Trissino's *Sofonisba*).

Sadoc notices a striking similarity between the two when he meets Florio.)

As they hang naked from the same umbilical cord, both of them think of their parents, and regret the day they were born. Biancifiore laments: «Ahi, dolorosa me, perchè insieme con la mia madre non morii quand'io nacqui?» (130, 5) and adds, «Maledetta sia l'ora ch'io nacqui [...] poi che a questo fine ne dovevi venire [...] Oimè misera, che quel giorno che ci diede al mondo, quel giorno la cagione di questa morte ne porse» (132, 2-4). Likewise, Florio tells his executioners: «un medesimo giorno ci diede al mondo: piacciavi che, poi che una ora ci toglie, che similmente una medesima fiamma ci consumi» (131, 3). By juxtaposing their birth to this encounter with death, the protagonists are framing their life while examining it in retrospect. By looking at their past from what they believe is going to be their last hour on earth, the two lovers acquire a totally new perspective of their life. In the ensuing four lamentations each lover realizes that (s)he, not «fortuna» or other external forces, is to blame for what has happened. Furthermore, they both realize, for the first time, how adversely their love affair has affected the person they love the most. They are now aware of how their «intellect» and «reason» have been affected: addressing her beauty, Biancifiore laments, «Tu principale cagione fosti dello ardente amore che costui mi porta; tu gli levasti la luce dello 'telletto, e la ragione, per la quale conoscere doveva me, femina vile, non essere da essere amata da lui» (130, 4). Whereas *ingenium* and *memoria* were dominant before consummation, *ratio* becomes prevalent after consummation.

This birth of self-knowledge in the face of death contrasts sharply with their carnal knowledge during the procreative consummation scene. The fact, however, that this moment of truth is coincidental with a visual reenactment of the protagonists' birth suggests that both lovers are undergoing a Pauline death of their old self which will later be followed by a spiritual rebirth when they convert to Christianity. Boccaccio, however, has deliberately distanced the two events from one another as if to underscore the protagonists' need to turn completely away from the idolatrous worship of the god Amor (i.e. Cupid) in preparation for their worship of the God of *caritas*.[95]

---

[95] One could say that their spiritual death is Providence's answer to the Admiral's earlier desire for the death of the two lovers.

The first changes in the protagonists' lives become apparent after the battle, when they are freed from the stake. We never again see them behaving the way they did prior to and during consummation. Furthermore, Fortuna and all the pagan gods disappear completely from their lives. Venus, in fact, makes her last appearance when she miraculously saves her two protégés from the flames of the burning stake. She gives them an olive branch as a sign of peace, while wearing laurels as a sign of her victory: «Questa sarà ultima ingiuria a voi e fine delle vostre avversità, dopo la quale voi pacificamente, avendo vinta la contraria fortuna, viverete» (134, 3). [96] With the lovers' triumph over adversity, Venus promises an end to Fortuna's trials and tribulations. Her protégés have proven themselves as lovers, steadfast in their devotion throughout their adversities. The fact, however, that this moment of victory, conferred on the protagonists by Venus herself, is immediately followed by the destructive consequences of Mars, as a direct result of the lovers' consummation, adds ambiguity to both their victory and the courtly ideal that love is a valid means of attaining «nobiltà di cuore». [97]

Mars, in fact, enters for the last time and makes a devastating exit. When Dario and Florio's six companions fear that harm has come to the two lovers, they become victims of their irascible appetite and lose that wisdom which characterized their conduct until now: «i più savi, storditi dell'avvenimento, hanno perduto il saper consigliare» (137, 4). Mars takes advantage of their «dubbio» and, dressed as a knight in shining armor, exhorts them to take up arms against the Admiral. The seven sages soon become «furiosi tori» filled with «focoso disio». When they see the burning stake, they are filled with «rabbiosa ira». Ascalion, the protagonists' teacher and closest friend, attempts to look through the smoke which has engulfed the stake: «Pinge si avanti Ascalion e ficca gli occhi per l'oscurità del fummo, disiderando, se in alcun modo esser potesse, di veder Filocolo, ma per

[96] As Quaglio has indicated, Venus's last appearance in the *Filocolo* recalls her first appearance to Biancifiore in Book II 48, 16 when she also appeared with a laurel crown and an olive branch; see BOCCACCIO, *Filocolo*, pp. 789-790 & 906. Both moments are linked to the two moments in which Biancifiore is condemned to the stake.

[97] Florio tried to make a similar point to his father in II 15, and to Ascalion in II 44, when he defends his love for Biancifiore as an ennobling force. However, the fact that this scene is very similar to the one in Book II, when Venus and Mars came to rescue Biancifiore from the stake, suggests that the final results are quite ambiguous (especially Mars' cruel punishment of the offending party).

niente s'affatica: per che dirizzatosi sopra le strieve, vede i compagni pure a lui guardare» (138, 1). His obfuscated vision is literal and metaphoric: «gli occhi della mente» are unable to penetrate the «smoke» caused by his irascible appetite. Thinking that the two lovers have been killed, Ascalion decides to die avenging their deaths (137, 8). [98]

The description of the ensuing «vendetta» contains allusions to Statius' *Thebais*, the most notable of which is the epithet «i sette compagni», used repeatedly when referring to Dario, Ascalion and Florio's other companions. These «sette compagni» in fact recall the seven champions against Thebes. But instead of attacking Thebes, they attack Alexandria. If Thebes was considered the city of libidinous passion in the Middle Ages, Alexandria could be considered its irascible counterpart. [99] Named after Alexander the Great (a figure for the irascible and violent man in *Inferno* XII 107), this city has no place for the concupiscible appetite. The Torre dell'Arabo is an ivory tower in which one hundred virgins are protected by a large number of eunuchs. Even the Admiral of that city carefully represses his concupiscible appetite in favor of his irascible appetite. When Florio and Biancifiore exercise their concupiscence in a place which forbids it, they unleash the irascible appetite of everyone in the city, including Ascalion, whose paternal love for Florio and Biancifiore («O cari a me più che figliuoli») is transformed into a suicidal desire for vengeance by a melancholy that is similar to the Admiral's.

After the battle, when both sides discover that the two lovers are still alive, an uneasy peace is reached by the Admiral and Ascalion. It is strengthened by the subsequent recognition scene and by the protagonists' public marriage. This second marriage is clearly meant to be juxtaposed to the secret marriage which took place in the tower prior to consummation. Whereas the secret marriage was meant to sanction the forthcoming consummation of their love affair, the public marriage is meant to mark an end to the disastrous consequences of the secret one. The Admiral, in fact, insists on having them remarry in

---

[98] This moment recalls the battle between Lelio and Felice. Just as Felice had been spurred by the false vision of Pluto and the prodigy of Mars, Ascalion is now moved to wrath by a vision (136, 3-4) and by Mars himself.

[99] As Boccaccio states in his *Chiose* to the *Teseida* I 134, 2, Venus's abode is located on mount Citeron just outside of Thebes. See BOCCACCIO, *Opere minori in volgare*, II, ed. Mario Marti, Milano, Rizzoli, 1970 («I Classici Rizzoli»), pp. 668-669. The association of Thebes with Venus is prevalent throughout the *Teseida*.

the open, not because he does not recognize the validity of their secret marriage, but because he wishes to use the occasion to appease his people for the wrongs they have suffered at the hands of Florio's men. On the day of the wedding the Admiral assembles all his people on the field where the slaughter had taken place, and narrates to them the misfortunes of his nephew and Biancifiore. When he tells his people how he almost killed the two lovers, he says that he was prevented from doing so by the gods:

ma gl'iddii, a cui niuna cosa s'occulta, conoscendo che ancora da loro gran frutto dovea uscire, li difesero dal mio colpo. Ma non però mancata la mia ira, con furore li giudicai come vedeste; e quanto gl'iddii gli aiutasse, ancora vi fu manifesto. Venuti adunque per tante avversità e per si fatti pericoli com'io v'ho narrato, aiutati in tutto dagl'iddii disideranno sotto la nostra potenza di congiugnere quell'amore che insieme si portano per matrimoniale legame. Alla qual cosa, conoscendo noi che degl'iddii è veramente piacere, abbiamo voluto che voi siate presenti, e rallegrandovi di ciò che gl'iddii si rallegrano, ciascuno secondo il suo grado faccendo festa li onori, considerando che l'uno figliuolo e di re, e la sua testa è a corona promessa, l'altra d'imperiale sangue e discesa. — (159, 5-6)

By repeatedly attributing his people's misfortune to the gods, the Admiral is actually justifying why he has made peace with the enemy without demanding some kind of retribution for his people's suffering (identified as a divine punishment).

The second marriage is done in the name of reconciliation: a reconciliation between Florio and his uncle, between Florio's men and those of the Admiral, and between the Admiral and his injured people. The fruits of the first marriage are the devastating consequences of Mars and Venus (the concupiscible and irascible appetites). The fruits of the second marriage are the preservation of existing family ties (between uncle and nephew), and the renewal of life after the death and destruction brought about by the first marriage. (The second marriage is in fact performed on the same field where the battle took place several days before.) If Amore (alias Cupid, the son of Mars and Venus) and its negative consequences are to be associated with the first marriage, generation and procreation are strongly suggested by the second one. In fact, Biancifiore gives birth to Lelio in Alexandria, and Florio later succeeds his father on the throne in Cordova.

Although Florio learns his lesson in Alexandria and admits his wrongdoing, he still has a long way to go before attaining Christian *caritas*. Nowhere is this more evident than in his remarks to the Admiral after the *agnitio*:

A me non è meno caro con tanti e tali pericoli avere Biancifiore racquistata, poi che sani e salvi siamo, ella e io e i miei compagni, che se con più agevole via racquistata l'avessi. Le cose con affanno avute sogliono più che l'altre piacere: e però a tutte queste cose considerando, sanza più delle passate ricordarci, faremo ragione come se state non fossero, e delle nostre prosperità facciamo allegra festa. (IV 153, 2-3)

No matter how sincere his apology may be, his concluding remarks are obviously out of place considering the numerous dead and wounded which have resulted from the battle between his companions and the Admiral's men. The fact that Florio's remarks come straight from Andreas Capellanus and Ovid suggests that Florio is still conditioned by his Ovidian education. [100]

In conclusion, the protagonists have a choice between two kinds of conjugal love after their second marriage: one mediated by their appetites, the other mediated by reason. The future success of their love depends on which of these two paths they will follow. After Alexandria, the lovers' future is in *their* hands, and no longer «nelle mani della fortuna». This fact alone, coupled with their eventual conversion to Christianity, enables them to attain their ultimate end both as lovers and rulers.

---

[100] The words «Le cose con affano avute sogliono più che l'altre piacere» can be traced to Andreas Capellanus' *De Amore*, as we can see in the *regulae amoris*, «XIV Faciliis perceptio contemptibilem reddit amorem, difficilis eum carum facit haberi», and in his dialogues: «non enim potest bonum plenare cognosci nisi mali prius percepta notitia» (p. 182), and «et carius habetur, quod pluribus est laboribus acquisitum, quam quod sollicitudine modica possidetur» (p. 32).

Chapter Six

THE *FILOCOLO* IN THE *DECAMERON*

I. *Decameron* V 6 and the *Filocolo*

Almost a quarter of a century separates the *Filocolo* from the *Decameron*, but, as Vittore Branca has shown, parts of the former appear throughout the latter. [1] In addition to a number of linguistic and narrative details which appear in many of the one hundred *novelle*, and which first appeared in the *Filocolo*, three of the *novelle* are actually based on the *Filocolo*: *Decameron* X 5 (*Filocolo* IV 31), *Decameron* X 4 (*Filocolo* IV 67), and *Decameron* V 6 (*Filocolo* IV 80-165). Of these *novelle*, *Decameron* X 4 and X 5 are based on two similar *novelle* which are told at Fiammetta's court of love in *Filocolo* IV; only *Decameron* V 6 is actually based on the tale of Florio and Biancifiore. The novella is an abridged version of the consummation episode; and, as Vittore Branca has shown, it contains a number of verbal echoes. [2] There are, however, also a number of significant differences, not the least of which is the difference in length: *Decameron* V 6 is one tenth the length of the consummation episode in the *Filocolo*. Furthermore, the characters are not the same; instead of the legendary Florio and Biancifiore, we have the quasi-historical figures of Gianni di Procida (nephew of the more famous Gian di Procida) and Restituta (daughter of Marin Bòlgaro). More important, however, are the changes in the original plot.

Gianni is in love with Restituta, a young woman from the neighboring island of Ischia. When she is kidnapped by pirates and later sold to King Frederick II of Aragon for his harem, Gianni sets out to

---

[1] See Branca's notes to this novella and the other *novelle* which are based on the *Filocolo* in GIOVANNI BOCCACCIO, *Decameron*, edited by Vittore Branca, Torino, Giulio Einaudi, 1980. All quotations from the *Decameron* are taken from this edition.

[2] BOCCACCIO, *op. cit.*, p. 648.

find her. Once in Palermo, Gianni sends his ship back to Procida, and surveys the building in which his beloved is held captive (just as Florio had done in Alexandria). Unlike Florio, Gianni is by himself in Palermo «da amor ritenuto»; but like Florio, he sees his beloved «per ventura» looking out of a window in the Cuba (the pleasure dome of the kings of Sicily). [3] Unlike Florio, who rushes madly to the tower and runs into Sadoc, Gianni is actually able to speak to Restituta from outside the Cuba:

E veggendo Gianni che il luogo era solingo, accostatosi come poté, le parlò, e da lei informato della maniera che a tenere avesse se più dappresso le volesse parlar, si partì, avendo prima per tutto considerata la disposizione del luogo: e aspettata la notte e di quella lasciata andar buona parte, là se ne tornò e aggrappatosi per parti che non vi si sarebbono appiccati i picchi nel giardin se n'entrò, e in quello trovata una antennetta, alla finestra dalla giovane insegnatagli l'appoggiò e per quella assai leggiermente se ne saglì. (14-15)

Gianni gains access to his beloved with less difficulty than Florio: there are no guards or other obstacles that must be turned into mediators before the lover can attain his desired object. There is, however, an ironic use of the word «parlar» which recalls Florio's use of the word «vedere» in his encounter with Glorizia. The fact that Gianni is already speaking to Restituta makes it obvious that he wants to be «più dappresso» for reasons which have little to do with conversation.

Once Gianni is inside, Restituta agrees to make love to him in return for his promise to free her from captivity. [4] Unlike Biancifiore, Restituta is not nearly as possessed by love as her lover is. [5] For Restituta, sexual intercourse is a means to her desired end (freedom). [6]

---

[3] For a description of the Cuba, see JOHN JULIUS NORWICH, *The Kingdom in the Sun: 1130-1194*, London, Longman, 1970, p. 354n.

[4] Gianni is quick to promise Restituta freedom without, however, having any idea of how to free her. In this respect he is similar to Florio who, prior to consummation, had never planned to marry or free Biancifiore.

[5] The only indication that Rustituta loves Gianni is at the beginning of the novella: «la quale un giovanetto [...] era e nominato Gianni, amava sopra la vita sua e ella lui» (4). However, when she decides to make love to Gianni, her reasons for doing so have little to do with love: «pensando a niuna persona più degnamente che a costui potersi donare e avvisando di poterlo inducere a portarla via, seco aveva preso di compiacergli in ogni suo disidero» (16).

[6] Restituta's *amor utile*, as Fiammetta would have characterized it, is not Biancifiore's coy means of getting Florio to marry her. The idea of prostitution, however, is not new: it was implicitly present in the chess games Florio and Sadoc played.

Similarly, her captivity is the means to Gianni's desired end since she is more willing to make love to him now that she is a captive:

La giovane, parendole il suo onore avere ormai perduto, per la guardia del quale ella gli era alquanto nel passato stata salvatichetta, pensando a niuna persona più degnamente che a costui potersi donare e avvisando di poterlo indurre a portarla via, seco aveva preso di compiacergli in ogni suo disiderio e per ciò aveva la finestra lasciata aperta, acciò che egli prestamente dentro potesse passare. (16)

The desired end of one becomes the means by which the other can attain his or her own desired end: each lover, in effect, seeks a release from a state of bondage by taking advantage of the other's bondage. Their condition prior to consummation is, in fact, a concupiscible bondage: Gianni is a slave of his passion, Restituta a slave of the king's concupiscence.[7] The eventual attainment of their desired ends recalls the exchange of «mistresses» that Sadoc and Florio strive for during their chess games. Like Florio and Sadoc, Gianni and Restituta mediate their desire through the primary desire of their partner. This alterity of desire, however, is not communicated through a mediating sphere (e.g. the chess games and Parmenione); instead, the two lovers communicate their desire directly to one another.

Gianni and Restituta's game of desire is also a power game: each exercises a subtle form of sexual coercion and control over the other. The nexus between desire and power is made more vivid by the fact that the two protagonists attempt to find a release from their respective bondages in the Cuba — a place that symbolizes unrestrained concupiscence and the shackled will. As a place which frees the concupiscible at the expense of the intellectual appetite, the Cuba is the antithesis of the Torre dell'Arabo where the concupiscible was repressed in favor of the irascible.[8] As we shall see, however, both Restituta and Gianni exercise their free will even within the confines of their restrictive bondages.

When the two lovers are caught *in flagrante delicto* by Frederick, who had gone to the Cuba with the intention of deflowering Resti-

---

[7] The idea that passion can lead a person to a state of mental and physical bondage is a fairly common topos in medieval literature: see STEPHEN A. BARNEY, *Troilus Bound*, «Speculum: A Journal of Medieval Studies», XLIX, 1974, pp. 445-458; and LOUISE GEORGE CLUBB, *Boccaccio and the Boundaries of Love*, «Italica», XXXVII, 1960, pp. 188-195. Augustine discusses it in *The City of God* XIX 15 and XIV 15-17.

[8] This is supported by the fact that Frederick later goes to the Cuba to deflower Restituta, whereas the Admiral of Alexandria goes to the Torre dell'Arabo just to look at Biancifiore.

tuta, they are sentenced to die at the stake for their transgression. They are saved at the last moment when Ruggieri di Loria, the king's admiral, recognizes Gianni and convinces the young king to spare their lives. The protagonists are thus saved by the *agnitio* itself, not the *deus ex macchina* (Mars and Venus). The novella concludes with Gianni and Restituta's marriage in the presence of the king whose authority they had tried to circumvent.

The thematic similarities between the novella and its source are also revealed in the verbal echoes from the *Filocolo*. Before actually beginning her novella, Pampinea prefaces it with a short statement regarding its theme:[9]

— Grandissime forze, piacevole donne, son quelle d'amore, e a gran fatiche e a istraboccchevoli e non pensati pericoli gli amanti dispongono, come per assai cose raccontate e oggi e altre volte comprender si può; ma nondimeno ancora con l'ardire d'un giovane innamorato m'agrada di dimostrarlo. (V 6, 3)

Pampinea's opening statement echoes the same thematic statement Boccaccio made in the *Filocolo*: like Florio, Pampinea's «giovane» (Gianni di Procida) is a lover whose «ardire» enables him to engage in «istraboccchevoli e non pensati pericoli» (the words are identical to those used by Dario and Sadoc to describe Florio's dangerous endeavor to enter the Torre dell'Arabo). Both Gianni and Florio are compared to the mythic figure of Leander who swam the Dardanelles in order to be with his beloved Hero.[10] Gianni actually swims the two miles between Procida and Ischia just to see the walls of Restituta's home, a deed which is reminiscent of Florio's mad rush to the tower walls in Alexandria.[11] The comparison of Gianni and Florio to Leander underscores the dangerous and almost foolhardy nature of their deeds, while at the same time suggesting that their passion may end in tragedy.[12]

A closer look at the way Gianni is portrayed clearly indicates that

---

[9] These short prefaces may be thought of as secondary themes since they expand on the general theme chosen by the king and queen of that day.

[10] Both Branca and Quaglio trace these allusions either directly or indirectly to the myth of Leander. See BOCCACCIO, *Decameron*, p. 650n; and BOCCACCIO, *Filocolo*, p. 890n. Janet Smarr, instead, traces Pampinea's comment to Vergil's *Georgics* III 258-63; see SMARR, *Boccaccio and Fiammetta*, p. 185.

[11] The lover who goes to see the walls which conceal his beloved is a common courtly love topos which also appears in the *Filocolo* II 26, 19-21.

[12] For a similar interpretation of Gianni's love madness, see SMARR, *op. cit.*, p. 185.

his faculty of reason, like Florio's, is dominated by his concupiscible appetite. Like Florio, Gianni thinks only of being in the arms of his beloved, no matter what the consequences to him and Restituta. His purpose for coming to Palermo was never to liberate Restituta: he enters the Cuba for exactly the same reason any other man entered that building. When Restituta asks him to free her, Gianni's response barely masks the selfish nature of his passion: «alla quale Gianni disse niuna cosa quanto questa piacergli, e che sanza alcun fallo, come da lei si partisse, in sì fatta maniera in ordine il metterebbe, che la prima volta ch'el vi tornasse via la ne menerebbe». Had his intentions been honorable, Gianni would have come to free her that very night. (He is not a courtly knight who comes to rescue a virgin from a fate worse than death). [13] Furthermore, he too, like Florio, has made no contingency plans should his mission fail: by ordering the ship to return to Procida, Gianni has no way of escaping from Sicily. Gianni is alone on an island where he knows no one except Restituta; therefore he cannot expect the same kind of help Florio got. These few but significant details reveal the extent to which Gianni's will has been swayed by his concupiscence: all his actions are directed towards only one end – sexual gratification. [14]

Restituta's conduct, on the other hand, may best be characterized by her intellectual appetite. Her will has been forced several times, first by the pirates who kidnapped her, and then by a king who has made her his slave and is about to deflower her. Her options are limited: she either becomes Frederick's concubine, or exchanges her virginity for her freedom. She chooses the latter and, in so doing, she exercises what little free choice she has left. Her sexual act, therefore, is largely an act of the intellectual appetite, and has little to do with her concupiscence. [15] The result of the ensuing intercourse, however, does not totally free either sex partner from their bondage, but rather transforms their opprobrious bondage into the more acceptable bonds of matrimony and vassalage.

---

[13] Even the narrator's use of a common courtly-love conceit to describe Gianni's love for Restituta, «la quale [...] amava sopra la vita sua», is ironic in light of Gianni's less than noble conduct. Gianni's love madness, like that of his counterpart in the *Filocolo*, puts both him and Restituta in danger.

[14] For a different interpretation of Gianni's actions, see MARGA COTTINO-JONES, *Order from Chaos: Social and Aesthetic Harmonies in Boccaccio's «Decameron»*, Washington, University Press of America, 1982, pp. 92-93.

[15] See footnote 5.

If Gianni and Restituta each represent the concupiscible and intellectual appetites in action, Frederick is a figure for the irascible appetite. When the king discovers the two lovers in bed, his concupiscence gives way to his irascibility. Like the Admiral of Alexandria in the *Filocolo*, Frederick's irascible appetite manifests itself in direct proportion to the frustration of his concupiscible appetite:

> Il re, al quale costei era molto nel primo aspetto piaciuta, di lei ricordandosi, sentendosi bene della persona, ancora che fosse al dì vicino diliberò d'andare a starsi alquanto con lei; e con alcuno de' suoi servidori chetamente se n'andò alla Cuba [...] in quella con un gran doppiere acceso innanzi se n'entrò: e sopra il letto guardando, lei insieme con Gianni ignudi e abbracciati vide dormire. Di che egli di subito si turbò fieramente e in tanta ira montò, senza dire alcuna cosa, che a poco si tenne che quivi con un coltello che allato avea amenduni non gli uccise. (20-22)

His wrath is provoked when he sees another man claim as his what the king thought belonged only to him (i.e. Restituta). Since Frederick was sick and therefore unable to deflower Restituta, Gianni acts as his surrogate much the same way Florio was a surrogate fulfilling the Admiral's repressed desire for Biancifiore.[16] Gianni unwittingly challenges Frederick's «power» by taking advantage of the king's momentary impotence. In so doing, he takes advantage of his rival's condition at the same time that he is taking advantage of his beloved's condition. While Gianni challenges Frederick at the level of the concupiscible appetite, Restituta challenges the king at the level of the intellectual appetite by being the one to decide which man will sleep with her that night. The king is thus punished for his abuses of power by being beaten at his own game: he is left holding a phallic-like «doppiere» like the proverbial «terzo incomodo che tiene la candela».

Like the king, Restituta and Gianni are also punished with a «contrapasso» which defines the nature of their transgressions. The two lovers find themselves in a new state of bondage (bound to the stake), about to burn by a different flame. Furthermore, what was concealed from the king's attention is now disclosed to the public. As Branca and Quaglio have shown, the lovers' discovery and public exposure in both the *Filocolo* and *Decameron* V 6 are patterned after Vulcan's discovery and exposure of the adulterous affair between

---

[16] The «gran doppiere» he holds in his hand as he stealthily enters her bedroom could easily be viewed as a phallic symbol.

Mars and Venus. [17] In both works this reenactment of the myth not only recalls the classical archetype of all disclosed love affairs, it also draws our attention to the role that the two sensitive appetites have in these affairs. When Ruggieri di Loria asks Gianni why they are condemned to the stake, Gianni's terse reply («Amore e l'ira del re») is, as Janet Smarr has shown, an acknowledgement of the role the concupiscible and irascible appetites play in determining the lovers' fate. [18] Here, as elsewhere in the *Decameron* V, Boccaccio demonstrates the opposite of Andreas Capellanus's thirteenth rule of love («Amor raro consuevit durare vulgatus»): had their affair been concealed from the public, it would have died along with the two lovers. [19] By exposing it, instead, the two lovers are able to get married and live happily ever after: «E fatti loro magnifichi doni, contenti gli rimandò a casa loro, dove con festa grandissima ricevuti lungamente in piacere e in gioia poi vissero insieme» (42). This happy ending is itself a contradiction of Andreas Capellanus' first and most famous rule of love, «Causa coniugii ab amore non est excusatio recta». [20] As in the case of Florio and Biancifiore, the protagonists' public marriage is both the solution to and resolution of their social and sexual bondage. [21]

The three appetites, each represented by one of the characters in this triangle, are finally brought under the control of reason through the wisdom of Ruggieri di Loria. After recognizing Gianni, the admiral goes to Frederick and explains to him the negative aspects of the king's wrath and the compelling nature of Gianni's love:

E io voglio che tu gli conosca, acciò che tu vegghi quanto discretamente tu ti lasci agl'impeti dell'ira trasportare. Il giovane è figliuolo di Landolfo di Procida, fratel carnale di messer Gian di Procida, per l'opera del quale tu se' re e signor di questa isola; la giovane è figliuola di Marin Bolgaro, la cui potenza fa oggi che la

---

[17] See BOCCACCIO, *Filocolo*, p. 655n; and BOCCACCIO, *Filocolo*, p. 904n.

[18] See SMARR, *op. cit.*, p. 185.

[19] Practically all the love stories in the *Decameron* deal with the exposure of a love affair by a third party (usually a jealous party). The relative merits of its concealment and disclosure are one of the key themes of these novelle.

[20] This *regula amoris*, which is based on Marie de Champagne's earlier ruling that true love cannot exist in marriage, is a cardinal point in the courtly-love code which Boccaccio is debunking both in the *Filocolo* and in *Decameron* V.

[21] For a slightly different interpretation of the conclusion, see SMARR, *op. cit.*, p. 185. For a more detailed study of the way matrimony is used for purposes of accommodation, see THOMAS GREENE, *Forms of Accommodation in the «Decameron»*, «Italica», XLV, n. 3, 1968, pp. 297-312.

tua signoria non sia cacciata d'Ischia. Costoro, oltre a questo, son giovani che lungamente si sono amati insieme, e da amor costretti, e non da volere alla tua signoria far dispetto, questo peccato, se peccato dir si dee quel che per amor fanno i giovani, hanno fatto. Perchè dunque gli vuoi tu far morire dove con grandissimi piaceri e doni gli dovresti onorare? (ll. 38-40)

The wise admiral teaches the impetuous young monarch the importance of bringing the sensitive appetites under the control of reason. Instead of making a moral case on behalf of Gianni and Restituta, which might offend the king and jeopardize the lives of the two lovers, Ruggieri di Loria proposes a strictly pragmatic solution. Pragmatic reason thus becomes a way of overcoming both sensitive appetites: Ruggieri uses it to free the two lovers, and the king in turn uses it to rectify his position vis-à-vis his two captives. The king does this by expressing his regal power in more acceptable terms: instead of imposing his will on them, he allows them to get married on their own free will («sentendo che di pari consentimento era»). He not only respects their *liberum arbitrium*, but he also redefines their social status. Restituta is no longer a slave, but a subject: the bonds of vassalage between her family and the king are reaffirmed, and take the place of her opprobrious bondage in the Cuba. Gianni's enslaving passion, in turn, is channeled into the socially accepted bond of matrimony, a bond which, in the ironic words of Ruggieri, will be just as burdensome: «Io farò sì che tu la vedrai ancora tanto, che ti rincrescerà».

Instead of exercising his power over Restituta and Gianni by succumbing to his sensitive appetites, as he had originally planned to do, Frederick exercises an even greater power over his two subjects through this pragmatic use of reason. Like the second marriage in the *Filocolo*, Frederick uses this marriage to reconcile himself with his two vassals and to consolidated his alliance with Ischia and Procida, thereby strengthening the bonds between all three islands (Sicily, Procida, and Ischia). Just as Gianni and Restituta had known how to take advantage of each other's plight in order to attain their most desired end, Frederick too takes advantage of the couples' desire for freedom and sexual gratification to reaffirm his power over them. In so doing, he too exercises a subtle form of sexual control over others (e.g. Gianni and Restituta) as well as over himself. Even though the new relationships between sovereign and subjects, and husband and wife reaffirm the notion that power must be used through «pari consentimento», the actual line separating coercion from consent has been blurred. Frederick's original intention to abuse Restituta and Gianni by invoking the *lex regia* is rectified by human reason, rather than by the *lex divina* or the *lex naturalis* (as was the case when Felice persecuted Biancifiore). However, it is the use of pragmatic reason, not right reason, that now governs the *lex humana*.

The thematic importance of marriage in this novella is similar to that in the *Filocolo*: marriage becomes the means by which the lovers' sexual transgressions cease to be precarious and dangerous. By getting married with the king's blessing, no one, not even the king, can disrupt or disapprove of their sexual activities: what was once illicit and dangerous, has now become normative and innocuous. Sex and the *lex regia* are realigned so as to conform to more pragmatic and, as Smarr has pointed out, expedient forms of conduct. [22] As in the case of Florio and Biancifiore's second marriage, Gianni and Restituta's marriage is followed by an end to the trials and tribulations which characterized their condition prior to matrimony.

Another theme from the *Filocolo* which is retrieved in this novella is the idea of nobility. The lives of Gianni and Restituta are spared because they belong to two important families, each of which represents a small island allied to the greater island of Sicily. Just as their hidden identity brought them within a hair's breadth of their death, the disclosure of their noble birth is what saves their lives. If Gianni and Restituta had belonged to a lower class, they would have certainly died. As in the case of Ruggieri's reasoning, the characters' nobility has a strictly pragmatic purpose for both the king and the two lovers. Now that they are married, Gianni and Restituta will presumably have children and thus provide future vassals for their king, thereby fostering this purely utilitarian form of nobility. Unlike the *Filocolo*, where «nobiltà di cuore» and «nobiltà di sangue» either clash or are closely interwoven, in *Decameron* V 6 there is only one kind of nobility, «nobiltà di sangue».

While modifying several themes that appeared in the *Filocolo*, Boccaccio also eliminates those themes which have no place in the *Decameron*. For example, there is a complete absence of pagan gods, both as symbols for the sensitive appetites and as supernatural beings whose role in the lives of the two lovers is part of a larger providential plan. Nowhere in the *Decameron* does there seem to be such a plan,

---

[22] See SMARR, *op. cit.*, pp. 185.

much less a supernatural presence which affects the lives of the characters. This would be in keeping with what Branca has characterized as the strictly immanent world of the *Decameron*, one which is deliberately juxtaposed to the transcendent world of Dante's *Commedia*. [23] In this novella, as elsewhere in the *Decameron*, human actions are largely determined by sublunary forces (fortune, nature, and human nature). As a result, the power of free choice in each character is no longer affected by a providential plan which determines between a right and wrong course of action. Unlike the characters in the *Filocolo*, who choose from several possible courses of action, make the wrong choice and are eventually obliged to follow the right course, the characters in the *Decameron* are not affected by an overriding moral force with supernatural powers. There is no visible connection between the characters' *liberum arbitrium* and Providence.

Another significant difference between this novella and its source is in Boccaccio's choice of characters. In the *Filocolo*, as in so many other medieval romances, the characters are only marginally connected to the realm of history. In this novella, however, many of the characters are historical. As Branca has shown, Ruggieri di Loria was in fact the admiral of King Frederick II of Aragon from 1296-1297. [24] Gianni is the nephew of the famous Gian di Procida (39), and Restituta the daughter of Marin Bolgaro who, as Branca points out, built galleys for Charles I and later became a knight of Robert of Anjou. [25] Although no one has been able to determine whether Gianni and Restituta are themselves historical figures, we can assume that they are meant to be regarded as such. [26] Practically all the historical and quasi-historical characters in the *Decameron* (including King Frederick and Ruggier di Loria) function as ambiguous «exempla» of human conduct. History may have already determined, in large part, the way in which these characters will be remembered, but Boccaccio's portrayal of them always reveals a lesser known, and usually negative aspect in their *notatio*. Pampinea's initial portrayal of Frederick is a case in point: «vennero a concordia di doverla [Restituta] donare a Federigo re di Cicilia, il quale era allora giovane e di così

---

[23] See BRANCA, *Boccaccio medievale e nuovi studi sul «Decameron»*, Firenze, Sansoni, 1981 [5], pp. 28 sg.
[24] See BOCCACCIO, *Decameron*, pp. 655n-656n.
[25] See BOCCACCIO, *op. cit.*, p. 657n.
[26] For a recent discussion of this, see PIER MASSIMO FORNI, *Forme innocue nel «Decameron»*, «Modern Language Notes», CIII, 1989, pp. 40-47.

fatte cose si dilettava» (8). Frederick's less than exemplary practice of keeping a harem is attributed, in part, to his youth. Pampinea's initial *notatio* of Frederick prepares the readers for his conduct in the rest of the novella. Like the novelle about Can Grande della Scala (I 7) and Tancredi (IV 1), Pampinea's novella focuses on a negative moment in the life of an otherwise «respectable» historical or quasi-historical figure. As in the case of the *Filocolo*, Boccaccio wants to focus on the ambiguous aspects of these characters, aspects which medieval chronicles conveniently ignore in their attempts to transform historical figures into superficial *exempla* of either good or bad conduct.

The idea that Boccaccio might be undercutting the attempts of medieval historiographers to represent human behavior in simplistic, Manichean terms is also suggested by his choice of names for his quasi-historical lovers. As we have seen, Gianni is named after Gian da Procida, but his daring labors of love (including his swimming feats and his assault of the Cuba) do not compare to the naval exploits of his famous uncle. Restituta, on the other hand, is named after Ischia's most revered saint. [27] Her adventures are a parody of the exemplary life of Santa Restituta. [28] According to a Neapolitan saint's life which predates Boccaccio's time, Saint Restituta lived in Africa at the time of Diocletian. [29] Brought before the tribunal on charges of being a Christian, the young virgin confesses her faith, whereupon she is sent to prison. While in prison she is consoled by an angel. The provincial governor Proclinus hardens his heart against her and orders her to be burned alive in a boat filled with pitch and resin. As her executioners are about to light the boat, they are submerged by a wave. While all this takes place, Restituta is comforted by her angel until she dies. (It is not clear how she dies.) The boat miraculously departs from the African shores and arrives on the shores of Ischia where a pious matrone named Leta buries the remains.

Since Boccaccio spent a good part of his youth in Naples, it is quite likely that he was familiar with some version of the saint's life.

---

[27] See BOCCACCIO, *op. cit.*, p. 649n.

[28] By naming his female protagonist Restituta, Boccaccio not only adds local color to a novella which is set, in part, on the island of Ischia, but he also establishes a parodic nexus between Restituta and the saint after whom she is named.

[29] For a summary of the eleventh century «passione» see, FRANCESCO LANZONI, *Le diocesi d'Italia*, «Studi e Testi», XXXV, 1933, pp. 152-ff. This Neapolitan «passio» is the oldest extant life of Santa Restituta. Other accounts of the saint's life may be found in the *Acta Sanctorum: Maii*, VII, pp. 781-ff. and in the *Bibliotheca hagiografica latina antiquae et mediae aetatis*, Bruxelle, Editions Soc. Bollandiana, 1898-1911, III, pp. 7190-91.

Like Saint Restituta, Boccaccio's Restituta is imprisoned by the leading authority in the land and is «consoled» by her own «angel» while in prison (much the same way madonna Lisetta is «comforted» by frate Alberto disguised as the angel Gabriel). Like her namesake, Restituta is sentenced to be burned alive and awaits her execution with her «angel» by her side. As in the saint's case, Restituta's death sentence is not carried out. Following an itinerary similar to that of her namesake, Restituta finally arrives in Ischia, thereby living up to the literal meanings of her name: *returned, restored*, and *paid back*. Restituta, in fact, is paid back for her suffering, restored to her previous social position, and returned to her native land. The fact that she only lives up to the literal meaning of her name, rather than to its spiritual analogue, suggests that she is «Restituta» in name only (much the same way Gianni da Procida is a «Gian da Procida» in name only). The two lovers are a poor *imitatio* of the *exempla* after whom they are named. By debunking these *exempla*, Boccaccio creates a more realistic and ambiguous form of character portrayal.

Boccaccio's parody of the saint's life is also reflected in the different meanings of the word «passio» (*saint's life, martyrdom, suffering*, and *passion*). The *passio Sancta Restitutae* is a narrative account of a saint's suffering and martyrdom. *Decameron* V 6, on the other hand, is a narrative account of a different kind of passion which also can lead to death. Since Restituta, like the saint after whom she is named, is virtually free of concupiscence, her «passio» consists of suffering the passions of others. Her freedom from the bondage of concupiscence, however, does not make her a Santa Restituta: there is no edification in her suffering, as we find instead in Biancifiore's suffering. [30] The somewhat utilitarian nature of Restituta's love (Fiammetta's *amor utile*) and the excessively passionate nature of Gianni's love (Fiammetta's *amor per diletto*) are distant from the *amor onesto* which Fiammetta advocated in her court of love. However, the fact that love, like reason and nobility, is put to a pragmatic and utilitarian use that is devoid of its courtly connotations does not necessarily imply moral condemnation as it did in the *Filocolo*. The fact that Restituta and

---

[30] The fact that the amorous activities in this novella are self-serving and self-centered might reinforce the position of those critics who have seen in Boccaccio's *Decameron* a condemnation of sexual love outside of matrimony; see THOMAS M. GREENE, *op. cit.*, pp. 297-312; ROBERT HOLLANDER, *op. cit.*, pp. 37-38; and VICTORIA KIRKHAM, *op. cit.*, pp. 47-59. For a completely different view, see WARREN GINSBURG, *The Cast of Character*, Toronto, Toronto University Press, 1983. Ginsburg suggests that Boccaccio is reflecting both sides of this issue without actually taking sides.

Ruggieri are the only two characters who are not slaves of their sensitive appetites, and are therefore capable of making rational and pragmatic use of both love and reason in order to overcome the irrational actions resulting from Gianni and Frederick's sensitive appetites, suggests that Boccaccio is not condemning them for their actions. Restituta's choice of *amor utile* over a fate worse than death, and Ruggieri's choice of pragmatic reason over right reason are ambiguous but effective means used to attain what they consider to be their ultimate good. [31] Even though these means may not be good in an absolute sense, Boccaccio seems to justify them in relation to their end. In the *Filocolo* such actions would have been regarded as morally wrong (at least from a Thomistic point of view), but in this novella Boccaccio does not seem to be as concerned with what is morally right or wrong in an absolute sense. Instead, he seems to be more interested in a relativist portrayal of morality and human conduct (not unlike Machiavelli's «verità effettiva»). The characters in *Decameron* V 6 may be as morally ambiguous as the characters in the *Filocolo*, but the way in which Boccaccio wants us to judge them seems to have changed since he wrote the *Filocolo*.

Similar perspectives can be found in the other novelle of the fifth day. As Thomas Greene has shown, marriage is the ultimate resolution to the lovers' plight in each novella of that day. [32] This is in sharp contrast to the tragic novelle of the preceding day where most of the lovers' affairs end tragically because matrimony was denied to them by a third party. Had marriage or some other form of acceptance been granted to the majority of lovers in the fourth day, their affairs would have ended differently. Boccaccio seems to view matrimony as a remedy which is often denied to those who need it most: it makes prodigious and dangerous deeds such as Gianni's unnecessary. When marriage is denied, the sexual experience usually results in something that is either morally ambiguous or socially unacceptable. [33] Rather

---

[31] Gianni's love for Restituta may be mistaken for courtly love, but it is neither edifying nor idealized. His ambiguous conduct proves to be more reprehensible than Restituta's «amor utile». Similarly, Frederick's nominal right over Restituta, both as king and as slave owner, is initially more reprehensible than Ruggieri's lack of right reason in his pragmatic speech to the king.

[32] See GREENE, *op. cit.*, p. 298.

[33] As Greene pointed out, the only novella of the fifth day which suggests that marriage can be an impediment towards sexual gratification is the last one. It is told by the unruly Dioneo, the only one of the ten narrators who is allowed to deviate from the established theme of the day. In his tale a married woman has an affair with a young man; when her husband

than being a moral end in itself, marriage becomes the means towards an end which ultimately acknowledges the compelling force of sexual love while recognizing its social importance. If, in the *Filocolo*, Boccaccio analyzes the nature of human love in relation to a divine love that governs the universe, in the *Decameron* he analyzes it strictly in terms of its immanent, rather than transcendent nature.

II. *Filocolo* IV 31

The two novelle in the *Filocolo* which Boccaccio revised and included in the *Decameron* are part of two *questioni d'amore* told at Fiammetta's court of love. The first novella is told by Menedon, and begins with a love triangle:

— Nella terra là dov'io nacqui, mi ricorda essere un ricchissimo e nobile cavaliere, il quale di perfettissimo amore amando una donna nobile della terra, per isposa la prese. Della quale donna, essendo bellissima, un altro cavaliere chiamato Tarolfo s'innamorò; e di tanto amore l'amava, che oltre a lei non vedea [...] (*Filocolo* IV 31, 2-3)

The alliterative formulas «amore amando» and «amore l'amava», used to describe the love the two knights share for the same woman, suggest that their love is similar despite the fact that one man is happily married to his beloved whereas the other is not. This is Menedon's first departure from the typical courtly-love triangle: the husband has successfully combined love and matrimony despite Andreas Capellanus' assertion that the two are incompatible. The notion that true love is possible in matrimony reinforces the central theme of this novella that nothing is impossible. [34] In fact, Menedon's novella and many of the «questioni d'amore» discussed at Fiammetta's court

---

discovers his wife's infidelity, rather than punish her and wreak vengeance on her lover (as his jealous counterparts had done in the fourth day) he establishes an unusual *ménage à trois*. Dioneo's retelling of Apuleius' tale reflects his own ironic interpretation of the theme of that day. Dioneo too debunks, in an ironic manner, Andreas Capellanus' first rule of love («Causa coniugii ab amore non est excusatio recta»). If marriage is the ultimate solution to sexual desire, who says that a triangle cannot exist within it so long as it is «di pari consentimento»? Dioneo's ironic novella actually asks a question which is only addressed by the novelle of the last four days: what remedy does a lover have when his/her beloved is married to someone else?

[34] The wife's promise to Tarolfo establishes a seemingly impossible relationship between the two of them: «E 'l dono il quale ella dimandò fu questo. Ella disse che volea del mese di gennaio, in quella terra, un bel giardino e grande, d'erbe e di fiori e d'alberi e di frutti copioso, come se del mese di maggio fosse, fra sé dicendo: "Questo è cosa impossibile: io mi leverò costui da dosso per questa maniera"» (IV 31, 8). Her «cosa impossibile» is immediately picked up by

of love take issue with the more established and better known «questions d'amour» of Andreas Capellanus and the courtly love tradition.

Tarolfo's attempts to win his lady's affection by jousting, promising gifts, and sending her «messagieri [...] per sapere il suo intendimento» are met with neither a «yes» nor a «no». The wife incorrectly assumes that by neither encouraging nor discouraging Tarolfo he will cease and desist:

Le quali cose la donna tutte celatamente sostenea, sanza dare o segno o risposta buona al cavaliere, fra sé dicendo: «Poi che questi s'avedrà che da me né buona risposta né buono atto puote avere, forse elli si rimarrà d'amarmi e di darmi questi stimoli». (IV 31, 4)

The wife's behavior, instead, prompts Tarolfo to persevere; and his perseverance in turn prompts her to make a rash promise:

Ma la donna, dubitando non queste cose venissero a orecchie del marito, e esso pensasse poi che con volontà di lei questo avvenisse, propose di dirgliele; ma poi mossa da miglior consiglio disse: «Io potrei, s'io il dicessi, commettere tra costoro cosa che io mai non viverei lieta: per altro modo si vuole levare via»; e imaginò una sottile malizia. Ella mandò così dicendo a Tarolfo, che se egli tanto l'amava quanto mostrava, ella volea da lui un dono, il quale come l'avesse ricevuto, giurava per li suoi iddii, e per quella leanza che in gentile donna dee essere, che essa farebbe ogni suo piacere; e se quello che domandava, donare non le volesse, ponessesi in cuore di non stimolarla più avanti, se non per quanto egli non volesse che essa questo manifestasse al marito. (IV 31, 6-7)

Like the protagonists of the *Filocolo*, the wife has several courses of action to choose from. She makes what she believes to be the right choice, but when it proves to be the worst of the options at her disposal, she is compelled to choose again. As in the case of Lelio and Florio, the course of action which seemed least likely to succeed (i.e. speaking to her husband about Tarolfo) is the only one which does succeed. [35]

_____

the narrator in the following line: «Tarolfo, udendo questo, ancora che impossible gli paresse e che egli conoscesse bene perché la donna questo gli domandava, rispose che già mai non riposerebbe né in presenza di lei tornerebbe, infino a tanto che il dimandato dono le donerebbe». In return for an impossible garden, she promises an equally impossible love, since she does not love him.

[35] This is even suggested by the way she makes her promise to Tarolfo: she threatens to report his behavior to her husband if he fails to abide by the terms of her proposal. If she had wanted to, she could have made the same threat without promising him anything.

Whereas Tarolfo's conduct is typical of the traditional courtly lover, the wife's behavior is not: her promise violates the code of *onestà* that all courtly lovers are expected to follow, according to Andreas Capellanus:

We believe we must firmly hold that when a woman has granted any man the hope of her love or has given him any of the other preliminary gifts, and she finds him not unworthy of this love, it is very wrong for her to try to deprive him of the love he has so long hoped for. It is not proper for any honest woman to put off without good cause the fulfillment of any of her promises; if she is fully determined not to listen to a suitor, she must not grant him hope or any of the other preliminary gifts of love, because it is considered very deceitful for her not to do what she has promised him. [36]

If we can assume that the wife loves her husband as much as he loves her, then her rash promise is also a violation of Andreas' third *regula amoris*: «Nemo duplici potest amore ligari». [37]

Throughout the novella the wife oscillates between being a virtuous wife in the presence of her husband, and an uncertain object of courtly desire in the presence of Tarolfo. At times she even substitutes the conventions of marital love with those of courtly love. For example, by asking for an impossible «dono» in return for her love, the wife has replaced the exchange of nuptial rings with the «guiderdone» a courtly lover receives from his beloved in return for his devotion. Furthermore, by promising to become Tarolfo's lover if he succeeds in performing a seemingly impossible labor of love, the wife replaces her vows of fidelity and love to her husband with similar vows of «leanza» and «amore» to her suitor. Her conflicting promises, however, compromise her «amore» and «leanza» to both men. [38]

The wife's noncommittal behavior at the beginning of the novella and her ensuing promise are all attempts to attain her desired end while deferring Tarolfo's desired end. [39] When she realizes that she

---

[36] ANDREAS CAPELLANUS, *The Art of Courtly Love*, trans. John Jay Parry, New York, W. W. Norton & Company, 1969, p. 166.

[37] Janet Smarr has suggested to me that the wife's conduct may be a sign of proper behavior, since medieval discussions of love usually say that any response from the lady is a good sign for the lover, who should persist even if she says no.

[38] Her conflicting promises are not unlike the conflicting vows and ensuing struggle between the protagonists' «lealtà» and «amor» in Book II of the *Filocolo*.

[39] This *dilatio* is made more suggestive by the length of this novella (the longest of the thirteen told at Fiammetta's court of love) and by the narrative itself which emphasizes the slow passing of time and the prolonged search for the attainment of each character's desired end. (By contrast, Tebano and the husband spend considerably less time accomplishing what

can no longer defer his desire after he has given her the garden, she reaffirms her promise like a willing courtly lover; but when she returns home and is asked by her husband the reason for her «melanconia» (a word which is traditionally associated with lovesickness), she responds like a virtuous wife, telling him the truth and declaring that she would rather kill herself than dishonor him. Unlike Lucrezia, however, the Roman noblewoman who actually killed herself after being raped by her husband's friend, this wife acts in a totally different manner when her husband tells her to keep her promise to Tarolfo: «Vedendo la donna la volontà del marito, ornatasi e fattasi bella, e presa compagnia, andò all'ostiere di Tarolfo, e di vergogna dipinta gli si presentò davanti». When Tarolfo asks her the reason for her visit, the wife tells him, «Per essere a tutti i tuoi voleri sono venuta; fa di me quello che ti piace». The fact that she makes no attempt to resist his desire, coupled with the fact that she has come to him in broad daylight in the company of other women, prompts Tarolfo to ask:

«Sanza fine mi fate maravigliare, pensando all'ora e alla compagnia con cui venuta siete: sanza novità stata tra voi e 'l vostro marito non può essere; ditemelo, io ve ne priego». Narrò allora la donna interamente a Tarolfo come la cosa era tutta per ordine. (48-49)

It is obvious even to Tarolfo that he would create a scandal if he tried to consummate his love under these circumstances. He has no choice but to free the wife from her promise. As in the case of the consummation episode in the *Filocolo* and the novelle of *Decameron* V, it is the disclosure rather than the concealment of love which provides the possibility for a resolution to the crisis.

Robert E. Kaske suggested in his compelling interpretation of Chaucer's *Franklin's Tale* (a tale that is similar to Menedon's novella) that the husband was probably aware that his rival would not go

---

Tarolfo and the wife were unable to do by themselves.) The concise and carefully worded speeches of the *Decameron* (each of which creates a desired effect) seem to be lacking in the *Filocolo* where the speeches produce quite a different effect, one of dilation. In Menedon's novella the «dilatio» is reflected not only in the length of the novella, but also in the narrative: the procrastination we see in both the wife and Tarolfo is similar to that of Florio and Biancifiore. Since courtship is a form of delayed gratification, Tarolfo's perseverance in it can also be viewed as a form of «dilatio». The lady's indecisiveness and her attempts to defer Tarolfo's desired end by asking him for the magic garden are also forms of «dilatio». As for her husband, the result of his long meditation is also deferred to the end of the novella, since it is by ordering his wife to undertake the course of action she kept deferring that he succeeds in making Tarolfo aware of his «follia».

through with such an opprobrious deal.[40] In the *Filocolo* this is suggested by the following:

La qual cosa udendo il cavaliere lungamente pensò, e conoscendo nel pensiero la purità della donna, così le disse «Va, e copertamente serva il tuo giuramento, e a Tarolfo ciò che tu promettesti liberamente attieni: egli l'ha ragionevolmente e con grande affanno guadagnato».

Had he any doubts about his wife's fidelity, the husband would have not decided, after so much thought, to have her keep her promise. The husband probably assumed that his wife would tell Tarolfo the truth (just as she had told it to him), and that Tarolfo, in turn, would not dare do anything dishonorable, especially now that his love has been exposed (*Amor raro consuevit durare vulgatus*[41]).

If the husband's conduct can be characterized as staying one step ahead of his wife, as Kaske suggested, the wife's behavior can best be characterized as being the result of fear. Her real dilemma is not how to avoid, at all costs, the fulfillment of her promise, but how to avoid displeasing her husband and Tarolfo. This is suggested by the fact that she gives equal importance to both her marital vows and her promise to Tarolfo without ever considering the obvious disparity between the two. As if to draw our attention to this, Boccaccio has Fiammetta declare that the wife's promise to Tarolfo was invalid because it went against her nuptial vows to her husband.[42] The fact that the wife does not use similar reasoning to solve her dilemma suggests that her reason and will have both been affected by her initial fear of evil (located in the irascible appetite), rather than by concupiscence or by a deliberate attempt to deceive the two knights. As in the case of the other characters in the *Filocolo*, the wife's will and reason are affected by one of the sensitive appetites.

No matter how bold the husband's effective gesture may be, the most striking aspect of this love triangle is the way in which the desire of both Tarolfo and the wife changes at the end of the novella. The wife's desire to free herself from her promise disappears the moment

---

[40] See ROBERT E. KASKE, *Chaucer's Marriage Group*, in *Chaucer the Love Poet*, edited by Jerome Mitchell and William Provost, Athens, Georgia, University of Georgia Press, 1973, pp. 63-4. For a more recent discussion on the relationship between these two works, see GERALD MORGAN, *Boccaccio's «Filocolo» and the Moral Argument of the «Franklin's Tale»*, «The Chaucer Review», XX, 1984, 4, pp. 285-306.

[41] ANDREA CAPPELLANO, *op. cit.*, p. 282.

[42] In Manzoni's *Promessi sposi* Fra Cristoforo makes a similar point in order to convince Lucia that she can marry Renzo.

her husband frees her from the constraints which prevented her from keeping it. She is now prepared to do what she was afraid of doing before; she does not even try to dissuade Tarolfo from exercising his nominal right over her. Ironically, it is by making his wife feel free to consummate Tarolfo's love that the husband enables her to attain her initial desire *not* to consummate it. As in the case of the wife's original desire, Tarolfo's original desire disappears the moment he too has the opportunity to fulfill it. It would seem that, just as the wife's deferral of Tarolfo's desire made it stronger, her newfound willingness to satisfy it has made it weaker: *Facilis perceptio contemptibilem reddit amorem, difficilis eum carum facit haberi.*[43] It is, however, the husband's daring course of action that actually brings an end to Tarolfo's initial desire, just as it brought an end to his wife's initial fear of either keeping or breaking her promise to Tarolfo. Desire and fear (emotions that reside in the concupiscible and irascible appetites respectively) disappear when all the constraints which nurtured them are removed.

The novella concludes with an apology and a promise by Tarolfo to the husband:

«Gentil donna, lealmente e come valorosa donna avete il vostro dovere servato, per la qual cosa io ho per ricevuto ciò che io di voi disiderava; e però quando piacerà a voi, voi ve ne potrete tornare al vostro marito, e di tanta grazia da mia parte ringraziarlo, e scusarglimi della follia che per adietro ho usata, accertandolo che mai per inanzi più per me tali cose non fiano trattate». (50)

This promise rectifies his relationship with the husband and wife, while eliminating the dangers which the two previous promises (the wife's promise to Tarolfo and Tarolfo's promise to Tebano) posed on the first and most important promise – the love and fidelity the husband and wife promised each other.

Although the relationships between Tarolfo, the husband and wife are central to Menedon's novella, the necromancer's role in this love triangle is just as important. Tarolfo's impossible labor of love brings him to Thessaly where he meets Tebano, a man whose knowledge of the occult allows him to make the impossible possible.[44]

---

[43] CAPPELLANO, *op. cit.*, p. 282. For a related discussion on the dynamics of desire, see RENÉ GIRARD, *Deceit, Desire, and the Novel: Self and Other in Literary Structure*, trans. Yvonne Freccero, Baltimore: The Johns Hopkins University Press, 1965, pp. 1-52.

[44] Thessaly was famed for witchcraft in the classical world.

Tarolfo's ensuing relationship with Tebano, like his relationships with the husband and wife, is determined by a promise: Tarolfo swears to give Tebano half of everything he owns in return for the magic garden. Initially, this new relationship is portrayed with an ominous tone: the two men meet on «lo misero piano che già tinto fu del romano sangue», which, according to Quaglio, is an allusion to the famous battlefield at Pharsalia. [45] As Quaglio has shown, this encounter recalls the encounter between Pompey's son Sextus and the witch Erictho in Book VI of Lucan's *Belli civilis*. [46] What it suggests is that if Tebano succeeds in creating the impossible garden, the consequences might be similar to the ones Erictho predicted on the eve of the battle which brought down the Roman republic. The civil war in Lucan's epic, which centers around Caesar and his son-in-law Pompey, is juxtaposed to the strife which might result on a smaller scale through the machinations of Tarolfo and Tebano. [47] The cataclysmic forces at the battle of Pharsalia have been replaced by Tebano's supernatural powers and Tarolfo's passion. Furthermore, the fact that Tebano comes from Thebes (as his name indicates and as he himself tells Tarolfo) establishes a nexus between the city of lust (Thebes) and the region of necromancy (Thessaly). [48] Tebano's Thessalian witchcraft will make it possible for Tarolfo to consummate his forbidden passion. Once the means to Tarolfo's desired end are established, the marital relationship between the husband and wife will be seriously threatened.

Menedon's allusions to Lucan's *Belli civilis* are not limited to Pompey, Caesar, and Erictho. The husband's gesture of lending his wife to another man distinctly recalls Cato's act of giving his wife Martia to his friend Hortensius, in Book II of the *Belli civilis*, so that Hortensius can sire children and not die childless. [49] Cato's noble gesture toward Hortensius is in sharp contrast to the hostile and ignoble deeds inflicted by Caesar on his son-in-law Pompey. What seems to be suggested by these allusions to Lucan's epic characters is

---

[45] See BOCCACCIO, *Filocolo*, p. 859n.

[46] See BOCCACCIO, *op. cit.*, p. 861n.

[47] The lady herself fears that she might be the cause of strife between her husband and Tarolfo.

[48] The association of lust with Thebes is not unusual in medieval literature. Venus had her abode in Mount Citeron just outside of Thebes (see note 99 in the previous chapter).

[49] This impressive act of «liberality» by Cato is narrated by Lucan in the *Belli civilis* II 374-6, and is later picked up by Dante in the *Convivio* IV XXVIII, 97-ff.

that the fate of the relationships between Tarolfo, the husband, and wife can go in either direction: ultimate liberality or civil and family strife.

The ominous tone which pervades Tarolfo's encounter with Tebano is also heightened by the latter's spectral appearance and by his warning to Tarolfo about the dangers of walking on the battlefield at dusk: «Non sai tu la qualità del luogo come ella è? Perché inanzi d'altra parte non pigliavi la via? Tu potresti di leggieri qui da furiosi spiriti essere vituperato» (15). Tarolfo is misled by Tebano's appearance in part because of his estimative power («la stimativa») and in part because he assumes that Tebano's «virtù» is proportionate to his poverty. [50] Tebano, in fact, reproaches Tarolfo for his social prejudice:

Tu e molti altri il sapere e le virtù degli uomini giudicate secondo i vestimenti. Se la mia roba fosse stata qual è la tua, tu non m'avresti tanto penato a dire la tua bisogna, o se forse appresso de' ricchi prencipi m'avessi trovato, come tu hai a cogliere erbe; ma molte volte sotto vilissimi drappi grandissimo tesoro di scienza si nasconde: e però a chi proffera consiglio o aiuto niuno celi la sua bisogna, se, manifesta, non gli può pregiudicare. (18)

Notwithstanding his reproach, Tarolfo's attitude toward Tebano remains unchanged:

Tarolfo rimirava costui nel viso, dicendo egli queste parole, e in se dubitava non questi si facesse beffe di lui, parendogli incredibile che, se colui fosse stato Iddio, ch'egli avesse potuto fare virtù. Non per tanto egli li rispose così: «Io signoreggio ne' miei paesi più castella, e con esse molti tesori, i quali tutti per mezzo partirei con chi tal piacere mi facesse». (IV 31, 19)

He treats Tebano in the same dismissive manner that the wife had treated Tarolfo; and his promise to the necromancer, like the wife's promise to Tarolfo, is made only after the «stimoli» he applied to the wife are now applied to him. [51] Like the wife, Tarolfo assumes that his

---

[50] As Quaglio has shown, Boccaccio refers to the same inner sense of the soul («la stimativa») when he explains why Biancifiore was unable to recognize Florio disguised as a knight (II 65 7); see BOCCACCIO, *Filocolo*, p. 797n. This seems to be one of the few Aristotelian parts of the soul which Boccaccio refers to by name in the *Filocolo*. It suggests that his understanding of the soul was not limited to the tripartite Galenian structure of Bernardus Silvestrus.

[51] His promise is also expressed in terms of an exchange: Tarolfo promises to give Tebano half of everything he owns in return for the garden. Although he does not tell Tebano what the garden is for, Tarolfo ultimately hopes that by giving up half of everything he owns he will be able to have the husband's «better half».

interlocutor is incapable of creating such a garden. Both Tarolfo and the wife are indirectly criticized by the narrator for underestimating the actual «virtù» of the people they shun, and for making false assumptions based on external appearances and everyday realities.

Unlike Tarolfo, however, Tebano *is* capable of doing the seemingly impossible. The expression used to indicate this, «fare virtù», refers to Tebano's supernatural powers; but the repeated use of the word «virtù» during their encounter suggests that Tebano is also capable of virtuous deeds despite appearances to the contrary. The figure of Tebano, in fact, is drawn on the topos of wisdom masked by ugliness. (The topos can be traced to Plato's *Symposium* where Alcibiades compares Socrates to the images of Silenus--ugly on the outside, but wise within.) [52] Like Socrates, Tebano's inner worth («virtù») is greater than what his external appearance suggests. This is supported by Fiammetta's commentary to Menedon's novella when she claims that Tebano's actions and motives reflect his wisdom rather than his liberality.

The fact that Menedon intended to portray Tebano as a noble individual is also supported in the discussion between him and Fiammetta. Menedon claims that Tebano is the most liberal of the three men; but Fiammetta disagrees, claiming instead that the liberality of the three men is based on what each man has at stake: the husband's honor, Tarolfo's labor of love, or Tebano's chance to become rich. For Menedon, Tebano's superior liberality seems to be based on his moral superiority. Compared to Tarolfo and the husband, Tebano is the only man whose «liberal» gesture is neither a moral imperative (as in the case of Tarolfo) nor a dubious moral act (as in the case of the husband). Menedon's portrayal of Tarolfo, in fact, debunks typical courtly-love conceits about the ennobling power of love. Tarolfo is ennobled by virtue of the husband's gesture, not by the wife's questionable behavior. Furthermore, the courtly ideal that a true lover is always generous («X Amor semper consuevit ab avaritiae domiciliis exsulare») takes on a totally new meaning: the «liberality» of Tarolfo and the husband has little to do with their love for the wife. [53] Here too, the courtly-love code is criticized. Ultimately, it is Tebano's

---

[52] It is unlikely that Boccaccio knew the *Symposium*, but this classical topos might have been familiar to him through other works.

[53] For this *regulae amoris*, see ANDREA CAPPELLANO, *op. cit.*, p. 282.

nobility of heart that proves to be less ambiguous than the question-able gestures of the two knights. [54]

As we have seen, it is through the mediation of a third party (Tebano and the husband) that Tarolfo and the wife attain their initial goal. Like the husband, Tebano works behind the scenes and triumphs when his deeds are revealed. The concealed and disclosed activities of these two men reflect the theme of concealment and disclosure which permeates this novella. Just as Tebano's concealed *probitas* is eventually disclosed through his deeds at the end of the novella, his long incantation discloses the concealed «virtù» of the occult:

O notte, fidatissima segreta dell'alte cose, e voi, o stelle, le quali al risplendente giorno con la luna insieme succedete, e tu, o somma Ecate, la quale aiutatrice vieni alle cose incominciate da noi, e tu, o santa Cerere, rinnovatrice dell'ampia faccia della terra, e voi qualunque versi, o arti, o erbe, e tu qualunque terra producente virtuose piante, e voi aure, e venti, e monti, e fiumi, e laghi, e ciascuno iddio de' boschi o della segreta notte, per li cui aiuti io già rivolsi i correnti fiumi faccendo gli tornare nelle loro fonti, e già feci le correnti cose stare ferme, e le ferme divenire correnti, e che già deste a' miei versi potenza di cacciare i mari e di cercare sanza dubbio i loro fondi [...] (31, 26)

His «versi», like those of Orpheus, are capable of extraordinary things including the resurrection of the dead («e nè morti corpi tornare dà paduli di Stige le loro ombre e vivi uscire dè sepolcri»). Tebano, in fact, makes it possible for Tarolfo to have his Eurydice; but like Orpheus, Tarolfo ultimately renounces his claim on his beloved.

The nexus between life and death in the lover's attempt to attain his desired end is as present in Menedon's novella as it is in the myth of Orpheus. We not only see it in the way his desire ceases once the desired object is within his grasp, but we also find it in the rites Tebano performs when he creates his magic garden. After erecting an altar to Hecate and one to Ceres, he evokes the two goddesses in his prayers. The goddesses symbolically represent seasons: Hecate, the goddess of the underworld, represents winter, and Ceres, the goddess of harvests and fertility, represents spring and summer. Tebano unites both seasons in a single magic moment: life returns to a season which is known for its barrenness. The certainty of death has been replaced by this unique and unreal recreation of life.

---

[54] Nor can Tebano be accused of pandering to Tarolfo's concupiscence since he is never told why Tarolfo wanted the garden in the first place.

Tebano's debunking of commonly held assumptions about reality with his creation of unprecedented new realities is also revealed in the allusive and symbolic connotations associated with his garden. This unique garden recalls the *locus amoenus* of courtly romances, where lovers are united: it gives Tarolfo the possibility of consummating his love. The unusual qualities of this garden also recall the classical Golden Age before the rape of Proserpina, when there was no winter. It is also a terrestrial paradise similar to Adam and Eve's prelapsarian world where death did not exist and where sexual intercourse was free of lust, shame, and sin. [55] Like Proserpina eating the pomegranate, or Adam and Eve eating the apple, the wife's companions eat the fruit in Tebano's garden while she gathers flowers and herbs. Unlike Eve or Proserpina, however, the wife does not partake of anything forbidden. Tebano's garden, in fact, is a place where nothing is forbidden. It is by means of this garden that Tarolfo may consummate, if he wishes, his love without the moral constraints commonly associated with an adulterous relationship. Since the lady's husband has allowed her to fulfill her promise to Tarolfo, there is no subterfuge, no transgression, and no *in flagrante delicto*: all three parties consent to the promised sexual union. This impossible garden has brought about an otherwise impossible moral state. What at first seemed forbidden within the traditional moral code of the protagonists' world, has now become morally acceptable by virtue of the garden. Tebano has transformed reality to the point that the impossible and the illicit have now become possible and licit.

As we have already seen, the transformation of moral and ethical codes brought about by the garden is accompanied by a similar transformation in the wife's attitude towards these codes. As will be the case of so many novelle in the *Decameron*, Menedon's novella illustrates how the most widely accepted codes of conduct can be easily altered and then accepted in their new form. The absence of the Tree of the Knowledge of Good and Evil in Tebano's garden, like the absence of anything forbidden, suggests that there is no distinction between good and evil in this terrestrial paradise: it is a place where malice and virtue are absent because of the total absence of moral constraints. The garden can thus be seen as representing a state of

---

[55] This is how Saint Augustine viewed Adam and Eve's prelapsarian state; see *The City of God* XIV 23-26.

moral neutrality. Ultimately, it is what Tarolfo decides to do with the garden that determines whether good or evil will come of it.

If the creation of this garden represents an attempt to return to the Golden Age (or to the prelapsarian state of Adam and Eve in Eden) by eliminating all moral constraints, Tarolfo soon realizes that this is morally impossible. (Only the naive wife believes that it is possible to do away with such constraints). In the end, neither Eden nor the Golden Age are regained. Unlike Adam, Tarolfo does not take the fruit of his desire: he already knows what is good and what is evil, and acts accordingly. Reason overcomes nature: the moral laws governing human conduct overcome the natural instincts which characterized man and woman in the Golden Age. No matter how successful Tebano is in changing realities, the moral world of the four characters can never be fully separated from the Edenic world of the magic garden. As long as the covenants which made the supernatural garden possible (e.g. the wife's promise to Tarolfo, and Tarolfo's promise to Tebano) are in conflict with the covenants of natural law which govern the social world of the characters, there can neither be a return to the Golden Age nor an Edenic fulfillment of one's desire. [56] The novella ends with a reversal of the myths of Proserpina, Adam and Eve: none of the promises are broken, just altered. Tarolfo frees the wife from her promise to him, and makes a new promise which restores the status quo; and Tebano frees Tarolfo of his promise to him, and returns to his state of poverty. The only terrestrial paradise these four characters can make for themselves in the natural world is not through the supernatural, but through human and natural laws designed to preserve the social fabric.

These thematic statements are made more suggestive by a very precise allusion to Medea's resurrection of Aeson, Jason's father. As both Zingarelli and Quaglio have shown, the lengthy description of Tebano's creation of the magical garden is taken almost verbatim from Ovid's *Metamorphosis* VII. [57] The fact that Boccaccio followed his

---

[56] For a similar interpretation, see MILLICENT JOY MARCUS, *An Allegory of Two Gardens: The Tale of Madonna Dianora* («*Decameron X,5*»), «Forum Italicum», XIV, 1980, pp. 162-174:169. Marcus sees the magic garden in *Decameron* X 5 as both a «false Eden, promising an illusion of peace, leisure, an end to all desire in the paradise of adulterous embraces» and «the *in bono* paradise of innocent love» which brings about Ansaldo's conversion from concupiscence to *caritas*. See also COTTINO-JONES, *op. cit.*, pp. 184-186; ROSARIO FERRERI, *Innovazione e tradizione nel Boccaccio*, Roma, Bulzoni Editore, 1980, pp. 63-80; and MARIO PETRINI, *Nel giardino del Boccaccio*, Trieste, Del Bianco Editore, 1986, pp. 137-144.

[57] See NICOLA ZINGARELLI *La fonte classica d'un episodio del «Filocolo»*, «Romania», XIV,

source so closely suggests that he may have meant to give this episode the same thematic significance it has in Ovid's tale. In *Metamorphosis* VII Medea uses her magic to satisfy all the wishes of her beloved Jason. The ensuing tragedy results from her excessive devotion and from Jason's proverbial infidelity, which Ovid alludes to the moment Jason plights his troth to Medea (*Metamorphosis* VII 80-ff). Medea believes Jason's promises despite his reputation; and after they are married, she rejuvenates Aeson because she is moved by Jason's devotion to his father. Medea projects on Jason her own devotion to him without realizing that he is not devoted to her. Medea thus becomes a figure of the devoted wife who is prepared to sacrifice everything and anyone, including her own brother, for her husband. She is as antithetical to the wife in Menedon's novella as Jason is to the husband.

For Medea, as for Tarolfo, the supernatural becomes the means by which she hopes to win the heart of the person she loves most. For both, however, the love they seek and wish to have is never actually attained because it is not shared by the person they love. [58] Despite the fact that both Jason and the wife in Menedon's novella promise freely, their promises do not follow the dictates of their hearts. Unlike Medea, however, Tarolfo does not avenge himself when he realizes that he cannot actually have his heart's desire. The allusions to Medea and Jason, like those to Ceasar and Pompey, point to the possible destruction of a family: this novella could have ended tragically.

These classical allusions to death and rebirth also have Christian overtones which are similar to those found in the description of Tebano's garden. Tebano works three day and three nights before creating the magic potion which brings to life the dead olive branches he stuck in the ground (even the odor of the potion is powerful enough to rejuvenate the dragons that pull his chariot). [59] The words «rinno-

---

1885, pp. 433-441; and see Quaglio's notes to his critical edition of the *Filocolo*, *op. cit.*, pp. 860-864.

[58] «Amare etenim alibi nemo potest, nisi ubi spiritus trahit amoris et voluntas cogit», says the lady of the upper nobility in Andreas's eighth dialogue; see CAPPELLANO, *op. cit.*, p. 192. This precept is in turn picked up in the ninth rule of love: «Amare nemo potest, nisi qui amoris suasione compellitur» (*op. cit.* p. 282).

[59] Ceres has a chariot drawn by dragons (*Metamorphosis* VIII 788-815). The image of Tebano's dragon-drawn chariot, however, also recalls Dante's vision in the Garden of Eden (*Purgatorio* XXXII 130-sg.) of the dragon (a figure for Satan) taking out the bottom of the chariot (a figure for the Church). When Tebano returns from his chariot ride with the magic potion, and pours it on the olive sticks in the ground, one cannot help think of Dante's dead

vellante» and «rinnovellati» and the resurrection imagery at the end of the third day recall Christ's death and resurrection. Christ's sacrifice, like the blood sacrifices Tebano makes on the altars of Ceres and Hecate, was also done so that life could come after death, and so that man could return to his prelapsarian state in Eden. Christ's sacrifice, however, is totally absent in Menedon's pagan tale. Instead, we have three pagan sacrifices--honor, desire, and wealth (as illustrated by the three kinds of «liberality» Fiammetta discusses in her commentary to the novella). Christ's human sacrifice will eventually supersede these pagan attempts at returning to a state of lost innocence: it is only through supernatural grace (not the supernatural forces of the occult) that the characters in the *Filocolo* can return to Eden. The rejuvenation and renewal must be a spiritual death followed by a spiritual rebirth through conversion (i.e. Saint Paul's death of the old man [self] followed by the birth of the new man [self]). In this novella, the closest thing to a conversion is the change of attitudes we find in all four characters; but it falls short of the Christian conversion Florio and Biancifiore will undergo in Book V.

When we look at Menedon's novella in relation to the events which have taken place in the *Filocolo*, we are reminded of the love triangle between Florio, Fileno and Biancifiore. The promise the wife makes under pressure recalls the veil Biancifiore was pressured to give to Fileno. Florio failed to handle the ensuing love triangle as discreetly as the husband in Menedon's novella. Since Fileno is Menedon's friend, this could be Menedon's way of blaming Florio for his friend's exile. [60]

This novella also anticipates the problems Florio encounters on his *peregrinatio amoris*. By concealing his identity and his love for Biancifiore, Florio fails to avert the disastrous consequences of his «lunga follia». The end of his love madness comes only after the civil strife between Florio's companions (Menedon included) and his uncle's men. The exposure of Tarolfo's «follia» through the husband's subtle move averts, instead, the civil strife that ominously loomed over the

---

Tree of the Knowledge of Good and Evil being rejuvenated when the Griffin (a figure for Christ) ties the chariot (the Church) to it; see *Purgatorio* XXXII 49-60. If Boccaccio had this Edenic episode in mind, then the analogies to Tebano's garden are quite suggestive. By bringing to life the dead olive branches (symbols of peace), Tebano is also providing the means by which the three parties of this love triangle can restore peace. In other words, his magic garden has the power of producing something good (by enabling the husband to make his impressive *donatio*) or something evil (by providing Tarolfo with the means to his desired end).
[60] As we have seen in the previous chapter, it is Menedon who solicits Florio in V 35 to help Fileno regain his human form.

characters in the novella. Finally, the idea of conversion, as it appears in the allusions to Tebano's garden and in the characters' change in attitude toward each other, will become preeminent in Book V where all the episodes reflect physical and spiritual transformations of one sort or another: from the four disdainful women who were transformed into statues, to the metamorphoses of Idalogos and Fileno, to the transformation of the rustic Caloni and Cireti into urban dwelling citizens of Calocepe, to the Christian conversions of Biancifiore, Florio, Felice, and Felice's entire empire. All these transformations reflect the characters' changing attitudes and beliefs, as well as the changing realities in their life. The fact that all the themes in Menedon's novella are echoed elsewhere in the *Filocolo* suggests that the novella was meant to be considered within the same thematic context as the adventures of Florio and Biancifiore.

III. *Decameron* X 5

Decameron X 5 differs from Menedon's novella in several respects. Whereas Menedon's novella is set in Spain and Thessaly, *Decameron* X 5 is set in Udine, a city which is too cold in winter to have a garden like the one the wife asks of her suitor. The region of Friuli has also been known for necromancy. [61] In his study on sorcery and agrarian rituals in Friuli during the sixteenth and seventeenth centuries, Carlo Ginzburg states that nocturnal battles between groups of peasants representing the forces of good (the «benandanti») and evil (usually witches and demons) took place at various times of the year in order to protect and augment the fertility of the land. [62] The Church tried to eradicate these formerly pagan rites by branding them as necromancy and by trying as sorcerers the peasants who practiced them. Although pagan agrarian rituals survive to this day in various parts of Italy, these particular nocturnal rites seem to have been unique to Friuli. Ginzburg does not have data on this «sorcery» before 1500, but it probably existed during Boccaccio's time, and it probably was regarded as necromancy even then. Although it would

---

[61] Giosuè Carducci's well known poem *Il comune rustico* alludes to witchcraft in this region. To this very day, popular tales about the occult are still told in northern Friuli.

[62] CARLO GINZBURG, *I Benandanti: Stregoneria e culti agrari tra Cinquecento e Seicento*, Torino, Giulio Einaudi editore, 1966. This work has been translated as *The Night Battles: Witchcraft & Agrarian Cults in the Sixteenth & Seventeenth Centuries*, trans. John and Anne Tedeschi, Baltimore, The Johns Hopkins University Press, 1983.

be hard to prove that the «nigromante» in *Decameron* X 5 is a «benandante», the garden that he creates is ultimately what the «benandanti» hoped to achieve through their nocturnal rites.

Besides the difference in setting, there are also differences in the characters, all of whom have a name except the «nigromante». The role of the necromancer in this novella is minimal compared to that of Tebano; and the themes associated with Tebano (*probitas* versus «nobiltà di sangue», family and social bonds versus civil strife, rejuvenation and conversion, etc.) are virtually absent in *Decameron* X 5. In fact the lengthy description of Tarolfo's encounter with Tebano and the even longer description of Tebano's creation of the garden are replaced by two sentences:

Il cavaliere, udita la domanda e la proferta della sua donna [...] in più parti per lo mondo mandò cercando se in ciò alcun si trovasse che aiuto o consiglio gli desse; e vennegli uno alle mani il quale, dove ben salariato fosse, per arte nigromantica profereva di farlo. Col quale messer Ansaldo per grandissima quantità di moneta convenutosi, lieto aspettò il tempo postogli; il quale venuto, essendo i freddi grandissimi e ogni cosa piena di neve e di ghiaccio, il valente uomo in un bellissimo prato vicino alla città con sue arti fece sì, la notte alla quale il calen di gennaio seguitava, che la mattina apparve, secondo che color che 'l vedevan testimoniavano, un de' più be' giardini che mai per alcun fosse stato veduto, con erbe e con alberi e con frutti d'ogni maniera. (X 5, 9-10)

Whereas Tarolfo travels far and wide to find Tebano, Ansaldo asks others to find a necromancer. In fact most of Ansaldo's «fatti e parole» are mediated by a third party: in addition to having others look for the «nigromante», Ansaldo also has someone speak on his behalf to madonna Dianora throughout his courtship (X 5, 6 & 11). The only time Ansaldo's words, deeds, and desires are unmediated is when Dianora comes to fulfill her promise, at which point the narrator shifts from indirect to direct discourse in order to report what Ansaldo said. [63] As in Menedon's novella, whatever is opprobrious is concealed and mediated, and whatever is honorable is disclosed and unmediated (e.g. Dianora's attempt to free herself from her promise, and Ansaldo's act of releasing her from it).

Significant differences can also be found among the characters that make up the triangle. There is a social disparity between the two men: Gilberto (the husband) is simply described as «un gran ricco

---

[63] This climactic moment, in fact, is the first and only time in the novella that Ansaldo speaks.

uomo nominato Gilberto, assai piacevole e di buon aria», whereas the man in love with his wife is described as «un nobile e gran barone, il quale aveva nome messere Ansaldo Gradense, uomo d'alto affare e per arme e per cortesia conosciuto per tutto» (4). Whereas «messere Ansaldo» (as he is referred to throughout the novella) belongs to the higher nobility, Gilberto (who never has a title before his name) belongs, in all probability, to the upper middle class. This contrasts sharply to Menedon's novella where both men are described as «cavalieri» (the husband is even referred to as a «nobile cavaliere») and where their social parity is mimetically reflected in the wife's ridiculous attempt to please them both. In the *Decameron* the social disparity between the two men makes Gilberto's situation more difficult than that of his counterpart in the *Filocolo*. Since Gilberto is at the mercy of a more powerful man, he cannot act the way his counterpart does in Menedon's novella. In fact, when Gilberto finds out about Dianora's rash promise, he reacts in a totally different manner:

Gilberto primieramente ciò udendo si turbò forte: poi, considerata la pura intenzion della donna, con miglior consiglio cacciata via l'ira, disse: «Dianora, egli non è atto di savia né d'onesta donna d'ascoltare alcuna ambasciata delle così fatte, né di pattovire sotto alcuna condizione con alcuno la sua castità. Le parole per gli orecchi dal cuore ricevute hanno maggior forza che molti non stimano, e quasi ogni cosa diviene agli amanti possibile. Male adunque facesti prima a ascoltare e poscia a pattovire; ma per ciò che io conosco la purità dello animo tuo, per solverti da' legame della promessa, quello ti concederò che forse alcuno altro non farebbe, inducendomi ancora la paura del nigromante, al qual forse messer Ansaldo, se tu il beffassi, far ci farebbe dolenti. Voglio io che tu a lui vada e, se per modo alcun puoi, t'ingegni di far che, servata la tua onestà, tu sii da questa promessa disciolta: dove altramenti non si potesse, per questa volta il corpo ma non l'animo gli concedi. (14-16)

Gilberto's irascible appetite is aroused by messer Ansaldo's concupiscible appetite and the threat it poses to his marriage. This typical juxtaposition of the two sensitive appetites never appears in Menedon's novella: Gilberto's impulsive reaction to his wife's revelation is in sharp contrast to his counterpart's long moment of meditation («il cavaliere lungamente pensò»). The knight in the *Filocolo* is in complete control of both himself and the situation: he does not even ask his wife to try to free herself from her promise (probably knowing that she is not clever enough to do so). [64] Whereas the wife in Menedon's

---

[64] Furthermore, had the wife not gone to Tarolfo prepared to keep her promise, the

novella relies on her husband for a solution to her dilemma, in *Decameron* X 5 it is the husband who tells his wife to do her best to resolve her problem.[65] It is madonna Dianora, not Gilberto, who comes up with a carefully thought-out plan to get out of her agreement with Ansaldo.[66]

Part of her plan is to tell Ansaldo a lie, unlike her naive counterpart in the *Filocolo* who tells Tarolfo the truth:

La donna vergognosa e quasi con le lagrime sopra gli occhi rispose: «Messere, né amor che io vi porti né promessa fede mi menan qui ma il comandamento del mio marito, il quale, avuto più rispetto alle fatiche del vostro disordinato amore che al suo e mio onore, mi ci ha fatta venire; e per comandamento di lui disposta sono per questa volta a ogni vostro piacere». (20)

Gilberto never showed any respect for Ansaldo's love labors. By lying, however, Dianora is able to make her plan succeed while making her husband look good in the eyes of Ansaldo. (Had Dianora told Ansaldo the truth, she would have compromised her husband and jeopardized her chances of getting out of her promise.) By emphasizing her husband's allegedly noble gesture of sacrificing both his «onor» and hers for a member of the higher nobility, Dianora is able to expose Ansaldo's ignoble desire without offending him in the process.[67]

The fact that Dianora had carefully planned all this is confirmed by what she tells Ansaldo after he has freed her from her promise:

---

surprise effect of her visit would have been minimal and Tarolfo's change of heart might not have occurred.

[65] The fact that Dianora, not her husband, becomes the key player in this game of wits is significant. As her title indicates, «madonna Dianora» is «una nobile donna», and thus belongs to the same social class as her admirer, messer Ansaldo. Due to her husband's lack of nobility, it seems all the more appropriate that she should assume responsibility for her own actions: her chances of success are greater because she is closer to messer Ansaldo's rank than her husband is. In the *Filocolo*, however, the husband's social rank matches that of his rival, thereby enabling him to display his true nobility while exposing Tebano's less than noble conduct.

[66] It is worth noting that the characters which are portrayed as the strongest figures in the two novelle (Tebano and the knight in the *Filocolo*, Dianora and Ansaldo in the *Decameron*) are the ones which belong to the nobility.

[67] By accusing Ansaldo of a «disordinato amore», when instead the narrator makes it clear that Ansaldo gets up to greet her «senza alcun disordinato appetito», madonna Dianora is able to bring to messer Ansaldo's attention the fact that his love threatens everyone's honor, including his own. Dianora is deliberately portraying Ansaldo as someone who is using his superior social station to claim a form of «rispetto» from Gilberto and Dianora which fails to take into account their «onor»: by punishing her for her rash promise, Ansaldo would actually be punishing an innocent man (Gilberto). In so doing, Dianora, like Fiammetta, juxtaposes what each man has most at stake (Gilberto's «onore» versus Ansaldo's allegedly «disordinato amore») as a way of exposing Ansaldo's inappropriate conduct.

«Niuna cosa mi potè mai far credere, avendo riguardo a' vostri costumi, che altro mi dovesse seguir della mia venuta che quello che io veggio che voi ne fate» (23). In Menedon's novella it is the husband who knows that his wife's suitor will not take advantage of her when she ingenuously comes to fulfill her promise. In *Decameron* X 5, however, it is the wife who knows that her suitor will not take advantage of her if she says and does the right things. In Menedon's novella there is no indication that the wife expected Tarolfo to free her from her promise (her blushing shame suggests just the opposite). When Dianora goes to Ansaldo, the situation is quite different: as Branca has pointed out, Dianora does not dress up «e fattasi bella» the way her counterpart did in the *Filocolo*. [68] Even though the wife in the *Filocolo* visits Tarolfo with unspecified «compagnia», it does not seem to be as deliberate as Dianora's «due suoi famigliari [...] e con una cameriera». The detail Boccaccio gives to the time of day and the three people who accompany Dianora suggests a sense of purpose behind her actions. It is her choice of proverbial scandalmongers for «compagnia» and the odd time of day (dawn, when lovers part from one another rather than come together) that prompt Ansaldo to question her action: «non vi sia noia d'aprirmi la vera cagione che qui a così fatta ora v'ha fatta venire e con cotal compagnia». His question in turn provides Dianora with the opportunity to tell him her carefully worded lie. It is clear that Dianora is eliciting this question from Ansaldo in order to be able to tell him her lie.

Dianora, however, is not the only player in this game of wits. Messer Ansaldo is as intent on exposing her rash promise as she is on exposing his «disordinato amore». When Dianora tells him the things her husband allegedly said, Ansaldo uses the occasion to indirectly criticize her for her lack of compassion by praising her husband's «compassione». Unlike Tarolfo, who believes that he can actually gain his lady's favors by doing the impossible, messer Ansaldo does not seem to delude himself about madonna Dianora's promise: «Il cavaliere [...] conoscesse per niun'altra cosa ciò essere dalla donna addomandato se non per torlo dalla sua speranza» (9). [69] Ansaldo knows that she is acting in bad faith when she tells his messenger, «E se io potessi esser certa che egli cotanto m'amasse quanto tu di', senza fallo

[68] See BOCCACCIO, *op. cit.*, p. 1153n.
[69] One should also keep in mind that prior to her promise, Dianora had rejected him in no uncertain terms (unlike her indecisive counterpart in Menedon's novella).

io mi recherei a amar lui e a far quello che egli volesse; e per ciò dove di ciò mi volesse far fede con quello che io domanderò, io sarei a' suoi comandamenti presta» (6). After the garden is made, Ansaldo gives Dianora fruit and flowers from it, «acciò che per quel potesse lui amarla conoscere e ricordarsi della promission fattagli e con saramento fermata, e come leal donna poi procurar d'attenergliele» (11). The fact that he is surprised when she actually comes to him the following morning suggests that he never actually expected her to «far fede» to her promise any more than she expected him to «far fede» of his love. Ironically, there is a certain amount of bad faith in both parties involved: neither Ansaldo's *amor* nor Dianora's *lealtà* has anything to do with why they are engaged in surprising each other.

The bad faith behind Dianora's promise may in fact be the motivating force behind Ansaldo's actions. Unlike Tarolfo, who travels from Spain to Greece in order to look for help, Ansaldo does not do much to give Dianora the garden she wants: he is not engaged in a labor of love. In fact his reasons for creating the garden and reminding Dianora of her promise seem to stem more from an irascible desire to punish his *dame sans merci* than from a concupiscible desire to consummate his unrequited love. If that is the case, then the garden becomes the means by which Ansaldo reaffirms his *onor* after being offended by Dianora's less than honorable conduct. [70]

The fact that he gives greater importance to his honor than to his unrequited love is suggested by the first words he says in the novella:

Il quale udendo la sua donna a lui esser venuta si maravigliò forte; e levatosi e fatto il nigromante chiamare gli disse: «Io voglio che tu vegghi quanto di bene la tua arte m'ha fatto acquistare»; e incontro andatile, senza alcun disordinato appetito seguire, con reverenza onestamente la ricevette, e in una bella camera a un gran fuoco se n'entrar tutti; e fatto lei porre a seder disse: «Madonna, io vi priego, se il lungo amore il quale io v'ho portato merita alcun guiderdone, che non vi sia noia d'aprirmi la vera cagione che qui a così fatta ora v'ha fatta venire e con cotal compagnia». (18-19)

The corresponding scene in the *Filocolo* is slightly different: «Tarolfo come la vide, levatosi da lato a Tebano con cui sedea, pieno di maraviglia e di letizia le si fece incontro, e lei onorevolmente ricevette, domandando della cagione della sua venuta». Tarolfo's «letizia» con-

---

[70] In this respect he is very similar to Gentile Carisendi in the preceding novella. In both novelle, *onor* becomes the motivating force which overrides passion.

trasts with Ansaldo's «sanza alcun disordinato appetito».[71] The fact that Tarolfo leaves Tebano in order to meet his lady, instead of asking the necromancer to be present, suggests that the lover still hopes to consummate his love. Had messer Ansaldo placed similar hopes in madonna Dianora's visit, he probably would not have asked the «nigromante» to be present since this would only compromise his *onor* and hers.[72] Whereas Tarolfo's «letizia» disappears when he realizes that the lady revealed her secret promise to her husband, the change in messer Ansaldo is not the same:[73]

se prima si maravigliava, udendo la donna molto più s'incominciò a maravigliare: e dalla liberalità di Gilberto commosso il suo fervore in compassione cominciò a cambiare e disse: «Madonna, unque a Dio non piaccia, poscia che così è come voi dite, che io sia guastatore dello onore di chi ha compassione al mio amore [...]» (21-22)

Branca translates «il suo fervore» as «il suo amore fervente»; but the word could refer to Ansaldo's irascible appetite.[74] Ansaldo curbs his irascible appetite towards Dianora the same way Gilberto had curbed his the day before. The «compassione» Ansaldo attributes to Gilberto is actually a common suffering («compassio») they share as a result of Dianora's lack of «rispetto»: the *onor* of both men is either menaced or put in doubt by her conduct.[75]

By having Dianora speak to him in the presence of the «nigromante», Ansaldo publicly reveals his honorable intentions while ex-

---

[71] The narrator's remark «sanza alcun disordinato appetito» belies Dianora's earlier accusation about Ansaldo's «disordinato amore» (20) just as her false claim about Gilberto's «rispetto» for Ansaldo's love labors is a projection of her own lack of respect for him and his deeds.

[72] The fact that messer Ansaldo's first words in the novella are his remark to the necromancer, «Io voglio che tu vegghi quanto di bene la tua arte m'ha fatto acquistare» suggests that the necromancer's presence is not gratuitous. The presence of a third party in this episode no longer functions as a mediator of desire, but rather as a witness to Ansaldo's honorable behavior and Dianora's less than honorable conduct.

[73] Unlike Tarolfo, who deduces that the wife told her husband about her rash promise, messer Ansaldo does not make the same assumption: it is madonna Dianora who makes it for him («né amor che io vi porti né promessa fede mi menan qui ma il comandamento del mio marito»). This difference is significant since it underscores the fact that madonna Dianora is attempting to free herself of her promise, whereas her counterpart in the *Filocolo* was naively doing what her husband told her to do. Gilberto and the wife in Menedon's novella let the members of the nobility play a game in which they are merely pawns. In the end both women obey their husbands (one of several marriage vows they took when they got married), but each does so in a very different way.

[74] See BOCCACCIO, *Decameron*, p. 1154.

[75] Here, as in the *Filocolo*, an open lie reveals a concealed truth.

posing her lack of «compassione» towards him. Furthermore, by giving her the proof she wanted of his love, Ansaldo exposes her bad faith with his own act of «fede». By lying to Ansaldo when she asked for this proof and when she said that Gilberto was motivated by «rispetto», Dianora fails to be *onesta* (as her husband had wanted) and *leale* (as Ansaldo had asked of her). Unlike her naive and indecisive counterpart in the *Filocolo*, Dianora proves to be both deceptive and dishonest, which may be why Ansaldo's feelings for her change from *amor* to *ira*.

At the end of Menedon's novella, Tarolfo asks to be forgiven for his «follia» (50), whereas in *Decameron* X 5 messer Ansaldo shows no sign of shame, nor makes any apology to Dianora or Gilberto. His conduct may be attributed in part to a nobleman's «sprezzatura», but it is also possible that he saw no need to apologize, especially if his intentions for commissioning the garden were honorable. The fact that messer Ansaldo welcomes her «onestamente» (18), whereas Tarolfo welcomes his beloved «onorevolmente», recalls Gilberto's earlier remarks to his wife about *onestà* and what constitutes an «onesta donna» (14-16).[76] Boccaccio's use of the words *onesta, onestà*, and *onestamente* (taken from the Stilnovist poets) mitigates any sexual threat the meeting between Dianora and Ansaldo might have, while highlighting the novella's loftier themes of *onor, lealtà*, and *onestà*. These words are also indicative of what the relationship between Dianora and Ansaldo ought to be--an honest and chaste one.[77] Madonna Dianora's *onestà* is twofold: as Gilberto points out to her, it is tied to both her word of honor and her «castità».[78] But her two conflicting promises (fidelity to her husband and her «promessa» to messer Ansaldo) have compromised both her *onestà* and *lealtà*. It is only when Gilberto and Ansaldo free her from these conflicting promises to them that both her *onor* and theirs are restored.

More than a revision of Menedon's novella in the *Filocolo*, this

---

[76] Branca suggests that this particular sentence recalls the courteous manner with which Federigo degli Alberighi receives monna Giovanna when she visits him; see BOCCACCIO, *Decameron*, p. 1153n. If Boccaccio intended for us to associate Ansaldo with Federigo, then this would be one more detail which mitigates the idea of sexual indebtedness during this encounter.

[77] The confrontation ends with the remark «ma sempre per lo tempo avvenire avendo per fratello e per servidore». For a similar interpretation see MARCUS, *op. cit.*, pp. 169-170.

[78] Honor is as important for Dianora as it is for her husband. This is because she has the same social importance as messer Ansaldo. Her counterpart in the *Filocolo*, instead, is more of a lay figure.

novella is actually a palinode to *Decameron* VIII 7.[79] In the latter novella, Rinieri falls in love with Elena, a widow who already has a lover, but uses Rinieri's love to make her lover jealous. When Rinieri discovers that he has been duped by Elena's false promise, his love is transformed into a violent hatred which is appeased by an act of vengeance attained «per alcuna nigromantica operazione» (47). The tension that exists between Dianora and Ansaldo certainly cannot be compared to the cruelty that Elena and Rinieri show each other. However, *Decameron* VIII 7 shows how violent even the best educated suitor can become on account of the «ingiuria fattami in premio del grande amore che io le portava» (49). The fact that Ansaldo neither takes advantage of Dianora's foolish promise nor attempts to make her suffer for her lack of compassion is indicative of his ability to keep both his concupiscible and irascible appetites under control. As a result, none of the characters in this novella suffer the insult and injury their counterparts suffer in the first nine days of the *Decameron* for similar temptations and transgressions. Instead, Dianora and Ansaldo expose each other's wrongdoing in such a way as to rectify their actions. This union of justice and mercy is itself a palinode to the retaliatory «beffe» of the *Decameron*. However, the fact that Dianora uses ambiguous means to attain her honorable end, while Ansaldo attains his ambiguous end with honorable means, suggests that their actions, in the end, are not quite as «noble» as they would appear to be. Like the other novelle of *Decameron* X, this one too suggests that there is a certain amount of ambiguity behind the actions «di chi liberalmente o vero magnificamente alcuna cosa operasse intorno a' fatti d'amore o d'altra cosa» (the theme of *Decameron* X).[80]

Both Menedon's novella and *Decameron* X 5 are, to a certain extent, the story of the *brigata* itself. The ten narrators have fled from Florence in an attempt to defer something that must eventually be confronted (i.e. death and the horrors of the plague). They have created a terrestrial paradise in which they hope to find their desired end; but as the tenth Day nears its end, they too, like Dianora and the wife in Menedon's novella, can neither defer nor deny the conse-

---

[79] For two recent discussions of this novella see Millicent Marcus, *Misogyny as Misreading: A Gloss on «Decameron» VIII, 7*, «Stanford Italian Review», IV, 1984, 1, pp. 23-40; and Robert M. Durling, *A Long Day in the Sun: «Decameron» VIII 7* in *Shakespeare's «Rough Magic»: Renaissance Essays in Honor of C. L. Barbar*, ed. Peter Erickson and Coppélia Kahn, Newark, University of Delaware Press, 1985, pp. 269-275.

[80] See Boccaccio, *Decameron*, p. 1106 and 1111.

quences of their actions. They therefore abandon their Edenic world, as Ansaldo and Tarolfo did, and return to a world from which one can never fully escape. The escapist tendencies of the *brigata*, as reflected in their lifestyle and the novelle they tell during the first nine days, have been replaced by a novella which signals the end of their idyllic interlude while revealing the impossibility of creating an Edenic world which is totally divorced from reality.

IV. *Filocolo* IV 67

The thirteenth and last «questione d'amore» in the *Filocolo*, contains several themes and motifs which appeared in Menedon's novella. Like Menedon's novella, this one is also about a love triangle in which the husband risks losing his wife to another man. In Messaallino's novella, however, it is the husband's negligence, not that of the wife, that threatens the marital bond that unites them. As in Menedon's novella, Messaallino's novella begins by narrating how one man «avea per sua sposa una bellissima e giovane donna, la quale egli sopra tutte le cose del mondo amava» and how another man tried to win her love in vain. Whereas the wife in Menedon's novella neither rejects nor accepts Tarolfo's suit, the wife in Messaallino's novella rejects her suitor in no uncertain terms. Unlike Tarolfo, however, the knight does not pursue his suit. Instead, he accepts to rule a city at the request of its citizens, thereby adopting a well-established *remedia amoris* to cure his *aegritudo amoris*. [81] While serving his term in office, he is told that the woman he loved is dead: «Signor mio, siavi manifesto che quella donna la quale voi sopra tutte l'altre amavate nella nostra città, questa mattina, volendo partorire, per grave doglia non partorendo morì, e onorevolemente co' suoi padri in mia presenza fu sepellita» (IV 67, 3). The woman allegedly died as she was about to give birth, and was buried beside her ancestors («padri»). The chain of generation and succession has been temporarily interrupted because the woman was unable to give birth to the son who would outlive her and continue the succession of her «padri». As the knight soon finds out, however, the woman is buried alive along with her still unborn child. The womb/tomb imagery underscores the thematic importance of the life/death

---

[81] This anticipates Caleon's rulership of Calopcepe, which, as Janet Smarr has pointed out, serves to help him overcome his unrequited love for Fiammetta; see SMARR, *Boccaccio and Fiammetta*, p. 54.

theme which pervades this novella. [82] In fact, the worlds of the living and the dead are separated by a blurred line which recalls Tebano's world of the occult.

Immediately after hearing about her death, the knight enters her tomb to take from her in death what she refused to give him in life:

entrò in quella e con pietoso pianto dolendosi cominciò a baciare la donna e a recarlasi in braccio. E dopo alquanto, non potendosi da baciare costei saziare, la cominciò a toccare e a mettere le mani nel gelato seno fra le fredde menne, e poi le segrete parti del corpo con quelle, divenuto ardito oltre al dovere, cominciò a cercare sotto i ricchi vestimenti: le quali andando tutte con timida mano tentando sopra lo stomaco la distese, e quivi con debole movimento sentì li deboli polsi muoversi alquanto. Divenne allora questi non poco pauroso, ma amore il facea ardito: e ricercando con più fidato sentimento, costei conobbe che morta non era; e di quel luogo la trasse con soave mutamento (IV 67, 6-8).

The act of entering her tomb corresponds to his desire to enter her womb. The description of the erogenous parts of the lady's presumably dead body and the knight's growing sexual desire reach an anticlimactic moment when he discovers that her body is not a corpse. The discovery is made as he moves his hand down towards «quel luogo ove ogni dolcezza si richiude» (IV 118, 6). [83] The locus of fulfilled sexual desire is also the locus of life: when the knight reaches the «stomaco» he discovers the «deboli polsi» (presumably those of the child in the lady's womb) at which point his erotic desire ceases. The sexual desire which was stimulated by the body of a woman presumed dead, disappears the moment the knight discovers that both the body and «quel luogo ove ogni dolcezza si richiude» are filled with life. [84] The knight's necrophilia is therefore a sterile love — a desire for

---

[82] For a detailed analysis of the life/death ambiguity which centers on the figure of the lady and permeates the whole novella, see DENNIS DUTSCHKE, Boccaccio: A Question of Love: A Comparative Study of Filocolo IV 13 and Decameron X 4, «Humanities Association Review», VI, 1975, pp. 300-312.

[83] This periphrasis is, in fact, almost identical to the one used to describe Florio's fondling of Biancifiore's body while she is asleep; see Filocolo IV 118, 6. In both accounts, this is the first time the lover comes in physical contact with his beloved.

[84] As Dutschke has pointed out, «life and death appear so intertwined [...] in the oscillating thoughts thereby expressed that the expected action in life (the consummation of love) becomes possible only in death. Normal reality has been replaced with a new one, so that life and death, no longer merely equivalent to one another, totally reverse their positions [...] Ordinary moral and emotional considerations (sorrow, respect for the dead, fear) as well as physiological perception do not suppress the cavalier's excesses»; see DUTSCHKE, op. cit., p. 303.

something dead. It is soon replaced, however, by a nobler, platonic love which gives life to both the lady and her child.

After bringing her to his mother's home, the knight has her placed in a warm bath (itself a womb symbol) in order to bring her back to life:

onde la donna risentendosi cominciò a chiamare la madre di lei, domandò dove ella fosse. A cui il cavaliere in luogo della madre rispose che in buon luogo dimorava e ch'ella si confortasse. E in questa maniera stando, come fu piacere degl'iddii, invocato l'aiuto di Lucina, la donna, faccendo un bellissimo figliuolo maschio, da tale affanno e pericolo si liberò, rimanendo chiara e fuori d'ogni alterazione, e lieta del nato figliuolo [...] Ritornata adunque la donna dopo il grave affanno alla vera conoscenza, essendo già nato nel mondo il nuovo sole, davanti si vide il cavaliere che l'amava e la madre di lui a' suoi servigii ciascuno di loro presto; e de' suoi parenti, miratosi assai dintorno, niuno vide. (IV 67, 10-12)

The lady's resuscitation is described as a rebirth: the knight becomes her surrogate mother («il cavaliere in luogo della madre»). Her rebirth and the ensuing birth of her son reestablish the chain of generation and succession which had been disrupted by her own family. The fact that the lady's family is conspicuously absent during this important moment («e de' suoi parenti, miratosi assai dintorno, niuno vide») further underscores their failure to insure the continuity of their lineage. By contrast, the fact that both the knight and his mother are present when the lady gives birth to her son suggests a doubling of kin since the survival of the younger mother and son depends on the deeds of the older mother and son.

In return for having saved her life and that of her new born son, the knight asks the woman not to reveal her identity to anyone (not even to her husband), and to wait for him to complete his term in office. She agrees, and after the knight has completed his mayorship, he invites the husband and the wife's brothers to dinner. In the ensuing banquet scene, the knight has the wife sit by her husband dressed as she had been when her relatives buried her alive. [85] The purpose for doing this prior to the *agnitio* is not simply to create a surprise effect, but to see if the same «parenti», who had declared her dead, are now capable of declaring that she is alive. They fail to do so: for them it is easier to pronounce her dead than alive. Even her

---

[85] As a sign of the knight's honorable intentions, Messaallino makes a point of saying that the wife sat on one side of her husband while the knight sat on the other. Similarly, the knight's mother is always present throughout the wife's resuscitation and convalescence.

husband, the man who should know her better than anyone else, fails to acknowledge her as his wife:

Era questa donna dal marito sovente riguardata, e i drappi e gli ornamenti, e fra sé gli parea questa conoscere essere sua donna, e quelli essere i vestimenti co' quali sepellita l'avea, ma però che morta gliele parea avere messa nella sepoltura, né credea che risuscitata fosse, non ardiva a far motto, dubitando ancora non forse fosse un'altra alla sua donna simigliante, estimando che più agevole fosse a trovare e persona e drappi e ornamenti simiglianti ad altri, che risuscitare un corpo morto; ma non per tanto sovente rivolto al cavaliere domandava chi questa donna fosse. A cui il cavaliere rispondea: «Domandatene lei chi ella è, che io non lo so dire, di sì piacevole luogo l'ho menata». (IV 67, 19-20)

His doubts («dubitando») and lack of daring («non ardiva»), qualities which instead appeared in the knight, reveal basic flaws in his character. [86] The husband, in fact, did not give his wife the same importance the knight gave her at the time of her alleged death. Had the husband actually loved her «sopra tutte le cose del mondo», he too would have gone to the sepulcher and discovered that she was either alive or missing. [87] The husband's failure to fully ascertain his wife's death and his complete abandonment of her after her alleged death are tantamount to repudiation and benign neglect. When he eventually acknowledges his wife during the *agnitio*, the husband is ultimately acknowledging his failures as a husband.

Like the other novelle told in Fiammetta's court of love, this one too can be seen as reflecting an aspect in the lives of Florio and Biancifiore. The king and queen's rejection of Biancifiore (like the husband's unintended repudiation) jeopardizes their lineage since Florio does not want anyone but Biancifiore as his wife and consort. The king and queen's hatred of Biancifiore throughout the first four books of the *Filocolo* is antithetical to all the principles of love, generation, and succession illustrated in Messaallino's novella. Furthermore, the lady's false death and actual burial recalls Biancifiore's false death and burial which the queen devised in order to hide the fact that Felice had sold her as a slave. Like the knight in Messaallino's novella, Florio too saw the tomb in which Biancifiore was allegedly buried. The knight's invective against death and his subse-

---

[86] The knight's «ardire» is consonant with the qualities associated with a true courtly lover.

[87] Messaallino in fact states that after the knight removed the lady from the tomb, he departed «lasciando la sepoltura aperta» (8).

quent discovery that his beloved is alive recalls Florio's despair and subsequent discovery that Biancifiore is not dead. Like the husband, however, Florio does not ascertain whether or not Biancifiore is actually dead. (Could this be Messaallino's way of criticizing Florio for wanting to commit suicide the moment he heard that Biancifiore was dead?) Finally, the knight's mother in Messaallino's novella plays a role that is diametrically opposed to the role played by Florio's mother. Rather than seek the death or bondage of her son's beloved, the mother in this novella helps her son bring his beloved back to life. Since Messaallino is fully aware of the events surrounding Florio's star-crossed love for Biancifiore, he may have wanted to tell a tale which alluded to the events that brought about their journey to Naples. [88]

As in the case of the other stories told at Fiammetta's court of love, Messaallino's novella not only alludes to problems in the lives of Florio and Biancifiore, but also suggests some solutions. For example, the eventual return of Biancifiore to the king and queen is anticipated by the wife's return to her husband and brothers: in both cases the dynastic succession is guaranteed by virtue of the woman's return to her family. Furthermore, just as the knight succeeds in having the husband reacknowledge his repudiated wife, Florio too will succeed in eventually having the king and queen accept Biancifiore after years of repudiation. In both cases, this acknowledgement fulfills the ultimate desire of all parties involved.

V. *Decameron* X 4

Decameron X 4 follows the *Filocolo* more closely than the other two novelle we have seen. There are, however, several significant differences. [89] One of the first things to strike the reader is that Boccaccio is able to give us a more complete picture of the characters and their actions with a limited, yet pertinent use of detail. For example, whereas Messaallino's novella is set in his native town of

---

[88] His veiled way of alluding to Florio's mishaps is not unlike Florio's own «coperto parlare» (IV 16, 10) when he speaks to Caleon about his misfortunes.

[89] In addition to Dennis Dutschke's comparison of this novella with its source in the *Filocolo*, see MARIO BARATTO, *Realtà e stile nel Decameron*, Vicenza, Neri Pozza Editore, 1970 («Nuova Biblioteca di Cultura», XXXIV), pp. 145-48 and 146n; GIORGIO PADOAN, *Il Boccaccio, le muse, il Parnaso e l'Arno*, Firenze, Olschki, 1978 («Biblioteca di "Lettere Italiane" Studi e Testi», XXI), pp. 22-24 and 110-112; and especially LAURA SANGUINETI WHITE, *op. cit.*, pp. 139-160.

Grenada, *Decameron* X 4 is set in Bologna, a city famous for its university — the most important one in Europe for jurisprudence. The significance of this setting becomes apparent later in the novella when Niccoluccio, the husband, is asked to make a ruling on a particular «questione» asked by Gentile, the man who rescued his wife. Like the extraneous «questione» in the *Filocolo*, the «questione» and «sententia» in *Decameron* X 4 are given quasi-legal importance. [90]

As for the characters, the three members of the triangle are all referred to by name (unlike their nameless counterparts in *Filocolo* IV 67), thus revealing their noble caste. Gentile Carisendi and Niccoluccio Caccianemico belong to two noble families who lived in Bologna during Boccaccio's time. [91] As for the apparent death of Catalina, it is described in greater detail: we are told that she is pregnant and living by herself on one of her estates three miles from Bologna, while her husband is out of town. Catalina's isolation and the fact that her relatives do not know about the advanced state of her pregnancy convey a sense of neglect even before her alleged death: [92]

e per ciò che le sue più congiunte parenti dicevan sé avere avuto da lei non essere ancora di tanto tempo gravida, che perfetta potesse essere la creatura, senza altro impaccio darsi, quale ella era, in uno avello d'una chiesa ivi vicina dopo molto pianto la sepellirono. (7)

Unlike her counterpart in the *Filocolo*, who is buried beside her «padri», Catalina's simple burial in a local church underscores her family's «senza altro impaccio darsi», and diminishes the importance of succession and generation which we found in Messaallino's novella.

The shift away from the themes of life and death, succession and generation, etc. can also be seen in Gentile's descent into Catalina's tomb: [93]

Ma sì come noi veggiamo l'appetito degl'uomini a niun termine star contento ma sempre più avanti desiderare, e spezialmente quello degli amanti [...] Vinto

---

[90] As Sanguineti White has pointed out, «E proprio in quanto decisione unanime, raggiunta attraverso il libero dibattito, essa assume il valore di *sententia* finale e inappellabile. Il gruppo che la emette assurge al ruolo di assemblea con valore decretale irreversibile: il fraseggio con cui la concordanza in un medesimo parere è espressa ("tutti in una sentenzia concorrendo" 28) è infatti mutuato dalla terminologia della corte suprema ("concurrere in sententiam")», *op. cit.*, pp. 159-160.

[91] BOCCACCIO, *Decameron*, pp. 1138.

[92] For a related discussion of this passage, see COTTINO-JONES, *op. cit.*, p. 177-78.

[93] For an interesting interpretation of Gentile's descent into the underworld, see MAZZOTTA, *The World at Play in the Boccaccio's Decameron*, pp 70-72.

adunque da questo appetito le mise la mano in seno: e per alquanto spazio tenutalavi gli parve sentire alcuna cosa battere il cuore a costei. (X 4, 10-11)

Unlike his counterpart, Gentile stops at her breast rather than at her belly. This more discreet description minimizes the morbid necrophilia of *Filocolo* IV 67, while de-emphasizing the importance of the unborn child. In fact, the actual birth of the child takes place after Catalina has agreed, at Gentile's request, to wait three months before returning to her family. This detail further diminishes the thematic importance of succession and generation while giving greater importance to the pact Gentile makes with Catalina, a pact which is based on the *onor* of both parties.

The thematic focus of *Decameron* X 4 is, in fact, the preservation of the nobility's *onor* through their noble deeds: it is their *probitas*, not their «nobiltà di sangue», that will enable them to survive in an age when their power and prestige are eroding. [94] Furthermore, the civil order and commonweal of cities like Bologna depend in large part on noble families respecting and helping each other, rather than killing one another in their quest for wealth and power: whereas one family (the Caccianemico) would accidentally bring about Catalina's death, another family, and potential rival (the Carisendi) saves her life. [95] Rather than illustrate the different kinds of love the two men have for the same woman, Lauretta's novella emphasizes the need to redefine the love each man has for Catalina so that both families remain intact along with their honor and good name. [96]

Like madonna Dianora, madonna Catalina too expresses concern for her good name and that of her husband the moment she returns to her senses:

---

[94] Sanguineti White alludes to the motif of «onore» when she analyzes the way Gentile actually *honors* his guests (*op. cit.*, pp. 152-53). The theme of honor, however, extends itself beyond the banquet scene itself.

[95] The fact that Gentile not only invites Niccoluccio, but also «molti e gentili uomini di Bologna» (23), suggests that this gathering of noblemen («gentili uomini») is meant, among other things, to reaffirm the bonds that tie them together. As Sanguineti White has stated, «i sentimenti di pacificazione e amicizia si estendono anche alle famiglie in una visione di raggiunto equilibrio sociale [...] La generosità che porta al sacrificio del sentimento personale in favore di quello sociale, è una forma attiva e coesiva dell'istituzione sociale [...] Il microcosmo del convito assurge a macrocosmo della società ideale in quanto i convenuti, per qualità («gentili») e codice di comportamento, forniscono la rappresentazione della comunità completa e perfetta che discute, controbatte e si concorda armoniosamente e liberamente in una unanime opinione», *op. cit.*, pp. 158-59.

[96] If Gentile and Catalina had wanted to, they probably could have eloped and justified it on the grounds of Niccoluccio's «culpa» (negligence). This, however, would have brought shame to both families, and possibly a blood feud.

Di che ella dolendosi, dopo alquanto quelle grazie gli rendé che ella poté, e appresso il pregò, per quello amore il quale egli l'aveva già portato e per cortesia di lui, che in casa sua ella da lui non ricevesse cosa che fosse meno che onor di lei e del suo marito e, come il dì venuto fosse, alla sua propria casa la lasciasse tornare. (16)

A similar concern is not expressed by her counterpart in the *Filocolo* (family *onor* does not have the same thematic importance in Messaal-lino's novella that it has in *Decameron* X 4 & 5). Gentile promises to treat Catalina as a sister but adds «questo mio benificio operato in voi questa notte merita alcun guiderdone». The sexual connotations of the word «guiderdon» are mitigated by his promise.[97] Catalina, in turn, promises to grant him his wish on the condition that «ella potesse e onesta fosse». Her Dantean *onestà* further mitigates any sexual in-nuendo which might result from her indebtedness to Gentile.[98] Like madonna Dianora, Catalina finds herself in a situation where she could lose her good name to her unrequited lover.

Like the true nobleman that he is, Gentile (whose very name means *noble*) tells Catalina that he would like her to wait for his term as *podestà* to expire before returning her to her family.[99] Catalina, however, has misgivings about waiting that long:

La donna, conoscendosi al cavaliere obligata e che la domanda era onesta, quantunque molto disiderasse di rallegrare della sua vita i suoi parenti, si dispuose a far quello che messer Gentile domandava; e così sopra la sua fede gli promise. (19-21)

Like the true noblewoman that she is, Catalina promises to carry out Gentile's «domanda [...] onesta» even though she would prefer to lessen the sorrow of her relatives by letting them know right away that she is alive. Her noble concern for her family and relatives contrasts sharply with their «senza altro impaccio darsi» (7). Her Vergilian *pietas*, which is absent in her counterpart in the *Filocolo*, is another

---

[97] We need only recall the sexual connotations that the word «guiderdone» has in the love poetry of the Scuola Siciliana to see how Gentile's request might be misinterpreted as a sexual favor.

[98] Messaallino's knight makes a point of reminding the wife that she and her child are indebted to him (14-15). Gentile, on the other hand, is more discreet when he asks Catalina to grant him this «grazia».

[99] His counterpart in Messaallino's novella does not tell her what he plans to do after he has completed his term in office (Gentile, instead, does). This difference could be another case of *dilatio*: by waiting for his term in office to come to an end, the knight in Messaallino's novella has more time to think about what he should do with the lady.

detail used to highlight Catalina's *nobiltà di cuore*. Her concern for her family's sorrow eliminates any suggestion that she wants to play on her husband's sorrow as a way of reprimanding him for his negligence. Like Gentile, Catalina too proves to be «per virtù e per nobiltà di sangue raguardevole assai» (5). Both acquired and achieved nobility are fused together in Catalina and Gentile: they both embody the courtly ideals of their class. The trick they play on Niccoluccio can therefore be seen as a way of teaching him to appreciate both forms of nobility since, by discarding his wife and unborn son, Niccoluccio was, in effect, discarding both his own and Catalina's nobility. This harmless trick, therefore, becomes a palinode to the nasty «beffe» in the *Decameron* which adulterous wives and their lovers play on their unknowing husbands. The trick Gentile and Catalina play on Niccoluccio does not add insult to injury (as in the case of the adulterous «beffe»), but rather it makes Niccoluccio appreciate Gentile and Catalina's true nobility.

The three months which separate the day of Catalina's burial from the day Gentile invites Niccoluccio to dinner and completes his term as *podestà* can be viewed as a case of *dilatio*. One can assume that during that time Niccoluccio felt Catalina's absence more than if she had been returned to him the day after her burial. Does Gentile wait this long so that Niccoluccio will feel Catalina's absence and better appreciate her return from the dead («Facilis perceptio contemptibilem reddit amorem, difficilis eum carum facit haberi» [100])? Or is the delay due to the fact that, as mayor of a neighboring city, Gentile cannot play such a trick on one of Bologna's noblest families without creating the impression that he is using his office and power to a personal end? [101] It is possible that Gentile had both reasons in mind when he asked Catalina to wait those three months.

As in *Decameron* X 5, the family's good name is preserved through a trick that two members of the love triangle play on the third

---

[100] Andreas Capellanus's cardinal rule seems to be the *raison d'être* for most forms of *dilatio* in the courtly romance. In this case it illustrates how Niccoluccio took his wife for granted.

[101] This seems to be supported by the fact that Gentile has Niccoluccio over for dinner the same day his term in office expires. Had he played this game while he was still mayor, Gentile could have been accused of dishonestly using his public office for an amorous matter, something Lisimaco is guilty of in *Decameron* V 1: «Questo gli parve agevole per lo uficio il quale aveva, ma troppo più disonesto il reputava che se l'uficio non avesse avuto: ma in brieve, dopo lunga diliberazione, l'onestà diè luogo a amore, e prese per partito, che che avvenir ne dovesse, di rapir Cassandrea» (53). Gentile is obviously not like Lisimaco.

member. In *Decameron* X 4, however, it is the husband who becomes the focal point of the game, whereas the wife is merely a prop. The game consists of a banquet at which Gentile promises to honor his guests «alla persesca» by showing them his most prized possession; but first they must respond to a «questione». Gentile's «questione», like its thirteen counterparts in the *Filocolo*, is based on an anecdote: a very sick servant is abandoned by his master and left to die in the middle of the road. A compassionate stranger finds him, brings him home and nurses him back to good health. The «questione» Gentile asks is whether the first master has any right to have his servant back if the second master refuses to give him back. On behalf of all the guests, Niccoluccio answers that the first master has forfeited his rights on his servant after abandoning him. Pleased by his reply, Gentile proceeds to honor his guests «alla persesca» by showing them Catalina and her child. What ensues corresponds more or less to *Filocolo* IV 67:

I gentili uomini, onoratola e commendatala molto e al cavaliere affermato che cara la doveva avere, la cominciarono a riguardare; e assai ve n'eran che lei avrebbon detto colei chi ella era, se lei per morta non avessero avuta. Ma sopra tutti la riguardava Niccoluccio, il quale [...] sì come colui che ardeva di sapere chi ella fosse, non potendosene tenere, la domandò se bolognese fosse o forestiera. La donna, sentendosi al suo marito domandare, con fatica di rispondersi tenne; ma pur per servare l'ordine posto tacque. (32-33)

Unlike his counterpart in the *Filocolo*, Niccoluccio does not hesitate to ask Catalina where she is from. His ardent desire to know this («ardeva di sapere») contrasts sharply with his lack of ardor to ascertain her death. However, instead of believing that she is his wife, Niccoluccio prefers to believe in the «judgment» of the doctor who pronounced her dead («da alcun medico morta giudicata fu»). In fact, both he and the other guests stand by this faulty judgment: «assai ve n'eran che lei avrebbon detto colei chi ella era, se lei per morta non avessero avuta». The words «avessero avuto» (a synonym for «sapere») recall an earlier use of this idiomatic expression in the novella: «e per ciò che le sue più congiunte parenti dicevan sé avere avuto da lei non essere ancora di tanto tempo gravida, che perfetta potesse essere la creatura» (7). The fact that her closest relatives did not know about the advanced state of her pregnancy (and therefore could not have anticipated its possible consequences) is paralleled by the guests' inability to accept a new reality on account of their faulty knowledge:

the certainty of death and the uncertainty of life alter their perception of reality. Even after Catalina is restored to her family, the people of Bologna find it hard to believe that she is alive: «La donna con maravigliosa festa fu in casa sua ricevuta e quasi risuscitata con ammirazione fu più tempo guatata da' bolognesi» (46). The context in which the words «sapere», «avere avuto», and «avessero avuta» appear suggests that neither knowledge nor death are certain.

After Catalina's identity is revealed to the guests, Gentile challenges Niccoluccio to stand by his «sentenzia». As a punishment for accepting the doctor's faulty judgment concerning Catalina's death, Niccoluccio must now accept the judgment he has unwittingly passed upon himself: «Per le quali cose, se mutata non avete sentenzia da poco in qua, e Niccoluccio spezialmente, questa donna meritamente è mia, né alcun con giusto titolo me la può radomandare» (40). [102] Gentile's claim that Catalina now belongs to him by virtue of Niccoluccio's own «sentenzia» would probably have been questionable within the legal system of that time. [103] Like messer Ansaldo, Gentile does not exercise the nominal right he has been granted by the other parties involved in this matter; and, like Ansaldo, Gentile frees his beloved from her promise to him so that she can return to her husband («Madonna, omai da ogni promessa fattami io v'assolvo e libera vi lascio di Niccoluccio»). Just as messer Ansaldo taught madonna Dianora a lesson in courtly «rispetto», Gentile teaches Niccoluccio a similar lesson. For Gentile, Catalina is indeed the most precious thing in the world, whereas for Niccoluccio she was, until now, someone he took for granted.

The ritualistic act of giving Catalina to Niccoluccio, the pseudo-legal «questione» Gentile asks, and the «sentenzia» which Niccoluccio makes in agreement with the leading men of Bologna («molti e gentili

---

[102] In accordance with her promise to Gentile, Catalina does not answer any of the questions the guests ask her (not even those of her husband). Her total silence, like the silence of a dead person, contrasts with Niccoluccio's numerous questions and his reputation as an orator («che bello e ornato favellatore era»): it also heightens the sense of separation between the two of them. Catalina's counterpart in the *Filocolo*, however, answers her husband's questions: «Io sono stata menata da codesto cavaliere, da quella vita graziosa che da tutti è disiata, per non conosciuta via in questo luogo»; the wife's veiled reply to her husband accentuates the life after death theme. In the *Decameron*, instead, Catalina's silence mocks Niccoluccio's silence at her grave: unlike Gentile, Niccoluccio did not open her grave in order to cry over her dead body.

[103] The fact that Gentile waited for his term as «podestà» to expire before creating this mock trial suggests that he had no intention of exercising the power of his office to attain the object of his greatest desire.

uomini di Bologna») are all part of a mock trial by which Niccoluccio condemns himself for his «culpa» (negligence) towards his wife. Aside from the fact that it would have been inappropriate for Gentile himself to pass such a judgment on one of his peers, the purpose for the mock trial and mock «sentenzia» is not just to serve as Niccoluccio's «contrapasso» for accepting as real Catalina's false death, but also as a warning to him of what could have become a reality, but did not. Niccoluccio, in fact, could have lost Catalina to death or to Gentile, and he could have even been sentenced for his «culpa» much the same the way Biancifiore was sentenced for hers. The line separating certainty from uncertainty, life from death, appearances from reality, and what is from what might have been, has been blurred to the point that all these distinctions are put in doubt.

The significance of Gentile's «questione» and Niccoluccio's «sentenzia», however, is not limited to this. When Gentile gives Catalina and her son to Niccoluccio he says:

«Leva sù, compare; io non ti rendo tua mogliere, la quale i tuoi e suoi parenti gittarono via, ma io ti voglio donare questa donna mia comare con questo suo figlioletto, il qual son certo che fu da te generato e il quale io a battesimo tenni e nominàlo Gentile [...]» (42)

Gentile has redefined the relationships among the three parties of the love triangle. Catalina is no longer considered Niccoluccio's wife, but rather Gentile's «comare». Gentile is not *returning* a wife to Niccoluccio, instead he is *giving* him his *comare*. On the basis of Niccoluccio's own «sentenzia», Catalina no longer *belongs* to him: when she *died*, so did her status as Niccoluccio's wife. Gentile, therefore, cannot *return* someone who is no longer tied to Niccoluccio or who is considered dead. However, since Catalina is now related to Gentile by virtue of the *comparatico*, Gentile can in fact give Niccoluccio someone who actually belongs to him: someone he treats as a sister (just as he said in line 17). As Laura Sanguineti White has suggested, Gentile's act of giving, rather than returning Catalina to Niccoluccio, is very similar to a wedding ceremony. [104] To this one should add that as the *compare*, Gentile is giving away his *comare* much the same way a brother might give his sister to her husband. Thus by becoming a godfather and a *compare*, rather than a lover or second husband, Gentile «possesses»

---

[104] See SANGUINETI WHITE, pp. 155-56.

his beloved metaphorically and spiritually, not carnally. The status quo has thus been redefined by virtue of both Niccoluccio's *sentenzia* and Gentile's *comparatico*.

This *possession* of the desired object is a palinode to *Decameron* VII 3. Unlike frate Rinaldo, who becomes a godfather and *compare* in order to make love to the child's mother (Agnesa), Gentile does not try to blur the line which distinguishes between the child's spiritual and carnal fathers. Instead, he redefines his previously carnal love for Catalina into a spiritual love: the child bears his name as a sign of Gentile's new relationship to Catalina. Furthermore, the bonds of the *comparatico* which now unite Gentile's and Niccoluccio's families will presumably maintain social harmony between two of the most prominent families in Bologna. [105]

From both Gentile's perspective and that of the narrator (Lauretta), his deed is meant to be seen as an *exemplum* that is closely linked to Niccoluccio's *sententia*. The fact that the *sententia* is made at a dinner table (instead of at the university or in a court of law) by a man «che bello e ornato favellatore era», suggests that it has something in common with the Quintilian «sententiae» which the poets and scholars of antiquity recited at banquets. [106] As Ernst Robert Curtius stated, *sententiae* in the Middle Ages were closely associated to the Aristotelian *exemplum* («an interpolated anecdote serving as an example») since both were intended for edification. [107] Besides being an anecdote, however, the *exemplum* could also be an «"exemplary figure" (*eikon, imago*), i.e., "the incarnation of a quality"». [108] The word *exemplum*, therefore, can refer to both the act and the account of it. [109] This is true of Gentile and the «novella» he tells his guests: both he and his deed are an *exemplum*, and his anecdote is an *exemplum* about himself. Even his name (Gentile) indicates that he is an «incarnation» of nobility, because, in Dante's words, «nomina sunt consequentia rerum». [110] Gentile has thus created the perfect union between

---

[105] For a more detailed analysis of this novella see my article *Frate Rinaldo's Paternoster to Saint Ambrose*, «Studi sul Boccaccio», XII, 1981-82, pp. 161-167.

[106] ERNST ROBERT CURTIUS, *European Literature and the Latin Middle Ages*, trans. by Willard R. Trask, New York, Harper Torchbooks, 1963, p. 58. Curtius says that the *sententia* of classical antiquity «put a psychological experience or a rule of life in the briefest form»; in the Middle Ages *sententiae* tended to have a strictly didactic purpose and were no longer used at banquets, but in schools and universities.

[107] CURTIUS, *op. cit.*, p. 59.

[108] CURTIUS, *op. cit.*, p. 60.

[109] CURTIUS, *op. cit.*, p. 60n.

[110] See Dante's *Vita nuova*, XIII 4.

res et verba and, more importantly, between «fatti e parole», a central theme of the *Decameron*.

Gentile's «novella», as well as his exemplary deed, become the source of yet another *exemplum* — Lauretta's novella. This shift from real life «exemplary figure» to narrative figure is significant because Gentile is fully aware that once people know that Catalina is alive, they will discuss his ambiguous role in her rescue. Had Gentile simply given Catalina back to Niccoluccio without all the pomp and ceremony of his *mise-en-scene*, the public might have viewed his deed differently: he might have been regarded as a fool who did not take advantage of the opportunity to elope with his beloved, or as someone who might have actually possessed her carnally before returning her to Niccoluccio. In either case, his *onor* would have been tainted and he would have been the object of gossip, if not of scandal. By creating this elaborately staged *donatio*, however, Gentile is not only edifying Niccoluccio through his *exemplum* and the ensuing *sententia*, but he is also making a virtue of necessity. [111] Catalina, in fact, does not desire Gentile: she wants to return to Niccoluccio. So instead of appearing as the unrequited lover who had no choice but to give his beloved back to her husband, Gentile gives Catalina to Niccoluccio as if she actually were his own «sorella». This in turn creates a situation whereby his magnanimity and magnificence outshine all the other events related to his deed (including Catalina's return from the dead, Niccoluccio's great joy at the discovery that both his wife and newborn son are alive, and Gentile's scandalous necrophilia). The fame and honor Gentile derives by «donating» Catalina in this manner not only reduce the chances that people might talk badly about him, but also convey to his peers at the banquet the idea that his *nobiltà* and *onor* are more important to him than his past love for Catalina. Gentile, in effect, is anticipating and preparing Lauretta's *exemplum*: he is making sure that history will record only what he wishes to be remembered for. Boccaccio's *exemplum* within an *exemplum*, therefore, not only reveals the genesis of the novella, but also the interdependence between self and history. What began as an attempt to find in Catalina's death what Gentile could not find when she was alive, has been reversed so that what Gentile does to his beloved after she has

---

[111] Critics have commented on the «sceneggiatura» of Gentile's deed, but their interpretation of it is different from mine; see MARIO BARATTO, *op. cit.,* pp. 146-147, SANGUINETI WHITE, *op. cit.,* pp. 155-158, and GIUSEPPE MAZZOTTA, *op. cit.,* pp. 71-72.

been brought back to life will live on after his death both through his exemplary *donatio* and his godson. Both the beginning and the end of this novella mark one man's attempt to overcome death's destruction of love and self. This novella becomes more meaningful when we realize that Lauretta and the nine other narrators will return to Florence and the Black Death the following day. They too will have to struggle against death as Gentile had done. From Lauretta's perspective, her *exemplum* suggests ways in which one's existence is made meaningful in the face of death through the noble ideals one lives by.

Despite Gentile's masterful attempt to shape history and his place in it, Boccaccio subtly undermines Gentile's narrative fiction of himself. The author does this by revealing that Gentile's «noble» deed is not done for the sake of *probitas*, but rather as a way of ascertaining that his *onor* will never be questioned by those who hear about his role in rescuing and returning Catalina to her husband. This nobleman's sense of honor moves him to perform a calculated deed whose ultimate end is as cold and sterile as the tomb from which it is born. By contrast, however, his deed becomes a source of warmth and life for Catalina, Niccoluccio, and their son. This dual perspective reflects the different points of view of the idealistic narrator and the more perceptive author. If from Lauretta's point of view this novella is an *exemplum* of true nobility, of carnal love giving way to spiritual love, etc., from Boccaccio's point of view Gentile's deed is too ambiguous to be truly noble. [112] In fact it is similar to the ambiguous deeds Felice, Florio, and the Admiral of Alexandria perform in the name of *onor* and *nobiltà*. Aside from the fact that Boccaccio still views the deeds of the nobility the way he did in the *Filocolo*, he also reaffirms his earlier belief that no man, no matter how powerful or in control of himself and his world, can ever control his «imago» or «eikon» (i.e. his *exemplum*): the public image of any individual is always volatile. [113]

VI. Conclusion

If one had to choose a governing theme around which both the *Filocolo* and the *Decameron* evolve, it would have to be the theme of

---

[112] Baratto alludes to a «quasi ambiguità di piani» in Gentile's deed (*op. cit.*, p. 147). For Baratto, «nella X 4 l'amore diventa costruzione insieme intellettuale e rituale; e quindi, per Gentile, possibilità di compensare sul piano sociale uno scacco amoroso sul piano personale» p. 148. See also PADOAN, *op. cit.*, pp. 23-24.

[113] For a related discussion of this idea in the *Decameron*, see MAZZOTTA, *op. cit.*, pp. 47-74.

desire. The *Filocolo* can be thought of as a teleology of desire: all forms of desire are ultimately a false reflection of the greater desire for God, and each form of desire is redirected by Providence so that it ultimately leads the characters to God. In the *Decameron* the desire of the characters does not have an ultimate end, nor a divine, governing force to redirect it. Whereas the *Filocolo* produces several different images of desire, each image being a partial reflection of the beatific vision, the *Decameron* represents several different attempts at redefining desire. Gianni da Procida's blind passion for Restituta is channeled into matrimonial love (a sure cure for such a passion according to Ruggier de Loria and Andreas Capellanus). Ansaldo and Gentile's courtly love for Dianora and Catalina respectively are channeled into *caritas*, whereby the bonds of matrimony are preserved. In the *Filocolo* such changes and redefinitions of desire appear as actual metamorphoses in the physical being of the characters (Fileno, Idalogos, etc.) or as mythological deities (Mars, Venus, Diana, etc.). In the *Decameron* desire is divorced from supernatural influences (with the possible exception of the novella of Nastagio degli Onesti). Despite these differences in representation, desire in both the *Filocolo* and the *Decameron* share several common denominators: in both works it is in a continuous state of flux (or as Andreas Capellanus would say, «Semper amorem crescere vel minui constat»), and it ultimately determines all human actions.[114] Love may be what makes the world go around in the *Filocolo*, but in the *Decameron* it represents man's ultimate condition in the postlapsarian world.

[114] For Andreas' famous fourth rule of love, see CAPPELLANO, *op. cit.*, p. 282.

INDEX

Satan (see also Pluto) 36, 43-45, 103, 105, 183, 218
Saturn 57-58, 60-61, 63, 149
Saxl, F. (see Klibansky)
Scaglione, A. 31
Schreiber, E. 44, 102, 157
Seneca 77, 159
seneschal (see Massamutino)
senhal 18, 34,
Seniff, D.P. 141
sententia 79, 122-123, 187, 234, 239-242
Sicily 194, 197, 200-201
signa amoris 143-144
Silenus (see Plato)
Silverstein, T. 156, 158
Sinon 45
Sirofane 183-184
slavery (see bondage)
Smarr, J.L. 19, 21, 24-27, 28, 29, 30, 31, 36, 40, 50, 57-58, 63, 66, 68-69, 196, 199, 201, 208, 229
Socrates (see Plato)
speranza (see hope)
Statius 20, 92
— Thebais 190
suicide 83, 88, 145, 190, 209, 233
Sultan 166, 187
summum bonum 51, 53, 55, 74, 78, 81-85, 103, 137, 158, 160
Sun 58-69
Surdich, L. 19, 29, 95, 100, 154-155, 173

Tarolfo 206-229
Tebano 209, 211-217, 221-223, 226, 230
Terpening, R. 93
terrestrial paradise (see Eden)
Thebes 190, 212
Theodoric 34, 48
theological virtues 36, 103, 105, 111
Thessaly 211, 220
Thorndike, L. 70
Titans (see Atalante)
Tizzone, G. 19,
topos 18, 78, 93, 98, 180, 195-196, 214
Torraca, F. 33
Torre dell'Arabo 95, 145, 180-181, 190, 195-196
traïson (see treason)
treachery (see also treason) 45, 89, 95, 98
treason 9, 48, 90, 108, 113-119, 126-129
Treubruch (see infidelitas)
Trissino, G. 187
Tristan 176

Troiolo (see Boccaccio, Filostrato)
Trojans (see Troy)
Troy 44-45, 92, 105
Turnus 107

Udine 220
ultimate end (see ends & means)
Ulysses 25, 26, 45
Usher, J. 16
usury 165
Ussani, V. 71, 83

vanti (see vows)
Vatican Mythographer 62, 66
Velli, G. 20, 37-38
vengeance (see also jealousy and Lex talionis) 49-50, 87, 106-107, 121-122, 125-126, 130-131, 190, 228
Venus 10, 23, 25, 26, 52, 58, 62-69, 71-73, 95, 100-112, 117, 129, 132, 136-139, 144, 149, 161-163, 173-176, 182, 185-186, 189-190, 196, 199, 212, 244
Verona 9, 34, 43-44, 46, 53, 63, 65, 76-77, 80, 86-87, 96, 107, 111-112, 131, 146, 155, 169, 177-178
Virgil 19, 83, 178, 196
— Aeneid 20, 26, 44, 72, 74, 76, 83, 105, 157, 172, 179
Virgin Mary 25, 102-104
virtù (see virtue)
virtue (see also theological and cardinal virtues) 35, 41, 55, 109-112, 134, 213-214, 216
vis aestimativa (see estimativa)
vis memorativa (see memoria)
visions (see dream visions)
vows 86, 93-94, 98, 104-105, 114, 178, 207-214, 223-228, 239
vox popoli, vox dei 129-132
Vulcan 102, 186, 198

Wallace, D. 146, 149, 161, 183
Wetherbee, W. 156-158
will (see intellectual appetite)
witchcraft (see necromancy)

Yvain 128

Zacharias 37
Zingarelli, N. 72, 217
Zumbini, B. 44-45

CONTENTS

FINITO DI STAMPARE
NELLA TIPOGRAFIA GIUNTINA
IN FIRENZE
GENNAIO 1992

BIBLIOTECA DELL'«ARCHIVUM ROMANICUM»

Serie I: Storia - Letteratura - Paleografia

1. Bertoni, G. *Guarino da Verona fra letterati e cortigiani a Ferrara (1429-1460).* 1921.   (esaurito)
2. — — *Programma di filologia romanza come scienza idealistica.* 1922.   (esaurito)
3. Verrua, P. *Umanisti ed altri «studiosi viri» italiani e stranieri di qua e di là dalle Alpi e dal mare.* 1924. 234 pp., 2 tavv.
4. Cino da Pistoia, *Le rime.* 1925.   (esaurito)
5. Zaccagnini G. *La vita dei maestri e degli scolari nello Studio di Bologna nei secoli XIII e XIV.* 1926, (esaurito)
6. Jordan, L. *Le idées, leurs rapports et le jugement de l'homme.* 1926, X-234 pp.
7. Pellegrini, C. *Il Sismondi e la storia della letteratura dell'Europa meridionale.* 1926, 168 pp.
8. Restori, A. *Saggi di bibliografia teatrale spagnola.* 1927, 122 pp., 3 cc.
9. Santangelo, S. *Le tenzoni poetiche nella letteratura italiana dalle origini,* 1928, XII-462 pp.   (esaurito)
10. Bertoni, G. *Spunti e commenti.* 1928, VIII-198 pp.
11. Ermini, F. *Il «dies irae».* 1928, VIII-158 pp.
12. Filippini, F. *Dante scolaro e maestro. (Bologna-Parigi-Ravenna).* 1929, VIII-224 pp.
13. Lazzarini, L. *Paolo de Bernardo e i primordi dell'Umanesimo in Venezia,* 1930.   (esaurito)
14. Zaccagnini, G. *Storia dello Studio di Bologna durante il Rinascimento.* 1930. X-348 pp., 42 ill.
15. Catalano, M. *Vita di Ludovico Ariosto.* 2 voll. 1931.   (esaurito)
16. Ruggieri, J. *Il canzoniere di Resende.* 1931, 238 pp.
17. Döhner, K. *Zeit und Ewigkeit bei Chateaubriand.* 1931.   (esaurito)
18. Troilo, S. *Andrea Giuliano politico e letterato veneziano del Quattrocento.* 1932.   (esaurito)
19. Ugolini, F.A. *I cantari d'argomento classico.* 1933.   (esaurito)
20. Berni F. *Poesie e prose.* 1934.
21. Blasi, F. *Le poesie di Guilhem de la Tor.* 1934, XIV 78 pp.
22. Cavaliere, A. *Le poesie di Peire Raimond de Tolosa.* 1935.   (esaurito)
23. Toschi, P. *La poesia popolare religiosa in Italia.* 1935.   (esaurito)
24. Blasi, F. *Le poesie del trovatore Arnaut Catalan.* 1937.   (esaurito)
25. Gugenheim, S. *Madame d'Agoult et le pensée européenne de son époque.* 1937   (esaurito)
26. Lewent, K, *Zum Text der Lieder des Giraut de Bornelh.* 1938.   (esaurito)
27. Kolson, A. *Beiträge zur Altprovenzalischen Lyrik.* 1938.
28. Niedermann, J. *Kultur. Werden und Wandlungen des Bregriffs und seiner Ersatzbegriffe von Cicero bis Harder.* 1941.   (esaurito)
29. Altamura, A. *L'Umanesimo nel mezzogiorno d'Italia.* 1941.   (esaurito)
30. Nordmann, P. *Gabriel Seigneux de Correvon, ein schweizerischer Kosmopolit. 1615-1775.* 1947.

31. Rosa, S. *Poesie e lettere inedite.* 1950.   (esaurito)
32. Panvini, B. *La leggenda di Tristano e Isotta.* 1952   (esaurito)
33. Messina, M. *Domenico di Giovanni detto il Burchiello. Sonetti inediti.* 1952.
34. Panvini, B. *Le biografie provenzali. Valore e attendibilità.* 1952.   (esaurito)
35. Moncallero, G.L. *Il Cardinale Bernardo Dovizi da Bibbiena umanista e diplomatico.* 1953.   (esaurito)
36. D'Aronco, G. *Indice delle fiabe toscane.* 1953, 236 pp.
37. Branciforti, F. *Il canzoniere di Lanfranco Cigala.* 1954.   (esaurito)
38. Moncallero, G.L. *L'Arcadia - Vol. I: Teoria d'Arcadia.* 1953.   (esaurito)
39. Galanti, B.M. *Le villanelle alla napolitana.* 1954.   (esaurito)
40. Crocioni, G. *Folklore e letteratura.* 1954.   (esaurito)
41. Vecchi, G. *Uffici drammatici padovani.* 1954, XII-258 pp., 73 tavv. esempi mus.
42. Vallone, A. *Studi sulla Divina Commedia.* 1955. (esaurito)
43. Panvini, B. *La scuola poetica siciliana.* 1955. (esaurito)
44. Dovizi, B. *Epistolario di Bernardo Dovizi da Bibbiena. Vol. I (1490-1513).* 1955, XXIV-528 pp., 6 tavv. f. t.
45. Collina, M.D. *Il carteggio letterario di uno scienzato del Settecento (Janus Plancus).* 1957, VIII-174 pp., 5 tavv. f. t.
46. Spaziani, M. *Il canzoniere francese di Siena (Biblioteca Comunale HX 36).* 1957.   (esaurito)
47. Vallone, A. *Linea della poesia foscoliana.* 1957. (esaurito)
48. Crinò, A.M. *Fatti e figure del Seicento anglo-toscano. (Documenti inediti sui rapporti letterari, diplomatici e culturali fra Toscana e Inghilterra).* 1957, 406 pp., 10 tavv. f. t.
49. Panvini, B. *La scuola poetica siciliana. Le canzoni dei rimatori non siciliani. Vol. I.*
50. Crinò, A.M. *John Dryden.* 1957.   (esaurito)
51. Lo Nigro, S. *Racconti popolari siciliani. (Classificazione e Bibliografia).* 1958, XL-324 pp.
52. Musumarra, C. *La sacra rappresentazione della Natività nella tradizione italiana.* 1957.   (esaurito)
53. Panvini, B. *La scuola poetica siciliana. Le canzoni dei rimatori non siciliani. Vol. II,* 1958, 188 pp.
54. Vallone, A. *La critica dantesca nell'Ottocento.* 1958, 240 pp. Ristampa 1975.
55. Crinò, A.M. *Dryden, poeta satirico.* 1958.   (esaurito)
56. Coppola D. *Sacre rappresentazioni aversane del sec. XIV, la prima volta edite.* 1959, XII-270 pp., ill.
57. Piramus et Tisbè, *Introduzione - Testo critico - Traduzione e note a cura di F. Branciforti.* 1959, 310 pp., 5 tavv. f. t.
58. Gallina, A.M. *Contributi alla storia della lessicografia italo-spagnola dei secoli XVI e XVII.* 1959, 336 pp.
59. Piromalli, A. *Aurelio Bertola nella letteratura del Settecento. Con testi e documenti inediti.* 1959.
60. Gamberini, S. *Poeti metafisici e cavalieri in Inghilterra.* 1959, 270 pp.
61. Berselli Ambri, P. *L'opera di Montesquieu nel Settecento italiano.* 1960, VIII-236 pp., 6 tavv. f. t.
62. *Studi settecenteschi,* vol. I (1960). 1961, 220 pp.
63. Vallone, A. *La critica dantesca del '700.* 1961. (esaurito)

64. *Studi secenteschi,* vol. II (1961). 1962, 334 pp., 7 tavv. f. t.

65. PANVINI, B. *Le rime della scuola siciliana.* Vol. I: Introduzione - Edizione critica - Note. 1962, LII-676 pp. Rilegato.

66. BALMAS, E. *Un poeta francese del Rinascimento: Etienne Jodelle, la sua vita - il suo tempo.* 1962, XII-876 pp., 12 tavv. f. t.

67. *Studi secenteschi,* vol. III (1962). 1963, IV-238 pp., 4 tavv.

68. COPPOLA, D. *La poesia religiosa del sec. XV.* 1963, VIII-150 pp.

69. TETEL, M. *Etude sur le comique de Rabelais.* 1963. (esaurito)

70. *Studi secenteschi,* vol. IV (1963). 1964, VI-238 pp., 5 tavv.

71. BIGONGIARI, D. *Essays on Dante and Medieval Culture.* 1964. (esaurito)

72. PANVINI, B. *Le rime della scuola siciliana* - Vol. II: Glossario. 1964, XVI-180 pp. Rilegato.

73. BAX, G, *«Nniccu Furcedda», farsa pastorale del XVIII sec. in vernacolo salentino.* 1964, VIII-108 pp., 12 tavv.

74. *Studi di letteratura, storia e filosofia in onore di Bruno Revel.* 1965, XXII-666 pp., 3 tavv.

75. BERSELLI AMBRI, P. *Poemi inediti di Arthur de Gobineau.* 1965, 232 pp., 3 tavv. f. t.

76. PIROMALLI, A. *Dal Quattrocento al Novecento. Saggi critici.* 1965, VI-190 pp.

77. BASCAPÈ, A. *Arte e religione nei poeti lombardi del Duecento.* 1964, 96 pp.

78. GUIDUBALDI, E. *Dante Europeo, I. Premesse metodologiche e cornice culturale.* 1965. (esaurito)

79. *Studi secenteschi,* vol. V (1964). 1965, 192 pp., 2 tavv. f. t.

80. VALLONE, A. *Studi su Dante medievale.* 1965, 276 pp.

81. DOVIZI, B. *Epistolario di Bernardo Dovizi da Bibbiena.* Vol. II (1513-1520). 1965, 252 pp., con 3 tavv. (esaurito)

82. *La Mandragola* di Niccolò Machiavelli per la prima volta restituita alla sua integrità. (esaurito)
Edizione di lusso numerata da 1 a 370, su carta grave, con 2 tavv. f. t.

83. GUIDUBALDI, E. *Dante Europeo, II. Il paradiso come universo di luce (la lezione platonico-bonaventuriana).* 1966, VIII-462 pp., 2 tavv. f. t.

84. LORENZO DE' MEDICI IL MAGNIFICO, *Simposio.* 1966, 176 pp., 2 riproduzioni.

85. *Studi secenteschi,* vol. VI (1965). 1966, IV-310 pp., 1 tav. f. t.

86. *Studi in onore di Italo Siciliano.* 1966, 2 voll. di XII-1240 pp. compless. e 6 tavv. f. t.

87. ROSSETTI, G. *Commento analitico al «Purgatorio» di Dante Alighieri.* 1966, CIV-524 pp.

88. PIROMALLI, A. *Saggi critici di storia letteraria.* 1967, VIII-232 pp. (esaurito)

89. *Studi di letteratura francese,* vol. I, 1967, XVI-176 pp.

90. *Studi secenteschi,* vol. VII (1966). 1967, VI-166 pp., 6 tavv. f. t.

91. PERSONÈ, L.M. *Scrittori italiani moderni e contemporanei. Saggi critici.* 1968, IV-340 pp.

92. *Studi secenteschi,* vol. VIII (1967). 1968, VI-230 pp., 1 tav. f. t.

93. TOSO RODINIS, G. *Galeazzo Gualdo Priorato, un moralista veneto alla corte di Luigi XIV.* 1968, VI-226 pp., 9 tavv. f. t.

94. GUIDUBALDI, D. *Dante Europeo, III. Poema sacro come esperienza mistica.* 1968, VIII-736 pp., 24 tavv. f. t. di cui 1 a colori.

95. DISTANTE, C. *Giovanni Pascoli poeta inquieto tra '800 e '900.* 1968, 212 pp.

96. RENZI, L. *Canti narrativi tradizionali romeni. Studi e testi.* 1969, XIV-170 pp.

97. VALLONE, A. *L'interpretazione di Dante nel Cinquecento. Studi e ricerche.* 1969, 306 pp.

98. PIROMALLI, A. *Studi sul Novecento.* 1969, VI-238 pp. (esaurito)

99. CACCIA, E. *Tecniche e valori del Manzoni al Verga.* 1969, X-286 pp.

100. GIANNANTONIO, P. *Dante e l'allegorismo.* 1969, VIII-432 pp.

101. *Studi secenteschi,* vol. IX (1968). 1969, IV-284 pp., 9 tavv. f. t.

102. TETEL, M. *Rabelais et l'Italie.* 1969, IV-314 pp.

103. REGGIO, G. *Le egloghe di Dante.* 1969, X-88 pp.

104. MOLONEY, B. *Florence and England. Essays on cultural relations in the second half of the eighteenth century.* 1969, VI-202 pp., 4 tavv. f. t.

105. *Studi di letteratura francese,* vol. II (1969). 1970, VI-360 pp., 11 tavv. f. t.

106. *Studi secenteschi,* vol. X (1969). 1970, VI-312 pp.

107. *Il Boiardo e la critica contemporanea.* 1970, VIII-544 pp.

108. PERSONÈ, L.M. *Pensatori liberi nell'Italia contemporanea. Testimonianze critiche.* 1970, IV-290 pp.

109. GAZZOLA STACCHINI, V. *La narrativa di Vitaliano Brancati.* 1970, VIII-160 pp.

110. *Studi secenteschi,* vol. XI (1970). 1971, IV-292 pp., con 9 tavv. f. t.

111. BARGAGLI, G. (1537-1587), *La Pellegrina.* 1971, 228 pp., con 2 ill. f. t.

112. SAROLLI, G.R. *Prolegomena alla Divina Commedia.* 1971, LXXII-454 pp., con 9 tavv. f. t.

113. MUSUMARRA, C. *La poesia tragica italiana nel Rinascimento.* 1972, IV-172 pp. Ristampa 1977.

114. PERSONÈ, L.M. *Il teatro italiano della «Belle Époque». Saggi e studi.* 1972, 410 pp.

115. *Studi secenteschi,* vol. XII (1971). 1972, IV-516 pp., con 2 tavv. f. t.

116. LOMAZZI, A. *Rainaldo e Lesengrino.* 1972, XIV-222 pp., con 2 tavv. f. t.

117. PERELLA, R. *The critical fortune of Battista Guarini's «Il Pastor Fido».* 1973, 248 pp.

118. *Studi secenteschi,* vol. XIII (1972). 1973, IV-372 pp., con 11 tavv. f. t.

119. DE GAETANO, A. *Giambattista Gelli and the Florentine Academy: the rebellion against Latin.* 1976, VIII-436 pp., e 1 ill.

120. *Studi secenteschi,* vol. XIV (1973). 1974, IV-300 pp., con 4 tavv. f. t.

121. DA POZZO, G. *La prosa di Luigi Russo.* 1975, 308 pp.

122. PAPARELLI, G. *Ideologia e poesia di Dante.* 1975, XII-332 pp.

123. *Studi di letteratura francese,* vol. III (1974). 1975, 220 pp.

124. COMES, S. *Scrittori in cattedra,* 1976, XXXII-212 pp., con 1 ritratto e 1 tav. f. t.

125. TAVANI, G. *Dante nel Seicento. Saggi su A. Guarini, N. Villani, L. Megalotti.* 1976, 176 pp.

126. *Studi secenteschi,* vol. XV (1974). *Indice generale dei voll. I-X (1960-1969).* 1976, 188 pp.

127. PERSONÈ, L.M. *Grandi scrittori nuovamente interpretati: Petrarca, Boccaccio, Parini, Leopardi, Manzoni.* 1976, 256 pp.

128. *Innovazioni tematiche, espressive e linguistiche della letteratura italiana del novecento.* 1976, XII-300 pp.

129. *Studi di letteratura francese,* vol. IV (1975). 1976, 180 pp., con 2 ill.

130. *Studi secenteschi,* vol. XVI (1975). 1976, IV-244 pp.

131. CASERTA, E.G. *Manzoni's Christian Realism.* 1977, 260 pp.

132. TOSO RODINIS, S. *Dominique Vivant Denon. I fiordalisi, Il berretto frigio, La sfinge.* 1977, 232 pp., con 10 ill. f. t.

133. VALLONE, A. *La critica dantesca nel '900.* 1976, 480 pp.

134. Fratangelo, A e M. *Guy De Maupassant scrittore moderno*. 1976, 180 pp.

135. Cocco M. *La tradizione cortese e il petrarchismo nella poesia di Clément Marot*. 1978, 320 pp.

136. Mastrobuono, A.C. *Essays on Dante's Philosophy of History*. 1979, 196 pp.

137. *Primo centenario della morte di Niccolò Tommaseo (1874-1974)*. 1977, 224 pp.

138. Siciliano, I. *Saggi di letteratura francese*. 1977, 316 pp.

139. Schizzerotto, G. *Cultura e vita civile a Mantova fra '300 e '500*. 1977, 148 pp., con 9 ill. f. t.

140. *Studi secenteschi*, vol. XVII (1976). 1977, 184 pp., con 5 tavv. f. t.

141. Gazzola Stacchini, V.-Bianchini, G. *Le accademie dell'Aretino nel XVII e XVIII secolo*. 1978, XVIII-598 pp., con 18 ill. n. t. e 24 f. t.

142. Friggieri, O. *La cultura italiana a Malta. Storia e influenza letteraria e stilistica attraverso l'opera di Dun Karm*. 1978, 172 pp., con 5 ill. f. t.

143. *Studi secenteschi*, vol. XVIII (1977). 1978, 276 pp.

144. Vanossi, L. *Dante e il «Roman de la Rose». Saggio sul «Fiore»*. 1979, 380 pp.

145. Ridolfi, R. *Studi guicciardiniani*. 1978, 344 pp.

146. Allegretto, M. *Il luogo dell'amore. Studio su Jaufre Rudel*. 1979, 104 pp.

147. Misan, J. *L'Italie des doctrinaires (1817-1830). Une image en élaboration*. 1978, 204 pp.

148. Toaff, A. *The Jews in medieval Assisi 1305-1487. A social and economic history of a small Jewish community in Italy*. 1979, 240 pp., con 14 ill. f. t.

149. Trovato, P. *Dante in Petrarca. Per un inventario dei dantismi nei «Rerum vulgarium Fragmenta»*. 1979, X-174 pp.

150. Fiorato, A.C. *Bandello entre l'histoire ed l'écriture. La vie, l'expérience sociale, l'évolution culturelle d'un conteur de la Renaissance*. 1979, XXII-686 pp.

151. *Studi secenteschi*, vol. XIX (1978). 1979, 260 pp.

152. Bosisio, P. *Carlo Gozzi e Goldoni. Una polemica letteraria con versi inediti e rari*. 1979, 444 pp.

153. Zanato, T. *Saggio sul «Commento» di Lorenzo de' Medici*. 1979, 340 pp.

154. *Studi di letteratura francese*, vol. V. 1979, 204 pp.

155. Piromalli, A. *Società, cultura e letteratura in Emilia Romagna*. 1980, 180 pp.

156. Accademici Intronati di Siena, *La Comedia degli Ingannati*. 1980, 248 pp.

157. *Studi di letteratura francese*, vol. VI. 1980, 176 pp.

158. Harran, D. *«Maniera» e il Madrigale - Una raccolta di poesie musicali del Cinquecento*. 1980, 124 pp.

159. *Studi secenteschi*, vol. XX (1979). 1980, VI-214 pp.

160. Ussia, S. *Carteggio Magliabechi. Lettere di Borde, Arnaud e associati lionesi ad A. Magliabechi*. 1980, 243 pp.

161. Dal Col, I. *Un romanzo del Seicento. La Stratonica di Luca Assarino*. 1981, 244 pp., con 24 tavv. f. t.

162. *Studi secenteschi*, vol. XXI (1980). 1981, 294 pp.

163. *Studi di letteratura francese*, vol. VII. 1981, 224 pp.

164. Castelletti, C. *Stavaganze d'amore. «Commedia»*. 1981, 172 pp.

165. *Carteggio inedito fra N. Tommaseo e G.P. Vieusseux. Vol. I (1835-1839)*. 1981, cm. 18 × 25,5, 688 pp.

166. *Studi secenteschi*, vol. XXII (1981). *Indice generale dei voll. XI-XX (1970-1979)*. 1981, 184 pp.

167. *Il Rinascimento. Aspetti e problemi attuali*. 1982, VI-700 pp.

168. *Stendhal e Milano*. Atti del XIV Congresso Internazionale Stendhaliano. 1982, 2 tomi di complessive XXVI-972 pp., e 2 tavv. a colori.

169. *Studi secenteschi*, vol. XXIII (1982). 1982, 328 pp.

170. *Studi di letteratura francese*, vol. VIII. 1982, 210 pp.

171. *Studi di letteratura francese*, vol. IX. 1983, 274 pp.

172. Aonio Paleario, *Dell'economia, o vero del governo della casa*. 1983, 116 pp.

173. Dalla Palma, G. *Le strutture narrative dell'«Orlando Furioso»*. 1984, 228 pp.

174. *Studi secenteschi*, vol. XXIV (1983). 1983, 324 pp.

175. Raugei, A.M. *Bestiario valdese*. 1984, 362 pp., con ill. n. t.

176. Da Pozzo, G. *L'ambigua armonia. Studio sull'«Aminta» del Tasso*. 1983, 336 pp.

177. *Studi di letteratura francese*, vol. X. 1983, 208 pp.

178. *Miscellanea di studi in onore di V. Branca*. Vol. I: *Dal Medioevo al Petrarca*. 1983, XII-492 pp., con 1 tav. f. t.

179. — — Vol. II: *Boccaccio e dintorni*. 1983, VI-450 pp.

180. — — Vol. III: *Umanesimo e Rinascimento a Firenze e Venezia*. 1983, 2 tomi di complessive XII-848 pp.

181. — — Vol. IV: *Tra Illuminismo e Romanticismo*. 1983, 2 tomi di complessive XII-900 pp.

182. — — Vol. V: *Indagini Otto-Novecentesche*. 1983, VI-390 pp.

183. Rizzo, G. *Tommaso Briganti. Inedito poeta romantico*. 1984, 274 pp.

184. Poliaghi, N.F. *Stendhal e Trieste*. 1984 VI-202 pp., con 22 ill.

185. Michelangelo Buonarroti il giovane, *La Fiera. Redazione originaria (1619)*. 1984, 162 pp., con 4 tavv. f. t.

186. *I cantari. Struttura e tradizione*. 1984, 200 pp.

187. Bianchini, G. *Federigo Nomi. Un letterato del '600. Profilo e fonti manoscritte*. 1984, XVI-338 pp., con 11 tavv. f. t.

188. *Studi secenteschi*, vol. XXV (1984). 1984, 304 pp.

189. Zambon, F. *Robert De Boron e i segreti del Graal*. 1984, 132 pp.

190. *Fenoglio a Lecce*. 1984, 248 pp.

191. Schettini Piazza, E. *Giuseppe Chiarini. Saggio biografico di un letterato dell'Ottocento*. 1984, X-158 pp. con 1 tav. f. t.

192. *Studi di letteratura francese*, vol. XI. 1985, 326 pp., con 9 tavv. f. t.

193. Misan, J. *Les lettres italiennes dans la presse française (1815-1824)*. 1985, 210 pp.

194. Cairns, C. *Pietro Aretino and the Republic of Venice. Researches on Aretino and bis Circle in Venice, 1527-1556*. 1985, 272 pp.

195. Bertelà, M. *Stendhal et l'Autre. L'homme et l'œuvre à travers l'idée de féminité*. 1985, 352 pp.

196. Piglionica, A.M. *Dalla realtà all'illusione: «The tempest» o la parola preclusa*. 1985, 146 pp.

197. *Studi secenteschi*, vol. XXVI (1985). 1985, 352 pp.

198. Cervigni, D.S. *Dante's poetry of dreams*. 1986, 230 pp.

199. *Studi di letteratura francese*, vol. XII. 1986, II-282 pp., con 4 tavv. f. t.

200. Marco Polo, *Il milione. Edizione del testo toscano («ottimo»)*. 1986, XII-418 pp.

201. Delmay, B. *I personaggi della «Divina Commedia». Classificazione e regesto*. 1986, LVI-414 pp.

202. *Patronage and Public in the Trecento*. 1986, 180 pp., con 36 ill. f. t.

203. Mitchell, B. *The Majesty of the State. Triumphal Progresses of Foreign Sovereigns in Renaissance Italy, 1494-1600*. 1986, VIII-240 pp., con 8 ill. f. t.

204. *Ugo Angelo Canello e gli inizi della filologia romanza in Italia*. 1987, 276 pp., con 4 tavv. f. t.

205. *Studi secenteschi*, vol. XXVII (1986). 1986, IV-348 pp.

206. Dédéyan, C. *Diderot et la pensée anglaise*. 1986, IV-366 pp.

207. *La letteratura e i giardini*. 1987, 436 pp., con 9 tavv. f. t.

208. *Letteratura italiana e arti figurative*, 1988, 3 voll. di complessive VIII-1438 pp., con 60 ill. f. t.

209. *Studi secenteschi*, vol. XXVIII (1987). 1987, IV-332 pp., con 2 ill. f. t.

210. *Dante e la Bibbia*. Atti del convegno internazionale. 1988, 372 pp.

211. *Veronica Gàmbara e la poesia del suo tempo nell'Italia Settentrionale.* Atti del convegno. 1989, 442 pp.

212. *Studi di letteratura francese,* vol. XIII. 1987, 194 pp.

213. COLOMBO, A. *I «Riposi di Pindo». Studi su Claudio Achillini (1574-1640).* 1988, 228 pp.

214. *Letteratura e storia meridionale. Studi offerti a Aldo Vallone.* 1989, 2 tomi di complessive XVI-960 pp., con 7 tavv. f. t.

215. SABBATINO, P. *La «Scienza» della scrittura. Dal progetto del Bembo al manuale.* 1988, 256 pp.

216. *Studi di letteratura francese,* vol. XIV. 1988, 144 pp.

217. SCHETTINO, P. *Opere edite e inedite.* Edizione critica. 1989, 410 pp., con 4 tavv. f. t.

218. *Giorgio Pasquali e la filosofia classica del '900.* Atti del convegno. 1988, VI-278 pp.

219. *Studi secenteschi,* vol. XXIX (1988). 1988, IV-328 pp.

220. LANDONI, E. *La teoria letteraria dei provenzali.* 1989, XXXIV-168 pp.

221. *Il meraviglioso, il verosimile tra antichità e medioevo.* 1989, 360 pp., con 5 tavv. f. t.

222. PROCACCIOLI, P. *Filologia ed esegesi dantesca nel Quattrocento. L'Inferno nel «Comento sopra la Comedia» di Cristoforo Landino.* 1989, 266 pp.

223. SANTARCANGELI, P. *Homo Ridens. Estetica, filologia, psicologia, storia del comico.* 1989, VI-452 pp.

224. *Filologia e critica dantesca. Studi offerti a Aldo Vallone.* 1989, XVI-660 pp., con 2 tavv. f. t.

225. *Dantismo russo e cornice europea.* 1989, 2 voll. indivisibili di XXXVI-880 pp., complessive.

226. *Studi di letteratura francese,* vol. XXX (1989). 1989, IV-316 pp.

227. *Studi secenteschi,* vol. XXX (1989). 1989, IV-316 pp.

228. *Il tema della fortuna nella letteratura francese e italiana del Rinascimento. Studi in memoria di Enzo Giudici.* 1990, XX-550 pp., con 1 tav. f. t.

229. SEBASTIO, L. *Strutture narrative e dinamiche culturali in Dante e nel «Fiore».* 1990, 320 pp.

230. *Studi di letteratura francese,* vol. XVI, 1990, 248 pp., con 1 tav. f. t.

231. *Studi di letteratura francese,* vol. XVII, 1990, 156 pp.

232. *Studi di letteratura francese,* vol. XVIII, 1990, 332 pp., con 1 tav. f. t.

233. DOZON, M. *Mythe et simbol dans la Divine Comedie.* In preparazione.

234. VALLONE, A. *Strutture e modulazioni nei canti della Divina Commedia.* 1990, 226 pp.

235. COMOLLO, A. *Il dissenso religioso in Dante.* 1990, 154 pp.

236. BENDINELLI PREDELLI, M. *Alle origini del «Bel Gherardino».* 1990, 360 pp.

237. GUERIN DALLE MESE, J. *Egypte: La mémoire et le reve. Itineraires d'un voyage, 1320-1601.* 1990, 656 pp., con 7 tavv. f. t.

238. SORELLA, A. *Magia, lingua e commedia nel Machiavelli.* 1990, 264 pp.

239. *Studi secenteschi,* vol. XXXI (1990). 1990, XXVIII-296 pp., con 6 tavv. f. t.

240. *Miscellanea di studi in onore di Marco Pecoraro.* 1991. Vol. I: *Da Dante al Manzoni,* X-398 pp. con 7 tavv. f. t. Vol. II: *Dal Tommaseo ai contemporanei,* IV-414 pp.

241. *Lingua e letteratura italiana nel mondo oggi.* 1991, 2 tomi di XVI-732 pp. complessive.

242. SABBATINO, P. *L'Eden della nuova poesia. Saggi sulla «Divina Commedia».* 1991, 232 pp.

243. *Alfonso M. De Liguori e la società civile del suo tempo.* 1990, 2 tomi di VIII-682 pp. complessive.

244. *Famiglia e società nell'opera di Giovanni Verga.* 1991, VI-494 pp.

245. *Studi secenteschi,* vol. XXXII (1991). 1991, IV-332 pp. con 4 tavv. f. t.

246. HEIN, J. *Enigmaticité et messianisme dans la «Divine Comédie».* In preparazione.

247. SANGUINETI WHITE, L. *Dal detto alla figura. Le tragedie di Federico Della Valle.* In preparazione.

248. GROSSVOGEL, S. *Ambiguity and Allusion in Boccaccio's «Filocolo».* 1991, 254 pp.

249. *Studi di letteratura francese,* vol. XIX. In preparazione.

Serie II: Linguistica

1. SPITZER, L. *Lexikalisches aus dem Katalanischen und den übrigen ibero-romanischen Sprachen.* 1921, VIII-162.

2. GAMILLSCHEG, E. und SPITZER, L. *Beiträge zur romanischen Woltbidungslehre.* 1921, 230 pp., 3 cc.

3. [SCHUCHARDT, U.] *Miscellanea linguistica dedic. a Ugo Schuchardt per il suo 80° anniv.* 1922. 121 pp., 2 cc.

4. BERTOLDI, V. *Un ribelle nel regno dei fiori (I nomi romanzi del «Colchicum autumnale L.» attraverso il tempo e lo spazio).* 1923, VIII-224 pp., con ill.

5. BOTTIGLIONI, G. *Leggende e tradizioni di Sardegna.* 1922. (esaurito)

6. ONOMASTICA. - I PAUL AEBISCHER, *Sur l'origine et la formation des noms de famille dans le Canton de Fribour.* - II. DANTE OLIVIERI, *I cognomi della Venezia Euganea.* 1924, 272 pp.

7. ROHLFS, G. *Griechen und Romanen in Unteritalien.* 1923, VIII-178 pp., 1 carta top. e 6 ill. f. t.

8. *Studi di dialettologia alto italiana* - I. GUALZATA, M. *Di alcuni nomi locali del Bellizonese e Lorenese.* - II BLAUERRINI, A. *Giunte al «vocabolario di Bormio».* 1924, 166 pp.

9. PASCU, G. *Rumänische elemente in den Balkansprachen.* 1924, IV-112 pp.

10. FARINELLI, A. *Marrano. (Storia di un vituperio).* 1925, X-80 pp.

11. BERTONI, G. *Profilo del dialetto di Modena. (Con appendice di «Giunte al Vocabolario Modenese»).* 1925, 88 pp.

12. BARTOLI, M. *Introduzione alla neolinguistica (Principi - Scopi - Metodi).* 1926. (esaurito)

13. MIGLIORINI, B. *Dal nome proprio al nome comune.* 1927. Ristampa 1968. (esaurito)

14. KELLER. O. *La flexion du verbe dans le patois benevois.* 1928, XXVIII-216 pp., 1 c. ripiegata.

15. SPOTTI, L. *Vocabolarietto anconitano-italiano.* 1929. (esaurito)

16. WAGNER, M.L. *Studien über den sardischen Wortschatz. (I. Die Familie - II. Der menschiche Körper).* 1930, XVI-156 pp., 15 cc.

17. SOUKUP, R. *Les causes et l'évolution de l'abréviation des pronoms personnels régimes en ancien français.* 1932, 130 pp.

18. RHEINFELDER, H. *Kulptsprache und profansprache in den romanischen Ländern.* (esaurito)

19. FLAGGE, L. *Provenzalisches Alpenleben in den Hochtälern des Verdon und der Bléone.* 1935, 172 pp., 14 tavv.

20. SAINÉAN, L. *Autour des sources indigènes.* 1935, VIII-654 pp.

21. SEIFERT, E. *Tenere «Haben» im Romanischen.* 1935, 122 pp., 4 tavv.

22. TAGLIAVINI, C. *L'Albanese di Dalmazia.* 1937.(esaurito)

23. BOSSHARD, H. *Saggio di un glossario dell'antico lombardo.* 1938. (esaurito)

24. VIDOS, B.E. *Storia delle parole marinaresche italiane passate in francese.* 1939. (esaurito)

25. ALESSIO, G. *Saggio di toponomastica calabrese.* 1939. (esaurito)

26. FOLENA, G. *La crisi linguistica del '400 e l'«Arcadia» di I. Sannazzaro.* 1952. (esaurito)

27. *Miscellanea di studi linguistici in ricordo di Ettore Tolomei.* 1953. (esaurito)

28. VIDOS, B.E. *Manuale di linguistica romanza.* 1959, XXIV-440 pp. Ristampa 1974.

29. RUGGIERI, R. *Saggi di linguistica italiana e italo-romanza.* 1962, 242 pp.

30. MENGALDO, P.V. *La lingua del Boiardo lirico.* 1963, VIII-380 pp.

31. VIDOS, B.E. *Prestito, espansione e migrazione dei termini tecnici nelle lingue romanze e non romanze.* 1965, VIII-424 pp., 3 ill.

32. ALTIERI BIAGI, M.L. *Galileo e la terminologia tecnico-scientifica.* 1965. (esaurito)

33. POLLONI, A. *Toponomastica romagnola,* 1966, XVI-346 pp.

34. GHIGLIERI, P. *La grafia del Machiavelli studiata negli autografi.* 1969, IV-364 pp.

35. *Linguistica matematica e calcolatori.* 1973, XX-670 pp.

36. *Computational and mathematical linguistics.* Vol. I, 1977, 2 voll. di XLVI-796 pp., complessive.

37. *Computational and mathematical linguistics.* Vol. II, 1980, 2 voll. di VIII-906 pp., complessive.

38. SEMERARO, G. *Le origini della cultura europea. Rivelazioni della linguistica storica.* 1984, 2 voll. di LXX-956 pp., complessive.

39. *Fonologia etrusca, fonetica toscana. Il problema del sostrato.* 1983, 204 pp. con 1 tav. f. t.

40. LA STELLA, T.E. *Dizionario storico di deonomastica.* 1984, 236 pp.

41. RANDO, G. *Dizionario degli anglicismi nell'italiano postunitario.* 1987, XLII-256 pp.

42. *Lessicografia, filologia e critica.* 1986, 204 pp.

43. SEMERANO, G. *Le origini della cultura europea.* Vol. II. In preparazione.

44. SCAVUZZO, C. *Studi sulla lingua dei quotidiani messinesi di fine Ottocento.* 1988, 208 pp.

45. AGOSTINIANI, L. - HJORDT-VETLESEN, O. *Lessico etrusco cronologico e topografico dai materiali del «Thesaurus Linguae Etruscae».* 1988, XXXVI-224 pp.

46. O'CONNOR, D. *A History of Italian and English bilingual Dictionaries.* 1990, 188 pp.

47. BOSELLI, P. *Dizionario di toponomastica bergamasca e cremonese.* 1990, 346 pp.

48. DELMAY, B. *Usi e difese della lingua,* 1990, 154 pp., con 1 tav. f. t.